W9-CFB-943

Kosovo

Kosovo

War and Revenge

Tim Judah

Yale University Press
New Haven and London

For my parents
with love and thanks

Set in Stempel Garamond by Northern Phototypesetting, Bolton, Lancs.
Printed in the United States of America

Library of Congress Cataloging-in-Publication Data

Judah, Tim, 1962–
   Kosovo: war and revenge / Tim Judah.
   Includes bibliographical references and index.
   ISBN 0–300–08313–0 (hbk: alk. paper)
   ISBN 0–300–08354–8 (pbk: alk. paper)
     1.Kosovo (Serbia)—History—Civil War, 1998– I. Title.
   DR2078 J83 2000
   949.703–dc21   99–89404

A catalogue record for this book is available from the British Library.

10 9 8 7 6 5 4 3 2 1

For permission to quote from *All Things Considered* on National Public Radio the author and publishers would like to thank American Radio Works.

Photographic credits: by kind permission of Mrs Marina Rainey: 1; Tanjug Photo: 2, 3, 4, 6, 8, 16, 17, 24, 26, 28, 32, 40, 41; Tomislav Peternek: 5, 7, 10, 19, 22; Author's collection: 9, 11, 13, 36; Seamus Murphy: 12, 20, 23, 37, 38, 39, 42; UNCHR: 14 (F. Del Mundo), 25 (U. Meissner), 27 (H.J. Davies), 29 (R. LeMoyne), 34 (R. Chalasani); PA News: 15; NATO Photo: 18, 21, 30, 31, 33, 35.

Maps drawn by Jim Pavlidis

Contents

Preface

Migjen Kelmendi had been in hiding for a week. A well-known Kosovo Albanian writer and journalist, he feared that he might be marked down for execution by death squads when the NATO bombing of Yugoslavia began. Then the Serbian police began clearing Priština, the Kosovar capital. Kelmendi borrowed a baby and pretended to be part of a family. Others huddled around him so that he was less likely to be recognised. Kelmendi was used to foreign travel. But nothing in his experience had prepared him for the journey he was about to make.

The police gathered a group of two to three thousand people in the street and then prodded them in the direction of the station. 'They were driving us like cattle. The children were screaming and the elderly were very slow.' They marched down Priština's main street, past the theatre and the Hotel Grand. 'The saddest bit was that, along the way, I saw bunches of people, Serbs. They looked at us with complete indifference. It was unimaginable.'

Then they got to the station. There they found that there were already 25–30,000 people. 'What's going on?' Kelmendi asked. People replied: 'We are waiting for the train to take us to the border, to Macedonia.' By this time it was four o'clock. Over the next few hours three babies were born and two old men died. Just before midnight the huge crowd heard the noise of NATO planes wheeling across the night sky.

'People began to clap. They were shouting "NATO! NATO!" and saying, "They will help us." Then we heard shooting very close to us and realised we were surrounded. Everyone fell silent immediately.'

At one o'clock in the morning the train arrived. It was an ordinary passenger train with twenty carriages, each divided into cabins. At that moment, 'the animal instinct in everyone, including me, came out.' Everyone surged forward, fighting and shoving. 'The strongest got on and then got their families in through the windows.' In each cabin there were thirty people and the corridors were jam packed too. There was no air and there was no water. Children were crying while parents were hunting for the ones they had lost. There were about 7–10,000 people crammed on board.

After a couple of hours the train began to move and the motion sent the exhausted children to sleep. But the train kept stopping and starting. Apparently people kept pulling the emergency communication cord. So the train stopped at Kosovo Polje, close to the legendary battlefield where the Serbs fought the Turks in 1389. There, police stood on the platform while exasperated Serb railwaymen worked their way down the train with a mechanical key trying to turn off the emergency brake system.

While they were in the station the police ordered everyone to get off. 'There was panic. No one wanted to get out. They were frightened they would be separated.' In others words, that men would be shot. So, no one got off and after five minutes, the police said 'Stay there and be quiet!'

The train lurched off into the dark again. An hour later it stopped. People got off to get water for their children. 'The police hit them in front of their families.' Then, everyone was ordered out and told to walk down the tracks. This took them across the border into Macedonia.

Immediately over the frontier, Kelmendi turned on his mobile phone. He had been far too frightened to use it while he was hiding. It rang straight away. It was his wife. She was in Montenegro. She was crying: 'You're alive, you're alive!' Of course, the Kelmendis were lucky.

Tetovo, May 1999

*   *   *

Through the night of 27–8 April I stood on the border between Kosovo and Albania at a place called Morina. The people on the first tractors were surprisingly calm, considering that, that morning, they had been ordered from their homes at gunpoint and then saw them being torched. This group of about 2,000 came from a cluster of villages near the western Kosovo town of

Djakovica. The police were angry and shouting that the rebel Kosovo Liberation Army (KLA) had, a few days earlier, killed five of their men.

I talked to some of the people on one of the first tractor-trailers. They said that they had started their journey with 37 packed on the trailer but that, at a hamlet called Meja, the police took ten men off. A 15-year-old boy was then ordered to drive. They told me that, apart from small boys, he was the only male left on their trailer. This was not quite true.

A middle-aged man said: 'I have a bad leg. One policeman said "Get out" and the other said "Stay in."' They left a blind man too. Then I saw an old man sitting in the corner, still cutting a fine figure in his traditional felt cap and with a curly grey moustache. 'What about him?' I asked. 'We forgot the old man,' laughed Sevdie Rexha, the young woman I was talking to.

The people on the next couple of tractors said the same thing. Many of their men had been taken off at Meja and they had seen them sitting in a field under police guard.

Looking across the border I could see the lights of more tractors as their engines began to grumble and they started to roll across from Kosovo. A minute later their drivers stopped and stared, uncertain what to do when they saw the dozens of aid workers, Albanian officials and television camera lights looming out of the darkness.

A dog sniffed at the first one across. 'Did you see the men in the field at Meja?' I asked. The tractor was still moving. These people were in shock, their eyes red from crying. 'They killed them, they killed them,' shouted a woman as she passed. I ran to catch up. 'In a field ... in a field ... more than a hundred ... they took two from us ... They're dead! They're dead!'

A hundred metres away Sevdie Rexha, the old man, the blind man, the lame man and the rest of them sat on their trailer. A drunken Albanian soldier was abusing them. 'Stop crying, stop moaning ... why did you leave your kids behind?' They still did not know what the others now arriving knew. I wondered whether I should say something. I thought not. They would find out soon enough.

Everyone on the tractors now arriving had seen the bodies, but no one had actually seen the killing. Hasan Shabani, aged 73, sat on a sack waiting for his wife. They had been walking but a tractor-trailer picked him up and she was hauled onto a horse-drawn cart, which then got left behind.

He said he seen the men taken from the convoy at Meja lined up. 'They were punched and kicked.' Women were rushing forward, crying, trying to get their sons and husbands back, but the police and paramilitaries, some wearing masks, were firing in the air, swearing at them to get back on the convoy.

'How many years have you been married?' I asked Mr Shabani. 'Thirty-eight,' he replied, 'but that's a funny question to ask at a time like this.'

In the distance, over Mount Paštrik, there were flashes and rumbles. It could have been thunder and lightning. It could have been artillery. But it wasn't. It was NATO bombing the Serbs. For the fifth week running.

Morina, May 1999

*   *   *

On the hill near the Serbian village of Drsnik in central Kosovo I counted smoke billowing from eight houses. Or at least I thought they were houses. Some proved to be haystacks. Revenge meant that even Serbian haystacks had to burn.

In the northern town of Mitrovica I sat on a wall with Meli Uka, a pretty, 22-year-old Albanian student. We sipped Coke and watched a column of fleeing Serb families packed into cars and tractor-trailers. They looked no different from the Kosovars I had seen who had been expelled from Kosovo a few weeks earlier. Meli smiled benignly and said: 'They wanted Albanians out and now this is our revenge. I am very happy about it and I never want them to come back. Now we are free.'

Forty-five minutes later I saw the Serbian village of Samodreža on fire. Two Albanian brothers, Naim and Namun Bala, were watching it burn. The Serbs had left two hours earlier. 'The KLA did it,' they said. 'Those Serbs were our neighbours. We never had any problems with them. We grew up with them, played with them and ate with them. But, when the Serbian police came and burned our houses they turned their backs and said: "Fuck you!"' Namun said: 'There are 28 of us in our family. We asked the KLA not to burn the houses because we could live *in them, but still, they went ahead and did it.' Cars full of KLA fighters drove past, waving happily and tooting their horns in triumph.*

In Vučitrn Albanian families swarmed through the Serbian Orthodox priest's house. Mothers manoeuvred sofas down stairs, children roamed about with hammers smashing religious pictures while others piled food, church candles and anything else they could carry on to wheelbarrows. When they were done they moved to the church. A girl with a manic expression on her face smashed the windows. Women tugged on dark red velvet altar cloths and precious icons crashed to the floor. A man struggled to wrench the chandelier from the ceiling.

Outside, two French soldiers from the Kosovo Force, KFOR, the newly arrived international peace force which has NATO at its core, looked on amiably. Up the road a Gypsy house was on fire. Albanians accuse many Gypsies of having 'collaborated' with the Serbs. At that moment the local French commander drove past. According to the sticker on his jeep, his regimental motto was 'Avec le sourire.' He said: 'Our job is to reassure the population.' I said it didn't look like he was reassuring the few remaining Serbs. He replied, sans sourire, 'The orders are to let them pillage.' I said: 'That's mad.' He said: 'Of course it's mad, but those are the orders.'

As everywhere else in Kosovo, Serbs in Priština live in terror. I rented a flat and soon Mileva, the Serbian woman from next door, came over. Almost whispering she said: 'What am I going to do? Someone stuck an Albanian name on my door. It is a message that they want me out.'

Priština, June 1999

Author's Note

Don't look for biases in place names. There are none. Kosovo is Kosovo, as the region is known in the English-speaking world and not the Albanian Kosova or the full and official Serbian Kosovo and Metohija (or the abbreviated Kosmet) unless in a quote.[1] The same holds for the other place names. I have used the Serbian ones because, for the moment, people outside Kosovo are still more familiar with names like Peć and Djakovica rather than Peja and Gjakova. It is also the way the names are still spelled in all but Albanian maps, and once you start using one spelling you have to try to remain consistent or you risk confusion. To repeat: the choice of spelling is not a secret signal of support for one side or another!

Technically the world Kosovar should refer to any inhabitant of Kosovo, whatever their ethnic background. However, in recent years, the term has come to be used as a shorthand for Kosovo Albanians only. I have followed this practice. It is useful as a name because, unlike 'Albanians' it distinguishes between Kosovo Albanians and Albanians from Albania itself.

Unless footnoted, quotations are from my own interviews or from the local or international media written down at the time, in my notebook.

Throughout the former Yugoslavia the German Mark is the most widely used hard currency, hence the references to Deutschmarks.

Unless there was a particular reason, I decided not to spell out the full Albanian and Serbian names of every political organisation. The Albanian name of the Kosovo Liberation Army, the KLA or UÇK, should however be given. It is the Ushtria Çlirimtare e Kosovës.

What follows is a list of the names of the main towns and villages of Kosovo mentioned in the text in both their Serbian and Albanian versions.

Serbian	Albanian	Serbian	Albanian
Ćirez	Çirez	Mališevo	Malisheva
Dečani	Deçan	Mitrovica	Mitrovica
Djakovica	Gjakova	Orahovac	Rahovec
Donji Prekaz	Prekaz i Ulët	Peć	Peja
Glogovac	Gllogovc	Priština	Prishtina
Gnjilane	Gjilan	Prizren	Prizren
Gornje Obrinje	Obria e Epërme	Podujevo	Podujeva
Kosovo Polje	Fushë Kosovë	Srbica	Skenderaj
Lauša	Llausha	Uroševac	Ferizaj
Leposavić	Leposvaiq	Vučitrn	Uushtrri
Likošane	Likoshan		

Acknowledgements

My thanks are due, first and foremost, to my wife Rosie, for her love and support and frontline editing. Then to Ben, Esther and Rachel for all their real help and to Jacob and Eve, for being there. If it was not for Natasha Fairweather, this book would not be here. Thanks also to Robert Baldock of Yale for turning up at the right time, again, and Candida Brazil, also at Yale, for her patience and hard work – also again. Thanks to Robert Silvers, editor of the *New York Review of Books*, for sending me to the right places at the right time. For real help in different places at different times: Denisa Kostovičová, Daut Dauti, Migjen Kelmendi and Braca Grubačić for *VIP*.

This book could never have been completed as fast as it was without the help of Marc Weller, who kindly gave me an early copy of his extraordinary compilation of documents about Kosovo. It is the *sine qua non* of all future studies on Kosovo and the war. For their hospitality and help: Jonathan Landay and Vlatka Mihelić. For the songs and other help, Dan Reed. Thanks too, to Jonathan Marcus and Goran Gocić. Also, to Chris Stephen, connoisseur of the art of the taxi and Jim Paulidis for making the maps.

FEDERAL REPUBLIC

Novi Pazar

Predominantly Serbian area of Kosovo

Leposavi

S A N D Ž A K
(Area with substantial Slav Muslim population)

MONTENEGRO

Mitrovica

Ivangrad

Rožaje

The Drenica Valley

Donji Prekaz

Srbic

Lauša
Devič

Likovac
Gornje Obrinje

Peć

Klina

Glogova

Dečani

Kijevo

Komor

Klěc

Junik

Košare

Mališevc

Padesh
Tropoja

Ponoševac

Djakovica

Orahovac

Bajram Curri

Suva Reka

ALBANIA

Bujan

Mount Paštrik

Prizren

Žur

Morina

Kukës
(Wartime refugee camps)

Dragaš

Predominantly Slav Muslim area of Kosovo

Gostiva

Kosovo border

● Monasteries

▲ 1998-99 KLA training camps

✝ Airport

✕ Mine

0   Km   20

O F   Y U G O S L A V I A

Kuršumlija

SERBIA

✗ Trepča
✗ Stari Trg
Podujevo
⊣ Vučitrn
■ Samodreža
⊢ Ćirez
⊢ Likošane
⊢ Belaćevac
⊢✗
Kosovo
Polje
⊢✚
Slatina

■ **Priština** ✚
Gračanica
(predominantly Serbian)

■ Novo Brdo
✗

Vranje ■

Štimlje
Uroševac ■
Camp Bondsteel
(US military 1999-?)

Gnjilane ■

Bujanovac ⇦

Preševo ■ ⇐

Predominantly ethnic Albanian areas within Serbia proper

Brezovica ■
edominantly Serbian)

■ Kačanik

Blace ■
Stenkovec ■
(Wartime refugee camps)

Kumanovo ■

Tetovo ⇙

Predominantly ethnic Albanian areas of western Macedonia

Skopje

MACEDONIA

The Drenica Valley

Rudnik
Donji Prekaz
Gornja Klina
■ Galica
Srbica
Ćirez ■
Lauša ■
Likošane ■
✚
Dević ■
Jošanica ■
Polluža ■
Trstenik ■
Klina ■
Gornje Obrinje ■
Glogovac ■
R Klina
Drsnik ■

0   Km   10

Introduction

Kossovo Day

During the summer of 1916 London was covered in posters. They read: 'Think of Serbia, Pray for Serbia, Restore Serbia.'[1] Britain was commemorating 'Kossovo Day'. Although 28 June is the day when Serbs remember the famous Battle of Kosovo in 1389 in which their ancestors fought the invading Ottoman Turks, 'Kossovo Day' events were being held across Britain throughout late June and early July. More than 12,000 schools responded to calls to do something and thousands of children wrote essays on Kosovo and the Serbs. This was written by a 13-year-old boy, a pupil attending Southwold National School:

> Although the Serbians are a small nation, they are a fighting nation, and will never surrender unless they are forced. They have many poems of the fallen kings of Serbia. They go down from generation to generation. And will never be forgotten until the end of the world.

Delphis Gardner, aged 15, from St Felix School, also in Southwold, wrote: 'Serbia is one of those places that conquest has not destroyed. It has merely made it unconquerable.'[2]

On 7 July a service was held in St Paul's Cathedral in which the Archbishop of Canterbury was reported as saying: 'Two years ago, we had little knowledge of the Serbians, and little or no enthusiasm for Serbia.' Since then, however, Serbia had, he noted, 'by her courage taken a very high place in the minds of the English, and a very high place in European affairs'. Before the Serbian national anthem was sung he added that Serbia's hopes, 'like her Christian creed, were indestructible'.[3]

On 28 June a leader in the *Daily Mirror* said:

> Serbia is ruined. Serbia, as at Kossovo, is defeated. But that omen is now as then it proved to be – favourable, eternal,

as the omen of recurrent Spring after bleak Winter. Serbia
will rise again as she once rose from her magnificent
dust. We of the West have pledged ourselves to it. And
the broken fate of this struggling nation may well move
us strangely, as we reflect that her defeats precede her
resurrections.[4]

One of the more extraordinary things about Serbia and the Serbs
is the way in which their reputation has roller-coasted across the
last one hundred years. In 1916 'gallant Little Serbia', as she had
become known, was occupied by the Austro-Hungarians,
Germans and Bulgarians, and Serbian troops were fighting
alongside the British and French. But, as the historian Edward
Crankshaw wrote in 1963, this 'at once obscured the fact that for
the previous decade Serbia had been regarded generally as a
thorough-going nuisance, a nest of violent barbarians whose
megalomania would sooner or later meet the punishment it
deserved'.[5] Few in the West today would disagree that things
have changed again. Indeed, if Crankshaw had penned this
opinion for the 'op-ed' pages of a British or American newspaper at some point during NATO's 78-day bombing campaign
in Serbia, which began on 24 March 1999, he would only have
been voicing a widely held belief. Then again, since the flight and
ethnic cleansing of the Serbs of Kosovo following NATO's
victory, perceptions have begun to change again. People are
asking: 'Who are the victims now?'

How is it that the fortunes of Serbia, so inextricably linked
with Kosovo, have led to its downfall and isolation? This is one
of the questions that I hope to answer in this book.

In 1991, I was sent by *The Times* of London and *The
Economist* to cover Slovenia's declaration of independence.
Within days the first shots of the Yugoslav wars had been fired.
During the ensuing conflicts in Croatia and Bosnia I lived, with
my family, in Belgrade. Occasionally I would find time to break
away from frontline news reporting to visit Kosovo. But it was
hard to interest news editors in this then-obscure little province
of Serbia. Every now and then one might succeed in persuading
them to take a piece on the extraordinary political stand-off that
had developed there after 1990, between Serbs and the state on
one side, and the region's ethnic Albanian majority on the other.

However, with the situation frozen, little actually happened there in terms of news. After the first few pieces predicting impending doom, editors could be excused for saying: 'Call me when it happens.'

When it did happen, when war finally did break out in Kosovo, I was sent back there to report for various magazines and papers, foremost amongst them the *New York Review of Books*.

The idea of this book is to follow the conflict from its origins, especially in the 1980s and 1990s, to the immediate aftermath of the NATO bombing campaign. It is also to show how this was, to a great extent, a war of human error. That is to say that, of course with the benefit of hindsight, we can now see just how haphazard were the steps that led to war. How all of the leading actors, in Serbia and in the West, made mistake after mistake, hoping that somehow everything would be all right in the end. Of course, it not to be.

In Serbia, for example, those in power or with the power to shape opinion, simply refused to confront the fact that Serbia's position in Kosovo was untenable. Instead of trying to look for imaginative and brave solutions they just did nothing. They thought that if they repeated the mantra of 'Kosovo is Serbia' enough, the problem would go away. It did not. But then, when the war started, many simply opted to believe in irrational explanations, which divested them of any responsibility for the unfolding disaster. They wanted to believe that everyone else was responsible – a fantastically powerful Albanian 'narco-mafia' for example, or the eternally Serb-hating West – but never Serbia or the Serbs.

Before the war began a very few Serbs understood that, since it looked unlikely that an historic compromise could be struck with the Kosovo Albanians and the only way to hold the province was by force, the nation's choice was 'Kosovo or democracy'. Serbia's historic failure to find a way out of this dilemma has meant that in the aftermath of NATO's bombing campaign she has neither.

For the best part of a decade, Kosovo's Albanians, never wavering in their demand for independence, tried to bring their case to the attention of the world by peaceful means. It was a tragedy that this experiment failed and that violence prevailed. It was a tragedy because thousands would pay for this failure with their lives. It was also a tragedy because it sent a powerful message to others around the world. That was, that nobody notices peaceful protest – only violence pays.

But there was worse. That was that following the ending of Serb rule in the province, it became gripped by yet another of its historic cycles of revenge. 'Blood can be wiped out only with blood,' wrote Edith Durham, the redoubtable English traveller and writer following her trip to northern Albania and Kosovo in 1908.[6] She was discussing the tradition of blood vengeance, codified in fifteenth-century Kanun of Lek Dukagjini or Canon of Lek which enshrined, she said, 'the old, old idea of purification by blood. It is spread throughout the land. All else is subservient to it.'[7]

During her travels, at a time when Kosovo was still part of the Ottoman Empire, Durham wrote that she found that the Serbs there, 'regardless of the fact that in most places they are much in the minority, still had visions of the expulsion of all Moslems, and the reconstruction of the great Servian Empire.'[8] She added that the history of Kosovo had always been:

> an elemental struggle for existence and survival of the strongest, carried out in obedience to Nature's law, which says, 'There is not place for you both. You must kill – or be killed.' Ineradicably fixed in the breast of an Albanian ... is the belief that the land has been his rightly for all time. The Serb conquered him, held him for a few passing centuries, was swept out and shall never return again. He has but done to the Serb as he was done by.[9]

This book is really several stories. One is a narrative, factual account of Kosovo's descent into a war, which dragged in the most powerful military alliance on earth. It is the story of the diplomacy that sought to avert war and the wilful political gambling of Slobodan Milošević, the Serbian leader and Yugoslav President. It is the story of how Western leaders began a 'war' they thought would last three days. It is the story of how a few dozen political hardliners plus a few families of armed, militant, peasant farmers began an uprising which would make the KLA the most successful guerrilla movement in modern history. But it is also the story of how Serbs and Albanians failed to break the cycle of violence and revenge into which their nations have become locked and which may yet be far from over.

1 History: War by Other Means

For centuries, Serbian history, myth and tradition was passed down from generation to generation through the singing of epic poetry. This fragment comes from the tale of Serbian Prince Marko and the Albanian highwayman Musa Kesedžija. Marko, a vassal of the Sultan, has been sent by him to kill Musa, who has been preying on people at the gorge of Kačanik, close to Kosovo's modern border with Macedonia. On seeing Marko, Musa greets him.

> Pass, Marko, don't pick a quarrel,
> Or dismount and we'll drink some wine;
> But yield to you – that I will not,
> Though a queen did give you birth
> In a pavilion on soft cushions,
> And swaddled you in purest silk,
> Bound you with golden cords
> And fed you on honey and sugar.
> Though a stern Albanian woman gave me birth
> Among the sheep, on a cold flagstone,
> And swaddled me in a black cape,
> Bound me with bramble stems
> And fed me on oatmeal porridge,
> Yet she besought me often
> Never to make way for any man![1]

The poem is more than just an entertainment. It tells us more about Serbs and Albanians in Kosovo than a dozen history books written by historians of one side or the other. Above all, the words 'yield to you – that I will not' speak volumes, not just about a tradition of conflict, but about the way Serbs and Albanians have interpreted the history of the land they shared. In Kosovo, history is war by other means.

After NATO troops entered Kosovo on 12 June 1999, Albanians began toppling statues of medieval Serbian kings.

1

A few weeks earlier, when the Serbs were still in control, the preserved house in Prizren where meetings in 1878 had given birth to modern Albanian nationalism was blown up. The site was then bulldozed and trees were planted on the spot.[2] When it comes to destroying each other's monuments, there is more to these actions than simple nationalist vandalism. For, in Kosovo, history is not really about the past, but about the future. In other words, he who holds the past holds the future. That is not to say, however, that outsiders cannot build a picture of the past which does not pander to the nationalist bents of either side. It is just that it is more difficult to do here than it is in other parts of Europe.

Back to the future

The classical Serbian view holds that the people who lived in Kosovo were overwhelmingly Serb until barely a few generations back. If this were true, then the modern Serbian claim to the land would be that much stronger. On the other hand, Albanian historians have always claimed the right of 'first possession'. They argue that their ancestors, the ancient Illyrians and Dardanians, lived here long before the Slav invasions of the sixth and seventh centuries. In fact, the truth is unclear.

As always in the Balkans, and elsewhere for that matter, the truth is not what matters, it is what people believe it to be. And what people believe can be put to everyday use. To those of us who live in places like London or New York, who lived here before us, in say 600 AD, has no contemporary resonance. However the fact that Albanian-owned travel agencies, shops and companies in Kosovo are frequently called things like 'Illyria Tours' or 'Dardania Import–Export' are good examples of the way that, even through the name of your business, you could signal your resistance and defiance of Serbian rule.

Although still bitterly disputed, history becomes a little more focused during the middle ages. Under the dynasty of the Nemanjić monarchs a first identifiably Serbian kingdom began to be fashioned. The Nemanjas hailed from Raška, which is now, as often as not, known as Sandžak, its Turkish name. Raška lies just to the north of modern Kosovo and its main town is Novi Pazar. The founder of the dynasty was Stefan Nemanja who abdicated to become a monk in 1196. His third son was Rastko, also a monk, who was later canonised as St Sava.

In the history of Kosovo and Serbia, Sava must rank as one of its towering and most influential figures. Until 1219, the Serbs, or rather the people who were on their way to developing a national consciousness as Serbs, teetered on the brink between western Roman Catholicism and Byzantine, eastern Orthodoxy. When, for example, Sava's brother Stefan was crowned king in 1217, Sava asked the Pope in Rome for his blessing despite the fact that his brother was consecrated monarch in the Orthodox tradition. In 1219, however, Sava, a brilliant diplomat and politician, secured from the then enfeebled Byzantine emperor and the Orthodox patriarch, autocephalous status for what was then to become, in effect, the Serbian national church. Autocephaly meant autonomy within the Orthodox church. The consequences of this were to be fundamental.

What Sava's actions meant were that, at least until 1355, Nemanjić power was supported by two pillars, that is to say, the state and the church. When, however, the Serbian nobility was swept away by the Ottoman invasions, the church remained. In this way the idea that Serbia would be resurrected – like Christ – was one that was nurtured by the very existence of the church. As most of the Nemanjić monarchs were canonised, their images were painted on to the walls of Serbian churches and monasteries. So, for hundreds of years, the Serbian peasant went to church and in his mind the very idea of Christianity, resurrection and 'Serbdom' blended together.

Just like other monarchs across Europe at the time, the Nemanjićs were church-builders. Some of their most famous buildings stand in Serbia proper, some in Raška and some in Kosovo. In Kosovo the most prominent are the Patriarchate in Peć, Gračanica and the monastery of Visoki Dečani (High Dečani) in western Kosovo.

But, who actually lived in Kosovo at the time of the Serbian kings? Serbian history books argue that only Serbs lived here, and point to their churches as proof, while Albanian ones argue the opposite. The British historian Noel Malcolm has written that 'all the evidence suggests that [Albanians] were only a minority in Medieval Kosovo'. Clearly this is not a view that finds favour amongst Albanian historians who often argue that, despite the fact that the majority of names in church registers are Slavic, the majority of Kosovo's people were still Albanian. Malcolm dismisses this as 'not credible'.[3] But it is what the majority of Kosovars believe. In a paper on the Orthodox church, for example, the academic Mark Krasniqi writes that 'The Serbian state and church assimilated Albanians in different ways, besides outright terror and violence':

> the church also used the holy sacraments in order to accomplish its diabolical mission. It gave Slavic names to Albanian infants, and imposed wedding ceremonies and liturgies in the Slavic language. Under such pressure from the Orthodox Church, many Albanian families in Kosova, Macedonia and Montenegro were Slavicized.[4]

As we have noted, in Kosovo, history is war by other means.

1389: Flying hawk, grey bird

The Serbian epics hold that the Ottoman Sultan Murad summoned the Serbian Prince Lazar to do battle at Kosovo Polje – the Field of Blackbirds – because Lazar would not agree to submit and become his vassal. As the poem points out, with a certain chilling contemporary echo, there 'never can be / one territory under two masters.'

> The Sultan Murad falling like a hawk,
> falling on Kosovo, writes written words,
> he writes and sends to the city of Krushevats
> to the knees of Lazar, Prince of Serbia:
> 'Ah, Lazar, Lord of Serbia,
> this has never been and never can be:
> one territory under two masters,
> only one people to pay two taxes:
> we cannot both of us be ruler,
> send every key to me and every tax,
> the keys of gold that unlock the cities,
> and the taxes on heads for seven years.
> And if you will not send these things to me,
> then come to Kosovo meadow,
> and we shall do division with our swords.'

And when the written words come to Lazar
he sees the words, he drops terrible tears.[5]

The last great Nemanjić monarch had been Stefan Dušan who fashioned a short-lived empire, which stretched from the Danube to the Peloponnese. When he died, suddenly, in 1355, the empire fell apart. In 1371 a Serbian army fought the invading Ottomans at the Battle on the Maritsa river, a place which now lies in modern Bulgaria. The Serbs were defeated and historians regard this battle as being of far greater military significance than the famous Battle of Kosovo, which was fought on 28 June 1389.

By 1389, the Serbs were divided between numerous feudal lords who squabbled and allied with one another as they saw fit. In general, the Ottomans preferred not to fight if they did not have to. Their preferred tactic was to offer the local lord a deal. In exchange for his agreeing to submit as a vassal, which included the obligation to supply troops in time of war, he could continue to rule his domain. What might happen after his death was open to question. For whatever reason, Lazar, a minor noble, who had recently managed to carve out a large fief, decided not to submit. Most of his lands lay in the Morava valley, in modern central Serbia, although within the modern borders of Kosovo they included Novo Brdo. This mountain-top fortress city, now forgotten, was at the time one of the largest cities in Europe, because its wealth derived from its valuable silver and gold mines, which were one of the main sources of income of the medieval Serbian monarchs. During the fourteenth century it may have had as many as 40,000 inhabitants, which would have made it larger than Paris.[6] Today, the town and fortress are no more than crumbling windswept ruins.

The actual battle was fought on the plain of Kosovo Polje, close to Priština. These were lands which lay within the domain of Lazar's son-in-law, Vuk Branković. In the weeks before the battle, Lazar had managed to assemble a coalition. These troops included a contingent from Bosnia and probably some Albanians too.

According to the epics, Lazar made a fateful choice before the battle. Would he choose a kingdom on earth, with all the riches that that entailed, or would he die for the empire of heaven, that is to say, for truth and justice and the everlasting?

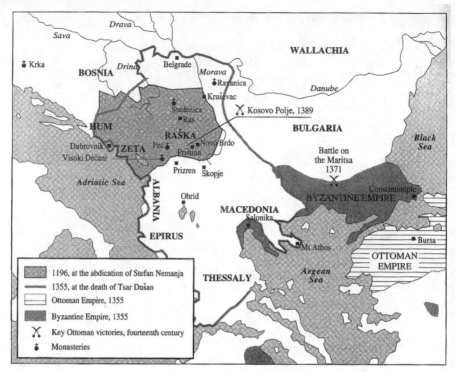

1196–1355: Medieval Serbia

This is how the question is posed in the epic called 'The Downfall of the Serbian Empire'.

Flying hawk, grey bird,
out of the holy place, out of Jerusalem,
holding a swallow, holding a bird,
that is Elijah, holy one;
holding no swallow, no bird,
but writing from the Mother of God
to the Emperor at Kosovo.
He drops that writing on his knee,
it is speaking to the Emperor:
'Lazar, glorious Emperor,
which is the empire of your choice?
Is it the empire of heaven?
Is it the empire of the earth?
If it is the empire of the earth,
saddle horses and tighten girth-straps,

and, fighting men, buckle on swords,
attack the Turks,
and all the Turkish army shall die.
But if the empire of heaven
weave a church on Kosovo,
build its foundations not with marble stones,
build it with pure silk and with crimson cloth,
take the Sacrament, marshal the men,
they shall die,
and you shall die among them as they die.'
And when the Emperor heard those words,
He considered and thought,
'King God, what shall I do, how shall I do it?
What is the empire of my choice?
Is it the empire of heaven?
Is it the empire of the earth?
And if I shall choose the empire,
and choose the empire of the earth,
the empire of earth is brief,
heaven is everlasting.'
And the emperor chose the empire of heaven
Above the empire of the earth.[7]

Before NATO deployed troops in Kosovo there was a Yugoslav army barracks by the battlefield and Serbian soldiers would often run exercises on the undulating heathland.

For a battle invested with so much significance, what is so odd is just how little we really know about what happened there. We do know that both Lazar and Sultan Murad died, but as to exactly how they met their ends we have only the unreliable testimony of the later much-embroidered epics and a few other unreliable sources. In trying to reconstruct what happened historians borrowed from the epics but, in fact, many of their tales were based on post-battle propaganda rather than fact. For example, the epics say that at a crucial moment the Serbs were betrayed by Vuk Branković. However there is no evidence for this and it is more than likely untrue. The epics laud the action of Miloš Obilić (Kobilić in earlier versions) who, to prove his loyalty to Lazar, managed to infiltrate his way into the Sultan's tent and murder him. There is, however, no evidence that

Obilić was even a real historical character. The Serbs 'know' that Kosovo was a great defeat. In fact, it seems to have been more of a draw and Serbia did not finally fall to the Turks until 1459.

What may have happened is that after the battle Milica, Lazar's widow, enlisted the church to help build up Lazar as a saint because she needed to bolster their small son's claim to power. So the great myth of Kosovo, so influential in Serbian history, may to a great extent be based on medieval propaganda. After the battle Patriarch Danilo recorded a speech, which he says Lazar gave on the eve of combat. 'It is better to die in battle than live in shame', he is reputed to have said. 'Better it is for us to accept death from the sword in battle than to offer our shoulder to the enemy … Sufferings beget glory and labours lead to peace.'[8] It is impossible to underestimate the power of these sentiments, even if these words were never actually spoken, especially as they came to infuse the fervour of nineteenth-century Serbian nationalism, which aimed to liberate Kosovo from the yoke of the Turks.

Piccolomini and the beasts

While it is certain that there were Albanians in medieval Kosovo, it would also seem certain, as we have noted, that the majority of the people who lived there were mainly Orthodox, and thus ancestors, in the main, of modern Serbs. A certain number, but how many is unclear, did convert to Islam, and either were assimilated into the later increasing numbers of Albanians or became Serbian-speaking Muslims, such as the Goranci, who live around Prizren. Over the centuries, however, a higher proportion of Albanians was to convert to Islam than Serbs. One of the main reasons for this was that the Albanians did not have a powerful national church like the Serbs, nor was the power of Catholicism as strong amongst them as it was in, say, the regions of modern Croatia.

That there was some conversion amongst the Serbs is important but does not really explain the fundamental demographic shifts which took place in Kosovo during the centuries of Ottoman rule. Under the Turks, Serbs moved northwards, to Bosnia, to Hungary – especially to the region of Vojvodina, now in northern Serbia, and to Dalmatia and Croatia. Classical Serbian history holds that, following the penetration of an Austrian army into Kosovo in 1689, the Serbs rose up to join the Austrians and then tens of thousands of them fled northwards after the Austrians met their defeat at a battle at highwayman Musa's Kačanik Gorge on 2 January 1690. After that, runs the classical line, the Turks encouraged Muslim Albanians to come down from the mountains to repopulate the land. In this way and about now, the population balance really began to change. In fact, the true picture is more complex.

Sir Paul Rycaut was an Englishman who, for 18 years, was the English consul in Smyrna, which is modern Izmir in western Turkey. He travelled through the Balkans and in 1700 published an extraordinarily detailed account of the wars that had been fought there since 1679. Of course, there is no reason for us to believe that everything he wrote was accurate or based on entirely reliable sources. Yet he obviously followed developments closely and so his book would seem to represent the sum of knowledge of one of the best-informed outsiders of the time. His account suggests that there were far more Albanians already in Kosovo – or Arnouts as he calls them, using a name derived from Turkish – than Serbian historians would have us believe. His graphic description of the aftermath of the Austrian retreat also paints a picture of reprisals horrifically similar to the contemporary conflict.

The Austrians, whom Rycaut calls the Germans, were led by Count Eneo Piccolomini. As the Austrians swept in to Kosovo, says Rycaut, they:

> hasted with all expedition possible toward Priština and Clina, where they understood from the advanced Guards that 6000 Arnouts, with 1300 Carts, and many Thousand Head of Cattle remained in expectation to joyn with the Germans, and to oppose the Turks with all the People of the country, and to yield themselves subjects and Vassals to His Imperial Majesty. Being arrived at Priština, they concluded a Treaty with those People.[9]

Interestingly Clina, now Klina, is a town on the edge of Kosovo's Drenica area – the heartland of the Albanian uprising of 1998 and 1999.

In Rycaut's time Serbs were more often than not called Rascians, a name derived from Raška. Here he quotes from a letter that he says Piccolomini sent at the end of October or early in November 1689:

> Ten Thousand Rascians with Arms in their Hand are come in to me without any Head or Commander, with intention to rob, and live on Violence and Rapin. I know not what to do with these Wild Beasts, for upon pretence of coming in to us, I know not how to restrain them, tho' they ruine and spoil all the country, and put me in some Fears and Apprehensions for them, whilst their Outrages affright others from coming in, to dismiss them out of our Army, I fear something worse, and to keep them is to suffer them to destroy all.[10]

In January, following the defeat at Kačanik, by which time Piccolomini was dead of the plague, the retreating Austrians, now in Niš (Nissa), heard of the appalling reprisals which were taking place. Cossova is the area of modern Kosovo Polje, and Prissina is Priština

> And now Advices came to Nissa, That the Turks had burnt Uranic, with all the Villages round that Place; as also Cossova, and their adjacent Places near Prissina; but some little time before this piece of Execution was performed the Turks had allured the poor Peasants, with their Wives and Children, to return from the Woods and Mountains, to their Dwellings, where they promised Quietness, Protection, and Safety; but the Tartars not having been concerned in this Guaranty, the poor People were no sooner returned to their Habitations, but they were barbarously attacked by the Tartars, who killed all the Old Men and women, and carried away young of both sexes into Captivity.[11]

The most miserable corner of Europe

'I left Uskub', (Skopje) wrote H.N. Brailsford, in his book published in 1908, 'with high expectations.' Brailsford, a journalist who was writing for what was then called the *Manchester Guardian*, today's *Guardian*, was to become one of the most distinguished British Balkan experts of his day. He left then for Kosovo asking: 'What might one not discover in that mysterious region, as strange as Arabia, as distant as the Soudan?' He was, he says, 'not disappointed'.[12] But, he reflected, in words which were often to be repeated by journalists following in his footsteps, almost a century later: 'I realise painfully that I have visited the most miserable corner of Europe.'[13] It would be a joy to write about Kosovo's golden age: the years of mutual tolerance and respect, the long years of peace and happiness. The problem is, they have not happened yet.

Although, of course, there were long periods of peace in Ottoman Kosovo, there were also long years of war and depredation. During the eighteenth and nineteenth centuries the vast majority of the people who lived in Kosovo, were peasants. Politically, however, the Serbs counted for little, but the case of the Albanians, or rather the Muslim Albanians, was different. Because it was Muslim, the Albanian aristocracy was the power in the land, and in constant struggle with the Sultan and the Turks. Ottoman troops were frequently campaigning to put down one revolt after another, but these were not uprisings which aimed at independence as such. Albanians could, and did, rise to the highest positions in the empire and many lived in Constantinople. However, Albanians had ambivalent feelings towards the Turks and the empire. On the one hand, they professed their loyalty and love of the Sultan. On the other, they wished to be left alone to run their own affairs as they saw fit. As the empire became increasingly sclerotic, the Albanians, as they began to contemplate their long-term future, became increasingly nervous. As the Christian states of the region, Serbia, Montenegro and Greece, slowly began to re-emerge as powers in their own right, all claimed land inhabited by Albanians. The empire was some form of guarantee that Albanians, if they could achieve autonomy within it, would thus be able to assure their continuing dominance in the lands where they lived and avoid being partitioned by the Christian states. The Albanians were, of course, right to fear for their future. From 1804, as Serbia began to emerge, first as a rebel province and then as an autonomous principality within the empire, Muslims, including Albanians who lived there, soon found themselves prevailed upon to emigrate or flee. In 1878, when the

Serbs retook Niš, the Albanian quarter of the town and the Albanian villages of the region were burned. Albanians in other areas of what is now southern Serbia experienced the same. Most of these people fled to Kosovo, which was to remain Ottoman until 1912. As the recent Balkan wars have underlined to a new generation, the influx of embittered refugees from one community always bodes ill for the innocent civilians of the other. In increasing numbers Serbs began to leave.

The Serbian historian Milan St Protić believes that the Serbian–Turkish wars of 1876–8 'caused the most massive migration process in the Balkans in the course of the 19th century'.[14] By his estimation, a million Christians and a million Muslims – including, of course, Albanians from those lands reconquered by the Serbs – fled their homes.

Serbian history books venerate 1878 as the year Serbia liberated Niš and other areas and was also officially recognised as a fully independent state. Albanians remember it as the year of the League of Prizren. Fearing the imminent loss of Albanian-inhabited lands to the new Christian states, including Bulgaria and Montenegro, intellectuals mobilised to call a meeting of Albanian leaders in Prizren in June 1878. Some wanted to defend Muslim and Albanian traditions, which they felt were being threatened by modernising reformers. Some wanted a fully autonomous Albanian state, including of course Kosovo, to be set up within the empire. Others were simply keen to fend off the encroachments of the Christian and Slavic states. By 1880, thanks to deteriorating relations between the politicians of the League and the Porte (the traditional name of the Ottoman government), the League in effect took over the running of Kosovo and some of its leaders, notably Abdyl Frashëri, began to think in terms of independence.[15] The spring of 1881, however, saw the insurrection crushed by Turkish troops. But the idea that Albanians, both Muslims and Catholics, and those hailing from both the northern Gheg and southern Tosk tribes, could or should unite as Albanians only and fight for either autonomy or even independence, could not be swept aside. As the Albanian poet Pashko Vasa put it: 'the religion of Albanians is Albanianism'.[16]

We are lucky that during the late nineteenth and early twentieth centuries these parts of the Balkans were well covered by journalists and travellers from Britain. Their books provide an invaluable source of information on life in Kosovo during the twilight years of Ottoman rule. These, for example, are Brailsford's impressions of Peć, Peja in Albanian (he uses the Turkish name Ipek), and of 'Djacova', Djakovica in Serbian or Gjakova in Albanian:

> In Ipek and in Djacova there is still literally no law and court of justice. The civil code, more or less on the Napoleonic model, which Turkey possesses, is not in force in these towns. Such justice as is administered is dealt out by religious functionaries whose code is the Koran. In all that belongs to the civil side of politics we are still in the heyday of Islam. The kadi administers the law as it was laid down by the Prophet, and his court observes the same maxims and the same ceremonies which prevailed when the Barmecides were Caliphs in Baghdad. It is still the world of 'Arabian Nights', and here in Europe, within a day's journey of the railway that leads to Vienna, we are in the East and in the Middle Ages.[17]

During her 1908 tour Edith Durham had lunch with the director of the Serbian Orthodox seminary in Prizren and his wife.

> The school, a fine building, recently enlarged and repaired, holds a hundred students. Many come from Montenegro even. I went over it sadly. It seemed sheer folly to make a large and costly theological school in a Moslem Albanian town, and to import masters and students, when funds are so urgently needed to develop free Serbian lands.
>
> The white castle of Tsar Lazar was but a dream in the night of the past. Around us in the daylight was the Albanian population, waiting, under arms, to defend the land that had been theirs since the beginning of time.

Durham felt uncomfortable with the director, though, and his wife was frightened because, earlier in the day, the Muslims in town (apart from Albanians, Prizren had substantial ethnic Turkish and Slavic Muslim minorities) had been up in arms, angry over a number of disputes involving Christians and Muslims.

I accepted his hospitality unhappily, for I felt that, so far as Prizren and its neighbourhood were concerned, the cause was lost, dead and gone – as lost as is Calais to England, and the English claim to Normandy. And the mere terror of his wife showed how completely she felt herself a stranger in an unknown land. Yet I could not but admire the imaginative nature of the Serb, who will lead a forlorn hope and face death for an idea.[18]

While it seemed clear to Durham, Brailsford and others that much of the southern and western parts of Kosovo were thoroughly Albanian, it was noted that other parts had compact Serbian populations, especially in the east and from Mitrovica to the then Serbian border. Brailsford wondered whether the area should not eventually be partitioned, an idea that was to resurface amongst Serbian intellectuals such as the novelist and briefly Yugoslav president, Dobrica Ćosić, in the 1990s and again after NATO's intervention in 1999.

All those who wrote about Kosovo in this period noted that these were bad times for its Serbs. 'There are few Servian villages which are not robbed periodically of all their sheep and cattle,' reported Brailsford:

> For two or three years the village remains in the slough of abject poverty, and then by hard work purchases once more the beginnings of a herd, only in due course to lose it again. I tried to find out what the system of land tenure was. My questions, as a rule, met with a smile. The system of land tenure in this country, where the Koran and the rifle are the only law, is what the Albanian chief of the district chooses to make it. The Servian peasants, children of the soil, are tenants at will, exposed to every caprice of their domestic conquerors. Year by year the Albanian hill-men encroach upon the plain, and year by year the Servian peasants disappear before them. Hunger, want, and disease are the natural accompaniments of this daily oppression.[19]

Avenging Kosovo

In 1876, when Serbia and Montenegro went to war with the Ottoman Empire, Montenegro's Prince Nikola said: 'This time we have to avenge Kosovo! Under Murad I the Serbian empire was destroyed – now during the reign of Murad V it has to rise again.'[20]

While the driving force of modernising and nationalist Albanian thinking was based in Constantinople, or Bucharest or Italy, wherever there were Albanian communities outside the homeland, the same syndrome was becoming less and less true for the Serbs. When all of what is now central Serbia had been part of the Ottoman Empire, the impetus for new thinking came from Serbian communities who also lived outside, for example in Novi Sad, the so-called Serbian Athens then inside the Austro-Hungarian Empire. In 1804, however, the first Serbian uprising, led by the erstwhile pig-dealer Karadjordje, had shown that it was possible to shake off the Turks. His revolt was eventually crushed but the second uprising of 1815 led by Miloš Obrenović secured autonomy for a small part of Serbia, which, as we have seen, was by 1878 far larger and recognised as an independent state. As far as Kosovo was concerned, this was to mean several things. We have already mentioned the fact that Albanians were chased out of this Serbia as it expanded. This resulted in an outflow of Serbs from Kosovo. Threatened or not, the autonomous and the independent Serbia also exerted a strong pull for the peasants of Kosovo and the other parts of the Ottoman Empire. Obrenović actively encouraged immigration by handing out land to peasants who came to live in what, by 1817, was his principality. In this way, and because there was no native aristocracy, Serbia was very much a peasant society. But, in Belgrade, there was something new too. This was an emerging middle class. And this demanded new ideas, literature and entertainment. Again Kosovo played a leading role. For example Vuk Karadžić, who worked on developing a standard Serbian literary language, began to record the Kosovo epic tales and to publish them. This meant that the epic tradition could continue to inspire people even though they no longer gathered around the fire and village bard to listen to him sing. So, Lazar, Obilić, Prince Marko and all the other heroes of the epics lived again for new generations, helping now to give focus to emerging Serbian nationalism. Nowhere is this better demonstrated than in the speech given by Cedomil Mijatović, Serbia's foreign minister, to the Royal Academy, in 1889, on the occasion of the 500th anniversary of the historic battle:

An inexhaustible source of national pride was discovered on Kosovo. More important than language and stronger than the Church, this pride unites all Serbs in a single nation ... The glory of the Kosovo heroes shone like a radiant star in that dark night of almost five hundred years ... There was never a war for freedom – and when was there no war? – in which the spirit of Kosovo heroes did not participate. The new history of Serbia begins with Kosovo – a history of valiant efforts, long suffering, endless wars, and unquenchable glory ... We bless Kosovo because the memory of the Kosovo heroes upheld us, encouraged us, taught us, and guided us.[21]

This was the era of Serbian national romanticism expressed in art and literature. Simultaneously though, Serbian scholars began to apply their minds to the Albanians. As the Croatian historian Ivo Banac pointed out in his seminal study *The National Question in Yugoslavia*, 'Not all Albanians could be expected to flee from their native homesteads,' when Kosovo was reconquered. 'As a result, Serbian propaganda simultaneously dehumanised Albanians, presenting them as utterly incapable of governing themselves and as the sort of element that ought to be exterminated, and elevated them to the standing that warranted their assimilation.'[22] While on the one hand, then, a theory was developed which explained that a large part of the Kosovo Albanian population were really Albanianised Serbs, on the other the Albanians were denigrated, as Banac puts it, as 'savages'. So,

> Dr Vladan Djordjević, a noted Serbian statesman and public health specialist, showed no restraint in this line of defamation. Citing various foreign travelers and doctors of anthroposcopy, Djordjević had his Albanians skinny and short, possessed of gypsy and Phoenician features – indeed reminding him of the 'prehumans, who slept in trees, to which they were fastened by their tails'.[23]

In our time, much of the Kosovo conflict can be related to the fact that too many Serbs have never been willing or able to rid themselves of the idea that the Albanians, with whom they shared a state for the best part of a century, were not to be treated as equals. Rather, they thought of them as people who could be patronised or dismissed as belligerent peasants who, instead of complaining, should have been grateful to be living in Yugoslavia.

The atmosphere of pre-Balkan-War Serbia helps explain why, in 1912, the Serbs were able to retake Kosovo while the Albanians were unable to secure a united Albania from the wreckage of the Ottoman Empire. The Serbs already had a state, which could, and did, cultivate a national myth and, just as important, Serbia and Montenegro had organised modern armies. Leon Trotsky, who was then working as a war correspondent for the *Kievskaya Mysl*, has left us valuable descriptions of Belgrade on the eve of war. 'Carriages, men, horses – have been snatched up by the machinery of mobilisation ... Factories and workshops stand silent, apart from those working to produce uniforms and munitions for the army, and the shops are empty.'[24] By contrast, the Albanian experience and tradition of risings against the Turks would not be enough to fend off the Serbs when the time came.

The war broke out in October 1912. The Turks had been weakened by yet another revolt in Kosovo, in which most of the area had been taken over by Albanian rebels. Bulgaria, Serbia, Greece and Montenegro attacked (almost) simultaneously. Within weeks the Turks had been driven back, virtually to the gates of Constantinople. Montenegro seized Peć and other parts of western Kosovo while Serbia took the rest. 'The single sound of that word – Kosovo – caused an indescribable excitement', wrote one Serbian soldier as his unit came to rest at the battlefield of 1389:

> When we arrived on Kosovo and the battalions were placed in order, our commander spoke: 'Brothers, my children, my sons!' His voice breaks. 'This place on which we stand is the graveyard of our glory. We bow to the fallen ancestors and pray God for the salvation of their souls.' His voice gives out and tears flow in streams down his cheeks and grey beard and fall to the ground. He actually shakes from some kind of inner pain and excitement.
>
> The spirits of Lazar, Miloš [Obilić], and all the Kosovo martyrs gaze on us. We feel strong and proud, for we are the generation which will realize the centuries-old dream

of the whole nation: that we with the sword will regain the freedom that was lost with the sword.[25]

The decisive battle of the war took place at Kumanovo in northern Macedonia. After that, a slogan was coined: 'For Kosovo – Kumanovo'. On 9 June 1999 Serbian commanders signed what was called a Military–Technical Agreement with NATO at Kumanovo. So, in a way, Kosovo was won, and lost again, at the same place.

While, of course, for Kosovo's Serbs, now between 30 and 40 per cent of the population of Kosovo, the return of a Serbian army was a liberation, for the Albanians it was a catastrophe. It meant that they could not unite with the now-emerging Albanian state which had been declared in 1912 and recognised the year afterwards.

As the Serbian and Montenegrin armies swept into Kosovo in 1912 and consolidated their rule, any attempt at resistance by the Kosovar leaders who had taken on the Turks earlier in the year was crushed with the utmost brutality. As many as 20,000 may have been killed and tens of thousands fled.[26] Horrified by events, including those of the Second Balkan War of 1913, which saw the erstwhile allies fall out and fight over their spoils, the American Carnegie Endowment organised a commission to visit the Balkans and report back. Amongst its eight members were the editor of *The Economist* and H.N. Brailsford. 'Houses and whole villages reduced to ashes,' it reported, 'unarmed and innocent populations massacred *en masse*, incredible acts of violence, pillage and brutality of every kind – such were the means which were employed and are still being employed by the Serbo-Montenegrin soldiery, with a view to the entire transformation of the ethnic character of regions inhabited exclusively by Albanians.'[27] As a general observation of the way that the wars were conducted, the report noted that:

> Since the population of the countries about to be occupied knew, by tradition, instinct and experience, what they had to expect from the armies of the enemy and from neighboring countries to which these armies belonged, they did not wait their arrival, but fled. Thus, generally speaking, the army of the enemy found on its way nothing but

villages which were either half deserted or entirely abandoned. To execute the orders for extermination, it was only
necessary to set fire to them. The population, warned by
the glow from these fires, fled in all haste. There followed
a veritable migration of peoples …[28]

Leon Trotsky came to the same conclusion. But one soldier,
talking about the war in general, told him that 'responsibility for
atrocities lies … only to a minor extent with the regular forces'.
He explained that 'as a general rule' they only destroyed the
houses of the *kaçaks,* the name for Albanian rebels, but that
then 'the reserves came up, and did their bit. And after them
came the militiamen and *komitadjis* to finish the job.' Today the
word *komitadji* would translate as a paramilitary force. 'The
komitadjis were worse than you can possibly imagine,' he
explained to Trotsky:

> Among them were intellectuals, men of ideas, nationalist
> zealots, but these were isolated individuals. The rest were
> just thugs, robbers, who had joined the army for the sake
> of loot. They sometimes came in handy, because they held
> life cheap – not only the enemy's but their own as well. At
> the village of Nagorican, near Kumanovo, no fewer than
> two hundred of them fell, fighting bravely. But in the
> intervals they were just out and out brigands.[29]

The parallels between the *komitadjis* of Trotsky's time and the
paramilitaries of today are striking. Now, one of the most vexed
questions when it comes to atrocities is just how high up the
chain of command the orders come from. As far as Trotsky was
concerned, there was little doubt. He recounts this episode
which he says had become well known. Serbia's King Peter
was on his way to Kumanovo where he met a party of Albanian
prisoners under escort. He 'stood up in his car, in all his
little height, and shouted: "What use are these men to me?
They should be killed – not by shooting, that would waste
ammunition, but with clubs."'[30]

The Albanians of Kosovo did not have to wait long before
they could exact their revenge. By 1915, after at first successfully
repulsing the Austro-Hungarians, the Serbian army was
defeated. The Austro-Hungarians, along with the Germans and

Bulgarians, occupied Serbia and her newly acquired territories. The response of the Serbian government and army was, quite literally, to walk out. With the Bulgarians having cut their escape route southwards, across Macedonia, many of the columns tramped across Kosovo, including the battlefield itself, while enemy planes circled above.[31] The Serbs were attempting to get to the sea, from where they could be rescued by allied forces. Tens of thousand were captured by the Austro-Hungarians and Bulgarians, but those that managed to escape by trekking across Kosovo, Montenegro and Albania were rescued by British and French ships which took them first to Corfu and then to the Salonika Front where they fought alongside the allies. The retreat across Kosovo, however, meant that the Albanians had an opportunity to take their revenge for 1912. One account, written by Nikola Petrović, a Serbian officer, describes how Albanian guerrillas picked off weak detachments. The army was already enfeebled by cold and hunger but, says Petrović:

> the worst thing was that unlike the enemy it could not take refuge in the houses of Albanian villages, because if one of ours dared to venture into one of these houses to warm up or rest, he would be sure to die there. The Albanians killed those who had become isolated, chopping off their heads with axe blows. Then they seized the uniform of the dead man and, disguised as Serbian soldiers so as to allay any suspicion, they killed other unhappy men by luring them into ambushes.[32]

The Serbian retreat was a truly heroic feat and thus the 1916 celebrations of 'Kossovo Day' should come as little surprise. Britain and the other allies were inspired by the Serbian David standing up to the Austro-Hungarian–German Goliath. On 23 February of that year Herbert Asquith, the British prime minister, told the House of Commons: 'We shall not sheath the sword, which we have not drawn lightly, until Belgium – and I will add Serbia – recovers in full measure all, and more than all she has sacrificed.'[33] Every-day, British foreign ministers are reminded of these times. At the top of the Grand Staircase in the Foreign Office is a mural painted during the First World War. It represents Britannia and her allies. Under Britannia's outstretched arm nestle the aggrieved children: Belgium, Serbia and little Montenegro.

By 1918 the pendulum had swung back again. Driving northwards with the allies, Serbian troops reoccupied Kosovo. On 1 December 1918 the new Yugoslav state, called, until 1929, the Kingdom of Serbs, Croats and Slovenes, came into being. Again, the Serbs, or rather the new authorities, were resisted. Bands of guerrilla *kaçaks,* many of whom had fought the Turks and Serbs in 1912 and 1913, and then the Austro-Hungarians and Bulgarians, carried on fighting. The crushing of the revolt was bloody. Thousands died. Banac, citing Albanian sources, writes that in November 1918 'the Serbian army ravaged the area of Podgor Metohijski (near Peć), massacring women and children and destroying 138 houses. The army massacred 700 Albanians in Rožaj (Sandžak) and 800 in the region of Djakovica and in mid-February 1919 used cannon fire to destroy fifteen villages in the Rugovo Gorge.'[34] Still the *kaçak* brigand-cum-freedom-fighter rebellions lingered on for years. In 1937 Rebecca West, the English writer, met the Scottish manager of the then British-owned Trepča mines. 'They used to sweep down on the roads round here and rob and murder,' he told her. 'It had to be stopped.'

> The only way the gendarmes could stop it, was by going up into these villages and killing every man, woman and child. Mind you, nothing less would do. If they'd let one child get away, as soon as it had grown up it would have to carry on the blood-feud against the gendarmes, or the people who were supposed to be responsible for the gendarmes' attack.[35]

First and foremost the *kaçaks* resisted the reimposition of Serbian or Yugoslav rule because they did not want Kosovo to be part of Yugoslavia. It was, after all, a state of the south Slavs, as it name suggested, and the Albanians are not Slavs. That aside, the antipathy that Albanians felt towards the new state was now fuelled by the fact that Albanian language schools were closed and, in an effort to redress the ethnic balance, the Serbian-dominated authorities encouraged Serbian and Montenegrin settlers to come to Kosovo.

The schools issue is a curious one, for when, after 1990, Albanians set up a parallel education system in the province, it was not as though this was the first time schools had been turned into an instrument of resistance. In what were known as 'Turkish schools' the authorities permitted instruction by imams and Catholic priests. The hope was that, by doing this, Albanians would remain, as one official wrote in 1921, 'backward, unenlightened and stupid,' and hence without the intellectual wherewithal to resist.[36] However, as Banac notes, this policy backfired, since these schools turned into 'formidable centers of underground national education and oppositional activity, stubbornly resistant despite frequent closings'. He also writes that 'Illegal organizations, such as Agimi (Dawn) and Drita (Light), operated through legal youth clubs and sports organisations, disseminating books smuggled from Albania.'[37] Some schools were also set up in private homes, a model which would be used again in the 1990s.[38]

Some 70,000 colonists were brought to Kosovo, and although dispossessed Albanians were supposed to be compensated for confiscated land, this in fact rarely happened.[39] In some places Albanians lost their land or were restricted to tiny plots because they could not prove their ownership with title deeds. This helped prod thousands into emigrating and some 150,000 people are believed to have left for Turkey in the years between 1910 and 1920. On precisely this question, the relationship between small plots and emigration, one official report noted 'this was precisely what we wanted; that is, to prevent them from living and thereby force them to emigrate'.[40] Noel Malcolm estimates that the number of Albanians and other Muslims who emigrated in the years 1918–41 lies between 90,000 and 150,000.[41] Turkey was delighted to take in Albanians because the emigration of Greeks from Anatolia had left whole areas underpopulated. Indeed, after the Treaty of Lausanne in 1923 saw the forcible exchange of those remaining Greeks and Turks from both countries, the total numbers who had left due to war and the treaty amounted to 1.3 million Greeks from Turkey and 350,000 Turks from Greece. In 1938 Yugoslavia and Turkey signed a convention which foresaw the emigration of some 40,000 families or 200,000 people to Turkey over the next six years. Officially the convention talked about the 'repatriation' of the 'Turkish Muslim' population but, apart from Yugoslavia's relatively small numbers of ethnic Turks and Slav Muslims from Macedonia, it was clear from the regions specified in the convention that the bulk of these people would be Albanians.[42] In the end the document remained a dead letter because of the outbreak of war.

Some clearly regretted this. Vaso Čubrilović was a distinguished historian at Belgrade University. As a young man he had taken part in the assassination of Archduke Franz Ferdinand in Sarajevo in 1914. In March 1937 he presented the government with a paper called 'The Expulsion of the Arnauts'. It is important to examine it because not only did it crystallise a strong stream of intellectual thought in Serbia but, in the wake of the events of 1998–9, we can see that its ideas proved to have enduring appeal. Čubrilović was highly critical of the colonisation programme because he simply did not believe it was working. 'The fundamental mistake of the authorities', he said, was trying to solve the problems of the 'bleeding Balkans' by Western methods.[43] He criticized the authorities for not having taken the opportunity of the rebellions, which followed the reoccupation of Kosovo in 1918, to expel part of the population to Albania. 'The only way and only means to cope with them is the brute force of an organized state ... if we do not settle accounts with them at the proper time, within 20–30 years we shall have to cope with a terrible irredentism, the signs of which are already apparent and which will inevitably put all our southern territories in danger'.[44] Čubrilović was nervous that Britain and France might object to forced removals but said they should be reassured, by pointing out that the result would be mutually beneficial, since a threat to Yugoslav security would be removed. 'At a time when Germany can expel tens of thousands of Jews and Russia can shift millions of people from one part of the continent to another, the shifting of a few Albanians will not lead to the outbreak of a world war.'[45] Čubrilović's suggestions as to how to prod Albanians into leaving are instructive since both ends of his spectrum, the legalistic and the violent one, were to be used by future generations.

The law must be enforced to the letter so as to make staying intolerable for Albanians: fines, and imprisonments, the ruthless application of all police dispositions such as on the prohibition of smuggling, cutting forests, damaging agriculture, leaving dogs unchained, compulsory labor and any other measure that an experienced police force can contrive.

If all of this was not enough he argued: 'There remains one more means, which Serbia employed with great practical effect after 1878, that is by burning down Albanian villages and city quarters.'[46]

The *kaçak* resistance was strongest in the years 1918–24. In the autumn of 1918 prominent Kosovo Albanians, based in Shkoder (also called Shkodra), in northern Albania, had founded the Committee for the National Defence of Kosovo which became known as the KK or Kosovo Committee. Just like the KLA in the early part of 1998, it smuggled arms across the border from Albania and coordinated, as best it could, raids within Kosovo and the two other areas of Yugoslavia with substantial Albanian populations, western Macedonia and parts of Montenegro.[47] The best-known of the *kaçak* leaders were Bajram Curri, Hasan Bey Prishtina and Azem Bejta. Significantly, bearing in mind that the heartlands of the revolt which began in 1998 were the villages of the central Drenica valley, fighting blew up there following a KK call to revolt on 6 May 1919. This was Azem Bejta's territory. He and his wife came from the village of Galica. According to Malcolm, 'it is estimated that there were 10,000 active rebels at this time. But the *kaçaks*, only half of whom had rifles, were no match against the machine-gun units of the Yugoslav army, which drove them off towards the mountains near Peć, destroying many villages as it did so and carrying out further reprisals afterwards.'[48] The legend of Azem Bejta lived on in Drenica, but even his fame was overshadowed by that of his wife Shota Galica, who had also taken up arms. In the event, apart from small groups which were never subdued, the end of major *kaçak* resistance came when the Yugoslav government helped Ahmed Zogu to return to power in Tirana in December 1924 in exchange for his suppressing the KK. Zogu, later King Zog, had opposed the KK and as minister of the interior in 1922 had run into conflict with it when he had tried to disarm the tribes of northern Albania. He became prime minister of Albania in 1923 but was overthrown, with KK help, in 1924.[49]

Although the authorities could break the *kaçak* back then, they could not, unsurprisingly, turn their Albanian citizens into loyal and happy subjects. Rebecca West travelled through Kosovo on her 1937 trip, paying virtually no attention to its Albanians whatsoever. She did, however, record this conversation in Peć with her cab-driver and his friend. First they asked her what countries she had visited and liked, a list which included France. 'They cried out against the name of France. The French they could not abide. They had fought against them in the Great War, they said and were glad of it. They liked, they said, the Germans and the Bulgarians, and hated the Serbs.' Indeed, so much so that:

> They both agreed that they would thoroughly enjoy another war if only it would give them a chance of shooting a lot of Serbs. They held up their left arms and looked along them and twitched their right thumbs against their left elbows and said 'Boom! boom! A Serb is dead!' I said, 'But what have you against the Serbs?' They said, 'After the war they ill-treated us and took our land from us.'

Grudgingly, West, who admired the Serbs, was forced to concede this point, noting, 'There was some justification for this, I knew.' She continued:

> The district of Petch [Peć] was handed over to an old man who had been [Serbian then Yugoslav] King Peter's Master of the Horse, and he appears, like our own followers of the Belvoir and the Quorn, to have offered conclusive proof of the powerfully degenerative effect of equine society on the intellect. 'But now what do they do to you?' I asked. 'We live so poor,' they said; 'in Albania our brothers live far better than we do.' It was as pathetic as the belief of the Bulgarian schoolboy in Bitolj [in modern Macedonia] that Bulgaria was a richer country than Yugoslavia; for everybody who comes out of Albania is amazed at the difference, which is all in Yugoslavia's favour, of the standard of living.[50]

What is especially interesting here is West's expression of the belief, which endures to this day, that when people hate each other, or have been manipulated into hating each other, that

relative wealth and standards of living have anything to do with
it. If this was the case, then the relatively prosperous Yugoslavia
would never have collapsed in blood in 1991.

Heavenly kingdom

On the night of 26–7 March 1941 Serbian officers in the
Yugoslav army overthrew the government. They objected to its
having signed up to Hitler's Axis pact. The government had,
after months of pressure, finally done so because it feared that if
it did not, then Yugoslavia would be invaded and dismembered.
On the radio, Patriarch Gavrilo spoke to the nation:

> Before our nation in these days the question of our fate
> again presents itself. This morning at dawn the question
> received its answer. We chose the heavenly kingdom – the
> kingdom of truth, justice, national strength, and freedom.
> That eternal idea is carried in the hearts of all Serbs,
> preserved in the shrines of our churches, and written on
> our banners.[51]

In London Winston Churchill rejoiced:

> Early this morning the Yugoslav nation found its soul. A
> revolution has taken place in Belgrade, and the Ministers
> who but yesterday signed away the honour and freedom of
> the country are reported to be under arrest. This patriotic
> movement arises from the wrath of a valiant and warlike
> race at the betrayal of their country by the weakness of
> their rulers and the foul intrigues of the Axis Powers.[52]

On 6 April Hitler took his revenge. Belgrade was bombed and
the invasion of Yugoslavia began. Resistance was feeble and the
country capitulated on 17 April. The country was now divided
up. A quisling 'Independent State of Croatia' (known by its
initials as the NDH) was formed which took in Bosnia and
Hercegovina. It was divided into German and Italian zones of
influence and much of the Dalmatian coast was directly annexed
by the Italians. Montenegro was occupied by the Italians and
most of Macedonia was occupied by Bulgaria. Serbia north of
the Danube was divided into a Hungarian zone, the Banat
was put under German control and the rest given to the NDH.

Central Serbia was German-occupied with a quisling government in nominal control.

Kosovo was divided into three sectors. The Bulgarians were given a small part in the east. Mitrovica and the zinc- and lead-producing Trepča mines were attached to German-occupied Serbia but the region was given a good measure of local control under Albanian leadership. The rest of the province, plus Albanian-inhabited areas of western Macedonia, were attached to Albania which had been conquered by the Italians in 1939.

At least to start with, the Kosovo Albanians were enthusiastic about the Italians. Although, of course, they were occupiers, they had also brought about the unification of almost all of the Albanian-inhabited lands. The swing of the pendulum also gave those Albanians who were minded to do so the opportunity to wreak revenge on the region's Serbs, and especially the Serbian and Montenegrin settlers who had come to Kosovo over the last twenty years. In the wake of the Yugoslav collapse, armed gangs roamed the countryside, burning Serbian villages and killing and expelling Serbs. Where Serbs could retaliate, they did, but, given the preponderance of power, there was presumably little opportunity to do so. Carlo Umiltà, the Italian 'Civil Commissioner' for Kosovo later described the horrific scenes that he had witnessed. 'The Albanians are out to exterminate the Slavs,' he wrote, saying that Serbs were begging passing Italian lorries and vehicles to take them to safety. In one region between Djakovica and Peć he found villages where 'not a single house has a roof; everything has been burned down … There are headless bodies of men and women strewn on the ground.'[53] Following the capitulation of Italy on 8 September 1943, Kosovo and Albania were immediately invaded by the Germans, who, although in control, maintained the fiction that Albania was an independent country.

Figures for the numbers of those killed in or expelled from Kosovo are highly contentious. The estimated number of those who were fled or expelled ranges from 30,000 to 100,000 while the number of Serbs and Montenegrins killed ranges from 3,000 to 10,000. In April 1942, however, 70,000 refugees from Kosovo had been registered in Belgrade. The numbers of Albanians who died is equally contentious. Most of them were killed when the communist Partisans reimposed Yugoslav rule in 1944–5 and these figures range from 3,000 to more than 25,000 within the boundaries of the province.[54]

While many Albanians collaborated willingly with the Italians and the Germans, they did so not out of love of the Axis, but out of hate for the Serbs. This meant, of course, that Tito's Partisans who first raised the standard of rebellion in Serbia in July 1941 found it hard to recruit in Kosovo. General Vladimir Velebit, a close associate of Tito, commented dryly in his account of the war that: 'The population was passive, their national aspirations having been satisfied by the removal of Great Serbian suppression.'[55] What this meant was that this made it 'difficult or well-nigh impossible to launch a national liberation struggle'.[56] Albeit under Italian or German tutelage, Albanians were in control and the occupiers encouraged the opening of schools which, of course, the former Yugoslav authorities had prohibited. Both the Italians and the Germans recruited various militias in Kosovo, where they found people more responsive than in Albania proper because of their fear of an eventual reversion to Yugoslavia. However, by all accounts, both proved to be disappointed. Some 600 to 700 Kosovars were trained by the Germans in Zemun, a suburb of Belgrade, and sent to Tirana at the end of September 1943. According to Bernd Fischer's recent study, 'their behaviour, however, did the Germans more harm than good, as they ravaged the countryside like a conquering army of old. The same was true of the twelve hundred armed gendarmes ... brought from Mitrovica to Tirana in December.'[57]

In February 1944 Hitler approved the creation of an SS 'Skanderbeg' division which was to serve only inside Kosovo. Named for the great Albanian hero who had resisted the Turks in the fifteenth century, the SS envisioned a force of up to 12,000 men, but only half that number were ever recruited. According to Fischer, 'Units of the division gained an unenviable reputation, apparently preferring rape, pillage, and murder to fighting, particularly in Serbian areas.' The Germans then had to disarm battalions in Peć and Prizren, while 'units that remained intact were sent against the Serbs, which is why many had joined, that is, to fight the hereditary enemy'. By October 1944 'more than half the original force had deserted' and the unit was disbanded.[58] Major-General August Schmidhuber, who commanded the

'Skanderbeg' division, was contemptuous of his men. He 'explained his failure by suggesting that Albanians had not developed culturally since the time of Skënderbeg in the fifteenth century':

> In his estimation, they had developed no concept of 'state' or 'nation', indeed, they had vegetated. He argued that the legend of Albanian military heroics was just a saga and that he personally could chase them all around the world with a light grenade launcher. They went on the attack only as long as there was something to steal.[59]

Perhaps the only thing the Germans had to be pleased about when it came to the 'Skanderbeg' division was their arrest of 281 Jews in Kosovo who were subsequently deported.[60]

If the Nazis were having problems with those they could recruit, Tito's Communists were having even more severe problems finding anyone to recruit at all. In September 1942 Tito wrote to the minute Partisan detachment that did exist in Kosovo, explaining that they had to point out to the Albanians that only by:

> fighting together with the other peoples of Yugoslavia, who are also struggling against the old regime, can the Albanian people of Kosovo and Metohija save themselves from a return of the oppression by the Greater-Serbia hegemonic clique ... It should be made clear to the Albanian masses that the Serbs and Montenegrins who live on their territory are not their enemies.[61]

Laudable though those sentiments might be, the problem was that most Kosovars did not believe in them. Communism was associated with the Serbs and thus with the future return of Yugoslav rule, a point skilfully played up by Italian and German propagandists. In the end, the Communists resorted to what amounted to a ruse in their bid to gain support. Meeting in Bujan, in northern Albania, over the new year of 1943–4, the two Yugoslav Communist committees which covered Kosovo issued a key declaration:

> Kosovo–Metohija is an area with a majority Albanian population, which, now as always in the past, wishes to be

united with Albania … The only way that the Albanians of Kosovo–Metohija can be united with Albania is through a common struggle with the other peoples of Yugloslavia against the occupiers and their lackeys. For the only way freedom can be achieved is if all the peoples, including the Albanians, have the possibility of deciding their own destiny, with the right to self-determination, up to and including secession.[62]

Right up to the end of the war, the Partisans were never able to recruit significant numbers of Kosovo Albanians to join them. However, those that did come to the colours in 1944 did so comfortable in the belief that they were fighting not just for Communism but for an Albania in which Kosovo would be included. They were to be betrayed. The return of Yugoslav forces was resisted in several areas, especially in Drenica. Here widespread fighting broke out when troops led by Shaban Polluzha, a former member of the Albanian nationalist Balli Kombëtar, who had gone over to the Partisans, refused to be sent north to help crush German resistance in Croatia. He had become angry because he, like others, had thought that the Yugoslav Partisans would soon be replaced by troops from Albania. At the same time it was discovered that a massacre of 250 men had taken place in Skenderaj, which is called Srbica in Serbian.[63] Skenderaj is a mile away from Donji Prekaz, where the 1998 uprising began, and five miles away from Galica – the village of Azem Bejta and his legendary wife, Shota Galica. Although Shaban Polluzha commanded much sympathy across Kosovo, the fighting that ended his resistance should not be interpreted in a simple Serb-versus-Albanian light. Many of those who took part in the fighting on the Yugoslav side were Albanians too.

In February 1945 martial law was declared while the Yugoslav authorities mopped up remaining pockets of resistance which included members of the Balli Kombëtar and the Serbian royalist and nationalist Chetniks. Both of these forces, in pursuing their anti-Communist struggle, had collaborated with the Italians and Germans.

The foundations of the new Yugoslavia were laid in Jajce, in Bosnia, in November 1943 at a meeting of the Second Anti-

Fascist Council for the National Liberation of Yugoslavia, known by its initials as AVNOJ. It stated that the new Yugoslavia was founded 'on the basis of the right of every people to self-determination, including the right to secede or unite with other peoples, and in conformity with the true aspirations of all the peoples of Yugoslavia'.[64] No Kosovo Albanians participated in the meeting, and, as we shall see, later constitutional refinements meant that the right of self-determination, meaning the right to secede from Yugoslavia, did not apply to Kosovo Albanians. In July 1945 Kosovo was formally annexed to Serbia. Kosovo was then declared to be an autonomous region of Serbia which in turn became a constituent part of the new Federal People's Republic of Yugoslavia.

After so much turmoil, ordinary Kosovars were more confused about the future than anything else. It was also not at all clear to them what the politicians were up to since any debates were not conducted in public.

According to an article published in an Albanian newspaper in 1981, in 1946 Tito told Enver Hoxha, the Albanian Communist leader: 'Kosovo and the other Albanian regions belong to Albania and we shall return them to you, but not now because the Great Serb reaction would not accept such a thing.'[65]

At this time the Albanian Communists, in Albania and Kosovo, were very much under Yugoslav tutelage. However, this is not the only reason why they did not oppose the reannexation of Kosovo. The other reason was that at this time, until Yugoslavia's break with Stalin in 1948, there was much talk about the creation of an all-embracing Balkan Federation, in which case, the issue of Kosovo might be resolved within that wider framework. 'Is it in our interests to ask for Kosovo?' asked Enver Hoxha in December 1946. 'That is not a progressive thing to do. No, in this situation, on the contrary, we must do whatever is possible to ensure that the Kosovars become brothers with the Yugoslavs.'[66]

One man who clearly doubted that this was possible was Vaso Čubrilović, who, as we have seen, had argued for the expulsion of the Albanians before the war. As early as November 1944, he reiterated his ideas in a new document which he presented to the new Communist authorities. Ethnic Germans, Hungarians, Albanians, Italians and Romanians should all be expelled, he said. And indeed, virtually all the ethnic Germans who lived in Yugoslavia were, along with many Italians and Hungarians too. Because the colonisation project in Kosovo had yielded such meagre results and indeed the colonists had all been driven out during the war, now, he argued, was the moment in a 'planned' way to 'unmercifully clean ... those territories which we wish to settle with our own national elements'. The interests of the state, he argued 'require that lands deserted by minorities be settled as soon as possible in order that they and the entire Europe be brought before a fait accompli'.[67] In his conclusion Čubrilović warned that 'we might never again have such an opportunity in order that we make our state ethnically pure ... the minority problem, if we do not solve it now, will never be solved.'[68] Čubrilović's advice was, on this occasion, ignored. It was clearly not forgotten.

2 Slobodan.Milosevic@gov.yu

Slobodan Milošević likes to think of himself as a thoroughly modern leader. He has an e-mail address, Slobodan. Milosevic@gov.yu and anyone who comes across it on the Yugoslav Government web site is invited to send him a message. I sent him one but he did not reply. You try.

What Mr Milošević really likes to do is make speeches about building high-speed railway lines. He likes to talk about being 'constructive' and 'resolute'. Typical speeches are full of bits like this:

> Our time, as all times in history, is not homogenous or uniform in any way. On the contrary, it is extremely varied. But every society that wishes itself good must endeavour to reach its peak in the material and spiritual sense in its time. Of course, to the extent to which this is possible. This effort, to attain the best a certain period can offer, will be our national, social and civilizational imperative.[1]

Milošević said this in his inaugural address to the federal parliament on 23 July 1997, when he became president of Yugoslavia. He had just traded in his old job as president of Serbia. But, as must be self-evident, Milošević did not rise to power on the strength of such stultifying banalities. He came to power by exploiting the issue of Kosovo. In this sense the cancer that killed Yugoslavia began in Kosovo. Milošević saw an opportunity and exploited it. In November 1988, for example, he told a rally of hundreds of thousands of adoring supporters, intoxicated by the nationalistic euphoria that he was then whipping up, that this was 'no time for sorrow'. It was, he said, 'a time for struggle'.

> We entered both world wars with nothing but the conviction that we would fight for freedom, and we won both wars ... We shall win the battle for Kosovo regardless of

the obstacles facing us inside and outside the country. We shall win despite the fact that Serbia's enemies outside the country are plotting against it, along with those in the country. We tell them that we enter every battle ... with the aim of winning it.[2]

But what was this battle for Kosovo? What was the issue in this tiny, forgotten corner of Europe? Surely Yugoslavia, for a Communist country, was a relatively prosperous and open society whose people could travel and work abroad just as they wanted? Weren't these obscure national quarrels in the Balkans something from the dim and distant past?

Kosovo – Republic!

The return of Yugoslav rule to Kosovo was, as we have seen, a far-from-welcome development for its Albanian population. Still, this was the era of orthodox Stalinism in both Yugoslavia and Albania, so there was precious little anyone could do about it, especially following the crushing of the anti-Yugoslav revolt which had centred on Drenica. There were at the time, however, a couple of factors which also softened the blow of reannexation. One was the fact that, until Yugoslavia's break with Stalin in 1948, the border between the two countries remained relatively open. The second, which we mentioned earlier, was that within the context of discussions about a Balkan Federation there was also talk of Albania itself becoming a Yugoslav republic in its own right. Unsurprisingly such talk never got very far but, as far as Stalin was concerned, Albania was a far-away country about which he knew little and cared less. Indeed, at one point he even encouraged the Yugoslavs to 'swallow' Albania whole.

Under the new constitution Kosovo was given regional autonomy. In fact, until the mid-1960s this meant little. Security lay in hands of Aleksandar Ranković, who until 1963 was minister of the interior and head of UDBa, the secret police. After that he became vice-president but remained *de facto* head of UDBa. Ranković was a Serb and many Serbs regarded him as 'their' man in Tito's inner circle. An old-fashioned Communist, Ranković believed in traditional old-style methods of repression and was particularly alert for any whiff of separatism. In

Yugoslavia: 1945–91

Kosovo, therefore, most key jobs in the immediate post-war era, especially in the police and security forces, went to Serbs. This was not only because they could be trusted as Serbs, but also because there were so few trustworthy Communist Albanians. Of those that had fought in the ranks of the Partisans many were now regarded with suspicion because of what they saw as the great betrayal of the Bujan promise, i.e., that post-war Kosovo would be allowed to determine its own future.

In 1956 there were trials of Albanians in Prizren who were accused of espionage and subversion. Violence was also a frequent feature of police raids, which aimed to gather in arms left over from the war. Despite this atmosphere of repression, as far as Ranković and other Yugoslav politicians were concerned Kosovo was not really a problem. There were some underground groups demanding union with Albania but politically they were insignificant. They included the Revolutionary Movement for Albanian Unity founded by Adem Demaçi and the People's Movement for the Republic of Kosova. Minuscule though they were, the long-term historical significance of these so called Marxist–Leninist and clandestine groups was immense. Indeed, the political ancestry of the KLA can be traced directly back to them. In 1964, Demaci and many of his followers were arrested and imprisoned.

Of far more immediate concern to Ranković were the long-term relations of the biggest of the Yugoslav nations, namely the Serbs and Croats. This related not just to the Yugoslav polity as a whole, but specifically to Croatia itself, with its substantial Serbian minority, and to Bosnia–Hercegovina.

Things began to change though, throughout Yugoslavia, after the fall of Ranković in 1966. The years preceding his fall had been dominated by quarrels between those who argued for centralism, as opposed to those who wanted more power, and especially economic decision making, to be devolved to the republics. Unsurprisingly it was the richer republics – Croatia and Slovenia – which were in favour of decentralisation. Tito was not particularly interested in economics but he was angered when he discovered that Ranković had been threatening individuals who had argued in favour of decentralisation. It was also alleged that Ranković was restricting access to Tito and had bugged his personal phones. He was ordered into retirement.

In the years following the fall of Ranković, Yugoslavia began to move, albeit haltingly, along the path of decentralisation and liberalism. One of the indirect results of this was that, by 1970, Croatia was being swept by waves of nationalist euphoria which eventually forced Tito to order a clamp-down in 1971. The long-term consequences of this were not to eradicate nationalism in Croatia, but to stifle it, temporarily. In 1968 Belgrade University was affected by the turmoil which was sweeping universities from Paris to Prague. There was no hint of nationalism here, but key figures in the protests, such as the philosophy professor Mihailo Marković, were later to play an important role in advising Milošević. In 1971, power in Serbia lay in the hands of economic modernisers like Latinka Perović and Marko Nikezić who took a tough line against nationalism. It was during their time in office, for example, that Mihailo Djurić, a law professor, was sent to jail. He had suggested that constitutional changes instituted in 1971 meant that the Yugoslav republics were on their way to becoming sovereign states and so the country's internal borders, which were obviously not then international frontiers, should be altered to take possible future developments into consideration. In the end Perović and Nikezić were purged, possibly through no fault of their own, but simply because Tito had to be seen to be even-handed following the ending of what had become known as the Croatian Spring.

With such important developments right at the centre of power, Kosovo was hardly in the limelight. It was, however, moving, relatively quietly, towards its own devolution. In 1968 those who had been convicted in the Prizren trials were rehabilitated. In November demonstrations broke out, led by students who demanded that the province be upgraded to a republic and that it be given its own Albanian-language university rather than remaining a provincial branch of Belgrade University. The protests spread to Albanian-inhabited areas of western Macedonia and, in what the authorities clearly regarded as an ominous development, radicals actually dared to shout slogans demanding union with Albania.

The question of a republic was easily dealt with. The answer was 'No'. Following the Soviet model Yugoslavia had devised a piece of constitutional sophistry to deal with precisely these questions. The peoples of Yugoslavia were classed as either 'nations' or 'nationalities'. The former were entitled to Yugoslav republics. They were the Slovenes, Croats, Serbs, Montenegrins and Macedonians. In 1971, they were joined by the Bosnian Muslims. By contrast, 'nationalities' were peoples who were, in effect, cut off from an existing motherland. The most important of the 'nationalities' were the Kosovo Albanians and the Hungarians who lived in Vojvodina in the north, both of whose people had existing states. This was, of course, so much legal gobbledegook because the real point was that nations – who had republics – were, under the constitution, theoretically possessed of the right to secede. So, under no circumstances could the Kosovo Albanians ever be allowed to become a republic lest one day they should actually try to exercise that right.

As to the second demand, that of a university, this was granted. Despite arrests and trials of some of the demonstrators of 1968, the authorities decided that the best way to deal with the Kosovars was to conciliate them. In 1970 Priština University opened and, given the dearth of Albanian-language academic materials in Yugoslavia, agreements were made with Albania itself to supply textbooks. Close links were also established between Priština and Tirana universities. While the authorities hoped that these concessions would dampen the attraction of poor, Stalinist, orthodox Albania, in fact they did quite the opposite. Along with the beginnings of the Albanianisation of the province a veritable Albanian national renaissance now began in Kosovo. Anton Logoreci, a writer on Albanian affairs, explained it this way:

> The main reason that things turned out the way they did was because, having been denied for many generations everything that helped to nourish a people's national consciousness and identity, the Albanians living in Yugoslavia, especially the post-war generation, were by the 1960s like a very parched sponge, immensely avid to absorb anything that helped to illuminate their past history and made some sense of their current situation.[3]

In 1974 Kosovo became a Yugoslav republic in all but name. That is to say it was represented on the federal presidency, along with its northern counterpart, Vojvodina, and the six republics. Power was by now very much in the hands of local Albanian Communists. Kosovo had its own assembly, police force, national bank and all the other accoutrements of republican status. Still, these were years of rising expectations and so it is hardly surprising that many wanted more. Throughout the decade there were waves of arrests and subversion trials. While the trials fitted in to a general pattern of repressing clandestine groups which objected to the de facto compromise between Kosovo's Albanian leadership and the authorities in Belgrade, some of those jailed did represent radical, hardline but minuscule groups which rejected Yugoslavia and demanded union with Albania. For them, Kosovo's Albanian Communist leadership was no more than a treacherous 'bureaucratic clique'.[4]

Tito died in 1980. With his death Yugoslav politics was deprived of its final arbiter, and, slowly but surely, the system began to unravel. In Kosovo, the first signs of this came in March and April 1981, when the province was rocked by demonstrations. They began in the university on 11 March, and at the very beginning had nothing to do with politics but with poor living conditions at the university and problems in the canteen. Daut Dauti, who was then a student and later became a journalist, recalls that 'actually the food was not that bad. The real problem was the service. There were so many students that sometimes you had to queue up for two hours to get a meal.' So, for the first few days, speakers complained about the canteen but then they began raising the issue of the university administration, saying that it was run by 'parasites' who were building themselves luxury houses in plush areas of Priština like Dragodan. Activists from the tiny Marxist–Leninist groups were moving in on what had begun as spontaneous protests.

Every day demonstrations took place in several different places at a time. As the denunciations shifted from the canteen to other issues, Dauti recalls that the atmosphere 'electrified'. Speakers began to say: 'We are rich enough, we should separate from Serbia. They take all our wealth.' Then Hydajet Hyseni, an activist, reputed founder of a Marxist–Leninist group and a journalist from the Kosovo Albanian daily paper *Rilindja*, who had recently been in hiding, climbed a tree and spoke to the demonstrators in front of the Communist Party building and urged them them not to stop. In this way he became known as the Che Guevara of Kosovo. Dauti says: 'People were saying we should be free from Serbian domination. There was a feeling that [despite autonomy] key positions were still held by Serbs and pro-Serb Albanians.'

Many years later Hyseni explained that, despite his association with the Marxist–Leninist groups, there were other influences as well:

> What was happening in Poland at the time had an indirect influence as well. It gave us hope. It showed us that a movement was possible. In general, democracy in Eastern Europe had a pro-western perspective. The opposition had an anti-Communist and social aspect in Poland. In contrast, in Kosovo the opposition had a national character. Instead of being anti-Communist, the Kosovo movement was anti-colonialist and nationalist.[5]

On the streets the students shouted for a republic. Arrests followed, which, by 26 March, sparked new protests by students demanding that those arrested be released. As demonstrators marched through the streets demanding a republic and union with Albania, onlookers cheered. As if things were not bad enough, they were now made worse by the fact that 26 March was Tito's birthday and, throughout Yugoslavia, a special celebratory youth relay was traditionally run on the day. Twenty-three demonstrators and fourteen policemen were injured in clashes.[6]

The situation began to spin out of control. High-school students joined their older brothers and sisters and workers in several factories downed tools. The slogans of the demonstrators were: 'Kosovo-Republic!', 'We are Albanians, not Yugoslavs!' and 'We want a unified Albania!'[7] Beginning to panic, the authorities called in units of special police, tanks appeared on the streets and a state of emergency was declared. When the unrest had been quelled the Yugoslav press reported variously that nine or eleven people (including policemen) had died and that 57 had been injured. However, the true casualty figure is unknown. Some insist that as many as 1,000 were killed, which is certainly an exaggeration, but the real figure might well have run into the hundreds.[8]

Arrests and trials now followed. According to Noel Malcolm, citing a 1986 survey published in the Belgrade magazine *NIN*, '1,200 people had been given substantial prison sentences, and another 3,000 sent to gaol for up to three months.'[9] Purges of Kosovo's Communist party now began and several of its leaders, such as its president, Mahmut Bakalli, were expelled. The authorities also constantly claimed they were unmasking (tiny) 'counter-revolutionary' groups, many of them even within the army.[10] Although these claims were certainly exaggerated, they were also, in some cases, not entirely without foundation. These groups usually came with some sort of Marxist–Leninist label and their members became known as the Enverists because of their publicly expressed admiration of Albania's Enver Hoxha.

Shkëlzen Maliqi, a Kosovar philosopher and political analyst, has written that, in this period, 'verdicts were harsh: eight to fifteen years' imprisonment. The police repression, not to mention the treatment of the whole issue in the Serbian press, was so unselective and chauvinistic – in relation to the entire Albanian population – that it produced a pattern of defensive homogenization on the part of Kosovo Albanians.'[11] According to one report, in the eight years after the protests, 584,373 Kosovars or 'half the adult population – were arrested, interrogated, interned or reprimanded. Seven thousand of these were jailed, hundreds more dismissed from school, university and work.'[12] It is vitally important to remember, however, that, at this crucial juncture, and indeed until 1989, it was not Serbs who were in charge in Kosovo. It was Albanians. This fact was to have enormous significance later on, as Western diplomats could never understand why it was so hard to bring together a Kosovo Albanian negotiating team which would represent a fair spectrum of opinion especially since they all agreed on the basic demand of independence. The answer often lay in who had done what, in and after 1981. Maliqi, for example, is well respected by Westerners and certain Kosovar circles. However, others will not forgive the fact that, in 1981, he was living in Belgrade and his father, a veteran Communist, was made Kosovo's secretary for internal affairs; in other words, its police chief. These are Maliqi's recollections about what his father said at the time. They tell us a lot about the psychology of the period. In June 1981, just after the riots, Maliqi senior was asked to take up the job. His son recalls:

> He told me that 'his legs felt numb' when they called him in and told him what they wanted …. He suggested that they find someone who was younger, better educated, etc. But when they called him in the second time, he agreed. He told me, 'I accepted that in 1941,' or, he said, '1942' … when he joined the Party. Since 1941 he had been a fighter in the movement, and he mentioned one of those two years, probably, because that's when he was accepted into the Party. In other words, he was a soldier of the Communist Party, and listened to everything those who were above him requested from him.[13]

His father's attitude to the demonstrations themselves is even more revealing:

> His argument was that Kosova practically already had what the demonstrators were demanding, and that only time was needed for … the legal status of a republic to be

achieved. He and his generation, Fadil Hoxha and the others, saw 1981 as the destruction of everything that they had achieved. In fact, 1981 implied precisely that. They adopted a defensive stance, thinking that an internal repression could break the 'Marxist–Leninists' and the organisers of the demonstrations, and that they could maintain a kind of *status quo* within Yugoslavia. They were excusing themselves for trying …. They were excusing themselves before the people, saying they were actually fighting for the very status of Kosova that the demonstrators were demanding, but that it could be achieved only by other means, and not 'in the streets'.[14]

Serbia is rising!

The events of 1981 were a turning-point, not just in the history of Kosovo, but for the whole of Yugoslavia. The death of Tito meant that, gradually, Communist power began to recede, or rather the fear of it receded, which amounted to the same thing. After the Kosovo riots, the steady number of Serbs already emigrating from Kosovo began to pick up and, even more importantly, the issue began to be discussed. In May 1982, for example, the Serbian Orthodox Church publication *Pravoslavlje* published an interview with Mother Superior Paraskeva of Dević monastery. Dević lies in the heart of Drenica, and, as we shall see, in 1998 it became a tiny island of Serbian territory in the middle of a KLA-controlled area. It had been burned down by Albanians in 1941 and some of its monks had been killed. After the war it had been taken over by nuns. In 1982, Dević was to play its role in history as Mother Paraskeva chronicled for *Pravoslavlje* how Serbs were leaving Drenica. 'Let us start with the village of Poljana, 48 or 49 [Serbian] families all gone; Ljubovats and Dugovats, around 60 homes, all gone; Gornje and Donje Prikaze, 30 homes …' The list continued. 'Prikaze' or as it has subsequently been transliterated, Prekaz, was the home of the Jashari family, and it was their massacre by Serbian police in March 1998 which sparked off the Kosovo uprising. Mother Paraskeva then told the reporter that the people had all left for Serbia; however, over what period she is talking about is unclear.

She then related how she and her sister nuns, 30 of them, lived since 1947. In a state of actual siege, battling the Albanian youths who harass them day and night, throwing stones, raiding the monastery forest, vegetable gardens, animal sheds. 'I was beaten, had broken ribs, my head was bloodied ten times ... We must say the militia [police] came often, but what's the use ...'[15]

Mother Paraskeva had data to hand because, ever since 1969, the church had ordered its people to compile it. The Serbian historians Alex Dragnich and Slavko Todorovich write that 'This order resulted from growing expressions of concern and alarm, both from members of the Serbian population of Kosovo and from Serbian priests who thought that the leadership in Belgrade was not doing enough to protect the Serbian faithful.' As early as February 1982, they note that a group of priests from Serbia proper wrote to their bishops asking 'why the Serbian Church is silent' and why it did 'not write about the destruction, arson, and sacrilege of the holy shrines of Kosovo'.[16]

It was true that Serbs were leaving Kosovo and that, especially after 1981, there were frequent expressions of hostility towards them. Some Serbian churches and graveyards were vandalised and many Serbs did indeed feel a pressure to leave. What was the peasant family to make of an incident if their cow was maimed in their field and the next day Albanians tried to buy their farm? The pressure on land and housing was, of course, demographic but it had political ramifications. Increasing numbers of Kosovars were also working abroad which meant that they could offer more and more money for Serbian homes. Still, Daut Dauti believes that, in the main, the general hostility towards ordinary Serbs was a 'boomerang' effect of the crackdown after 1981.

The problem was that what was and was not actually true now became lost in a increasingly bitter war of words – and lies. For example, while it is more than likely that the hated nuns of Dević were harassed, and even attacked, it is also equally unlikely that this happened 'day and night'. Serbian and Albanian propagandists now went to war armed with statistics, lies and half-truths, which far from helping either side in the long-run, were to embitter communal relations, pave the way for the rise of Milošević, the destruction of Yugoslavia and the deaths of tens of thousands.

The question of emigration was central in the evolving battle of lies. According to the census returns, the number of Serbs and Montenegrins in Kosovo remained relatively stable, moving between 200,000 and 260,000 in the post-war period. What does change though is that their numbers, *as a proportion of the population as whole,* dropped from a combined 27.5 per cent in 1948 to 14.9 per cent in 1981 and 10.9 per cent in 1991. This was not just due to Serb emigration, which in turn contributed to the lack of the natural growth of the population, but to the fact that the Albanian birth-rate was extremely high. Interestingly, if the 1991 census figures are more or less accurate (a projection of the numbers of Albanians was made because they boycotted the census), then the Albanian proportion of the population was 82.2 per cent. This means that the oft-quoted figure of the Albanian population constituting 90 per cent of Kosovo's population was, until 1999 anyway, not true.[17]

Not only is it difficult to work out exactly how many Serbs were really leaving but it is also difficult to work out why they were leaving. During the 1970s and 1980s Kosovo's administration, and just about everything else in the province, was progressively Albanianised. This meant that the Serbs lost their privileged status in the administration and state sector. One reason for this was that Priština University was producing thousands more graduates every year than the economy could possibly absorb. Family and other contacts inevitably meant that they would get jobs before Serbs. This in turn meant that young families tended to leave for Serbia proper because there were jobs in the factories of central Serbia and besides, there was no hassle there about being a Serb. But whether the majority of people left because they were discriminated against, felt threatened or simply felt that they or their children had no future in an Albanian-dominated Kosovo is a moot point. Probably the push factors were a combination of all of these, despite what propagandists of either side would like to pretend. The other crucial point to remember is that, ever since the war, there had been considerable demographic shifts across Yugoslavia. So, for example, peasants from poor areas of Montenegro and Bosnian and Croatian Serbs had moved in considerable numbers to the rich farmlands of Vojvodina and eastern Croatia where they were given homes and land which had belonged to the some 350,000 ethnic Germans who had been expelled, or fled, after the war. Industrialisation in Serbia and Croatia had also acted as a magnet for Bosnian Serbs and Croats respectively, and as mentioned, Serbs from Kosovo. Higher education was a pull factor too. Intelligent young Serbs would gravitate to Belgrade University, Croats to Zagreb and Muslims, from the Sandžak area of Serbia, which has a considerable Muslim population, to Sarajevo. Few of them would ever return home because the jobs for skilled people were in the big cities.

As if the emigration debate was not complicated enough, a number of related questions were frequently mixed in with this bitter battle of statistics. Serbs charged that a great injustice was done when pre-war Serbian colonists were, in March 1945, prohibited from returning to Kosovo. Initially this ruling was made as a sop to the Albanians, to soften the blow of re-annexation. In fact the accusation is a classic half-truth. There was a ruling, which was then adjusted, meaning that many, but not all, could return.[18] But, a good number also had no wish to come back since, during the war, they had had to flee for their lives. In turn, a good number of them were given former German homes and land in Vojvodina. By contrast, many other Serbs, who had not been colonists in the sense of farmers working the land, but administrators, teachers or people with other jobs, could and did return.

The other side of this quarrel was one over the numbers of Albanians who had emigrated to Turkey in the post-war years, during the Ranković era when Serbs dominated life in Kosovo. Was this was a form, as Albanians later charged, of what we now call ethnic cleansing or the willing emigration of people who wanted to live with family already there or simply did not want to live in a Communist country? Between 1952 and 1967, 175,000 Muslims emigrated from Yugoslavia to Turkey, but exactly how many of those were Albanians (probably a major-ity), as opposed to, say, Slav Macedonian Muslims or ethnic Turks, is unclear.[19] As with the debate about Serbian emigration, there were probably push and pull factors intertwined but the propagandists would find use for all of this, regardless of the facts. Similarly bitter polemics were traded over the question of how many Albanians had immigrated to Albanian-inhabited parts of Yugoslavia during the war, or in the early post-war years, when the border was still relatively open.

To a certain but unquantifiable degree, the hostility that was brewing in the 1980s was connected to the relative poverty of Kosovo. Albanian polemicists claimed that Kosovo was either exploited or not getting its fair share of Yugoslav development money. By contrast, the Serbian and Yugoslav authorities would use various statistics to 'prove' quite the opposite, that is to say that Kosovo was receiving disproportionate amounts of subsidies and direct investment. This in turn helped fuel other Yugoslav quarrels. For example, other comparatively under-developed regions, such as Macedonia and Bosnia, would say that the Kosovars were getting more than their fair share. By contrast, the largest contributors, Slovenia and Croatia, complained bitterly of the money they said was being spent propping up white-elephant industrial complexes which had only been built to employ and hence keep occupied people who might otherwise be unemployed and channel their anger against the authorities. There was also simmering anger because of the widespread belief that a lot of the development money channelled to Kosovo was in fact ending up in the bank accounts of its Albanian bosses rather than on the projects for which it had been designated. Whatever the truth of these allegations, what was clear was that Kosovo remained the poorest part of Yugoslavia. In 1979, average per capita income was $795. The Yugoslav national average was $2,635 while that of Slovenia was $5,315.[20]

As power began slowly but surely to ebb from the Yugoslav centre all of these elements began to poison the general political atmosphere. For every real incident, the rumour mill manu-factured a thousand more. For example, otherwise serious academics contend that in Kosovo 'the rape of little Serbian girls was an everyday occurrence'.[21] This charge, among others, came to be widely believed amongst Serbs, even though subsequent research revealed that the incidence of rape in Kosovo was two-and-a-half times lower than in Serbia proper and that the rape of Serbian women by Albanian men was extremely rare.[22] Bizarrely however, one of the most infamous such cases, and one which did much to conjure up all sorts of historical demons, was that of the Kosovo Serb farmer Djordje Martinović. In May 1985 he was taken to hospital with a broken bottle shoved up his rear. He claimed he had been attacked by two Albanians, but the local authorities asserted that the injury was self-inflicted. The case became a *cause célèbre* in Serbia with eminent academics opining that the incident was 'reminiscent of the darkest days of the Turkish practice of impalement'.[23]

The first sign that the issue of Kosovo was beginning to have a widespread impact in Serbia proper came in 1983. The occasion was the funeral of Aleksandar Ranković, who had lived in obscure retirement since his fall in 1966. To widespread shock, tens of thousands turned up for his funeral, some of them shouting nationalist slogans such as 'Serbia is rising!' Ivan Stambolić, then head of the powerful Belgrade branch of the Communist Party and later president of Serbia, said afterwards: 'All across Yugoslavia they criticised me for not controlling it – should I have put tanks around the cemetery?'[24]

A secret voice

In 1968, bones discovered in Prizren which were believed to be those of the Tsar Stefan Dušan who had died in 1355 were reburied in the great St Mark's Church in Belgrade. Candles have burnt there, ever since. Tens of thousands turned up for the ceremony at which Patriarch German said: 'A secret voice is still heard in Kosovo today, a powerful voice from a hallowed place.'[25] As we have seen, it was the church that first began to raise the alarm about the Serbs in Kosovo, but even as far back as 1968 they were not the only ones. In May of that year the novelist Dobrica Ćosić, a Partisan commissar during the war, was expelled from the Communist Party for warning that Kosovo's Albanian leaders were separatists. He levelled the same charge against Vojvodina's Hungarian leaders and denounced as 'senseless' moves to promote Yugoslavia's Slav Muslims (the vast majority of whom lived in Bosnia) to the status of a fully fledged Yugoslav nation. Far from disappearing from the political scene, Ćosić began to play an increasingly influential role on its periphery. During the 1970s he, along with others, organised the so-called Free University in which talks, mostly on philosophical questions, were given in private flats. Vojislav Šešelj, later to emerge as the leader of Serbia's extreme nationalists, said that Ćosić was a role model 'for all us younger dissidents'. In 1984 he became one of the prime movers in the Committee for the Freedom of Speech which had been formed to protect dissidents.[26] Ironically, some of its best-known cases turned out to be amongst the leading characters in the drama of the destruction of Yugoslavia. They included Šešelj, Franjo Tudjman, later president of Croatia, and Alija Izetbegović, later president of Bosnia. Within Serbia, Ćosić was also giving discreet help to a small group of Serbs from Kosovo who had turned to him for advice.

In 1982, a first petition from Kosovo Serbs was circulated, but it only managed to gather 79 signatures. A second one, in October 1985, gathered 2,016. In January 1986 more than 200 Serbian intellectuals signed a petition demanding action over the 'unbearable condition of the Serb nation in Kosovo' and 'decisive measures ... to halt Albanian aggression in Kosovo and Metohija'.[27] Later in the year another petition gathered 50,000 signatures. Sporadic Kosovo Serb demonstrations began to break out. Things were beginning to move.

In 1984, Ćosić suggested that the venerable Serbian Academy of Sciences and Arts discuss various national and social problems. In June 1985, sixteen prominent academics, including economists, scientists, historians and philosophers were appointed to begin work on a document which has, ever since, been referred to simply as the *Memorandum*. Ćosić was not one of the sixteen; however, it is clear that, in key parts, the man who was later dubbed the 'father of the nation' was its main inspiration.

On 24 and 25 September 1986 the newspaper *Večernje Novosti* published extracts of what was still a draft document. To this day no one knows how, or why, it was leaked. The paper attacked the *Memorandum*, calling it: 'A Proposal for Hopelessness'. Very soon, photocopied versions of the typewritten document began to circulate and to be attacked by officials across Yugoslavia. Its main theme was that decentralisation was leading to the disintegration of Yugoslavia and that the Serbs were discriminated against by Yugoslavia's constitutional structure. It pointed out that 24 per cent of Serbs lived outside Serbia while 40.3 per cent lived outside the boundaries of central Serbia, that is to say either outside Serbia itself or in Kosovo and Vojvodina.[28] Part of the rationale of giving power to Serbia's provinces had been that otherwise Serbia, by the far the most populous republic, with some 10 million people as opposed to 4.7 million in Croatia, would inevitably dominate the rest of Yugoslavia and thus provoke an anti-Serb and anti-Yugoslav reaction. Now the policy was beginning to rebound. As the *Memorandum* put it, this policy of 'a weak Serbia ensures a strong Yugoslavia' was provoking a backlash amongst Serbs.[29]

The language of the *Memorandum* was strong and many of its points addressed areas of legitimate concern. However, the reason that it provoked such a strong reaction and that its publication is rightly seen as major step on the road to war, is the extraordinary language it used to examine the situation of the Serbs in Croatia and Kosovo. While most might have agreed that Serbs in Kosovo were living through difficult times, the *Memorandum* asserted that they were being subjected to nothing less than 'genocide':[30]

> The expulsion of the Serbian people from Kosovo bears dramatic testimony to their historical defeat. In the spring of 1981, open and total war was declared on the Serbian people ... This open war has been going on for almost five years ... we are still not looking this war in the face, nor are we calling it by its proper name.[31]

In one of its most infamous paragraphs the *Memorandum* asserted that 'The physical, political, legal, and cultural genocide of the Serbian population of Kosovo and Metohija is a worse historical defeat than any experienced in the liberation wars waged by Serbia from the First Serbian Uprising in 1804 to the uprising of 1941.' And the people responsible for this were Serbia's politicians. The *Memorandum* accused them of 'inveterate opportunism' and of always being 'on the defensive and always worried more about what others think of them and their timid overtures at raising the issue of Serbia's status than about the objective facts affecting the future of the nation they lead'.[32] It claimed (without any supporting evidence) that 200,000 Serbs had been forced to leave Kosovo in the last two decades, and then, in a paragraph which has an ironic ring to it now given the *Memorandum*'s role in the catastrophe which was about to begin to unfold, it said:

It is not just that the last remnants of the Serbian nation are leaving their homes at an unabated rate, but according to all evidence, faced with a physical, moral and psychological reign of terror, they seem to be preparing for their final exodus. Unless things change radically, in less than ten years' time there will no longer be any Serbs left in Kosovo, and an 'ethnically pure' Kosovo, that unambiguously stated goal of the Greater Albanian racists ... will be achieved ... Kosovo's fate remains a vital question for the entire Serbian nation. If it is not resolved ... if genuine security and unambiguous equality for all peoples living in Kosovo and Metohija are not established; if objective and permanent conditions for the return of the expelled nation are not created, then this part of the Republic of Serbia and Yugoslavia will become a European issue, with the gravest possible unforeseeable consequences.[33]

So, what should be done? 'The Serbian people cannot stand idly by and wait for the future in such a state of uncertainty ... Naturally, Serbia must not be passive and wait and see what the others will say, as it has done so often in the past.'[34]

Nothing ... but the darkest nationalism

On 4 June 1987 Slobodan Milošević, then the leader of the Serbian Communist Party, denounced the *Memorandum* and everything it stood for. Speaking to a group of secret policemen, he denounced the document as 'nothing else but the darkest nationalism' which 'means the liquidation of the current socialist system of our country, that is, the disintegration after which there is no survival for any nation or nationality'. Indeed, he argued, 'Tito's policy of brotherhood and unity' was the 'only basis' which 'could secure Yugoslavia's survival'.[35]

The odd thing about this statement is not that he made it, but that he made it two months *after* his campaign, based on the grievances of the Kosovo Serbs, had already begun. Milošević has proved past master at telling people what they want to hear and, in this way, enlisting their support.

Milošević was born on 20 August 1941 in the little town of Požarevac close to Belgrade. His parents were recent

Montenegrin immigrants. Svetozar, his father, had trained to be an Orthodox priest, first in Cetinje and then in Belgrade, but instead became a teacher of religious education, Serbo-Croatian and Russian. The family home was not a happy one. Soon after the war Svetozar returned to Montenegro where, in 1962, he shot himself. Slobodan and Borislav, his elder brother, were raised by their mother Stanislava. She was a 'strict woman, diligent and an ambitious communist activist'.[36] Like her husband, she committed suicide, in 1972.

Schoolboy Slobodan was serious and studious. He dressed in a shirt and tie and had gained a reputation for lecturing other children for not being well-dressed enough. Apart from that, however, his youth, according to Slavoljub Djukić, his (unofficial) biographer, passed 'unremarkably even monotonously for a boy'.[37] Barring one thing, that is. While at school he met Mirjana Marković (Mira), the love of his life from whom he has never been separated. Many believe that she is the driving force behind him. Long before anyone had ever heard of Milošević, Mira would boast to her friends that her Slobodan would one day be as glorious a leader as Comrade Tito himself. Mira came from a distinguished Partisan family, although a cloud hung over the memory of her mother who had died during the war. It was believed that, under Nazi torture, she had revealed the names of other Communists, but Mira always rejected this.

Standing solidly behind him, Mira began to push her man. Gradually he began to climb the career ladder. At university he headed the ideology section of its Communist Party branch. There the couple met with another ambitious young Communist called Ivan Stambolić, the nephew of one of the grandees of Serbian politics. As Ivan climbed the greasy pole, he hauled Slobodan up too, always one step behind him. In 1968 Milošević got a job in the Technogas company where Ivan was already working. In 1973 he became its head. One day, about this time, Milošević was sprawled in an armchair in the office of Belgrade's mayor when a lady who worked for Beobanka, one of Yugoslavia's biggest banks, paid a working visit with a colleague. The lady was called Borka Vučić. She told her colleague: 'Watch that man.'

Sure enough, by 1978 Milošević was the head of Beobanka. Milošević travelled to New York and Paris and other places but his real job was that of a political–financial fixer. The banking brains behind him was Borka Vučić. When she returned from trips with her colleague she 'always made sure that she had bought a present for Mira'. The colleague added: 'In my time I saw many presidents of Beobanka but the only one who was not on the take and who never had affairs was Milošević.'

By 1984 Milošević was moving into mainstream politics. Stambolić was now the Serbian Communist Party chief, so he secured Milošević his former job of Belgrade party chief. There, according to the historian and analyst Aleksa Djilas, he earned a reputation as a hardliner:

> He frequently attacked dissident intellectuals, firmly opposed all demands for liberalization, and punished any manifestation of Serbian nationalism. He also resisted any attempt by reformers to cut excessive time devoted in schools and universities to the teaching of Marxism, promoted dogmatic professors at Belgrade University, and prevented the publication of books by politically proscribed authors.[38]

In January 1986 Stambolić became president of Serbia and Milošević succeeded him as head of the Serbian Communist Party. Over the last few years Stambolić had been complaining about what was widely regarded as the constitutional injustice done to Serbia by the 1974 constitution. That is to say, that Kosovo and Vojvodina had a say in the running of Serbia as a whole, but Serbia was unable to interfere in the internal affairs of the provinces. So, while Kosovo frequently voted against Serbia on the federal presidency, the collective body which had replaced Tito, Serbia itself was constitutionally unable to do anything about what was increasingly being considered the parlous condition of the Kosovo Serbs. Stambolić did understand, however, that Serbia needed to proceed with caution, since fanning the flames of Serbian nationalism would be a disaster. Until now Milošević was regarded as his sidekick, and although in a powerful position, he had never expressed any particular interest in the national question.

All this was about to change. On 24 April 1987 Milošević, at Stambolić's behest, went to listen to the grievances of Kosovo Serbs who were threatening to come and demonstrate in Belgrade. As he entered the building, in the Priština suburb of

Kosovo Polje, thousands of angry Serbs were clashing with the mainly Albanian police and throwing stones at them – which were being supplied by protest organisers from a truck parked around the corner. The protestors shouted: 'Murderers' and 'We are Tito's. Tito is ours.'[39] Milošević came out of the building and said: 'No one should dare to beat you!' Miroslav Šoljević, one of the Kosovo Serb leaders, said later: 'This sentence enthroned him as a Tsar.'[40]

Back inside the building, Milošević listened to the angry Serbs who demanded that action be taken to protect them and to deal with the province's Albanian leadership. Milošević told them:

> Comrades ... you should stay here. This is your country, these are your houses, your fields and gardens, your memories. You are not going to abandon your lands because life is hard, because you are oppressed by injustice and humiliation. It has never been a characteristic of the Serbian and Montenegrin people to retreat in the face of obstacles, to demobilise when they should fight, to become demoralised when things are difficult. You should stay here, both for your ancestors and your descendants. Otherwise you would shame your ancestors and disappoint your descendants. But I do not suggest you stay here suffering and enduring a situation with which you are not satisfied. On the contrary! It should be changed, together with all progressive people here, in Serbia and in Yugoslavia ... Yugoslavia does not exist without Kosovo! Yugoslavia would disintegrate without Kosovo! Yugoslavia and Serbia are not going to give up Kosovo.[41]

Far from it being a spontaneous show, Milošević had prearranged the whole drama. Four days earlier he had come to Kosovo to organise this trip. Back in the capital Dušan Mitević, deputy director of Belgrade Television, showed the clip of Milošević saying 'No one should dare to beat you' over and over again. From being a grey apparatchik Milošević was emerging from the shadow of Stambolić. Very soon he would betray his friend. However, as the speech to the secret policemen shows, he hesitated, or at least was telling different people different things.

By the end of the summer, though, Milošević knew what he was going to do. On 3 September Aziz Kelmendi, an Albanian conscript in the army, went berserk, killing four other conscripts before turning his gun on himself. Only one was a Serb, but the Serbian media, which was increasingly coming under Milošević's influence and control, unleashed a barrage of anti-Albanian venom, describing the act of this deranged individual as a premeditated Albanian separatist attack. Ten thousand then turned up to mourn Srdjan Simić, the young Serb who was killed. Now, Stambolić could hardly believe what was coming, especially since Milošević owed him everything. He was stunned when, at the Eighth Session of the Central Committee of the League of Communists of Serbia, speaker after speaker attacked Dragiša Pavlović, the Belgrade party chief.[42] Everyone understood that an attack on Pavlović was an attack on Stambolić. After twenty hours of debate Pavlović resigned and Slobodan told Stambolić: 'I'm sorry, but your position has become untenable.'[43] Stambolić lingered on as president until 14 December of that year. Milošević was triumphant; however, he only formally assumed the position of president of Serbia in May 1989. But the Eighth Session was the turning-point for far more than just Milošević's career. As the academic and analyst Denisa Kostovičová argues, by shifting the political debate from ideology to the Serbian 'national interest' – above all other issues – Milošević and his allies 'destroyed the prospects of Serbia's transition to democracy. Instead, Serbia edged closer to confrontation not only with Albanians in Kosovo, but with other Yugoslav republics as well.'[44]

The two years following the Eighth Session were ones of frantic activity, of building and consolidating power. Using the Kosovo Serbs as his shock troops, Milošević organised rallies around Serbia, so-called 'Meetings of Truth' to whip up support for him. According to the writer Robert Thomas, between July 1988 and the spring of 1989, one hundred of these meetings took place across Serbia, 'involving an estimated cumulative total of 5 million people'.[45] The myth of Kosovo, which had in the post-war years been eclipsed by those of heroic Partisans, now began to re-emerge. The slogans chanted by pro-Milošević demonstrators included: 'Who betrays Kosovo, betrays the people.'[46]

But words, however intoxicating, were not enough. Milošević had to do something to make concrete his promise to 'unite Serbia' by abolishing the autonomy of the provinces and protect the Serbs of Kosovo. On 5 October 1988 Milošević scored his first major victory. His demonstrators brought about the resignation of the government of Vojvodina. Two days later the government of Montenegro also resigned and a Milošević protégé, Momir Bulatović, was promoted to take over. With these two dealt with, Milošević turned his sights on Kosovo, an altogether more formidable nut to crack.

On 17 November Milošević secured the dismissal of Kosovo's Albanian communist leaders. This move, however, had to be endorsed by the local party committee. Two thousand Albanian miners from Trepča now marched the 55 kilometres to Priština to protest in front of the party headquarters, where they were joined by tens of thousands of students and others. On 19 November Milošević told a giant rally in Belgrade: 'Every nation has a love which eternally warms it heart. For Serbia it is Kosovo. That is why Kosovo will remain in Serbia.'[47] The Kosovo dismissals were endorsed. Early in the new year preparations were made to alter the constitutional status of Kosovo, in order to 'reunite' it with Serbia. To make everything legal Kosovo's own assembly had to vote, in effect, to endorse Milošević's policy and approve the necessary constitutional amendments. In the run-up to this, on 20 February 1989, in a last-ditch effort to save the province's autonomy 1,350 Trepča miners began an underground hunger strike. Their first demand was: 'No retreat from the fundamental principles of the 1974 constitution.' Despite Serbian speculation that the hunger strike was bogus, the miners' example was followed by other miners, and demonstrations and strikes spread rapidly across the province. On 27 February Shkëlzen Maliqi wrote: 'The whole of Kosova has risen – desperate, frightened and angry … a kind of Albanian intifada has begun.'[48]

In fact, eight days after they had begun, the protests ended when Milošević's three placemen in the Kosovo Communist Party resigned. Their resignations were then rescinded. Azem Vllasi, the former Kosovo Albanian party leader, who had defended the province's autonomy, was arrested. On 23 March

the Kosovo assembly, surrounded by tanks and police, voted for
the constitutional amendments, which were then ratified in the
Serbian parliament five days later. Demonstrations in Kosovo
cost the lives of 22 protestors and two policemen. Although,
legally, the provinces still existed, the changes meant they were
no longer autonomous. There was a simple reason why, on
paper, they had to continue to exist at all. This was because, with
Montenegro under his control and with the votes of Vojvodina
and Kosovo now in his gift, Milošević now held four out of the
eight votes on the federal presidency. In May, the Serbian
parliament elected Milošević president of Serbia. On 28 June, at
Gazimestan, part of the historic Kosovo battlefield, Milošević
celebrated his triumph on the 600th anniversary of the battle.
Before an estimated 1 million Serbs, he cited Miloš Obilić, the
knight who the legends say had killed the Sultan, by saying:
'After many decades Serbia has her state, national and spiritual
integrity back. Today it is not difficult for us to answer the old
question: how shall we face Miloš?' Using the diminutive for
Slobodan the crowd chanted: 'Tsar Lazar, you were unfortunate,
not to have Slobo on your side.'[49] Milošević then said:

> Serbs in their history have never conquered or exploited
> others. Through two world wars, they have liberated
> themselves and, when they could, they also helped others
> to liberate themselves ... The Kosovo heroism does not
> allow us to forget that, at one time, we were brave and dig-
> nified and one of the few who went into battle undefeated
> ... Six centuries later, again we are in battles and quarrels.
> They are not armed battles, though such things should not
> be excluded yet.[50]

Milošević had won the battle of Kosovo, but the war had not
even begun. He was now the undisputed master of the Serbs of
Yugoslavia, but by his actions he was precipitating the destruction of Yugoslavia. It seems unlikely that Milošević realised this.
Everything he has done since would appear to indicate that the
only thing he cares about is power and that, while brilliant at
manoeuvring on a day-to-day and week-to-week basis, he has
no long-term vision. Milošević realised that the issue of the
Kosovo Serbs was one which he could use. This does not, by any
means, imply that from the very beginning he was thinking of

creating a Greater Serbia. There is no indication of this whatsoever. However, the appetite grows with the eating. Once he
had achieved his aim of abolishing provincial autonomy, he came
to believe he could dominate the rest of Yugoslavia. The
problem was that the very act of abolishing the provinces'
autonomy, and the fact that the federal police and the army – i.e.,
men from all the other republics – were now involved in
suppressing violent demonstrations across Kosovo, was setting
the stage for disin-tegration of the country as a whole. Why,
thought Croats and Slovenes, should their men be involved in
policing Kosovo so as to help out Milošević who might soon try
to dominate them too? Indeed, people like Miroslav Šoljević,
who had organised the Kosovo Serbs for Milošević, boasted of
what they were about to do. As Kosovo's autonomy was being
abolished he told the Croatian weekly *Nedeljna Dalmacija*:
'Revolution in Bosnia–Hercegovina is inevitable: this is a sure
thing, and will be implemented by the spring. The same thing
will then happen to you in Croatia and Slovenia.'[51]

Ines Sabalić, who was then reporting the situation in Kosovo
for the Croatian magazine *Start*, reflected, ten years later, that
'observing what was going on there, we were convinced that
Serbs were mad and uncontrollable.' She says she was shocked,
not just by the political developments in Serbia, but also because,
at Milošević's rallies, she saw people turning up in wartime
royalist and nationalist Chetnik regalia, looking, she says, 'as if
they had just walked out of Partisan movies, dressed as the very
people we had been brought up to think of as the baddies'. At
the same time the church was now moving the remains of Lazar,
the Kosovo hero, around the country, attracting large crowds of
pilgrims. What was worse, though, was the 'silent approval' of
what was happening in Kosovo, from people who would otherwise be considered democrats in Belgrade. Warren Zimmermann, the US ambassador in Belgrade from March 1989 to May
1992, makes precisely the same observation in his memoir of his
time there, *Origins of a Catastrophe*. 'During my first few weeks
in Yugoslavia I found that Milošević's trampling on Albanian
rights was almost universally popular among Serbs, and not just
those with a limited grasp of political issues.' Discussing the way
the *Memorandum* 'dehumanised' Albanians, he writes:

There was no use dismissing these crackpot ideas as the maunderings of intellectuals; they were prevalent throughout Serbian society, from shopkeepers to peasant farmers to journalists. I remember meeting an art historian at a dinner party. A tall, attractive, and sensitive woman, she had been to New York many times and loved America and its culture. After a wide-ranging and fascinating conversation on a variety of subjects, I asked her how she would deal with the Kosovo problem. 'Simple,' she said. 'Just line all the Albanians up against a wall and shoot them.'[52]

Sabalić recalls: 'The terror down there made people outside Serbia sick. Everybody who understood a bit of politics was frightened.' In fact they were waiting for party officials, either at the republican or federal levels, 'to do something to stop the violence, after all Yugoslavia was rather a peaceful place. But, and this was news for us, the old communist leaderships and the reformed ones revealed themselves as being incapable of solving the problem – Milošević.' And it was precisely this inability to tackle Milošević which led to the uncontrollable spiral of competitive nationalism across Yugoslavia which would soon lead to war.

Serbia and Slovenia were already increasingly at odds over political and constitutional questions but, buoyed up by the euphoria sweeping the republic, few Serbs took the Slovene problem seriously. They had no historic quarrel with the Slovenes; and in fact, Slovenes and Serbs generally liked one another and relations had, in the past, been good. So, when Milan Kučan, the president of Slovenia, declared that the Trepča miners were 'defending' Yugoslavia by striking, most Serbs were horrified. Far from understanding that this meant a policy of caution and that reflection was needed, it simply enraged them. The Slovenes were insolent and if they didn't like the new Yugoslavia in which the Serbs would get what they deserved, they could simply get out. In an arrogant way, they could hold to this belief, since few really understood that the Slovenes – followed by the Croats, the Bosnians and the Macedonians – would choose to do just that. It was simply inconceivable. Still, Serbs reasoned, if the others so much as dared to think in such a way, then *tant pis,* because as Serbia's leading intellectuals now argued in public, Serbia would simply redraw her borders to include Serbian areas in Croatia. Then, with luck, Bosnia would see sense and avoid risking a war by submitting to Serbia's will and staying united with it. 'The peoples who wish to go will do so and the peoples who do not wish to go will stay in Yugoslavia,' explained Mihailo Marković, one of the authors of the *Memorandum*, who was now emerging as a close advisor to Milošević.

> Yugoslavia must determine its new state frontiers – because at the moment it seems that we are the only state in the world which on the major part of its territory does not have a state frontier. The new state frontier must in Croatia follow the line of separation between the Serbian and Croat people.[53]

Dobrica Ćosić said that Milošević was devoting 'himself bravely to the renewal of the Serbian state and for the salvation of the Serbian people from new slavery and annihilation ... Slobodan Milošević has done more for the Serbian people than all Serbian politicians in the last five decades.'[54]

Yugoslavia's descent into war has been well covered elsewhere. Milošević chopped and changed his policies to suit himself. If he could not dominate the whole of the old Yugoslavia then he would carve out a Greater Serbia. When that did not work he opted to play the peacemaker, because that suited his needs at the time. It had been predicted that, if there was to be war, it would break out in Kosovo. In the event, it was the dynamics of the political conflict in Kosovo which resulted in war, first briefly in Slovenia, then in Croatia and then in Bosnia–Hercegovina. But there was no war, for the moment, in Kosovo, because the Albanians did not have the wherewithal to wage one and because they opted instead for a policy of passive resistance. It was an extraordinary experiment and it failed. Still, while the situation was quiet most Serbs could delude themselves into thinking that, because it was quiet, it would remain so. In other words that they could ignore it. The fact that it was quiet also meant that Serbs never had to face the vital contradiction in Serbian policy. This was that the carving out of Serbian enclaves, in Croatia and Bosnia, was justified on the basis of an ethnic principle, which also declared that the republican boundaries of Yugoslavia had no international status because they were simply 'administrative boundaries' within a state. By contrast Kosovars were not entitled to this same right to self-determination because Kosovo was Serbian thanks to 'historical right'. In this case, then, the 'administrative boundaries' were inviolable. Failing to come to grips with this contradiction was, of course, to have more than just theoretical consequences. In the long run, and because they were led by a man who cared about his power and not his people, the Serbs would lose everything. On the eve of war the Serbian rallying cry was 'All Serbs in One State!' The irony was, of course, that in the old Yugoslavia all Serbs were in one state. By his violent challenge to that fragile entity Milošević created a situation in which almost all Serbs are again in one state. That is to say, with the exception of the couple of hundred thousand Serbs in the Republika Srpska, the Serb half of Bosnia created during the war there, 800,000 Serb refugees from Croatia, Bosnia and Kosovo are now in Serbia, a small, broken and impoverished pariah in south-eastern Europe.

3 Phantom state

Ibrahim Rugova, the man who came to dominate Kosovo Albanian politics from 1990 to 1998, had several distinguishing quirks and characteristics. His trademark was, and is, a silk scarf, which he wears everywhere he goes, except in August, when he does not wear it at all. He has a collection of rocks which he likes to show to foreign visitors and, oddly for a man who commanded such fantastic loyalty and devotion from his people, is extraordinarily dull. In the end, Rugova misjudged Kosovo's mood, but in the early 1990s, he was politically adept and far-sighted.

After Milošević had begun to destroy the province's autonomy, the arms which had belonged to its reserve Territorial Defence forces had been confiscated.[1] So, writing on the eve of the Bosnian war in 1992, Rugova explained why the Kosovars did not have a military option. 'We are not certain how strong the Serbian military presence in the province actually is, but we do know that it is overwhelming and that we have nothing to set against the tanks and other modern weaponry in Serbian hands.' And then, prophetically, he added: 'We would have no chance of successfully resisting the army. In fact the Serbs only wait for a pretext to attack the Albanian population and wipe it out. We believe it is better to do nothing and stay alive than to be massacred.'[2]

Reunification

Kosovo remained wracked by demonstrations and violence until the spring of 1990. In the meantime, and for the next two years, both Serbian and Albanian politicians were busy laying the groundwork for the future. Although Kosovo's autonomy had now been abolished, several hundred new laws and decrees were passed by the end of 1992. The Serbian authorities needed these to consolidate their reimposition of rule from Belgrade and to eliminate any vestiges of the province's former status.[3]

Among the more important of the raft of laws passed were those that in effect prevented Albanians buying land or houses from Serbs. This was aimed at slowing the Serb exodus from the Kosovo. In March 1990 the Serbian parliament passed the Programme for the Attainment of Peace, Freedom and Prosperity in the Socialist Autonomous Province of Kosovo which was followed in July by the so-called 'temporary measures' or Law on the Activities of Organs of the Republic in Exceptional Circumstances. These included incentives to encourage Serbs who had left Kosovo to return, and regulations that were to lead to the dismissal or resignation of most Albanians in public sector, civil service or managerial jobs. The police force was rapidly purged, making it in essence an all-Serb force. Public companies which had operated under the aegis of the provincial government, for example the local electricity firm, were taken over by their Serbian counterparts. Where workers were not technically sacked they were forced to resign by being presented with loyalty oaths which they were supposed to sign. Some 1,855 doctors and other medical staff were dismissed and local facilities in the countryside were shut down. In the all-important media field, the police moved in to take over television and radio buildings and 1,300 Albanian journalists and others lost their jobs, plus another 250 when *Rilindja*, Kosovo's main Albanian-language daily was shut down. All cultural and other institutions were also closed or merged with their Serbian counterparts.[4]

The most dramatic application of the new measures came in the field of education. Autonomy had meant that Kosovo's authorities had the power to shape the local school curriculum. This was now swept away, as Serbia's much-trumpeted 'reunification' also meant that the Serbian curriculum was now imposed on Albanian students. While this would not have made much difference in the teaching of maths, say, it did, of course, make a difference in history, geography, music and language. Albanian teachers rejected this. This led to a round of sackings, a restriction on the numbers of children who could be taught in Albanian (as opposed to Serbian) and, eventually, to the police being deployed to prevent teachers and students from entering schools. 'As of March 1991,' writes Denisa Kostovičová, who has made a special study of education in Kosovo, 'the financing of all Albanian schools, including 21,000 teaching staff, ceased. The closure of companies that published textbooks and teaching materials in Albanian followed.' This in turn was followed by the policy of 'rationalisation' which meant that while 36,000 Albanian students finished primary school 'only 6,000 places were envisioned in Kosovo's secondary education for them. All 4,000 Serbian and Montengrin students got a place.'[5] The authorities soon moved on Priština University which by the beginning of the academic year in 1991 had, to all intents and purposes, become a Serbian-only institution. Eight hundred and sixty-three teachers and staff were sacked.[6] In March 1993 Professor Ejup Statovci, the former university rector, was arrested and jailed for a public order offence which consisted of having demanded that the university authorities return its buildings which he said: 'were taken by force'. In May of that year Radivoje Papović, the new Serbian rector, gave his version of events:

> Our first task was to remove the hatred for all that is Serbian which had been accumulated here for decades ... This factory of evil, established with the basic intention of destroying Serbia and the Serbian name ... is now destroyed thanks to the coordinated action of the Government and university personnel ... Our university has the ultimate object of renewing Serbian thought in Kosovo and Metohija.[7]

Reaction

The destruction of Kosovo's autonomy resulted, unsurprisingly, in Albanian rage. Shkëlzen Maliqi has written that:

> the feeling prevailing among Albanians was ... one of revenge: they waited for a moment of maximum mobilization to start a massive armed uprising. Some political agitators who subsequently had an important role in the formation of political parties believed that an uprising was inevitable, irrespective of casualties. 'We will lose 50,000 or 100,000 people, but we will be finally free,' they said.

But it was not to be, at least not for the moment. 'Overnight,' writes Maliqi, 'warriors went out of fashion.'[8] In the aftermath of the war of 1998–9 one might be tempted to conclude that Maliqi had just got things wrong. In fact, he was right. Bearing in mind the violence which invariably accompanied the changes of regime in Kosovo, which as a subtext meant the passing of the whip from Serb to Albanian and back again, what now began, on the Albanian side, was an extraordinary break with tradition and the beginning of a unique experiment in passive resistance. When it failed the warriors came back into fashion.

Today, as we trace the story of the developments in Kosovo from 1989 onwards, it seems curious that so little is known about these years, outside the region. Indeed, bearing in mind the grand finale of the NATO bombing raids of the spring of 1999, it may seem odd just how little was reported in the Western press at the time. In fact, it should not seem strange if we remember the context in which these events were taking place. For example, the Democratic League of Kosovo (LDK) was founded on 23 December 1989. The party was to dominate Albanian political life in the province until 1998. That week, Romania was in full and spectacular revolution and indeed, in the general aftermath of the fall of the Berlin Wall, the founding of yet another political party in an obscure province of another country moving away from Communism was hardly front-page news. What was news, just, was the final congress of the League of Communists of Yugoslavia, which met in Belgrade from 20 to 22 January 1990. The Croats and Slovenes walked out, and for the first time many, but not a majority by any means, suddenly began to comprehend that the end of the Party might also herald the end of Yugoslavia too. The authorities responded to fresh demonstrations in Kosovo by ordering out the army at the beginning of February.

In Kosovo, Albanian politics began to develop along two different tracks that would ultimately run together. The first involved Albanian politicians who were still part of the structures that were now being dismantled by Milošević. Although deputies in the provincial parliament had been intimidated into voting through Milošević's demands, they now appeared to lose their fear and repent. In May 1990, those Kosovars who remained in the increasingly toothless regional government resigned. On 2 July, 114 out of 123 Albanian members of the provincial parliament, who were unable to get into the locked building, voted to declare Kosovo a republic, that is to say independent from Serbia but still part of Yugoslavia. Three days later the Serbian parliament voted to dissolve the Kosovar parliament for this 'illegal act'. At the same time Slovenia and Croatia were accelerating various changes which would, in the end, lead to their independence. Although Kosovars understood that their situation was different from those of the northern republics, there was no particular reason then to believe that the final outcome of any pan-Yugoslav settlement, be it for example some form of confederation, would not affect them too if they took advantage of current developments.

On 16 July 1990 the Serbian League of Communists officially transformed itself into the Socialist Party of Serbia (SPS) and elected Milošević as its head. Throughout August, tensions in Croatia led to the beginning of the carving out of what was eventually to become the secessionist, but ultimately short-lived, enclave of the Republic of Serbian Krajina. On 7 September, gathering secretly in Kačanik, the Kosovar deputies voted for a constitution for their own Republic of Kosovo. At this point the Albanian deputies did not envisage an independent republic. They still assumed that Yugoslavia would continue to exist and that any outright declaration of independence from Yugoslavia, as opposed to Serbia, would give the authorities an excuse to crush their movement. In that sense, what was happening in Kosovo paralleled, albeit briefly, Serb moves in Krajina. It was only when war was raging out of control in Croatia, one year later, on 22 September 1991, that the deputies voted for the Resolution on Independence and Sovereignty of Kosovo. A referendum was then organised, which, although illegal, the authorities did not make much of an effort to stop. Unsurprisingly, of the 87.01 per cent of the 1,051,357 eligible voters who cast their ballots (i.e., the Serbs did not vote) 99.87 of them voted for independence. On 19 October 1991 the 'parliament' voted to confirm the result of the resolution and declared Kosovo to be the independent 'Republic of Kosova'.

Kosovo's independence was, of course, a state of virtual reality. In other words it existed in some form, but definitely not in the sense of Kosovo Albanians running Kosovo. Serbian and

Yugoslav institutions remained, Albanians carried Yugoslav passports and the Yugoslav army and Serbian police remained very much in control. But, this is where the experiment began, guided by the LDK. Instead of trying to mount a violent insurrection to realise this independence, the party began to simulate it in the hope that, by force of demographic and other pressures, Kosovo would, one day, simply drop into Albanian hands like a ripe fruit.

The two bodies that were the driving force behind the creation of the LDK were the professional associations representing Kosovo's writers and philosophers. The core group who formed the party were 23 individuals who gathered in Priština's Elida café. Amongst them was Ibrahim Rugova, a professor of Albanian literature, Bujar Bukoshi, a surgeon, and Fehmi Agani, a professor of sociology. Rugova was born in 1944. His father had been executed by the Partisans when they restored control over Kosovo at the end of the war. He had studied at the Sorbonne and studiously cultivated a rather bohemian air, which included a penchant for drink. Like most of the other founders of the LDK, Rugova had been a member of the Communist Party, although he had been expelled for voting against amending Kosovo's constitution. Rugova was not particularly well known and was not the first choice of this select group when they looked for a party leader. Their first choice had been Rexhep Qosja, a well-known nationalist writer and a grandee of Kosovar politics. Bukoshi recalls that 'any of us could have been named but Rugova was acceptable because he was calm and cultivated and never had any conflicts with his colleagues'. Ajri Begu, another writer and member of the group of 23, takes a more acerbic line on why Rugova was selected. At the time, he says, 'it was just enough to give two or three interviews to the BBC, VOA and a few other newspapers to become famous'. In the early 1970s Begu worked with Rugova on a Kosovar student newspaper. 'We were both liberal,' he says, 'but I can describe him as a liberal anarchist. I don't think he is capable of organising things.' Ramiz Kelmendi, a journalist and writer who also took part in the meetings in the Elida café, says:

> Rugova was a total outsider. He was a kind of loser who sat in the corner drinking too much coffee. He was charged

with contacting his friend Rexhep Qosja to ask him to become leader. He tried for three weeks but Qosja did not accept. He did not want to be in politics. Then there was a dilemma. One man called Jusuf Buxhovi, a writer, wanted to be leader but everyone was against him. There were 'suspicions' about his background and we tried hard to avoid him. So, Rugova was a compromise candidate. He had been a member of the Communist Party, he was head of the writers' union and he had given some brave interviews. Because of this background and because we thought he was a man of compromises and, as Yugoslavia still very much existed, he got the job.

Many other parties were also set up at this time but none matched the LDK in terms of size or influence. In the same way as the SPS would take over the functions and influence of the former Communist Party in Serbia proper, the LDK absorbed much of the former Communist Party membership in Kosovo. Its aims, however, were purely couched in terms of the national question. While the old Yugoslavia still existed, its aim was republican status; once it had gone, it demanded independence. But, how was it that the LDK decided on a policy of passive resistance? Shklëzen Maliqi answers the question by saying that, at the time, it was thought that 'the key to the solution of the Kosova problem and the Albanian national question lay in democracy'. The formula, he argued, appeared 'simple', that is to say, 'pluralism, market-economy, parliament and democratic institutions.' If you had these, then there was 'no need for war.' It would be enough to know that all Albanians favoured independence and once that was clear then its achievement would 'not be far away'.[9]

The problem was that Serbia was still very much in control. It was all very well holding a referendum on independence and having the deputies of the old Communist-era parliament confirming the vote but, as was becoming clear, this did not bring independence any closer. Besides, as the wars in Croatia and Bosnia showed, opting to fight for independence without sufficient arms or preparation could be deadly. In the meantime, then, something had to be done. The idea was that, with the LDK essentially in charge, new institutions would have to be created to fill the void left by the dismantling of the old ones. There were two levels at which this was done. On the one hand, new political bodies were created and, on the other, practical measures were instituted to make up for the effective loss of health care and educational facilities.

On the first level, the LDK created a whole simulated government structure. On 24 May 1992 elections were held for a new Kosovar parliament and to elect a president. Although the Serbian police interfered in a couple of places, in general the Albanians were left to hold their election. The poll was not clandestine, in the sense that it was held secretly, but it was not held completely openly either. Polling stations were in private houses, hidden away in discreet alleyways, and on the streets there were no signs that an election was in progress. However the fact that the Serbian authorities decided not to try and arrest the organisers was presumably related to the simultaneous beginning of the Serbian siege of Sarajevo. In other words, it was better to let Kosovo be, to avoid provoking violence in the province lest Serbian forces found themselves overstretched. The results of the election were an overwhelming victory for the LDK, which picked up 76.44 per cent of the votes. Rugova was elected by 99.5 per cent of those who voted, but, in fact, no one had stood against him. At least eighteen parties contested the election but, since none contested the basic issue at stake, which was independence, their existence owed more to personalities and interest groups than anything else. Fourteen seats were left vacant for Serbs and Montenegrins.

Although the authorities basically ignored the poll, it was decided that the convening of a parliament would be a step too far and so, on 24 June, the police prevented the newly elected deputies from meeting. After that, it never convened, but thirteen commissions were created, made up of small groups of deputies to give some direction to policy.[10] Despite this, the elections had given some legitimacy and authority to Rugova and his party. Rugova was now described by virtually all Kosovars as the president of the republic. In theory, Rugova now oversaw a government. In fact, a government made up of six ministers had already been created on 19 October 1991. Until May 1992 it sat in Ljubljana in Slovenia, but it then moved to Germany, finally making its headquarters in Bad Godesberg, a pleasant suburb of Bonn. Its prime minister and foreign minister was the urbane former surgeon Bujar Bukoshi who had been LDK secretary-general before being nominated to the post. There was more to setting up this government-in-exile than simply an exercise in institution-building or gesture politics. In fact its real role was to collect money from the large and growing Kosovar community abroad.

From the 1960s Kosovars, like other Yugoslavs and Turks too, had flocked to Germany, Switzerland, Austria and Scandinavia as *Gastarbeiters* or 'guest workers', mainly in industry. It was their remittances which enabled their families to build comfortable houses, buy cars and generally make a better life for themselves than if they had stayed at home. These communities now provided a destination for Kosovars who in the wake of the ending of autonomy, police repression and economic sanctions imposed by the UN on Serbia because of the war in Bosnia now left in search of asylum or work or both. Exact numbers are hard to determine, especially because Albanians from Albania proper also began to search for work abroad too, but always asked for asylum as Kosovars. For example, by the end of 1998 Kosovars in London estimated that there were some 30,000 Albanians in the city, only half of whom were Kosovars. In 1989 there were believed to have been a mere 30 Albanians in the city. The great concentrations lived in Germany, where estimates of the numbers of Kosovars fall within a range of 230,000 to 350,000. In Switzerland, according to Bujar Bukoshi, there were as many as 150,000, with another 20,000 living in Austria. Another major concentration of Kosovars was in Sweden, with, according to another source, 30,000 people.[11] Whatever the true figures, what was clear was that these people could provide a substantial source of income and, like their compatriots back home, they were now asked by the government to pay 3 per cent of their salaries or up to 10 per cent of business profits into government coffers. Although technically it would be hard for any government-in-exile to make sure that those in the diaspora paid up, it was understood that it would be dishonourable not to. Although not everyone did pay, life could be hard for your family back home if it was discovered that you were refusing to and, besides, it was also understood that, following independence, questions would be asked about who had contributed what. So, there was always the veiled threat that accounts could be settled in the future.

No one knows how much money was raised by the government-in-exile. However, the numbers of people involved suggests it must have been substantial. Besides, not all Kosovars were simple industrial workers or unemployed exiles existing on social security. Some, like Bexhet Pacolli, who lived in Switzerland and presided over a major construction company working in Russia, were extremely rich. Some Kosovars were also sucked into crime and the drugs trade. With family connections in Turkey, Germany and Switzerland, some Kosovars began to play a linking role in the international drugs trade, coming to dominate, for example, the heroin business in Zurich. The opening of Albania itself from 1991, coupled with sanctions on Serbia in 1992, also meant that a major new drugs route, passing through Albanian-inhabited parts either in Macedonia, Kosovo, Serbia proper or of course Albania itself, now opened up. The significance of this, in terms of the Kosovo question, should not be overestimated, but still the fact that some 'dirty money' helped finance the Kosovar cause is more than likely, and is a fact which, for the record, should be noted. But what was this money used for?

In the main, the cash raised had to finance the second level of Kosovar institution-building that was mentioned above. This meant funding the emerging parallel education system.

The sacking of teachers and the imposition of the unacceptable unified Serbian curriculum meant that radical steps had to be taken with regard to education. A parallel system now began to emerge. This meant that teachers, using the old pre-1990 curriculum as a base, continued to teach it, but where students were barred from their old schools they taught in private homes, garages or other buildings. In general, primary school children could continue to use their old school buildings and, where there were also Serbian children using the buildings, they were either divided or a system of shifts was worked out. To a lesser extent, secondary school children could also use the old buildings but a higher proportion of them had to be taught in private houses. All university students had their lessons in private buildings. Resources were scarce, and while this was problematic enough when it came to books, it became a chronic problem in the teaching of sciences to older pupils and especially subjects like medicine to university students. In 1998 there were 266,413 primary school pupils, 58,700 secondary school pupils and 16,000 university students studying in the parallel system.[12] Money to pay teachers came, as we have noted, from the 3 per cent income tax that Rugova's government levied as best it could, both inside Kosovo and in the diaspora, but in the early 1990s, when the system began, the teachers went unpaid. They were also unpaid in the run up to the war in 1998, a situation which reflected the poor state of relations between Rugova and Bukoshi in Germany.

Politically speaking, the schools had a tremendous impact because school papers were all stamped as being issued by the 'Republic of Kosovo'. Thus the schools became one of the few symbolic aspects of what was otherwise nothing more than a phantom state. The schools were also important because, as we shall see, the education issue consumed a lot of diplomatic energy which would ultimately turn out to have been wasted. Equally, they had an important effect on the mind-set of a new generation who were only taught that Serbs were the occupying enemy who, by one means or another, must be got rid of. The numbers enrolled in the parallel system, however, dropped by a considerable amount over the years. The school year 1995–6, for example, showed a drop in enrolment in primary schools of 11.9 per cent compare to 1989–90. In the same year, the number of secondary school students was down by a factor of 21.44 per cent compared to 1990–1. Even more dramatic was the drop in the number of university students which was almost halved by 1995–6 compared to the 1989–90 levels.[13] This did not mean that people were beginning to send their children back into the state system. Far from it. What it did reflect was an increasing number not going to school; but, almost certainly, the greatest drop can be attributed to emigration, which also explains the steepest drop when it comes to university students. In the early days of the parallel system a small number of primers paid for and printed up by the Kosovar diaspora were smuggled into the province on donkey trails from Albania. Symbolic perhaps of the shifts that were to take place over the next few years, the same donkeys later found themselves strapped up with guns.

After education the second substantial pillar of Rugova's republic was health care. As was noted above, many doctors and medical staff had already been or were being sacked throughout 1990. In spring of that year, however, in a bizarre and never-explained occurrence, several thousand children succumbed to attacks of nausea, stomach pains and other illnesses. While the Serbian authorities claimed this was a case of mass hysteria, Albanians believed that the Serbs were trying to poison their children by puffing some form of toxic gas into classrooms via ventilation systems.[14] In the end, these extraordinary events led to two outcomes. One was that already poor inter-communal relations between Serbs and Albanians were embittered even further and many Albanians now determined that under no circumstances could they or their children see a Serbian doctor or enter a Serbian-run hospital or health clinic. This in turn accelerated the expansion of what was to become an alternative health system in Kosovo.

The mainstay of the organisation was the Kosovar humanitarian organisation named for Mother Teresa, who was herself an ethnic Albanian, born in Macedonia. According to a report by the US-based International Crisis Group, published in 1999, it had '239 general practitioners, 140 specialists and 423 nurses working voluntarily in clinics set up in 86 private houses throughout Kosovo, supplying food, medicine and hygienic materials to some 350,000 people'.[15] Although foreign visitors to Kosovo were often given the impression that the Albanian boycott of the Serbian health care system was total, this was never fully the case, and, as the 1990s wore on, less and less so. Despite the sackings, half the doctors and medical staff in the state system remained Albanians. While the Mother Teresa clinics could provide a useful service at a basic level, for anything more complicated, involving serious surgery or the need for sophisticated medical equipment, patients had no choice but recourse to the state system. For this reason, Albanian doctors who remained working in hospitals were not ostracised by the rest of the community as they would have been had they remained in any other comparable state job. When they needed to, Kosovars also went to doctors and hospitals in Serbia proper, where they were generally well treated, because they could afford to pay well.

A married couple who hate each other

The striking thing about Kosovo between 1992 and 1997 was what an odd place it was. Simultaneously it was both dull and bizarre. Police repression was constant, but Rugova drove around Priština in a presidential Audi. Applications to see him had to be made as if to a real president and then, if he received you, he did so not in a presidential palace but in a modest wooden bungalow which used to be the headquarters of the Kosovo writers' association. People went about their daily business, but armoured personnel-carriers prowled the streets and policemen in flak jackets directed traffic. Cafés were full and roads were open for anyone to go anywhere. The trouble was, of course, that all of this was a kind of looking-glass world. Cafés were full, not because people were relaxing after a hard day's work, but more often than not, because they had no work to go to and nothing else to do. A little money from family abroad went a long way back home.

During this period Kosovo received relatively little attention in the outside world, in great measure because of the wars in Croatia and then Bosnia. The second reason was that not much that was newsworthy actually happened. This is not to say that war was not a possibility that people discussed. It was, but neither Albanians nor Serbs had any interest in starting one. Albanians feared if that if conflict began they would be driven from their homes like hundreds of thousands of Bosnian Muslims had just been, and the Serbs did not want to fight a war on two fronts. Besides, for what it was worth, President George Bush's White House had cabled Milošević on 24 December 1992 in what became known as the 'Christmas Warning'.

The famous cable was actually sent by Lawrence Eagleburger, a former US ambassador to Belgrade who knew Milošević and who was, in the dying days of the Bush presidency, the acting secretary of state. It was brief and to the point. It said: 'In the event of conflict in Kosovo caused by Serbian action, the US will be prepared to employ military force

against Serbians in Kosovo and in Serbia proper.' Accompany-
ing the cable was an instruction to the US chargé d'affaires –
there was no ambassador at this point – that the message be read
to Milošević 'verbatim, without elaboration, and face to face'.[16]
The problem, though, was not that Milošević was preparing to
use force to solve the problem but that he was doing absolutely
nothing about it at all – and so it festered.

Kosovar politics in this period were driven by several
considerations. The first was staying alive and avoiding giving
the Serbs a chance to ethnically cleanse the province. The second
was to keep – or rather put – Kosovo on the international agenda
and the third was to build a certain legitimacy for the 'Republic
of Kosovo'. While at first Milošević was, of course, the enemy, a
rather grotesque symbiosis now evolved between Belgrade and
Priština. This began to become clear as the Serbs in Croatia and
then in Bosnia carved out their separate republics in 1991 and
1992. As far as the Albanians were concerned this was a question
of hearts and minds. That is to say that, in their hearts, the
Albanians wanted nothing more than to see the Serbs crushed –
and mercilessly at that. Indeed, many Albanians who remained
in the Yugoslav army defected during the war in Croatia to join
the fledgling Croatian army. Many Albanians who lived in
Croatia, where they were renowned as pastry-makers, gladly
joined the army too. Many of these men later fought in Bosnia.
But while the heart dictated one thing, cool logic dictated quite
another outcome. What the Kosovars wanted, secession with the
option of union with the mother country, was, after all, exactly
what the Krajina and Bosnian Serbs wanted too. At every
opportunity Serb propagandists would proclaim that it was no
longer possible for the Croatian Serbs, some 12 per cent of the
pre-war population of Croatia, or the Bosnian Serbs, 33 per cent
of Bosnia's pre-war population, to continue to live in the same
state with people whom they now professed to hate and who
hated them. So, if this was the case, thought Kosovars, it would
be hard, if the Serbs won and succeeded in changing frontiers to
make a Greater Serbia, for the international community to
object to Albanians asking for the same. The Serbs demanded
that all Serbs should live in one state. Albanians could not disagree with this since they wanted the same thing for themselves.
They did not believe that a couple of hundred thousand Kosovo

Serbs, a tiny percentage of the total number of Serbs, could stand in their way, especially as they themselves represented one-third of the total Albanian population of the Balkans.

Actually, some Albanians were irritated by this line of argument. They protested that they possessed rights based on being a pre-existing federal entity, while the Serbs of Krajina and the Republika Srpska had seized what they had by force. Still, it was clear that the argument did have an impeccable logic to it and, in its way, it imposed a certain way of thinking on the Kosovar leadership. Quite simply, this was that Milošević was good for them. If he won they would have a strong international claim to secession based on what the Serbs had secured. But, what if he lost? Then, the calculation was that Serbia would be so enfeebled that Kosovo would, one way or another, be able to escape from Belgrade's grip. Besides, it was assumed that since they had adopted a stance of passive resistance, and since it was self-evident that the majority of Kosovars wanted independence, then any future international conference on the former Yugoslavia would recognise the justice of this and reward the Albanians for their 'good behaviour'.

On the assumption that Milošević was good for the Kosovo Albanians, the worst thing that could happen was that he might be replaced by a Western-minded democrat. In 1992, in the wake of the international recognition of Slovenia, Croatia, Bosnia and Macedonia, this became a key issue. The reason was that this recognition was based on the legal opinion that the republics had the attributes of statehood and therefore could be recognised. By contrast Kosovo, which had failed in its campaign to become a republic, did not have this right because it was just a province of Serbia. So long as Milošević remained in power, the Kosovars had a perfect foil to the argument that they must live in the same state with Serbia. As Maliqi expressed it so eloquently:

> Europe's determination and that of the other international actors that the Albanians must live under the jurisdiction of Serbia may produce a desperate situation – like a court order to a married couple who hate each other, and who can no longer live together, to share a flat. And if one of them wanted to partition the flat, the judge would say

cynically: you will have your little autonomous corner in that flat where you can cry your heart out.[17]

But what would happen if the Serbian spouse changed? If he no longer beat his wife? There was not much chance of Milošević being toppled but, as we shall see, it was not absolutely impossible either. Still, in the short term there were other considerations. On 21 June 1991 James Baker, the US secretary of state, had come to Belgrade to tell the leaders of the six republics, then specifically Slovenia and Croatia, that the US would not recognise them if they tried to secede from Yugoslavia. But he also told them, and in this case specifically Serbia, that the US would oppose any attempt to prevent secession by force. The European Community (EC) – later the European Union (EU) – concurred with this rather weak policy. Seven months later it was in shreds and the EC led the world in recognising Croatia and Slovenia. It is impossible to under-estimate the importance of this radical reversal of policy – or rather recognition of reality. It meant that, from then on in, Kosovars never believed that US or European policy was immutable when it declared that Kosovo did not have the right to independence because of its provincial status. Fehmi Agani, the mild-mannered sociology professor, vice-president of the LDK and the man widely believed to be its *éminence grise*, always delighted in reminding visitors at this stage that: 'The attitude of Europe and the west can be changed.' Apart from the fact that he believed it was better for Albanians, Serbs and Europe in general for Kosovo to go its own way, he also based his confidence on his assertion that the EC's ill-fated Hague Conference which began in September 1991, chaired by the British Lord Carrington, 'started by trying to keep Yugoslavia alive and ended up by looking how to dissolve it'. Significantly, one of the stumbling-blocks at The Hague was the question of Kosovo, which had been raised by the Slovenes. Later Dimitrij Rupel, their foreign minister, recalled:

> The only question that really bothered the Serbs in The Hague was the question of Kosovo. In one of the commissions they started to talk about how to regulate the question of minorities, the Serbian minority in Croatia – at that time it was only Croatia under discussion – and how

painful it was for them, the Serbs, to live under Croatian rule. Then I said, we should design in this new arrangement equal rights for all minorities, including Albanians, ha. [Vladislav] Jovanović [the Serbian foreign minister] really got mad, that was really something I shouldn't have said. It was the end of our friendship.[18]

And, within weeks, the end of Yugoslavia. Germany announced on 23 December that it would recognise Croatia and Slovenia on 15 January 1992. On that day Britain, Belgium, Austria and the Vatican also recognised the two republics and other countries soon followed. On 6 April Bosnia was also recognised by EC states and full-scale war began immediately. One of the first acts of war was the despatch by the Serbian ministry of interior, for whom he worked, of Željko Ražnatović, also known as Arkan, the head of a ruthless paramilitary force. His job was to lead a blitzkrieg-style capture of Bijeljina and then Zvornik, two key towns commanding the roads from Serbia into Bosnia.

My hair stood on end

Kosovo's declaration of independence meant that, wherever possible, Kosovars boycotted Serbian and Yugoslav institutions. While they still had to use Yugoslav dinars and passports and pay taxes, they did not have to vote. Many Serbs who despise Milošević and everything he has done believe that if the Albanians had suspended their electoral boycott their 800,000 or so votes would have changed history. Of course, this is one of the great 'what ifs …?' of recent times. In theory, and at some crucial juncture, these Albanian deputies could have voted alongside Serbian opposition deputies and moved to topple Milošević. On the other hand the Milošević regime is an authoritarian one so it is questionable whether, if the Albanians had ever voted, their deputies would ever have been allowed to come to such a position where they held the balance of power. Still, this is all theoretical, since, as we have noted above, the Kosovar leadership worked on the Leninist principal of 'the worse the better' – that is to say, that Milošević was good for them. The only time that the issue ever came into sharp focus was in late 1992 when Milan Panić, the Yugoslav prime minister, came to Kosovo looking for votes. The Panić story was rather an extraordinary episode. As a young man and champion cyclist, Panić had defected from Communist Yugoslavia during a cycling competition abroad. Settling in the US, he prospered, building up a California-based pharmaceuticals firm called ICN. On 14 July 1992 Milošević had him installed as Yugoslav premier. Panić was, and is, a genuine democrat. He also really believed that business, money and economics could solve the problems of the Balkans. He was uninterested in ethnic conflict and genuinely wanted peace. Milošević wanted someone who would do what he was told and he believed that, by virtue of being rich and an American citizen, Panić had a direct line to the White House. At this point Dobrica Ćosić, the spiritual father of the infamous *Memorandum*, was president of Yugoslavia. The whole episode degenerated into a farce with Panić even visiting besieged Sarajevo promising to end the war but having no power whatsoever. As far as Milošević was concerned, the Panić episode was a disaster and he had to be got rid of as quickly as possible. The problem was that Panić was close to Ćosić and because he promised an end to the war, prosperity and was a living embodiment of the American dream, his popularity was soaring amongst ordinary Serbs.

As the conflict burst into the open the exuberant Panić hoped to capitalise on his popularity in Serbia. One tack was to build it up further. On 22 September, in New York, he asked the foreign ministers of the five permanent members of the UN Security Council, which had on 27 May imposed a total economic embargo on Serbia and Montenegro, to allow for an exemption for the import of winter heating oil. The request was refused. If it had been accepted, many Serbs believe, then Panić would have been regarded as a miracle-worker and would have received far more votes than he did when he challenged Milošević directly in presidential elections in December. And, of course, he could have received hundreds of thousands more votes if the Albanian leadership had suspended its electoral boycott policy and urged its people to vote for him in a bid to get rid of Milošević. But this was exactly what they did not want to do.

This was Panić's second tack: on 15 October he visited Priština and tried to cut a deal with the Rugova and the LDK. In exchange for a compromise over the question of the Kosovar school curriculum, which would lead to the reintegration of Albanian students into the state system, he hoped the Albanians could be persuaded to vote for him. There then followed an extraordinary press conference where Panić, acting like an ebullient circus ringmaster, announced that he and Rugova had agreed that talks must begin to get children back to school and people back to work. He then announced that 'Dr Rugova and I are going to democratise the Yugoslav system' and, for the benefit of the cameras, grabbed the by-now dazed Rugova and clasped him in an unwelcome bear hug.

There is no reason to doubt that Panić was genuine and that he meant what he said. But, above all, he was desperate for those Albanian votes. And there was no way he was going to get them. The night before, sitting in the gloomy presidential bungalow in the muddy car park behind Priština's sports stadium, Fehmi Agani, whose eyes always twinkled, gave a chilling expose of LDK policy. 'Frankly, it is better [for us] to continue with Milošević. He is not prepared for such a long war. Milošević was very successful in destroying Yugoslavia and, in the same way, if he continues, he will destroy Serbia.' But, he added, 'we don't want to destroy Serbia and go into war'. This was because the Kosovars wanted to achieve their independence without violence. And, of course, however cooperative and friendly Panić was, he could not offer Kosovo independence, but only 'enlightened hegemony ... Panić is offering crumbs but it is not enough to resolve the crisis,' said Agani. 'We can't give total support to Panić because his position is not total support for us. The position of Panić is to reduce problems rather than resolve them.' But surely, he was asked, getting rid of Milošević was a priority? 'The problem is not only weakening Milošević and helping Panić but finding a solution for us ...' As far as Agani was concerned, there could be an historic compromise with the Serbs. But this would not be within Serbia or Yugoslavia, 'but as a neutral state open to both Serbia and Albania ... [in which] Serbs could realise their cultural rights'. He continued: 'We haven't insisted on union with Albania as a sign of compromise. Serbs and Serbia would not accept that. This is not a small sacrifice.' And, as to the question of Panić's fishing for votes, he said: 'He thinks we will accept him because he is an opponent of Milošević. It's not enough. He may offer us to take part in the elections but without offering anything concrete. We are against Milošević but we also know he must fall, with or without Panić.' But was there not a risk that the longer Milošević remained in power, the higher the risk of war? 'If they want war they will have it just for one madman. War will not be avoided by giving concessions to the aggressors ...' At the time, this did not necessarily seem to be a recipe for avoiding war, but, if the situation remained frozen, then it did seem likely that more radical voices would begin to be heard within the Albanian community. Agani agreed with this. For now, he explained, the radicals were 'more verbal than real,' but he added that if the LDK's policy of passive resistance did not succeed, then the party 'would be radicalised'. Prophetically he added: 'If Albanians wanted to embrace the radicals we would have a lot more radicals here ... We are in a position of occupation. War is not inevitable but the risk is permanent.'

Panić's visit to Kosovo was greeted with horror by most Kosovo Serbs. By now the triumphal euphoria with which they had hailed the rise of Milošević and the demise of autonomy had given way to depression, despondency and the realisation that war might yet come to Kosovo. On Gazimestan, that part of the historic battlefield where Milošević had given his famous speech on 28 June 1989, you could climb the tower that commemorates the battle. In the brush, the army was waiting, exercising at the holy site. Tanks sat silently, their cannons aimed at the tower-blocks of Priština while smoke coiled upwards from the fires around which Serbian soldiers were cooking. In Kosovo Polje, the nearby Priština suburb with a large Serbian population, the gloom was everywhere. 'My hair stood on end,' said Drenjinka Pavlović, a hospital ward sister, commenting on Panić's embrace of Rugova. 'How could he do such a thing? Embracing a secessionist is too much.' Mrs Pavlović got her job in 1990 after the old ward sister, an Albanian, had left. She said that she thought that if there was deal with Panić, the old ward sister would get her job back, 'and take her revenge. I would probably have to leave, but I don't think our men will allow it, so it could be war.'

Budimir Savić was promoted to become director of his civil engineering firm when his Albanian boss was sacked. He said: 'If they get the jobs again by law, then there will be no life for Serbs here. They will demand Kosovo's independence and we'll either have to leave or it will be war.' Still, Mr Savić added, in the meantime he was far more concerned by a more immediate danger, that of the risk of his company closing thanks to the effects of international sanctions. Surely then the best way to have the sanctions lifted would be for the Serbs to get rid of Milošević? 'If it wasn't for Milošević we wouldn't be here,' he replied. 'He gave us hope. That's why we could survive.'

Priština University was, of course, by now an all-Serbian University. The head of its sociology and philosophy department was Aleksandar Matijašević, who had lived in Kosovo for 25 years. He too saw no room for optimism. 'A compromise is possible,' he said, 'but it would only be provisional and the Albanians would not keep their promises.' In fact, he believed that the future risked being 'worse than war'. He predicted:

> a constant pressure, murders and terrorism and the killings of soldiers which will make life impossible, just like Ireland, but much worse. There's little chance of its getting better. There are two parallel societies here. Each one has organised their own education. They control the private sector, the Serbs the public sector. There is even a double system of taxes. They have their own informal taxes. Our children don't play together anymore.

And neither did people even walk together any more. Professor Matijašević said that during the *corso*, in which families and friends strolled out of an evening, in Priština, 'they have one side of the main street and we have the other'. His observations about the economy were quite correct. The effect of the large-scale dismissals from the administration and state-owned companies was to help kick-start the private sector in Kosovo. Jobless, the more entrepreneurial amongst the Kosovars opened shops and small businesses. In terms of capital, Albanians, with their large families, often had access to hard currency, remitted by brothers and uncles and cousins already working abroad, and those who were now leaving to seek work in Germany and elsewhere in ever-larger numbers. This led to the situation whereby Serbs, who initially thanked Milošević because they now had all the public-sector jobs, cursed him because, thanks to the war, sanctions and hyperinflation which was now taking off, their salaries had dropped from the equivalent of perhaps DM1000 a month to DM100 which was not enough to support a family. By contrast, because of the Albanians' access to hard currency, goods which could not be bought in Belgrade could often be found in Priština. Milk was a classic example. By January 1994, just before hyperinflation was ended, by which time it had reached a *monthly* rate of 313,563, 558 per cent, even basic goods simply disappeared from the shops.[19] However, milk from Vojvodina could always be bought in Priština (but not Belgrade) because Kosovar businessmen paid for it in Deutschmarks at the factory gates. While Serbs got poorer, their resentment and hatred of their Albanian neighbours soared.

The coda to Panić's hunt for votes in Priština came in December. The election campaign in Kosovo underlined the stark division of the province into what was really two countries on one land. While the walls were covered in election posters and Serbs talked politics, ordinary Albanians were hardly aware that the poll they were boycotting was even taking place. There was no particular reason why they should have been, especially as the only Albanian news now on Serbian television and radio was simply a translation of the Serbian news, so nobody watched it. The campaign in Kosovo was not without interest, though, as several seats in the Serbian assembly were being contested by a 'group of citizens' headed by one Željko Ražnatović, the paramilitary leader known as Arkan. The fact that Milošević was encouraging him to stand, or perhaps even giving him the seats that he won, was clearly in part designed as a threat to the Albanians. The message was that Arkan was being rewarded for his sterling services in ethnically cleansing large areas of Croatia and Bosnia and woe betide any Albanian who even as much as thought about doing anything to make their independence real. For weeks, television adverts trumpeted Arkan's virtues. 'He's a good and honest man, who won't sell us down the river,' said Zoran, a Priština market stall-holder. Stories about Arkan's alleged Mafia links were dismissed by most Kosovo Serbs and the tales of his ethnic-cleansing prowess were generally greeted with approving satisfaction. 'Arkan and Milošević are defenders of the Serbian people and they are fighting fascism together,' opined Mileva, a café proprietor. Arkan's heavily armed men took up residence in the central Hotel Grand and drove around

Kosovo in unmarked four-wheel-drive cars. Few Serbs worried about what Arkan meant for the health of their democracy. Jelena, a teacher at Priština University, was an exception when she said:

> He looks such a lamb, but it worries me, because, wherever he's been there's been trouble. I heard he was involved in crime and wanted to enter parliament so that he could have parliamentary immunity. Who knows what to believe?

Edita Tahiri, a member of the Kosovar parliament who advised Rugova on foreign affairs, knew what it meant for her. Arkan's candidacy was a 'provocation' and 'a mirror of the future of Serbian democracy'.

The polls for the Serbian and Yugoslav parliaments and for the Serbian and Montenegrin presidencies were held on 20 December. According to the official statistics, 70.7 per cent of the electorate took part. Milošević won 2,515,047 votes (56 per cent of those voting) while Panić won 1,516,693 votes (34.02 per cent). A third candidate won 147,693 votes (3.31 per cent.) Because Milošević had got more than half of the votes cast, there was no need for a second run-off poll. If the Albanians had been told by their leaders to vote for Panić, and if he had received extra votes thanks to the kudos he could have gained if he had succeeded in winning sanctions relief over heating oil, then maybe he could have won. That must remain, as we have already noted, a 'what if …?' of history. As it was, Panić claimed that the poll had been rigged and that Milošević had really won only 49 per cent as against 43 per cent for himself. This result would have required a run-off. Panić also claimed that he had been handicapped from the start because of Milošević's control of the all-important state media. Having lost the election, Panić was duly sacked on 29 December. He continued to play a role in opposition politics in Yugoslavia and, until it was confiscated by the authorities in 1999, to run ICN-Galenika, the Yugoslav subsidiary of his pharmaceuticals enterprise.

Arkan won five of the 21 seats in Kosovo and celebrated with the optimistic announcement that 'Kosovo will no longer be a problem for Yugoslavia.'

Organising in case

Clearly, under wartime conditions, the Serbian authorities made the calculation that passive resistance, such that it was, was better than active resistance. In a way, then, Ibrahim Rugova and his associates had been put in a situation where, rightly fearing what might happen if they tried anything more robust, they effectively pacified the province, which was exactly what the authorities wanted. In return the authorities did not arrest Rugova who was free to travel the world to plead the Kosovar cause, as were other members of the LDK. They calculated that the unrest that might have been sparked by arresting Rugova or other prominent Kosovars and putting them on trial was simply not worth the bother. Besides, the international community backed the Serbian line that Kosovo could not secede.

Just because Rugova and well-known Kosovars had some measure of protection, this did not mean that this extended to the rest of the population. In fact, the police kept up a regime of constant surveillance, harassment, questioning, beatings and arrests. These had two aims. One was to keep the population cowed and the other was to crush any attempt, however feeble, at more robust resistance.

In retrospect the human rights question takes on some very interesting dimensions. The first is that many Kosovars success-fully convinced many Westerners that the question of Kosovo was really one of human rights. In fact it was not. At the heart of the matter was a fundamental struggle between two people for control of the same piece of land. In our times, however, human rights have become an influential factor in shaping international politics. This is not to say that the Kosovars did not suffer grievous human rights abuses at the hands of the Serbian authorities. They did. But it is to say that, with the benefit of hindsight, we can see how the question of human rights became another weapon in the arsenal of the Kosovars. In this they were amply aided by the Serbian authorities who, more often than not, ignored proper judicial practices, beat suspects up and hence turned what we now know could have been quite legitimate cases into legal farces which played into the hands of the Kosovars. As we shall see, these cases often involved groups of men who stood accused of plotting a violent insurrection and the secession of Kosovo. At the time, these cases looked doubtful. The reason for this was that the UN, the Conference on Security and Cooperation in Europe (CSCE) and groups like Amnesty International from London and Human Rights Watch from New York dutifully and correctly reported on the widespread abuses surrounding these cases.[20] The latter, for example, noted that 'Those tortured and beaten by the police have little recourse in Kosovo as the rule of law is practically nonexistent. In a state where the judiciary has been robbed of its independence, defendants are routinely convicted solely on "confessions" signed after prolonged torture.'[21]

Despite the fact that Kosovo simply could not compete in terms of news and foreign interest with developments in Bosnia, there was no shortage of human rights reporting during this period. Between September 1992 and June 1993, when the Yugoslav authorities refused to renew their visas, the CSCE had small missions in Kosovo, Sandžak and Vojvodina monitoring the situations there. The UN was also reporting on the situation and resolutions were passed in New York, but all to no avail – at least in the short run.

The question of human rights needs to be examined at several levels. On the first level we need to look at the constant and general low-level harassment which affected ordinary people. This included being brought into police stations for questioning and beatings. Whole villages were frequently surrounded and subjected to violent searches for weapons. In 1993, for example, Human Rights Watch reported in detail about a police raid on a village called Čabra. This is the testimony of Aziz Hasani, which was typical of the rest:

> About eight officers came to my house to beat me. I recognised some of the police from around town and knew at least one of them by name. They kicked me until I fell down from the blows. Two of them pinned me down with their legs and they started to ask, 'Where are your bunkers, your hiding places for weapons?' During the time I was on the ground, they continued to beat me. They kicked me in the mouth with their boots and kicked me in the left ear. I still don't hear well in that ear. I am very embarrassed because they beat me like that in front of my wife and children.[22]

Abusing their authority, the police frequently used raids of one form or another to steal money from ordinary people, motorists and businesses. Only on very rare occasions was a policeman reprimanded if an Albanian died from a beating or an innocent man was shot. The case of Adem Zeqiraj from Djakovica is a mundane example of one such death, as investigated by the CSCE and reported here by the UN. He was arrested, sent the next day to Djakovica hospital and then transferred to Priština hospital where he died. 'A medical report from Djakovica hospital recorded that he had been admitted with traumatic shock, internal bleeding and a serious kidney condition.'[23]

The authorities never bothered to try to win Albanian hearts and minds. This would have been virtually impossible anyway and may explain why they never tried. Still, the behaviour of the authorities and the police was ultimately self-defeating, as they simply stored up more and more trouble for themselves in the future. In view of the fact that the Kosovar leadership had opted for a strategy of passive resistance, the combination of an inability to hit back or seek recourse contributed to an ever-growing sense of frustration and hatred – ready to explode at any time. Abroad, such frequent and constant reports of abuses also had an effect. Report by report, drip by drip, they helped undermine Serbia's claim that Kosovo was its internal affair that merited no outside involvement. Even apart from the fact that the human rights situation was intolerable, the authorities also made it the affair of others, because as we have noted, hundreds of thousands of Albanians left the province during these years. Whether they were leaving because they personally had a 'well-founded fear of persecution' as the UN's definition requires of asylum seekers, or they were leaving for economic reasons, or a mixture of both was really irrelevant since they all asked for asylum. And, to make matters even more pressing, after 1991, increasing numbers of Albanians from Albania began to come to Germany and other countries all claiming to be Kosovars and thus eligible too for asylum and social benefits. In Britain, a 1996 court ruling meant that Kosovo Albanians were elevated to the same status as Bahais fleeing Iran. That is to say that they were effectively deemed eligible for asylum simply by virtue of being Kosovo Albanians, rather than having to prove, on an individual basis, that they were threatened personally.

In most countries where human rights are trampled on, human rights organisations are either illegal or find it extremely hard to function. Yet another of Kosovo's oddities was that two human rights groups operated legally, and despite being subjected to general harassment, police raids and occasional brutal beatings were, in the main, free to collate statistics and publicise the situation. The groups were the Council for the Defence of Human Rights and Freedoms, which was headed for many years by Adem Demaçi, and the Kosova Helsinki Committee headed by Gazmend Pula. While their work was invaluable in documenting the human rights situation, they have been criticised for conflating abuses. As a report of the International Crisis Group noted, 'their accounting system is misleading. For instance, of the 2,263 overall cases of "human rights violations" in the period from July to September 1997, they cite three murders, three "discriminations based on language ..." and 149 "routine checkings". By collating minor and major offences under the same heading, the same statistics fail to give a fair representation of the situation.'[24]

The second level of human rights abuses that we need to examine relates to the targeting of specific people and political trials. While the most senior LDK officials were generally left to their own devices, lesser officials frequently found themselves a target for interrogations and beatings. The same was true for trade union officials. While Albanians always presented these as simple human rights abuses, there may well have been more to some of this than met the eye. For example, in a rather loose fashion, Albanian policemen from among the 3,500 who were sacked in 1991 organised themselves in a trade union. They then began to try and act as a kind of shadow Albanian police force, discreetly acting, in fact, as a parallel police. The authorities moved to crush it as they understood that this was part of a game, albeit played by a very small number of people, to see how far the Albanians could push the boundaries of Serbian 'tolerance'. In November and December 1994 some 200 of them were arrested and accused of attempting to form the core of the 'Interior Ministry of the Republic of Kosova'. Officially, Bujar Bukoshi's government had six ministers, who were named, but, depending on whom you asked, the posts of the ministers of defence and of the interior had either not been nominated because the time was not right – or were secret. Beginning in spring and summer of 1995, a group of 159 of the former police officers were put on trial. The prosecutor said that their 'trade union' served 'as a shield for the forming of an illegal police force'.[25] Amongst other accusations, they were charged with spying on the police and army and stockpiling weapons. At the time, human rights observers, journalists and even organisations in Belgrade noted that many of the defendants said they had been tortured and reported their claim that they were undergoing a 'staged and political trial aimed at incriminating the Albanian democratic movement'. The latter was clearly true but it is also true that at least some of the police were indeed trying to construct some form of parallel police force. However, some or perhaps many of those convicted may not have known the full facts. One of those jailed during one of this series of trials, the former police chief of Uroševac (Ferizaj) told the journalist Daut Dauti that the policemen 'were organised in case something happened'. However, when they had visited Rugova to offer their services, he simply dismissed them saying: 'You do whatever you want.' Still, a small number did have contacts with Bujar Bukoshi, who, as the 1990s wore on, began to despair of what he saw as Rugova's increasing apparent political paralysis. Dauti also reported that he had met (former) policemen who did indeed bug police stations and debug the phones of political activists or others who suspected they were being listened to. They told him that most of the listening devices they found were manufactured in Britain. One of the main reasons why they bugged the Serbs, where they could, was to reveal the identities of Albanian informers.

Similar to the police trials were the 'Ministry of Defence and General Staff of the Army of the Republic of Kosovo' trials. They began on 23 September 1993.[26] Like the police trials, it would seem that a mixture of truth and fiction were mingled here. The prosecution alleged that Hajzer Hajzeraj, who had been the former chief of staff of Kosovo's reserve Territorial Defence forces, which were abolished in 1989, was the minister of defence and chief of staff of an army allegedly belonging to Rugova's government. Of the more than 100 arrested, many were former Yugoslav army officers. They stood accused of trying to organise an armed rebellion, organising military training, distributing weapons and, in many cases, of being members of a tiny militant group called the Popular Movement for the Republic of Kosovo (LPRK). Again, human rights activists and lawyers claimed that confessions had been extracted under torture and that there was little credible evidence against the accused. In fact, despite torture claims, which are undoubtedly true, there was, as in the police case, an element of truth to the Serbian accusations. As we shall see in the next chapter, Bukoshi, as opposed to Rugova, had indeed been trying to do business with the LPRK and some of their members had been sent to Albania for training. The prosecution charged that the defendants had been trying to build 'military formations up to the size of a brigade and collecting weapons for 40,000 people'. Of course, no such thing ever came about, but, if the Serbs had not continually cracked down, then there is little doubt that arms for 40,000 would indeed have been collected.

Apart from these set-piece trials which tried to link the shadow government with accusations of preparations for an armed uprising, and so smear Rugova by claiming his passive resistance policies were fraudulent, there were also several trials of small, individual groups. They too stood accused of plotting armed rebellions. Because of the allegations of torture and the clear attempts to ram home convictions, regardless of legal procedures, these were often reported in minute and often scathing detail in human rights reports. In 1992, for example, nineteen Albanians were convicted of founding an illegal organisation which 'conspired to purchase weapons to advance secessionists' aims'. A goldsmith and father of three called Mentor Kaqi was accused of being the founder of the 'illegal enemy organisation', the National Front of Albanians and of:

> coordinating with military experts abroad (Austria, Switzerland, Albania), and at home with a goal to separate Kosovo from Serbia and Yugoslavia ... [Visiting] Switzerland and Albania [to raise] money for the organisation ... [Acquiring] three machine guns, four revolvers, one pistol, one semi-automatic gun and five hand grenades as well as ammunition from an unidentified person in Switzerland.[27]

Pleurat Sejdiu was a doctor and activist from Podujevo who moved in these radical underground circles. In 1998 he lived in London where he was spokesman for the KLA. After NATO troops entered Kosovo he became deputy foreign minister in the self-proclaimed provisional government. Of the Mentor Kaqi trial he says simply that this attempt to start an armed group was 'cut short'. Of trials of others accused of plotting an uprising he says that in 'ninety per cent' of cases, the Serbs had caught the right people. During the early and mid-1990s there were occasional shootings of policemen and soldiers, but it seems that while members of various underground groups were arrested, by contrast, the real assassins escaped. Human Rights Watch reported that in the summer of 1993 the Serbian police:

> stepped up attacks against Albanian civilians; in doing so [the] authorities have pointed to several recent police killings as purported justification for detaining and interrogating Albanians. One Albanian human rights worker in Uroševac voiced the sentiment of many in stating: 'Police simply use any opportunity they can to beat us. Since late July, everyone who gets interrogated at the police station is accused of having wounded a policeman.'
>
> For example, on July 4, 1993, a policeman was killed at the police checkpoint entering Peć/Peja. No one was arrested in connection with the incident. Serbian authorities claim that the death was the work of Albanian terrorists. The Chairman of Human Rights Council of Peja, Tahir Demaj, says 'We don't know how the incident occurred, and we have no information on it.' According to Mr Demaj, police in Peć used the incident as a pretext to raid villages surrounding Peć, beating villagers, searching homes and detaining, interrogating and further beating suspected village leaders.[28]

Similarly, and typically, a UN report noted that, according to former detainees, in August 1993, they had 'been systematically beaten to induce them to confess to membership of an illegal Albanian separatist movements and to provide information about armaments. In each case, the individual was asked whether he had arms himself. When this was denied, he was told to obtain gun(s) and produce them to the police.'[29]

So, in this way, the spiral of violence was perpetuated. What is so striking about this period, though, is how so many Serbs really believed that such a situation could continue indefinitely.

Boško Drobnjak, the Serbian Kosovo secretary for information, told Human Rights Watch that 'in the past year [1992–3], there have been 130 terrorist attacks on police'.[30] Like the Kosovar figures for human rights abuses, it is hard to know what exactly constituted an attack and so this figure more than likely gives an inflated sense of the gravity of the problem. However, a UN report cites statistics supplied by the Serbian ministry of interior stating that between 1 January and 30 September 1993 there were 52 attacks against the police which resulted in two deaths and fifteen wounded.[31] Interestingly, however, given the official line and the way that the situation was to develop several years later, Drobnjak also told the human rights activists that:

> In his opinion, the attacks were committed by Albanian 'extremist groups, not by Mr Rugova'. Although no one has been charged in the attacks, Mr Drobnjak claims that police have determined that the bullets used were produced in China and 'it is well known that Albanians have Chinese arms and ammunition, probably delivered from Albania'.[32]

Humiliation, despair, fury, rage and hatred

Difficult though life was in Kosovo through the early 1990s, and as highly politicised as most Kosovars were, it is important to understand that until at least 1995, after the Dayton Conference which ended the war in Bosnia, as far as most people were concerned the province simply settled into a type of sullen stability. As for the attacks on the police, for most people the perpetrators were unknown extremists and frustrated, angry individuals. Above all, people were simply grateful that the horrors of war, which they had seen on their television sets just like everyone else in Europe, had not come to them. And, curiously, in this, they were often better informed than their Serbian counterparts. The reason for this was that, with the take-over of Priština television and the dismissal or resignation of its journalists, the vast majority of Kosovars simply tuned out. They did not turn off though. Because they had no television of their own and did not want to watch Serbian programmes they bought satellite dishes, meaning that a far higher proportion of people in Kosovo had access to satellite television than in the rest of Serbia. This did not confine them to foreign-language programmes, though, as they could watch the satellite broadcasts of Albanian television and, most importantly, its Kosovo news and features segments beginning at 6.30 every evening, a programme which the authorities in Tirana had given over to the parallel government. In this way Rugova and Bukoshi could speak to their constituents in a way which would have been impossible a few years earlier.

Television, though vitally important, was not everything. Following the closure of *Rilindja*, a paper which had previously served the agricultural community, *Bujku*, which means 'farmer', was turned into the mouthpiece of the LDK and more or less left alone by the authorities. A clutch of magazines also toed the LDK line in this period. What this meant was that most Kosovars became lulled into believing that not only was Kosovo high on the international agenda, but because it was high, it would soon be solved, and so therefore there was no need to do anything except put one's trust in Rugova. According to the news, the 'President of the Republic' was always meeting and greeting important and influential visitors or travelling the world doing the same. The fact was that, with 250,000 people under siege in Sarajevo, hundreds of thousands of Bosnians being driven from their homes and Europe and the US at loggerheads about what to do, Kosovo was always just an after-thought. It was the place that the diplomats knew they should do something about, but were not sure what and anyway had more important things to do. In its most grotesque form, this was demonstrated at the London Conference of August 1992, when the leaders of the Yugoslav republics were gathered to talk peace with world leaders. Rugova, as Kosovars were duly informed, had indeed been invited too, but in the most bizarrely English aristocratic-cum-laconic way possible. On 17 August Lord Carrington, the chairman of the conference, wrote to Dr (not President) Rugova. 'If you are planning to be in London at the time of the conference,' he told him, then it would be possible for him to have some meetings but it would not 'for practical and other reasons, be possible to grant your delegation access to the Conference chamber'. Still, Lord Carrington promised to set up a *salle d'écoute* for the Kosovars, which was diplomatic speak for a small side room with a live video link in it. This meant that the Kosovars could watch the fate of almost everyone else in the former Yugoslavia being discussed, except their own. 'We are thus making strenuous efforts to ensure that the views of the Kosovan Albanians are heard,' continued Lord Carrington. 'If you are interested in participating on this basis, I should be grateful if you would contact the Secretariat ... with details of your proposed delegation and accommodation in London.'[33]

Although the London Conference failed in its primary task of bringing peace to the former Yugoslavia, it was important in that it set up a crucial part of the institutional diplomatic structure which aimed at ending the conflict. Following the resignation of Lord Carrington after the conference, his place was taken by Lord Owen, who in turn was replaced by Richard Holbrooke and the Americans. They then used much of the work that had already been done by Owen's team in Geneva as a base from which they ultimately constructed the Dayton Accords for Bosnia. During this period, however, Kosovo continued as an 'add-on' to the main work of the diplomats. In this way the London Conference also set up a Kosovo Special Group which was chaired by Ambassador Geert Ahrens of Germany. In the words of Marc Weller, an international lawyer based at Cambridge University, the group 'quickly determined to circumvent the difficult issues of status, and instead attempted to focus on practical improvements of life in the territory. The issue of education was picked as one area where progress might be possible.' In the end it was not, and, as Weller points out, the talks 'quickly got bogged down'. But, he adds, 'Worse than the lack of progress on the education issue may have been that the mere existence of the Special Group gave the impression that the Kosovo problem was now being addressed in some way by an international forum.'[34]

Apart from the work of the Special Group there was one intriguing, but stillborn, idea which emerged from Geneva. That was to link the issue of Kosovo with that of Krajina in Croatia. The theory was that the Kosovo Albanians should have as much, or as little, autonomy as Krajina ultimately gained within the borders of Croatia. The idea was, of course, perfectly rational, from a Western peacemaking point of view, as it seemed to solve two outstanding cases of minorities, autonomy and sovereignty in one fell swoop. It was stillborn, however, since there was nothing in it for the Croats, and the Serbs still wanted to unite Krajina into a Greater Serbia, and keep full control over Kosovo. The Kosovars as well were against it because they did not want autonomy but independence. In the end, in August 1995, the Croats solved the Krajina problem by driving out the Serbs. As we shall see, Krajina was to have a profound influence on the future of Kosovo, but not in the way the diplomats had intended.

Even before the cleansing of the Krajina and the Dayton Conference of November 1995, disillusion was beginning to set in amongst the Kosovars. At first this manifested itself in increasing tension between various wings of the LDK. While Fehmi Agani represented those in favour of what one might a term a softly-softly approach, former political prisoners, amongst whom were former members of the old so-called Marxist-Leninist groups, were demanding more radical action. Gazmend Pula, the urbane head of the Kosova Helsinki Committee, described what was happening as a 'hidden struggle' in the sense that none of it took place in the open and the real meaning of what was happening was opaque. 'They are not clear-cut divisions,' he said, 'one wing wants a harder line – action, but it's not very clear what a harder line should consist of. They just say we need something tougher.'

> People are disillusioned, but they recognise that the LDK has managed to avoid conflict ... they are disillusioned by the results. People are simply asking for more. They are saying we need ... to see more action, not through provoking possible conflict but with a more realistic approach. No one is challenging the non-violent peaceful approach but, given that it has resulted in not much but avoiding conflict, they would like to see a more realistic approach to negotiations with relevant factors, including Belgrade. People are coming to realise that Belgrade is one of the key players and you cannot simply ignore it saying you have your own independent whatnot republic.

With the benefit of hindsight, we can see that what Pula was describing was the coming collapse of the widespread consensus in Kosovar politics that non-violence was the best way forward. Pula was right, in that people wanted more. He was also right in that people did not know what that meant. Ultimately the question was posed in far starker terms. 'People are beginning to realise,' said Pula, 'that sovereignty is something you get when you soak your soil with a couple of feet of blood, and they are not so keen on it.' As far as Pula was concerned, then, that meant that 'people are ready to bargain for the best they can get, but not yet for the suggestion that Kosovo is part of Serbia'.

In fact there was more to what Pula was saying than just educated speculation. At the time, he, Agani and a few others were being invited to functions at the Swiss embassy in Belgrade where, informally, they were meeting with the likes of the SPS grandee Mihailo Marković and others. The Swiss, with their large Kosovar community, and fearing the influx of more if the situation did not improve, had decided that if there was anything they could do to ease the parties into some form of dialogue, however informal, it had to be done. These meetings were conducted with the utmost discretion because the Kosovars feared being denounced as traitors if the news leaked out. The Swiss must also have hoped that, if these contacts matured, then real secret talks, emulating the Israeli–Palestinian Oslo negotiations, could begin. It was not to be, but this period did see people like Pula beginning to talk privately about the so-called 'Three Republic' solution. The idea was that, in the nature of an historic compromise, both the Serbs and Albanians would forfeit something in a bid to avoid war and achieve a settlement. The Albanians would renounce their demand for *de jure* independence but would gain it *de facto*. The Serbian republic would give up Kosovo but it would remain within Yugoslavia, in a loose federation as an equal republic alongside Serbia and Montenegro. The idea was to linger on for some time but, ultimately, was to wither, thanks to the prevailing cultural norm which dictated that politics was a zero-sum game and that nothing could ever be gained by compromise. When, in 1997, Pula began to talk openly about the 'Three Republic' solution – when others were in fact now considering it in private – he was indeed denounced for treachery. In the meantime, those who wanted Rugova to take a more robust approach, whatever that was, would soon part company with him and many of them were rapidly moving closer to the conclusion that the idea of gaining independence by peaceful means had been nothing more than a cruel delusion.

It was not just people like Pula, however, who at that time began to believe that the only way to break the deadlock was to try to initiate talks based on the idea of compromise. The same message was also coming from Tirana. When the Democratic Party led by Sali Berisha had come to power in Albania in 1992 Kosovars held high hopes of him, believing that, in him, they had strong ally. During his time in opposition against the former Communist Party, now the Socialist Party, Berisha had projected a strong nationalist image denouncing his opponents for not doing enough for Kosovo. As a heart surgeon, Berisha had been a member of the tiny Albanian élite under Enver Hoxha and Ramiz Alia, his successor after 1985. But Berisha's roots were in Tropoja, a village in northern Albania close to the border with Kosovo. This was a region which had suffered by the imposition of the border in 1912 and particularly its sealing after 1948. This was because people in these frontier areas had close family and clan links with those on the other side and also because they were now cut off from towns where they traditionally went to market such as Djakovica, Prizren and Peć.

When he came to power, however, Berisha had to grapple with the realities of Albania's situation. In 1994, in his modest presidential office in Tirana, he explained that, above all, Albanians wanted to avoid war: 'Our priority is the prevention of conflict. We are a country that has lost 50 years in the twentieth century, and making up for lost time is the main goal.' Berisha was also responding to strong Western or, more particularly, American pressure, not to play the nationalist card and to dampen Kosovar expectations that they could turn their declaration of independence into reality. Berisha told the Kosovars that they should try to come to an accommodation with Belgrade, although, as we shall see, he did allow some very limited Kosovar military training to take place in Albania.

Berisha's cautious Kosovo policy was very much in tune with the prevailing public mood. With the fall of Communism in Albania, a number of sharp Kosovar businessmen had come to Tirana and made themselves unpopular, as it became widely believed that they were taking advantage of Albanians' lack of business experience. This feeling was reciprocated by many Kosovars who believed themselves infinitely more sophisticated than their Albanian country cousins, who had, after all, been effectively locked up for 50 years and had little experience of the ways of the world. Albanians, in turn, thought themselves better educated than Kosovars whom the people of Tirana – the élite at any rate – tended to look down upon as peasants. Whatever their feelings towards one another, though, there is little doubt that Berisha had correctly assessed the Albanian mood. One of Tirana's new businessmen, Zef Rakacolli, expressed it this way: 'If war was to break out, all would be lost. Hundreds of thousands of refugees would flood in and Albania would lose its chance to join the European mainstream.'

Despite his cautious Kosovo policy Berisha forged close links with Bukoshi, also a surgeon turned politician and a frequent visitor to Tirana. These contacts were to have important ramifications in the future. This was because the KLA's contacts and friends in Albania tended to come from the Socialist side of the political divide. This was due to their so-called Enverist roots and their connections dating from the time when they could expect some modest help in terms of money and passports from the old Communist secret service, the *Sigurimi*.

Berisha's close ties with Bukoshi did not mean that he maintained a good relationship with Priština. Indeed, Bukoshi's relations with Rugova were steadily worsening. In Kosovo, then, Berisha's message of moderation was far from welcome and although Kosovars were happy that his diplomats would raise the issue wherever possible, they were not about to cede anything to him. This was manifested in a tussle for power and influence over Albanian politicians in Macedonia in the summer of 1994 between Berisha and Rugova. Berisha's envoy to the Macedonian Albanians was Dylber Vrioni, then the head of the central bank in Tirana. His view of how Albanians outside Albania should think was telling: 'There is no solution for them if they don't think like us.' Fehmi Agani responded tersely by saying: 'To tell us we have to be part of Serbia means we have to continue to suffer under Serbian occupation. This line has no perspective.'

For people like Shkëlzen Maliqi, who believed that there should be ways of solving conflicts peacefully, the situation was becoming increasingly desperate. 'The fact that war has not yet broken out in Kosova can be attributed to two factors,' he wrote:

> the decision by Albanian leaders to pursue a policy of non-violent resistance, and the fact that virtually all Serbian military capacities have been taken up in the conflicts in Croatia and Bosnia–Hercegovina. But the war has only been postponed – because nothing has been done to remove its root causes. In the meantime ethnic conflict in Kosova has turned into a kind of intense war of nerves, in which one side stops at nothing, committing the most brutal violations of human rights and civil liberties, completely ignoring the protests of the international organisations which for a while kept monitoring teams in Kosova, while the other side bottles up its humiliation, despair, fury, rage and hatred – but for how long before it explodes?[35]

4 Homeland Calling

When young men came to join the KLA they gave their *besa*. In a literal translation it means 'oath' but somehow, in our modern societies, that word seems too weak. In the Albanian mind it is something almost mystical, a word entwined with ancient notions of blood and honour.

> In front of my flag I give my *besa* and my life that I will die for freedom and for my land and I will obey my army. If I betray my comrades they have the right to kill me. Now I am a soldier who fights for freedom.

This should not be surprising. The first men to take up arms against the Serbs in 1990s saw themselves as the latest generation, carrying on the struggle of their fathers and their grandfathers before them. And nowhere was this more the case than in the rolling hills of the Drenica valley. Here, more than anywhere else, this sense of tradition ran deep. This was where Azem Bejta, the *kaçak*, sometimes called Galica after his village, came from, along with his Amazon wife, Shota Galica. In 1937 Rebecca West drove through Drenica. On the road she met a Serb who had stopped to pray. She asked him why. 'Because I am glad to be alive,' he replied. He explained that after the war he had travelled frequently along the road,

> and because of the brigands I was always very frightened, particularly just at this spot, for they used to come down this valley and lay a tree trunk across the road. I used to think of my dear wife and my three children, and pray to God for protection, and now there is no more danger I am thanking Him for giving it to me.

West, who was clearly rather uninterested in all of this, and anyway was accompanied by a government minder, explained:

> The brigands who had operated on this road were by way

of being political insurgents. They were Albanians claiming to represent the element which had been dispossessed by the redistribution of land made by the Yugoslavian Government after the war. All over the Balkans there is an association between highway robbery and revolutionary idealism which the Westerner finds disconcerting, but which is an inevitable consequence of the Turkish conquest …'[1]

It is of course a pity that West did not delve a little deeper. If she had, we might find an explanation as to why, only a few years later, this same valley would be up in arms again, with the Yugoslav Partisan army men being pinned down by Shaban Polluzha and thousands of his men. Some believe that there is less to this Drenica spirit than a loathing of Serbs. They believe it is just a rejection of any sort of authority whatsoever. In May 1981, for example, a man called Tahir Mehaj who came from a hamlet from where he could see down a hill to his neighbours, the Jasharis, took to his compound and fought off siege rings of police and even soldiers. They had come to arrest him after a gunfight in nearby Srbica (Skenderaj) market where they had tried to arrest him for skipping bail over a court case involving his possession of a pistol. Along with his father, Nebil, who had fought with Shaban Polluzha, Tahir held out for several days until the authorities dropped bombs on the Mehaj compound from a helicopter.

With this weight of tradition and history, it was only natural that ambitious young men who wanted to start an uprising against the Serbs and men who just wanted to shoot Serbs should eventually make common cause here. In the same way, it is hardly surprising that they should also go to war singing the old songs. One of first men to take up arms recalled a practice that must date from ancient times. His friend Adem Jashari would go into battle, attacking Serbian police patrols, singing:

When I fight I feel more powerful if I yell. I feel happy because I'm fighting the Serbs. Sabit would be on one hill and I was on another, with our comrades. We started the war-cry on our hill and he started on his – it wasn't coordinated but there and then the voices came together, from one hill to another. 'Stand fast, stand fast …' Adem sang too. When we were with Adem, he gave us willpower, he was a strong man.

As the KLA grew, modern songs were composed for it, but it also adopted old songs and modernized them too:

O red Kosova,
We will bring you light one day,
Through the red hot barrel of a gun!
Azem Galica comes back to life,
We are cleansing our burned land with blood!
We give our lives but that's too little,
We are building our castles and turrets with gunslits,
New Adems and Hamzas are growing,
Bent on victory,
With the gun.
We save Kosova and make Albania proud!

By this time Adem Jashari, whom the song refers to, along with his brother Hamza, was dead, but as we can see, there was no doubt in the minds of the person who composed the song that the Jasharis were simply carrying on the struggle of Azem Bejta-Galica. There was also no doubt that this was a struggle that had to be passed down from generation to generation. This song was sung by a Drenica man who later was killed as he tried to cross the mountains back from Albania to Kosovo at Christmas in 1998:

Sun and moon shine on our land,
Mother Kosova where I was born,
Where I grew up,
Where I shed my blood,
Where I drink the water from the land,
Mixed with our mother's tears.

When my mother rocked my cradle,
And sang me a lullaby,
'Bless you my son,
Keep your sword and your gun always in your lap.'
She stroked my eyes and my hands,
And covered my face with the banner,
The double-headed eagle.

'Listen to your Albanian mothers,
If you don't die for your homeland,
You'll never rise from the dead!'

I grew in stature,
From stone to stone,
My eyes and my gaze,
Came from the flag,
How can we get to freedom?
All the roads begin in the gun turret,
I was taught how to shed my blood,
By my old grandpa.

'O my son don't hesitate to die,
For this land and these mountains,
Our way is to wear the white hat,
If someone tramples it,
And you don't have a gun,
Attack him with your teeth!'[2]

The Enverists

As we saw in the last chapter, the Serbian police were coming
under occasional attack throughout the early and mid-1990s and
they were also often unearthing groups of conspirators and
would-be guerrillas. When the war began in Kosovo in the
spring of 1998, however, few people had any idea who the KLA,
a tiny and secretive group, actually were. And, as we shall see,
no one was more surprised by their sudden emergence and
explosion of popularity than they were.

On 5 July 1998, with the KLA uprising in full swing, a man
in a neat suit, with a bushy moustache, mobile phone and briefcase stood before a packed audience in the Conway Hall in Red
Lion Square in London. Hundreds of London's Albanians had
come to hear what Jashar Salihu had to say, and above all to find
out who on earth were these people leading the revolt. Salihu,
and a couple of associates who, like him, had come from
Switzerland, stood to attention during a minute's silence for
those who had died. Behind them was a KLA flag. In the audience were Agim Fagu, the Albanian ambassador to London, Isa
Zymberi, the *de facto* ambassador of Kosovo who worked with

Bujar Bukoshi, and a bearded man called Pleurat Sejdiu, a mini-cab driver who headed the London branch of an obscure political party called Popular Movement for Kosova or LPK.[3] At the end of the minute's silence everyone shouted '*Lavdi!*' – 'Glory to them!' and the speeches began. Jashar Salihu took the floor: 'We didn't come here to divide people. I'll tell you the truth and the facts. This is the reality.' The KLA had been founded in 1993, he explained, and took its first three casualties on 31 January 1997. But Mr Rugova and his comrades had spent the last couple of years denying that the KLA existed and even claiming that it was the creation of the Serbian secret police – who by such a dastardly, wicked plot, which involved killing Serbian policemen, were really trying to smear Rugova and his policies of passive resistance. And now he came to the point. Jashar Salihu was asking for money:

> Villages are burning, people are being massacred. This is war. We do not have weapons and, as you see, we need weapons. We have to make efforts to help our brothers and sisters end the national liberation war, because no one will give us arms as a gift. That is why we are here today, to help the KLA and all Albanians in Kosova.

From the floor a man asked about volunteering. Salihu said, 'There is no need for men. What we need are weapons and we are here to provide them. I can tell you that tonight 1,500 men have left Kosova for Bajram Curri [in Albania] to … collect "some things"!'[4] The hall broke out in wild applause. 'We can organize sending people to Kosova, but in small groups. But I repeat it is not so much men that are needed as weapons.' Mehmet Bislimi, another of the speakers from Switzerland, now announced: 'I'd like to open an account here in England. In Kosova they might have spent 5,000 bullets while we've been talking.' A man got up to ask about whether the KLA wanted NATO intervention. Salihu answered: 'The KLA did not start this to get help, but, to go to the end does not mean we don't need help.' Was the KLA just for Kosovo, asked someone, what about the other Albanian-inhabited lands, in Macedonia and Montenegro? Salihu replied:

> Kosova starts in Tivar [Bar in Montenegro] and ends in Manastir [Bitola in Macedonia]. We don't care what

America and England think about it, we should unite with actions, not with words. We don't care what Clinton and other devils think! We are going to tell the truth!

Salihu and his colleagues were from the LPK, a tiny party which had consistently denounced Rugova, Bukoshi and his government as sell-outs. Most of the audience were uncomfortable with this, especially as, until now, they and their families back home had not only loyally supported the LDK but also contributed to its funds. Many had also believed Rugova when he claimed that the KLA was nothing but a Serbian secret police front. If it wasn't, some asked, then who led it and how many members did it have? 'I can't answer this,' replied Salihu. 'Why doesn't the government help the KLA?' was the next question. 'Ask the government,' was the reply. There was no hiding the deep rift in the Albanian body politic. And, as the audience flowed out into the warm summer evening, writing their cheques as they did so, there was also no doubt about where their sympathies were moving.

Around the corner in the pub, Salihu told his story. He was the chairman of the LPK's Homeland Calling fund. Based in Switzerland, he collected money from branches set up across Europe and north America and channelled it on to the KLA. The KLA was, he explained, 'somehow the armed wing of the LPK'. He was scathing of Rugova and his comrades. 'They thought that with the break up of Yugoslavia they would achieve their aim. They were only waiting for western Europe to act for them.'

Some of us knew this would never happen 18 years ago. I was organising in 1979 and was already for an uprising back then with some of my friends, but they were killed in Germany. In 1981 I was imprisoned for distributing political pamphlets. I was in gaol in Sarajevo and Foča with Alija Izetbegović [later president of Bosnia].

Salihu's friends who died in Germany are a vital link in the story. One of them was Jusuf Gërvalla who was leader of one of the tiny Marxist–Leninist or so-called Enverist groups which existed underground. The Movement for the National

Liberation of Kosovo (MNLK) was founded in 1978 by Gërvalla and Salihu joined in 1979. Salihu said: 'Our aim was, and is, for Kosova to be apart from Yugoslavia.' Asked whether, back then, such a thing was realistic, he replied: 'For us it was realistic, to move step by step.' But, still, he admitted that 'At that time we thought it would be good if our grandchildren lived in a free Kosova.' Xhafer Shatri was also active in underground politics at the time, but in 1992 became Bujar Bukoshi's minister of information, based in Geneva. He says that, back then, no one really believed that anything more than republican status could be achieved. 'No one thought Yugoslavia could be destroyed ... it was the West's little darling.'

Especially for young Kosovars, Jusuf Gërvalla was something of an icon. He had worked as a journalist at *Rilindja*, was well educated, came from a good family, was good-looking, a poet and guitar player of some renown. Like other similar groups, the MNLK agitated amongst students and others and published underground leaflets and other publications. Gërvalla's brother, the less well-known Bardhosh, ran the group with him. Another was led by Hydajet Hyseni, the *Rilindja* journalist who, during the demonstrations of 1981, had denounced the authorities in his speech from the tree in front of the Communist Party head-quarters. All of these men held Adem Demaçi in awe because of his long-term imprisonment for forming the ancestor to all of these groups back in the 1960s.

As is natural with small, clandestine and secretive political groups, they were always evolving, splitting and merging. Hence, on the 17 January 1982 the Gërvalla brothers met in a village near Stuttgart in Germany with Kadri Zeka, another activist and journalist who led the Group of Marxist–Leninists of Kosovo. Their idea was to merge their two groups into one new one, which was to be called the Popular Movement for the Republic of Kosovo, the LPRK. That night, as they emerged from the house where they had been meeting, they were gunned down. While most Albanians assume that the unknown assassin was working for the Yugoslav intelligence services, some believe that they might have been killed by a hitman working for the Albanian intelligence services. The theory goes that their commitment to Enverism was less than total and that they had thought of opening new perspectives by framing their project for Kosovo in terms which held the contribution of Albania and Enver Hoxha himself in a less than central place.

The question of Marxism–Leninism or Enverism is a vexed one, especially as the KLA were later accused of having these roots and therefore, in a politically motivated *non sequitur*, of still being committed Enverists. However, according to Daut Dauti, the Kosovar journalist, who was at university at this time: 'The Marxist–Leninists were for an armed uprising in the 1980s. They had no idea what Enverism was – they just wanted to get rid of the Serbs.' Especially after 1981, these people believed that the Albanians running the autonomous province were simply Serbian puppets and were angered that some Serbs did hold important jobs. Bardhyl Mahmuti, a member of one of these underground groups, recalls that, 'It was not a question of ideology, rather Leninist theory on clandestine organisations.' Not to mention the fact that making the right revolutionary noises secured at least a little help and money from Tirana. Xhafer Shatri, who spent eleven years in prison, says that despite their bombast the Enverist groups were, in fact 'purely nationalist' but adds that 'Albania was our only help.' Part of the appeal of Enverism was that a purely nationalist cause could be wrapped up in terms of a fashionable radical leftism. This meant that it could not be tarred with the brush of Fascism by those who equated Albanian nationalism with the nationalist-cum-Fascist groups of the wartime period. There is another element to consider here. That is that during this period very few Kosovars were able to visit Albania. In the minds of many, therefore, it became an almost mythical land of socialism, equality and well-being for all. In fact, it was a vicious, poverty-stricken Stalinist hermit state. However, those few who visited either did not realise this, because they had little opportunity to mix with ordinary people, or would never dare say so openly for fear of putting at risk their interlocutors or the family they had visited. There was, however, an even more powerful taboo on speaking about Albanian realities, and that was that the political correctness ruling in Kosovo at the time meant that anyone who dared say publicly that Albania was not the promised land risked being branded as pro-Serb. Later, Hydajet Hyseni explained the Marxist–Leninist cum Stalinist issue this way:

of course we were not Stalinists – the greatest outside influence came not from Stalinists but from the west and Albanian immigrants in the United States. The identification with brother Albania was actually weak. It was on the level of fantasy. Most activists knew nothing about Albania. Since they had never been there, they could afford grand illusions. It is similar to the orphan child who has never known her mother; she can easily glorify her. I was one of those who once had those fantasies about Albania.[5]

The importance and influence of the Marxist–Leninists in Kosovo in the 1970s and 1980s was far greater than the small numbers of committed activists would have led one to believe. They were influential at Priština University, for example, and after the first few days of demonstrations in 1981, had mobilised to organise further protests. In one way, however, with their demands for radical action, they can in a certain way be compared to the radical leftists in western European universities in the same period. That is to say that, while they may have had many sympathisers, such sympathies tended to fade as the students went on to jobs and to start families. Such a comparison can only be taken so far, though. Firstly, as Salihu pointed out, even the most hardline of the Enverists hardly viewed independence or union with Albania as a realistic short-term option. Therefore most of their political energy was taken up, not with actually plotting a hopeless uprising, but rather with agitating and working towards persuading people that Kosovo had to become a republic, a far more realistic goal. Of course, if it was achieved, republican status would then have become the transitional phase towards independence, but they would meet that problem once they had achieved the first step. The second difference is that, after the demonstrations of 1981, the authorities swooped, arrested and jailed hundreds of activists. Salihu, for example, was imprisoned for four years in 1981 for distributing leaflets. This in turn had unintended consequences. It meant that many of the most able agitators were removed from the political scene during the early to mid-1980s, while the experience of jail radicalised and hardened them. Once released, some stayed in Kosovo but others went abroad where they continued their agitation amongst the *Gastarbeiter* communities in

Germany, Switzerland, Scandinavia and elsewhere. Amongst them was Bardhyl Mahmuti. In June 1998, sitting at an elegant terrace restaurant in Vevey, on the shores of Lake Geneva, Mahmuti explained that after the 1981 demonstrations, he was sentenced to seven years in prison because he had told a Macedonian television crew that he supported the creation of a Kosovo republic. Behind him, an elderly woman in a pink dress and wearing white gloves ordered an ice cream. At tables all around pensioners trilled happily, ordering more and more food. As yachts cut across the sparkling water Mahmuti's phone rang constantly with reports coming in from the front. Mahmuti was now the spokesman abroad for the KLA. And he made no secret of what had made the difference between the student who had supported an idea to the man who, ever since, had devoted all of his energies into overthrowing Serb rule in Kosovo. Seven years, he said bitterly, are: 'Eighty-four months or 2,555 days'.

Until 1997, men like Mahmuti and Salihu were widely regarded as the loony fringe of Kosovar politics. Before 1989 most Kosovars sympathised with calls for a republic but the idea of an armed uprising, however notional, against a strong, confident and world-respected Yugoslavia seemed patently ridiculous, especially since the Serbs were not even running Kosovo. After 1991, and the experiences of Croatia and Bosnia, it seemed like suicidal madness.

They did not stop working, though, and, even apart from the effect of prison on a small but important group, the death of the Gërvalla brothers and Kadri Zeka had an extraordinary impact. For people like Salihu and Mahmuti this incident was one of the defining moments of their lives. Firmly believing that the Yugoslav secret services were behind the deaths, they also understood that blood had been spilled, and blood required blood to expunge the original sin. For them, the war began that night in 1982 in the village near Stuttgart. In the months that followed Xhafer Shatri, who had just escaped from prison, and others held a series of meetings in Switzerland and Turkey to complete the last work of the Gërvallas and Zeka by founding the LPRK. Inside Kosovo, it was to distribute leaflets and agitate, and a tiny number of its members actually began to train for war. Outside, in smoky *Gastarbeiter* clubs from Zurich to Malmö, it tried to enlist support. But all to no avail. As Shatri recalls it, they were 'voices in the wilderness'.

Odd as it may seem, it was Milošević who then gave many of them the chance to come in from the wilderness. The irony of Milošević's ascent to power is that while it was a central tenet of his campaign to abolish Kosovo's autonomy, he could not, at the same time, prevent the birth and phenomenal growth of the LDK. While a good proportion of the leadership were former members of the so-called Titoist wing of the Albanian political spectrum, that is to say they were former members of the old ruling Communist party, an influential group were also their former Enverist enemies. They included Hydajet Hyseni and Xhafer Shatri. This would have a long-term and devastating impact on Kosovar politics. It meant that there were always tensions between the more moderate wing of the party, led by men like Fehmi Agani, and the former political prisoners. But, in another split, the fact that men like Shatri had left the LPRK meant that bad blood now existed between people like him and those who decided it was beneath their dignity to join a party that was legal and indeed registered as such by the Serbian authorities. Those who remained behind in the LPRK were embittered and accused their former comrades of political opportunism and treachery. In its own small but significant way, this bad blood was to contribute to the rivalry and suspicion that would later characterise the relationship between the government-in-exile, the LDK, and the KLA. It is important to keep in mind that Kosovo's population is so small that its active political class is minute. So political jealousies and enmity over the last few decades, even where they have been expressed in ideological terms, have also become intertwined with personal and family relationships. During the run-up to the Rambouillet peace talks in February 1999, Western diplomats were exasperated at the extraordinary difficulties they encountered when trying to get the Kosovars to put together a single negotiating team. They thought that it stood to reason that, whatever the means they chose to employ, passive resistance or violence, all the Albanian political leaders wanted the same thing, independence, and equally were all being asked to make the same sacrifice, that is to say, to accept autonomy. However, the fact was that they were trying to find agreement between people who had a long history of antagonism. Some, as former Communist Party officials, had been directly or indirectly responsible for jailing the others during the 1980s. Post-war Kosovo is still riven by that legacy.

For war

Looking back on the 1990s, until the rise of the KLA changed everything, Xhafer Shatri was rueful. In the end, he concluded, Rugova had been too timid. Passive resistance had not been the wrong strategy but it had not been taken to its logical conclusions. 'We should have been stronger,' he said.

> There should have been boycotts of Serbian goods, utility bills should never have been paid. They could arrest one, or ten people but never 100,000. We had too many illusions, we did not do enough.

Why was this? One of the simplest reasons was that the Kosovars expected that the international community would do more for them than it did. They also thought it wise to batten down the hatches while Serbs were at war in Croatia and Bosnia and assumed that their views would be taken into account during any final settlement of the Yugoslav conflict. There was a third reason, though, which those in the know had to take account of. That was that the first attempts by small groups of individuals to take up arms had ended in failure.

Two hardline activists, Rexhep Mala and Nuhi Berisha, who began gathering a militant group together in the early 1980s, died in a shoot-out with a police special unit in a Priština cellar on 11 January 1984. Nuhi Berisha, who was aged 24, was the nephew of Kadri Zeka, who had been killed in 1982. One of their group was the then 26-year-old Shaban Shala, an LPRK member who had studied to become a lawyer. In 1983 he had gone to the mountains to train with Mala. After the two leaders were killed, the group managed to wound a man from the secret police and plant a few small bombs. 'Within the LPRK we were the radicals, the military wing of that party.' The bombs did not kill anyone, according to Shala: 'they were just to say we existed'. Shala and most of his friends were arrested and jailed, though in late 1989 and early 1990 those LPRK members who were at large made contact with a militant family in the Drenica village of Donji Prekaz. Some photos show Adem Jashari, his father Shaban and brother Hamza, kitted out with bandoleers and in traditional headwear. Adem sported an extravagant beard. Pleurat Sejdiu, who from 1998 was the KLA's London spokesman, insists that 'he was well prepared politically' but also says that he was 'allergic to police uniforms'. The heart of the matter was that Adem Jashari was a *kaçak* for the 1990s.

Working with the LPRK, Jashari, his friend Sami Lushtaku and several others left for Albania in 1990 to begin serious military training. Their main, but not their only, camp was at Labinot, near Elbasan where there was an Albanian army base. According to Shaban Shala, the training was conducted by Albanian army officers, although officially, when they were training the Kosovars, they were 'volunteers'. At this point, Albania was still run by Ramiz Alia, Enver Hoxha's successor.

When the Kosovars returned, the Serbian police besieged Jashari's house but, in the ensuing gun battle, other LPRK members came to his aid, one policeman was killed, two of Jashari's daughters were wounded and the police withdrew. After that the police did not go back to Donji Prekaz.

Meanwhile, as Rugova now attempted to coordinate the parallel state structures on the inside, Bujar Bukoshi outside, in league with hardline elements in the LDK, was also making some sort of preparations for the future. For example, in 1993, along with Xhafer Shatri, he arranged for a group of twenty or so promising students to take a course in diplomacy in Switzerland. While the republic's future diplomatic service was one thing, he also had to consider whether the policy of passive resistance was something that he, abroad, had to be as committed to as Rugova. We have already mentioned that he had worked on organising former policemen and army officers inside Kosovo. However, in 1991, when his government was still in Slovenia, he struck a deal with the LPRK to begin training guerrillas, so that Kosovars would have at least some trained and organised men ready, when the right time came for an uprising. The experiment was a disaster. As Pleurat Sejdiu recalls, 'He wanted to supply his men, former policemen and officers, and we wanted to supply our members.' The LPRK were suspicious of the former policemen, because they feared infiltration by the Serbian secret police. Still, training for a small number of men, about 100 according to Sejdiu, took place in 1991 and 1992 in Labinot, where Jashari and his friends had been. Sure enough, though, many of them who trained there were arrested or killed when they tried to return. According to Sejdiu, there were to be no more joint ventures between the LPRK and Bukoshi. However, some training continued. At the end of June 1993, for example, the Serbian authorities claimed that 'an Albanian terrorist group of 72 members, which was sent from Albania for the purpose of practising terrorism in the municipality of Klina (the home municipality of these Albanians) and organizing an armed uprising, was thwarted'.[6]

As we have seen from trials during the 1990s, the Serbian police did, in fact, often catch the right people, and although their claims were often extravagant, they were usually not without some sort of basis in fact. For this reason, Serbian reports from this period make interesting reading, especially with the benefit of hindsight. In one article called 'Profile of an Average Albanian Terrorist', published in an English-language pamphlet intended for foreign journalists, the author claims that the Kosovars had three camps in Albania: Labinot and one each in Shkodër and in the northern town of Kukës. The 'average Albanian terrorist' was sent there by the LDK and underwent a six-month military training course.

> He is particularly trained for sabotage (use of explosives, poisons, knives and special-purpose weapons) and he is partly trained also in martial arts ... He is trained in keeping secrets to the maximum extent possible and is acquainted with 150–200 other terrorists who have been trained together with him.

These claims certainly exaggerate the scale of any training, but still, the next assessment is interesting because, several years early, it foreshadowed what would in fact happen with the KLA:

> On completing his training, he signed an undertaking that in the event of armed clashes in Kosovo and Metohija, he will respond to the mobilization call, irrespective of where he might be at the time. He will be mobilized by his local LDK activist when necessity arises. The plans of action of the rebel unit to which he has been assigned, are not known to him, but he is aware of their existence and knows that they have been well prepared.[7]

Whatever the extent of any training that took place in Albania at this time, and whether it was connected to Bukoshi, the LPRK or any other fledgeling guerrilla group, one thing can be said with certainty: it had no discernible impact whatsoever, apart from giving the authorities a chance to catch, kill and put on trial relatively small groups, whom it could accuse of terrorism. Curiously, a small number of men who had undergone training in Labinot in 1992 turned up in Britain in 1995–6 where they asked for political asylum. They complained (not in their asylum interviews of course!) that, following their training, they were effectively abandoned in Albania with no orders or organisation. They had gone to Germany where, after a lengthy procedure, their requests for asylum had been turned down, and now, fearing being sent back to Serbia by the authorities, they had moved on to London.

While Bukoshi toyed with the idea of military training in the early 1990s, one thing he firmly rejected was the request from the Croatians and later the Bosnian Muslims that the Kosovars open what was talked about at the time as the 'second' or 'southern front'. The theory was that, with the Serbs tied up along extended lines of communication from Serbia all the way to Croatia's Adriatic coast, an Albanian *intifada* or guerrilla campaign would split their forces and weaken them. However, since the net result might well have been a triumphant Serbian sweep though Kosovo resulting in the cleansing of hundreds of thousands, Bukoshi (in consultation with Rugova) firmly rejected this idea. 'First of all we were not interested in doing favours for others,' recalls Bukoshi, 'and secondly the Croats always thought that Kosovo was the internal affair of Serbia.' And, of course, it had to be, because if it was not, then Serbia could claim a far more legitimate case in defending the Serbs of Krajina. However, this was *realpolitik* and, according to Bukoshi, the real reason why the 'second front' was the 'wrong demand at the wrong address' was because 'we were defenceless'. Still, this is not to say that there was no real pressure on Bukoshi to reconsider.

During the summer of 1991 Kosovar officers and conscripts were deserting from Yugoslav army units based in Croatia. To make sure that young men did not find themselves either press-ganged into the new Croatian army or wandering the streets with no documents, Fehmi Agani from the LDK and a young and ambitious politician called Veton Surroi entered into secret negotiations with Josip Manolić, Croatia's security chief and the right-hand man of President Franjo Tudjman. The negotiations were successful and, following a combination of public and secret announcements, several thousand conscripts were issued with papers and left Croatia, mainly to work abroad. A number of them did however join the Croatian army. Among the new recruits that joined the Croatian army that summer were Captain Agim Çeku, later to become a general and head of the KLA, and Tom Berisha who also became a general in the Croatian army. Buskoshi says that Berisha:

> was for a second front and he tried to make a link between us and the Croats. But, Tudjman was never fair. He did not want to make a coalition, he just wanted to use Albanians as an instrument, however the most important element was that Albanians could not open a second front because they had no arms.

Sejdiu says the fact that there were no arms is the fault of Rugova. 'The Croats and the Bosnians began organising properly so why didn't Rugova? Tudjman and [Bosnian President Alia] Izetbegović believed that Rugova would act with them.' Agim Çeku was part of the team that worked with Berisha. 'I was for war all the time,' he recalls. As part of their preparations the Croats and the Kosovar officers organised 400 men into special Kosovar units of the Croatian army which were supposed to be sent to Kosovo. There were many other Kosovars in other ordinary units too. When, however, the negotiations with Bukoshi failed, the Croats disbanded the special Kosovar units, in October 1991. Çeku says that he is 'sure Bukoshi made a mistake. He said, "war is not our way" and we said, "we'll only free Kosovo by war, with active resistance." But, he did not believe in the morale of our people.'

While Tudjman had his contacts through men like Tom Berisha, Izetbegović knew some of the radical Albanians from his time in jail. Shaking his head, Sejdiu points out that 1991 and 1992 would have been the right moment for the Kosovars to start something because 'the Albanians were all united and the Serbs were in a critical position'. However, as he says, 'Rugova said he did not want to go to war for the Croats and Bosnians, and at that time it was very difficult for anyone else to do anything else.' And that was due, to a great extent, to the fact that, as Bukoshi pointed out, the Albanians did not have any arms and, being landlocked, they had no possibility of getting any significant quantities either. While Albanian President Sali Berisha was close to Bukoshi, and permitted some limited military training, neither would he, nor could he, jeopardise the economic assistance that Albania was getting. And, even more importantly, he did not wish to jeopardise its physical security – that is to say, inviting Serbian reprisals over the border – by allowing the Kosovars to acquire and smuggle large quantities of weapons.

Exasperated, the men of the LPRK decided to do something on their own, however limited that might be. In August 1993 the party called together a secret meeting of some 100 local branch heads who convened in Drenica. The meeting was held to consider three questions. The first was the party name, the LPRK – the Popular Movement for the Republic of Kosovo. Because the 'Republic of Kosovo' had already been declared, this name was deemed to be redundant. The second point to consider was the dropping of Marxist ideology, and the third, according to Sejdiu, was 'forming the armed forces'. The result was a split and the emergence of two new parties. They were the LPK, and the National Movement for the Liberation of Kosovo (LKÇK). Sejdiu, who joined the LPK, says that the LKÇK:

> did not want to abandon communist ideas. Also, they left because they did not agree on tactics. They wanted an uprising, an *intifada*, but the LPK wanted a guerrilla war. There had already been discussions in Kërçova (Kičevo, in Macedonia) about forming the KLA. At the meeting in Drenica a four-man 'Special Branch' was appointed by the LPK to prepare it.

While it was common knowledge in the LPK, and amongst people close to it, that a decision had been made for 'further work', very few actually knew what was being done or who was doing it. The name of the KLA was chosen in December 1993 but it was only in late 1996 that a wider group of members began to find out what was going on. The LPK's four-man group consisted of Kadri Veseli, who later became the chief of the KLA's security service, a student called Hashim Thaçi, who had been head of the student union in 1991, Xhavit Haliti, who had been an activist in Switzerland, and a man still known only by his pseudonym, Abaz Xhuka, because he continues to live underground in Macedonia. The four were ordered to begin building a network of secret cells across Kosovo and, according to Sejdiu, to make contact with well-known 'armed groups' such as the Jasharis.

The reasons for the split between the LPK and the LKÇK, bearing in mind that these were, at the time, tiny groups, may well have had more to do with personalities than real disagreements over policy. Both had publications and both used to trade insults over seemingly arcane points of insurrectionary theory. At the same time, they were both beginning to recruit their own units. The LPK's paper was called *Zëri i Kosovës* and published in Switzerland and the LKÇK's was *Çlirimi*, which was printed underground in Kosovo. Anyone found in possession of it could be jailed. Perhaps because *Zëri i Kosovës* was published abroad and easily available there (but not in Kosovo), the LPK had more of a presence amongst the *Gastarbeiter* than back home, where, in radical circles, the LKÇK was better known. Even LPK people admit that, during this period, their rivals were better organised, both in terms of propaganda and in beginning to kill policemen and people they deemed to be 'collaborators'. So, says Sejdiu, 'They just accused us of talking from Switzerland and, when the war started, everyone thought the LKÇK *was* the KLA!'

In fact, relatively soon after the end of the war in Kosovo, it is still very difficult to discern exactly who did what in these early days, especially as everyone wants to claim credit for as much as possible. Florin Krasniqi, who runs a construction company in Brooklyn and who set up the US branch of the LPK's Homeland Calling fund, says, for example, that Adem Jashari 'opposed Thaçi saying "you're just talking".' According to Krasniqi, while 'those guys just talked' the real action was being taken by others. Zahir Pajaziti, 'Chief of the Supreme Command of the KLA', died in a hail of Serbian police bullets along with Edmond Hoxha and Hakif Zejnullahu on 31 January 1997. It may have been a grand title for a man involved with such a tiny band. But, according to Krasniqi, Pajaziti was responsible for 'executing' many of the Serbian police who had died until then. Oddly, considering the suspicion that surrounded former policemen, Pajaziti had actually trained as one. Krasniqi adds that he believes that his death came after he had been betrayed. According to Krasniqi, and this point seems to be undisputed, the first KLA man to die *in uniform* was his cousin, Adrian Krasniqi, who was killed on 15 October 1997, while attacking a police station at Kličina on the road between Peć and Klina.

One of the key elements necessary for an understanding of the development of the KLA is to trace how, in the four years following its creation in 1993, small but different groups began to coalesce. In and of themselves they were relatively unimportant, but, as we shall see, the particular conjunction of circumstances that developed in just over two years after the Dayton Accords of November 1995 meant that an explosive cocktail was being mixed. To start with, you had the Enverist generation of radicals, many of whose political lives had been forged by the demonstrations of 1981 and the experience of jail. They included Jashar Salihu and Bardhyl Mahmuti, both of whom were now in Switzerland. The decision to start an armed group now brought them into contact with a younger generation whose numbers included people like Hashim Thaçi, Ramiz and Fehmi Lladrovci from Drenica, Sabri Kiçmari and Pleurat Sejdiu. Most of them were teenagers in 1981 but for much of the next decade they worked underground distributing leaflets and organising demonstrations. Sabri Kiçmari, for example, who was to become the KLA representative in Austria and then Germany, was first arrested in 1981 when he was only 13, for writing banners. He fled to Germany in 1989 after an arrest warrant for 'illegal activities' had already forced him into hiding for a year. Like Kiçmari, Thaçi was an active member of the LPRK and helped organise demonstrations in 1989. In 1991 he distributed leaflets and became head of the students' union and, as early as 1992, he began organising the military training of small groups working with his friends, the Lladrovci brothers. Between 1993 and 1994 he lived underground but then spent the next year in Switzerland studying politics and international relations in Zurich and working (after the LPRK had split with the LPK) on meetings with the diaspora.

Pleurat Sejdiu was 17 in 1981 and was punished for taking part in the demonstrations by being struck off the list of students due to enrol at the university that autumn. Banned then, he left for Bucharest, where after having learned Romanian he enrolled at university from where he was to graduate as a doctor. He returned home in 1990 but, after being taken in for questioning twice and having heard from a source inside the police that he was about to be arrested, he fled. After a period spent wandering in Romania, Sweden and Germany, 'there was a decision by the LPK to send me to London'. Unable to practise as a doctor, Sejdiu became a minicab driver and got himself elected as head of the city's Albanian social club. At time nobody knew that Sejdiu was an LPK activist, just that he was an ace table-tennis player. In 1998 Sejdiu, by now a member of the KLA's political directorate, which paralleled the rudimentary military hierarchy, 'came out' as the KLA's representative and spokesman in London.

What linked all of these people to the LPRK, and then the LPK, was not just membership and a strong identification with its policies. It had invested in them by helping fund Thaçi, Sejdiu, Kiçmari and others through their studies. In this way the older generation of LPRK activists, who were now *émigrés*, were cementing a relationship with a younger generation who in turn were beginning to create a network, at home and abroad, which would eventually turn Homeland Calling cash into guns and channel them to the right people. The younger generation were also linking up with men like Shaban Shala and families like the Jasharis, who were *kaçaks* to the core but who alone would have been just that – groups of rebellious families capable of not much more than shooting the odd policeman and making it unsafe for Serbs to go to villages like Donji Prekaz. It is important, however, not to give the impression that in this period the KLA was a rapidly expanding organisation. It was not. According to Mahmuti there were 'about 150' active KLA men in Kosovo up to 1997.

While these men were getting some military training, a little was also being done abroad. In 1994 for example, about 100 LPK-cum-KLA members, including Jashar Salihu, hired former army officers from three Western countries to give them a crash course in the art of war. He will not say where they trained and it is probable that there were more such courses organised. Sejdiu notes too that while 'gun laws in Britain are much tougher than elsewhere, in Switzerland or Germany anyone can go and join a gun club'. Small shipments of arms were also infiltrated into Kosovo. However, with constant police raids and good Serbian intelligence, arms were always a problem. Unless something changed there was never going to be a way to smuggle in enough guns to begin to make the option of an armed uprising credible, and this was well understood by everyone. Within a year, though, as we shall see, things were beginning to change.

While it is important to trace the roots of the KLA, it is equally important to stress that, as late as the autumn of 1997, few foresaw the threat of an imminent and major guerrilla-led uprising in Kosovo. There was an increasing number of attacks on the police and 'collaborators' but this was far from a popular movement, especially as no one had much of an idea who was carrying them out. By contrast, it was absolutely obvious to all outside observers and Kosovar analysts like Shkëlzen Maliqi that an explosion was inevitable; but when, nobody knew.[8] Equally, few in Belgrade, apart from the intelligence services, took the slightest bit of notice of what was happening in Kosovo. Consumed with their own problems, including the major anti-Milošević demonstrations over the winter of 1996–7, most Serbs could not have cared less what was happening in their southern province so long as the Albanians kept quiet. Because there was no apparent urgency then, and no all-important dead bodies on television to galvanise Western opinion, the very few diplomats who ventured down to Kosovo and who were beginning to realise that things were changing found that their reports were having little impact. They were ordered to concentrate on confidence-building measures and especially in trying to resolve the bitter education question. 'We wasted a lot of time doing that,' recalls one former Belgrade-based diplomat. He adds that 'if you tried to suggest to your superiors back home that you must have a Dayton-style conference *now* or there will be a bloodbath, it ended up like you were making an academic point because they said, "yeah, well, there might not be."' After the war was over, one of those Foreign Office bosses said that while his officials had been very conscious of 'rights denied' and 'simmering tensions' before the situation actually exploded, 'there was no sense of a critical mass … you could not say before then, that it was going to erupt.'

Perhaps not, but one has to wonder whether it was the bureaucracies of modern Western governments which meant that people who should have been getting the information were not getting as much as they should have done. Shaban Shala was by now a leading member of the human rights group, the Council for the Defence of Human Rights and Freedoms. This was a cover for his real work as an LPK activist and KLA member. In 1996 he travelled to Albania with Azem Syla, another senior KLA man (who also happens to be Thaçi's uncle), where he says that they met with representatives of the British, American and Swiss intelligence services. They did so as KLA members. 'These were not just one-way talks, they were exchanges of information.' According to Shala, these were not the first such meetings. Some had contacts from several years earlier. Since 1991 the LPRK had been in contact with 'friends' to whom they gave information and of course, they were always in contact with these 'friends'.

Dayton and the junkyard dogs

The fact that a tiny number of men inside Kosovo had decided that they were going to wage war on the Serbs, does not, of course, explain how and why the war broke out when it did. In fact, the KLA was to benefit from two events over which it had no control whatsoever, but which were to result in seismic shifts in the strategic landscape of the southern Balkans. The first was the Dayton Conference on Bosnia in November 1995 and the second was Albania's descent into anarchy in the spring of 1997.

By the time Serbs, Muslims and Croats were corralled into the US Airforce's Wright-Patterson base in Dayton, Ohio, war had been raging in Bosnia for more than three and a half years. After the initial weeks of war, in the spring of 1992, the frontlines had become more or less fixed and the fighting, though bloody, was relatively static. The summer of 1995 saw major shifts, however. In July, Srebrenica, a beleaguered Muslim enclave in eastern Bosnia, fell to the Serbs, who promptly massacred up to 8,000 men, either in cold blood or as they were trying to flee to Muslim-held territory in lightly armed columns. The situation was critical. Žepa, another enclave, which like Srebrenica had enjoyed the dubious status of a UN 'safe area', fell and a third and major enclave, Goražde, looked as if it was about to fall too. Now, at the beginning of August, the Croats, with effective backing from the US, attacked the rebel, Serb-held Krajina region inside Croatia, driving out some 170,000 Serbs in three days. Western countries mumbled their disapproval but nothing of substance was done to reverse the single greatest act of ethnic cleansing in the wars of the former Yugoslavia at that point. In fact, unspoken but ever-present was the feeling that if there were no more Serbs in Croatia, then, in future, there would be no more problem either. As we shall see, this failure to act would have important ramifications in Kosovo.

Despite the Serbian exodus, the drama of these weeks was far from over. On 28 August a shell fell on a market-place in Sarajevo killing some 37 people, and NATO finally received the green light. In major bombing runs, backed by a UN Security Council mandate, NATO planes pounded Bosnian Serb positions. During days of frantic diplomacy the Bosnian Serb leadership now agreed to mandate Slobodan Milošević as their negotiator at forthcoming talks. Time was of the essence because, as NATO planes pulverised their military communications network, the Bosnian Croat, Croatian and Bosnian Muslim armies surged forward in western Bosnia, capturing large swaths of previously Serb-held land. Everyone was to draw their own conclusions from these events, which they would then apply to Kosovo – only, too late, to find them irrelevant.

At Dayton, in talks led by Richard Holbrooke, the US special envoy, an agreement on Bosnia and eastern Slavonia, the remaining Serb enclave in Croatia, was struck. Bosnia's borders would not be changed but the republic was formally recognised as consisting of two entities, a Muslim-Croat federation and the Serbian Republika Srpska. The agreement was to be enforced by up to 60,000 NATO-led troops. Although all sides were exhausted and wanted a deal, the fact that one was struck is in great measure a tribute to Holbrooke's negotiating skills. Far from the stereotypical urbane diplomat, Holbrooke is to US diplomacy what Quentin Tarantino is to modern film. Soon after the bombs began to fall in August 1995 NATO generals began to get cold feet saying that they were now in favour of winding up the campaign. But Holbrooke argued that the Serbs had not been punished enough. They needed more bombs before they would take him seriously at the negotiating table. 'Give us bombs for peace,' he demanded. Of course, Holbrooke's character alone was not enough, and ultimately he succeeded where his predecessors, the Lords Carrington and Owen, had failed – because he could back up his threats with real military might.

Surprisingly perhaps, Holbrooke's background is pure State Department. Born in 1941, in New York of German Jewish descent, he was 16 when his father died. He was then taken under the wing of the family of Dean Rusk, the former US secretary of state. According to the *New York Times* correspondent Roger Cohen, who writes about Holbrooke in *Hearts Grown Brutal*, his book on Bosnia, 'Rusk came to embody the ideals of patriotism and public service that led Holbrooke into the Foreign Service after college at Brown and make up one element in his personality.' But Cohen is sharp in sketching the 'other' Richard Holbrooke:

> the driving ambition, the impatience with form, the bad temper, the manipulative circumlocutions, the insatiability about publicity ... created problems in Washington and sometimes placed his Ruskian ideal of service and self-effacement grotesquely at odds with the baroque reality of being Richard Holbrooke.[9]

In May 1968 Holbrooke was present in Paris when the US talked to the Vietcong. Later, he served in Asia, becoming President Carter's under-secretary of state for Far Eastern affairs. There he won plaudits but also brickbats as he was accused of becoming too close by far to Filipino President Ferdinand Marcos and his wife during negotiations over the renewal of the leases of the two big American bases there.

True or not, Holbrooke himself has always insisted that a foreign policy without an ideal is one that is doomed to failure. In his own book, his memoir of Dayton, called *To End a War*, he writes that the supposed choice in international relations between 'realists' and 'idealists' is a false one. 'In the long run, our strategic interests and human rights supported and reinforced each other, and could be advanced at the same time.'[10] It is, again, the clash of ideal and brute force which characterises the man. He is also not one to shirk the notion of US leadership.

At the end of his memoir he wrote, prophetically, in view of what was to happen in Kosovo:

> *There will be other Bosnias in our lives* – areas where early outside involvement can be decisive, and American leadership will be required. The world's richest nation, one that presumes to great moral authority cannot simply make worthy appeals to conscience and call on others to carry the burden. The world will look to Washington for more than rhetoric the next time we face a challenge to peace.[11]

So Dayton was a success, in that, despite its faults, the war was ended. In its wake an argument raged in Washington and other Western capitals. Surely, argued one camp, the success of Dayton was due to the fact that Western military might had been used to deliver the Serbs, who as soon as the bombs started falling had been pleading for peace. This, they claimed, proved that if they had been listened to and the Serbs had been bombed earlier, then evidently the war would have ended earlier. This was nonsense, argued the other camp, which pointed out that all sides were exhausted and that the Serbs had agreed to the principles of Dayton *before* the bombing began. And, besides, chipped in Europeans, Americans who argued that bombing should have happened earlier were hypocrites. This was because they conveniently forgot the fact that when they were calling for bombing the Serbs and arming the Bosnian Muslims, the so-called 'lift and strike' strategy, thousands of British and French UN troops, amongst others, were stationed in Serb territory and delivering food and aid. This made them potential targets for revenge attacks and hostage-taking. In fact, it was only after UN troops had been withdrawn from Serb territory, after several hundred had been taken hostage in the spring of 1995, that it was really feasible to switch to a policy which involved the real use of force. In the wake of the war in Kosovo, it is necessary to recall these arguments because they came to shape the way Western policy-makers looked at the question of how to deal with the Serbs when Kosovo became an issue. The fact that the Serbs had sued for peace immediately the bombs had started falling in Bosnia inevitably influenced calculations – or more accurately speculations – about how they would react two and half years later.

Dayton, and the events that preceded it, were to have a far more profound impact on the situation in the Balkans than simply giving Western leaders ideas about how they should deal with the 'junkyard dogs' as one of Holbrooke colleagues called its leaders. Indeed, by a twist of fate, the only reason Holbrooke was to return to play a role in the region was because Kosovo had not been addressed at Dayton. Strictly speaking, there was no reason it should have been. It was about ending the war in Bosnia and tying up loose ends in Croatia. It was not supposed to be a general settlement of all the outstanding issues of the former Yugoslavia. Also, no one but the Albanians themselves disputed that Kosovo was an integral part of Serbia and besides, since not much seemed to be happening there, there was no compelling reason to add it to the agenda. In his Dayton memoir, one of the few references Holbrooke makes to Kosovo is this:

> Once, as Milošević and I were taking a walk, about one hundred Albanian–Americans came to the outer fence of Wright-Patterson with megaphones to plead the case for Kosovo. I suggested we walk over to chat with them, but he refused, saying testily that they were obviously being paid by a foreign power, and that Kosovo was an 'internal' problem, a position with which I strongly disagreed.[12]

In the wake of the Kosovo war Holbrooke is defensive about the failure to discuss it at Dayton. He says, certainly accurately, 'Izetbegović and Tudjman had zero interest in Kosovo and if we had raised it they would have said, "get out of here" and Milošević would have said "screw you!"' In his view, 'Kosovo would have happened anyway, and it is part of the mythology that Dayton was responsible and I don't believe it. What really drove this thing was Rugova's failure to produce results and the Serb crackdown.'

In fact, Holbrooke has no reason to be defensive, because, as he says, the three presidents assembled in Dayton were not there to discuss Kosovo. Whether more could have been done after Dayton to try and forestall an explosion in Kosovo is another question entirely. However, whatever Holbrooke says, there is no doubt that, unrecognised in the West at the time, Dayton was an extraordinary trauma for the Kosovo Albanians. And it was a trauma because it confirmed to them in the most dramatic and humiliating way that Rugova's policy of passive resistance had failed. And not only that, but that his idea that they would be rewarded for their 'good behaviour' by Western countries had been just plain wrong. While they had had an entity, which had played its part as a federal unit in the old Yugoslavia, they were now without rights while, in their view, the campaign of genocide led by Bosnian Serb leaders was being rewarded. Few Kosovars believed that Dayton Bosnia was a viable long-term proposition rather than a face-saving cover for Western countries, and like many others in the region they thought that, sooner or later, the Serb and Croat parts would secede to join the respective 'motherlands'.

As if the Dayton Conference itself was not enough to encourage the Kosovars to believe that they had been forgotten, the full-scale UN embargo imposed on Yugoslavia in 1992 was lifted. It had been applied because of Serbia's role in Bosnia and was nothing to do with Kosovo, but such fine legal points appeared irrelevant in Priština. By contrast, the US blocked Yugoslavia's return to the World Bank and the International Monetary Fund (IMF), citing the issue of Kosovo as one reason for maintaining what became known as the 'outer wall' of sanctions. Although this did not look like much, in fact the 'outer wall' was to mean that Yugoslavia remained excluded from the world financial system and, unable to secure significant fresh credits, was unable in any real sense to reverse the trend of wartime economic decline. This, however, was not obvious to the majority of Kosovars and neither did it impress the hard men who were preparing to wage their war of liberation. More to the point, it did not impress Milošević who was not moved to initiate discussions on the future of Kosovo because Yugoslavia could not return to the IMF.

While the 'outer wall' remained for the vast majority of Kosovars a rather theoretical sanction, which had no evident effect on their aspirations, the EU's recognition of Yugoslavia after Dayton did. What the EU states recognised was the Federal Republic of Yugoslavia (FRY), born in 1992, which consisted of Serbia and Montenegro and, of course, Kosovo. Bujar Bukoshi recalls: 'It was a shock. We weren't expecting it and it was a fatal mistake.' What all of this meant was that Jashar Salihu, Bardhyl Mahmuti and all the agitators in the *Gastarbeiter* clubs and those who risked prison back home by distributing leaflets or had begun to train in the woods could say: 'We told you so.' And they did.

The end of the pyramids

The fact that Dayton began to undermine Rugova was not a phenomenon that was immediately obvious. It took time and incessant work by the LPK-cum-KLA to persuade people that there actually was an alternative to passive resistance. One of the reasons that this was so slow was that the LDK controlled, either directly or indirectly, most of Kosovo's Albanian-language news. It controlled *Bujku*, the only daily, it controlled the satellite television news programme broadcast from Tirana, and in an indirect way it controlled most weeklies, as they tended to follow the LDK line. No one wanted to be howled down or frozen out by their friends if they began to propagate unpopular opinions. Mahmuti and *his* friends did have unpopular opinions. In the summer of 1998 Mahmuti's view was that:

> Rugova applied a totalitarian politics aimed at preventing any resistance to the Serbs. He gave the illusion that the international community would resolve the crisis and that independence would come as a gift. The LPK always tried to persuade people that this illusion was dangerous and that no one would come and liberate us and that we would have to pay the price. But, our message only got through very slowly. We had no media and he has television, dailies, weeklies all giving the same message.
>
> The second thing is the message of the Bosnian war. If we can get a freedom without a struggle, why fight and risk massacres? Many really believed this, and so this strangulation of the KLA hurt it a lot. Without money and support no one wanted to help. After Dayton, when it was clear that the international community was not taking things in charge then our line was seen as valid. The LDK had controlled people's imagination but our room for manoeuvre opened up.

Still, as we have noted, every time a Serbian policeman was shot dead, Rugova and his associates would say that they thought that this was the work of the secret police which wanted to discredit his policy of passive resistance. In 1997, when Florin Krasniqi set up the Homeland Calling fund in the US, he says that 'people thought I was crazy, that I was out of my mind. They said: "The KLA is Serbian propaganda."' Another problem faced by the LPK in its bid to raise money was that its Enverist roots made it unpopular, especially since the fall of Communism had revealed, even to the most stubborn of believers, that Hoxha's Albania had not been a land worthy of their dreams. And although officially the LPK had divested itself of Marxist ideology it still clung to some of the old forms of language. In Switzerland, where the LPK in exile was led by Fazli Veliu, a portrait of Ramiz Alia, Hoxha's successor, hung on the wall. It was, of course, under Alia that the Jasharis and others had begun their training in Albania. Still, Florin Krasniqi was horrified. He says, 'I just wanted to help, I told them "I don't want to be in politics." I said I would open the fund in the US but not if they set up the LPK here.' Krasniqi suspected that the slightest whiff of Communism would be fatal for his fund-raising activities, and the LPK did not break their agreement. Unlike in Switzerland or Germany, where the bulk of the Albanians are *Gastarbeiter* from Kosovo, who only began to arrive in the 1960s, in the US the Albanian communities are far older, stemming from waves of emigration over the past century, most of it from Albania itself. As such, and as Krasniqi understood, they tended to be staunchly anti-Communist.

Although the KLA was now beginning to issue the odd communiqué and, slowly but surely, was beginning to be talked about, it faced a far greater problem than the fact that people were deeply suspicious. The fundamental problem was that it was all very well for LPK officials and others to talk about an armed uprising, but the simple fact remained that there was no way to obtain and import large amounts of weaponry.

The problem was now solved in the most unexpected and bizarre manner possible. In the spring of 1997 Albania, as state and country, simply imploded. Hundreds of thousands of people had invested their savings in pyramid or 'Ponzi' schemes, which the government failed to stop. As long as people kept putting in more and more money these schemes paid out enormous sums in interest. However, obviously, they could not carry on for long and so, inevitably, they collapsed. Outraged, Albanians took to the streets and rose in anger against President Berisha. Although Berisha had been warned that a collapse was coming, especially by Kris Luniku, the young head of the central bank, Berisha found himself in an impossible situation. The problem was that his Democratic Party, and the rival Socialists, had benefited from largesse donated to them by the so-called 'foundations' which ran the pyramid schemes. Apart from sucking in the savings of Albanians at home and those who had gone abroad to work since 1991, especially to Greece and Italy, the schemes were also widely believed to be major money-laundering machines for criminal syndicates and drug smugglers. Because Albania lacked the checks and balances of a modern democracy there was no way to avert the coming collapse if the president did not take decisive action. However, facing elections, there was little Berisha could do, since if he did take action to curb the pyramid schemes, there would be financial chaos, meaning he would lose the elections. So no action was taken, meaning that the longer the collapse was postponed, the worse it would be when it came.

And the collapse was indeed terrible. The Socialists, who had also taken money from the pyramid schemes, took advantage of popular anger and, especially in the south, where their Communist forebears had been strong, they activated networks of former secret policemen and army officers purged by Berisha who moved to seize local power. In other areas, mafia bosses helped organise discontent. In the ensuing chaos the government lost control, the army dissolved, the police ran away and arms depots were thrown open. Albania was suddenly awash with hundreds of thousands of Kalashnikovs. The significance of this was not lost on the Kosovars – guns and ammunition suddenly available for virtually nothing and no more central government in Tirana to prevent them smuggling as much they could carry back to Kosovo. Coupled with disillusion with Rugova following Dayton and, in the words of Xhafer Shatri, his continuing 'asphyxiating' domination of Kosovar politics, the LPK began to argue that not only was it the right time for an uprising, but now it actually had the means to achieve its aims.

The KLA, or rather the tiny number of men associated with

it, began buying guns. Although the vast majority of *émigré* Kosovars only began switching their contributions from Bukoshi's coffers to Rugova's after the conflict exploded in the spring of 1998, men like Krasniqi in the US were, to a modest extent, able to overcome the ingrained suspicion of the KLA and raise some cash. He says that in this period, including the sums he contributed himself, he was bringing in some $10,000 to $15,000 a month. In Europe the LPK was organising concerts for the Kosovar communities to raise money. One of the men in Albania to whom the funds were being channelled was Florin Krasniqi's cousin Adrian (the one who was killed in October 1997), who had been living there ever since he had fled Kosovo in 1995. In mid-1997, using the money raised, he was buying Kalashnikovs for $5 each. Despite this and the general frustration of the population, KLA activists were still finding it hard to win widespread acceptance for their idea of a general uprising which needed careful preparation and long-range planning. When he slipped back home undercover, Jashar Salihu found that few people were prepared to take the guns he was offering them from Albania, either for use now or later, and that everywhere the refrain was the same: 'Look what happened in Bosnia.'

First warnings

As we have seen, sporadic anti-Serbian actions were already beginning to take place before the founding of the KLA in 1993. In May 1993, for example, two policemen were killed and five wounded in Glogovac, in the heart of Drenica. After the founding of the LPK and the KLA, the occasional communiqués began to be issued, although it was only from 1996 that those of the KLA began to be published. They were always faxed from anonymous places like Frankfurt airport and were sent to organisations like the BBC's Albanian Service and of course the LPK's Swiss-based newspaper, *Zëri i Kosovës*. The early LPK ones were a clear call to arms. This one was published in *Zëri i Kosovës* on 1 September 1993:

> The LPK will put all of its energy and power at the service and the will of the people without which there will be no perspective for our people. The LPK invites all forces who

are sincerely interested in liberation to contribute in order
to create a united and popular liberation front.[13]

Two weeks later it issued another statement arguing that it was a
'necessity' for the Albanian people to fight 'by all ways and
means' for their liberation. It added that:

> the barbarity of the occupier and the failure of peaceful
> means to solve our national question are having an effect
> on the Albanian population and the only way to freedom
> is through a liberation war … the LPK is for a people's
> war but is against fascism, racism, anarchy and terrorism
> but is also against those exclusive forms of capitulationist
> pacifism.[14]

As time wore on, the KLA began to issue more frequent
statements. This is from communiqué 13 of June 1995. The
Serbian 'colonists' it refers to came from two places. A small
number were housed in a new settlement built for them in
Babaloć, where Serbs and Montenegrins from Albania who had
left the country after the collapse of Communism in 1991 had
been resettled. After the wars began in Croatia and Bosnia, small
numbers of Serbian refugees were also settled in Kosovo by the
authorities, their numbers swelling to some 16,000, mostly
highly unwilling, after the fall of Krajina in August 1995.

> During the last two months the central command ordered
> its armed units to act militarily and actions have been
> executed according to plan. In April a police station in the
> village of Izniq was attacked. At the beginning of May two
> houses were mined which had recently been built for
> Serbian and Montenegrin colonists. The explosions in
> Junik are warnings to those colonists who have accepted
> sacrifice at the hands of the ethnic cleansing policy of
> Belgrade. In the last week of May the Serbian spy Bexhet
> Muçiaku was executed. We call upon the Serbian and Mon-
> tenegrin civil population to think about their future in
> Kosovo and not to take part in the military and police
> forces which are terrorising Albanians.[15]

On 14 February 1996 communiqué 18 informed whoever was
able to read or hear it, that 'guerrilla units of the KLA' had

undertaken actions in 'Operational Zone One' against Serbian 'colonists' and in several other towns across the province. In retrospect, it is quite breathtaking in its insolence and confidence, bearing in mind that the KLA still only consisted of some 150 men and that most Kosovars, let alone people outside Kosovo, had never heard of it:

> We let the occupiers from Belgrade know that our actions up until now are just first warnings .... Dialogue about withdrawing the military and police from the Republic of Kosova should start immediately. We call on powerful international centres such as the USA to recognise the independence of Kosova for which the Albanians have declared themselves in a referendum otherwise war in Kosova is inevitable.

The same communiqué also issued a death threat to any Albanian leader who signed an autonomy agreement with Serbia.

Although KLA attacks on Serbian policemen and Albanian 'collaborators' were still sporadic, by the end of 1996 they were increasing. Ironically, however, it was an assassination attempt on 16 January 1997 on Radivoje Papović, the Serbian rector of Priština University, that really first began to focus both domestic and some foreign attention on what was happening in Kosovo. Ironically, that is, because despite a KLA claim of responsibility, it is extremely unlikely that the car bomb that destroyed Papović's car and severely injured him had anything to do with them. The KLA had not planted sophisticated car bombs before and would not do so in the future. In fact, the attempt on Papović's life was far more likely to have been connected to an inter-Serb quarrel and one possibly connected to the big business affairs of his brother. Still, many Kosovo Serbs believed at the time that the KLA was responsible and as Radovan Urošević, an official at the Priština branch of the Serbian ministry of information, said: 'When we're on the road now and we go to a restaurant, the drivers don't like to come in and eat because they are afraid of bombs.' This was the first intimation to outsiders that the KLA was a real threat and not, as Rugova said, a Serbian police conspiracy. On 5 March a bomb wounded two Serbs and two Albanians close to the university.

On 11 July a court in Priština convicted fifteen Albanians for 'terrorist acts'. One of them, convicted *in absentia*, was Adem Jashari.

The KLA threat to kill any Kosovar leader who signed any form of autonomy deal might seem odd since none was on the table in 1996. However, what was happening was that the 'Three Republic' idea was being discussed openly at the time, in a way that suggested that diplomats were floating the notion to test the waters. The 'Three Republic' idea was, as we have seen, the attempt to square the Kosovo circle by giving it virtual independence as a republic which would, however, remain within a Yugoslav federation alongside Montenegro. At the same time Adem Demaçi, the former Marxist–Leninist who had been released after a cumulative total of 28 years in jail in 1991, was discussing his idea for a Balkan federation to be called *Balkania*. He had even planned its flag. Whether these ideas could have amounted to anything seems unlikely, but any public discussion of them was cut short by a totally unrelated event. In November 1996 local elections were held in Serbia. During the count it became apparent that opposition parties had done extremely well, seizing power in cities across the country from Milošević's Socialists. When the results were announced, however, it appeared that these results had been readjusted so that the Socialists could remain in control of the town halls. Outraged, tens of thousands of Serbs – indeed hundreds of thousands at peak points – took part in daily marches and protests against the regime. For the first time since demonstrations in Belgrade in 1991 it really looked as though Milošević might fall from power.

The threat to Milošević's power seemed all the more credible since he simultaneously faced a threat from Montenegro. On 31 May 1996 Montenegrins had, by a very slender majority, voted out a pro-Milošević party and elected a coalition headed by Milo Djukanović, the former republican premier and a former Milošević loyalist. During the demonstrations, however, Djukanović came out against Milošević and argued forcefully that Yugoslavia's only chance of survival was to get rid of his former patron. This was, of course, extremely important because, if the Montenegrins could muster enough support inside Serbia, i.e., if the Serbian opposition could endure and win enough seats in the federal parliament, they could unite to remove Milošević from power. And, as Djukanović hinted darkly, if that did not happen then Montenegro might move towards secession which would leave the Yugoslav president unemployed since there would be no more Yugoslavia to preside over.

Milošević appeared uncertain what to do. Then, after 88 days of impressive and energetic demonstrations, he just gave up. The opposition were given their victories. They promptly began squabbling amongst themselves and thus destroyed the huge anti-Milošević momentum that they had built up during this period. Resignation and political apathy now set in, and people were anyway forced to turn their minds to making ends meet whilst Serbia's economy remained in a parlous state.

All of this was to have a tremendous, although at the time unrecognised, impact on Kosovo. What it meant was that the time, which might or might not have been used by the diplomats to prompt discussions on the 'Three Republic' solution or indeed spent in any form of negotiations about Kosovo at all, apart from on the question of education, was lost. There had simply seemed no point in engaging in discussions with Milošević, just at the point when he might actually fall.

One of those to miscalculate was Demaçi. Also convinced that Milošević's days were numbered, Demaçi made an overture to the Serbian opposition by sending them a message of support. He did so because he hoped that, if they took power, they would then be well disposed to discuss his *Balkania* plan. As he prepared to go on the stage to address the crowds, Vuk Drašković, one of the three main opposition leaders, wavered because he was uncertain how Demaçi's message would be received. He gulped back two stiff drinks and read it to widespread applause.

By the time Milošević had recovered his balance and had broken the opposition coalition by entering into negotiations with Drašković – by dangling an offer of a cabinet post in front of him – the chance to discuss *Balkania* or, more realistically the 'Three Republic' solution, had been lost. During the winter Bukoshi, exasperated at Rugova's passivity and together with Sali Berisha, who had now grasped the nationalist card in the months before the Albanian collapse, changed the political line of the daily satellite television news broadcast to Kosovo from

Albania and began attacking Rugova. By the spring Albania was in chaos and the KLA was buying as many guns as it could afford, although, as we have noted, there was still a great deal of reluctance on the side of ordinary people to take up arms. This was the case everywhere, except in the Drenica heartland which had given birth to Shaban Polluzha, Azem Bejta, Shota Galica and Tahir Mehaj. Within months, the first uniformed KLA men began appearing on the roads around the Jasharis' police no-go village of Donji Prekaz, nearby Lauša and one or two other villages. Equipped with Motorola walkie-talkies, spotters were organised to give advance warning of any police patrols and the first rudimentary 'liberated zone' began to emerge. The die was cast.

5   Friends from the woods

Things were going well, very well indeed in fact. By January
1998 the KLA decided it was time to get some serious publicity.
In Switzerland Jashar Salihu, Bardhyl Mahmuti and Visar Reka
(who had worked as a television cameraman and was the son-
in-law of Rexhep Qosja, the writer and nationalist politician),
began calling various news organisations. Because of its global
reach they targeted the BBC. But Owen Bennett Jones, the
BBC's Geneva correspondent, was irritated by the persistent
calls from these mysterious Albanians; the Balkans was not his
patch and besides he had far too much to do reporting on the
Swiss Nazi gold story. By chance, Paul Wood who had recently
finished a stint as the BBC's Belgrade correspondent, was
coming to Switzerland to attend a conference and so Bennett
Jones passed them on to him.

Wood met the three in a cafe near the station in Geneva. It
was early morning, seats were up on the tables and the floors
were being mopped. They told Wood that the KLA was going to
step up its attacks on the Serbs and indeed launch an armed
insurrection. Wood did not file a story. 'What could I tell the
BBC,' he says, 'that I met three Albanians in a café in Switzerland who told me they were about to start a war?'

What neither Wood, the KLA or indeed anyone else realised
was that all that was needed now was the spark that would light
the fire.

Terrorists and martyrs

The KLA men in Switzerland had good reason to be pleased. All
the indications were that things were finally beginning to go
their way. In August 1997 students in Priština began protests at
the failure of the authorities to implement a 1996 agreement on
education which had been broken by a Vatican organisation.
What was significant about the protesters, though, was the fact

that not only were they not controlled by the LDK and Rugova but that when in September he asked them to stop, they ignored him. Albin Kurti, one of the student leaders, complained that there had been no demonstrations since 1992, 'nothing has been going on,' that 'political parties lost credibility' and that this reflected the 'passivity' of Kosovo's politicians.[1] What no one knew at the time, however, was that the student leaders had, according to Shkëlzen Maliqi, been in touch with the LPK which was helping finance their double defiance of the Serbs and Rugova. On 1 October 1997 some 20,000 students faced down the police before violence broke out, resulting in students being beaten and their leaders being briefly detained. There were also demonstrations in other parts of the province.

If it had just been for the frustration of students, the KLA men would have little reason to find encouragement. However, they also knew that there was severe dissension within the LDK between those who still counselled caution and those who wanted more dramatic action. In February 1998 the bubbling animosity between the two wings of the party and the frustration of the hardliners boiled over. Several high-profile members, many of them former political prisoners including Hydajet Hyseni, stormed out of the party. Amongst the unknowns who left the party was a local LDK activist, also a former political prisoner and a history teacher from the town of Ćirez in Drenica. His name was Jakup Krasniqi and he had close family ties to Hashim Thaçi. He, Thaçi, the tiny band of KLA men and their supporters abroad could sense that things were going their way. There was mounting evidence that the KLA-cum-LPK message was finally getting through. The first real sign of this had been the funeral of Adrian Krasniqi, who, as we saw in the last chapter, became on 15 October 1997 the first KLA man to die in uniform. When his funeral was held a few days later, there were reports of up to 13,000 people attending. A few weeks later, on 28 November, an activist and teacher called Halit Gecaj was buried in the village of Lauša, deep inside Drenica, a village next to the Dević monastery. Gecaj had been killed by a stray bullet when the KLA had attacked a Serbian police patrol. This time, not only did 20,000 people turn up, but so did three uniformed and masked KLA men. Two of them took off their masks and one made a speech. 'Serbia is massacring Albanians. The KLA is the only force which is fighting for the liberation and national unity of Kosovo! We shall continue to fight!' The crowd were ecstatic and began chanting: 'KLA! KLA!'[2] One of the men was Rexhep Selimi, one of the first members of the KLA, who was soon to become one of its leading figures. The three then got into a car and drove off. The news of this naked defiance electrified Kosovo. The next day the daily *Koha Ditore* carried a report and photo on its front page. The funeral had also been filmed and was seen across the province on the evening satellite news broadcast from Tirana.

On 22 January 1998 the police tried to arrest Adem Jashari. They surrounded the Jashari family compound at 5.30 a.m. but, according to his father Shaban, they retreated when Adem's 'friends from the woods' came to his aid.[3]

Finally, it was becoming clear to everyone that the KLA was for real and was not, as Rugova had insisted, some form of bizarre Serbian conspiracy. Over the next two months the number of attacks on the police and on Albanian 'collaborators' escalated. Colonel Ljubinko Cvetković, the Serbian police spokesman, claimed that there had been 31 KLA attacks in 1996, 55 in 1997, but 66 in January and February 1998 alone.[4] According to a report by the International Crisis Group published in March 1998:

> Kosovar observers calculate that since 1996 the organisation has claimed responsibility for killing twenty-one citizens in the province, including five policemen, five Serb civilians and eleven Kosovars accused of collaborating with the Serbian regime.[5]

The KLA was finally emerging from the shadows. And, as it emerged, it could for the first time demand to be taken seriously, not only at home but also, even more importantly, by Albanians abroad. At the beginning of February a fund-raiser was held in Brooklyn. This is how it was reported in *Illyria*, an Albanian–American paper which used the Albanian initials of the KLA:

> A banner in big red letters on a white background hung over a mirrored wall reading 'Long Live UÇK – Honor to the Martyrs' as young men spoke at a microphone where a

picture of an armed UÇK member killed in an attack in Kosova last year hung in front of 150 sympathisers. Speakers, some of whom read poems commemorating those who have been killed in confrontations with the Serbian police, often drew energetic applause from the audience.[6]

At the same time, foreign journalists began criss-crossing Drenica. Some had heard that there were Albanian guerrilla 'training camps' out there and others that uniformed men were appearing on the roads at night. Foreign diplomats too were finally realising that, after years of warnings that conflict was imminent, this time it might actually be true. On 23 February Robert Gelbard, the US special envoy to the region, visited Priština. 'The violence we have seen growing is incredibly dangerous,' he said. He criticised the violence 'promulgated' by the Serbian police and then attacked the KLA. 'We condemn very strongly terrorist actions in Kosovo. The UÇK is, without any questions, a terrorist group.'[7] It was a turning-point. If the KLA were a terrorist group and the representative of the most powerful nation on earth said so, then there could be no objection to the Serbian police moving in to finish it off. No doubt unintentionally, the US had appeared to give Milošević a green light to act. In terms of the former Yugoslavia this was the second time that an American statement, given in good faith, had been or rather could be interpreted as invitation to act. In June 1991, James Baker, the US secretary of state, had come to Belgrade and told the leaders of Yugoslavia's six republics, specifically Croatia and Slovenia, that it did not favour secession. Four days later conflict began in Slovenia, the Yugoslav army believing that it could act, in part, because of what Baker had said.

Albanian politicians began pressing Rugova to step up the pressure, to call for demonstrations, to do something, anything, to get the attention of the world – but he did nothing. He appeared to have gone into a form of political paralysis. He drove around Priština in his presidential Audi and simply did nothing.

Fighting began at 11.00 a.m. on the morning of Saturday 28 February. A firefight broke out between four KLA men and a police patrol in Likošane, a small village close to Ćirez.

According to Shaban Shala, the LPK militant and KLA member, who at that point was still working under cover as a human rights activist, the police ambushed the KLA men by a curious oak tree with six connected trunks known as the 'Six Brothers'. As both sides traded fire, they both called for reinforcements. Five cars with KLA men converged on Likošane. Amongst the men inside were Adem Jashari and Sylejman Selimi. Selimi was the 27-year-old nephew of Rexhep Selimi who had appeared at Halit Gecaj's funeral. He would soon emerge as the KLA's Drenica commander, operating under the *nom de guerre* of 'Sultan', and from February to April 1999 he would be the KLA's chief of staff. By now the police had an attack helicopter overhead, two policemen were dead and several injured. Two of the KLA were hurt but they made a dash for a silver Audi that had come for them. It was hit by a rocket fired from the helicopter which injured everyone inside, but the KLA men were able to escape. Critically injured, two more policemen would soon be dead.

The police now turned on two nearby households. Exactly why they did so is not clear. It is not known if they just turned on these houses to take revenge for their dead or whether they were being fired at from the two compounds. Survivors, and Shala, insist that the two families had nothing to do with the KLA and in fact had stayed in their houses precisely because they thought they had nothing to fear. Two men died in the first house and then at 3.30 p.m. the police in an armoured vehicle rammed through the gates of the Ahmeti family, the richest people in Likošane. Everyone was forced to lie on the ground and then ten Ahmeti men plus one guest were taken outside and killed. Shala claims that, at most, one KLA man had fled past the Ahmeti houses.

On the same day, and as part of the same action, presumably to catch the KLA men fleeing Likošane, police in armoured personnel carriers and a helicopter descended on Ćirez. Amongst others killed was Rukie Nebihu, a 27-year-old pregnant woman. By the end of the day 26 Albanians from Likošane and Ćirez were dead. On 3 March at least 15,000 people attended their funerals. Most, if not all of them, were civilians. The KLA men had escaped – but the police had not finished yet.[8] This time, they decided, unlike their failed attempt in January, they would get Jashari.

On the hill behind the Jashari compound was an old and disused ammunition factory. The police moved in. Several houses belonging to various branches of the Jashari clan in Donji Prekaz now lay in the police gunsights as did the compound of the Lushtaku family, which was also associated with the KLA. Early on the morning of the 5 March, a column of police entered the village from one side while, using artillery, they began firing from the factory. The Lushtakus fled. The police called on the Jasharis to come out. When they emerged from one house the police gunned down two of them. No one came out from Adem's house. So the shelling and firing continued. In the end 58 died, including eighteen women and ten children under the age of 16.[9] The Jashari houses lay in ruins, their blood, congealed and dark, stained the walls. Adem was dead – but the KLA had gained a martyr.

At the same time Milošević had gained no friends. In one of the more spectacular diplomatic drubbings of recent times the Yugoslav president humiliated Robin Cook, the British foreign secretary. In the wake of the violence in Likošane and Ćirez, Cook flew to Belgrade for the EU to urge him to offer moderate Kosovars an alternative to violence. During the meeting Milošević angrily denied that his forces were overreacting. But events had bypassed Cook. While he was actually in the room with Milošević, Donji Prekaz was in flames. Of course, it is hard to weigh up the significance of personal factors in the way politicians make important decisions, but it is interesting that just over one year later Britain took a very tough stance against Milošević and Serbia. If by the circumstances of this meeting Milošević had earned Cook's eternal hatred he would only have himself to blame.

If they wanna war ...

The deaths of the Jasharis left Kosovo reeling. Years of accumulated frustration boiled over and demonstrations were held across the province. Within weeks everything began to change, the status quo that had held since 1990 began to collapse and everyone was shocked by what was happening – no one more so than KLA men themselves. Pleurat Sejdiu recalls that:

1. The way we were: *Britannia the Peacemaker* (detail) painted during World War I by Sigismund Goetze, which is prominently displayed at the top of the Foreign Office staircase in London. Britannia protects Belgium, Serbia and little Montenegro who is, in turn, being cuddled by Serbia.

2. Aftermath of the bombing of Belgrade, 6 April 1941.

3. Tito (*left*) visits the Serbian Orthodox monastery of Gračanica, close to Priština, 1950.

4. Albanians in flight from Enver Hoxha's regime in Albania cross the border, 1951. The numbers who fled during this period have never been established. This group is crossing into Montenegro.

5. Kosovo Serbs from the village of Batuše battle with police demanding protection from Albanian 'persecution', 1986.

6. Slobodan Milošević, 28 June 1989, the six-hundredth anniversary of the Battle of Kosovo.

7. Last ditch protest by Albanian miners against the ending of Kosovo's autonomy.

8. Voting for the phantom state. Ibrahim Rugova, head of the LDK, votes on 24 May 1992 in the parallel state's first parliamentary and presidential elections. He was elected president.

9. *From left to right:* Adem Jashari, his father Shaban and brother Hamza.

10. Waiting, Djakovica, February 1998. Serbian arms, Kosovo crows. Albania, and KLA camps, lie on the other side of the mountains.

11. Watching TV Tirana. Kosovars at the Priština Café-Club in Geneva. They gathered every evening, as did the family back home, to watch Kosovo news broadcast via satellite by Albanian Television. The bulk of the money to buy arms for the KLA was raised in clubs like this.

12. Jashar Salihu, head
of the KLA's Swiss-
based Homeland
Calling Fund.

13. Father Sava.
The monks at his
monastery of Visoki
Dečani led the fight
for peace via
cyberspace. Here Sava
stands at the open
sarcophagus of King
Stefan Dečanski, who
died in 1331. Peeking
out from under the
shroud is the king's
withered hand.

14. Albanian villagers survey their dead. The killings at Račak, on 15 January 1999, were a turning point in the conflict.

15. Not exactly the Congress of Vienna: Rambouillet château outside Paris where peace talks began on 6 February 1999.

16. Serb troops; dead KLA. March 1999, ten days before NATO's bombing started.

17. Richard Holbrooke meets Slobodan Milošević, March 1999.

18. Madeleine Albright, US Secretary of State.

19. The skies over Belgrade. Anti-aircraft fire during
NATO's 78-day bombing campaign.

20. Albanian refugees from Kosovo Polje arriving in northern Albania, April 1999.

21. General Wesley Clark, SACEUR, press conference, April 1999.

22. The heart of the regime. NATO bombs hit the Socialist party headquarters.

23. Over the top. KLA fighters leave Padesh in northern Albania and cross into Kosovo

24. Bombed bridge. Novi Sad, April 1999.

25. The UNHCR delivering food for refugees in Kukës in northern Albania. Milošević miscalculated the international community's will and ability to cope with the refugee crisis.

26. Serbian eye view. Novi Sad.

27. Makeshift camp on the border between Kosovo and Macedonia. Up to 65,000 Kosovar refugees were caught in a no-man's land in appalling conditions before being allowed to enter Macedonia several days later, April 1999.

28. NATO mistake. Grdelice Bridge and destroyed passenger train, 12 April 1999.

29. Albanians expelled or in flight from Kosovo cross into Macedonia at Blace.

the plan was for 1999, to start a war, bombing depots and so on. We considered that, by that time, we would have structures and people ready. But, the events in Albania speeded things up because of the availability of arms and Prekaz found us unprepared for a big war because it led to a big influx of volunteers, it was unstoppable ... we just couldn't stop it.

Of course, some preparations had been made but, as Sejdiu says, they were far from complete and the rudimentary KLA structures soon found themselves overwhelmed. From northern Albania the few men already in place began to dispatch arms and uniforms over the border, the sleepers that Thaçi and his group had recruited over the past few years 'awoke' and village elders, especially in Drenica, decreed that now was the time to fight the Serbs. Village militias also began to form and, whether they were KLA or not, they soon began to call themselves KLA. In this way a tiny armed group, which had been making preparations for war, suddenly found itself welded to a far older tradition of Kosovar *kaçak* uprisings.

For the first few weeks after the Jashari killings, though, there was a lull. It was clear, however, that these were the dog days and that a waiting game had begun. The province was paralysed with fear. Villages in Drenica found themselves blockaded by the police and, with people staying inside, mostly behind closed doors, they gave off an eerie feel. On a hill above Donji Prekaz, close by the ruins of Tahir Mehaj's house, destroyed in 1981, a small group of men explained that they could not leave. 'If we pass the police checkpoint they'll arrest us and say we're terrorists,' said Agim.

Across Drenica the police began digging in. They hauled sandbags to construct fortified bunkers and checkpoints. They were well armed but they were also deep inside hostile territory. They were nervous and under fire from snipers. Most of them were Serbs from Serbia proper. They said that if it came to war they would do their duty – but they lacked conviction. Compared to 1991, they lacked the nationalist swagger that Serbs had boasted when they went to war in Croatia and then Bosnia.

In western Kosovo, as icy night fell over the Serbian monastery of Visoki Dečani, the monks' evening chant drifted to heaven. It had been like this, every evening, since the 1330s. At the entrance to the monastery church is a sarcophagus, which is said to hold the bones of knights who fell at the fateful battle of 1389. Another sarcophagus holds the remains of the monastery's founder, King Stefan Dečanski. Dečani's monks are young, vigorous and well educated. But while the monks guarded the bones of their holy king and dreamt the dream of a Serbian 'Empire of Heaven' they also fought their cause in cyberspace. One monk explained: 'It is our "obedience". One day we might be told to chop wood, the next to work in the stables and the next to work on the computers.' But Dečani's web page, which talked of reconciliation, and its e-mailing monks could do little to appease the fear of their ever-dwindling flock. By now, barely 25 souls were turning up to worship with them on Sunday. Urbane and intelligent, the monastery's Father Sava said that local Serbs were frightened: 'For us monks it is different. We think about death every day.' He added:

> In my view the deaths in Drenica will be avenged. Their tradition of revenge is very strong. It is the tradition of Lek Dukagjini. Sooner or later they will take revenge. No one will kill Milošević's wife or daughter, but ... That's the logic of war ... but maybe that's the plan ... When they see you are strong they respect that, but when you are weak they attack.

In happier days UFO-crazy tourists would make a point of visiting Dečani because amongst its rich frescoes were a curious sun and moon which the UFO writer Erich von Daniken had once claimed were spacecraft. Even now, the monks could still find the wherewithal to chuckle about this.

A mile down the road, in the little town of Dečani, Albanian men sipped coffee at the Edona café. Ignored in their corner, three Serb policemen drank their espressos too. Then they picked up their machine-guns and left. They did not say goodbye. They would have been greeted with stares of silent, distilled hatred if they had. Drawing up a chair, Toni, who had worked 'in construction' in New York for 12 years, now felt free to vent his anger.

> You can hardly even drive around here! They stop you, and just rip you off demanding money for whatever they

can think of. They come into your shop, take stuff and say they'll pay you tomorrow. Of course they never do.

Toni said he had come home to protect his family. He said that he believed, even at this late stage, that a compromise with the Serbs was still possible, but lapsing into Bronx-cum-Rambo-speak he added: 'If they wanna war we gonna to give 'em a war. If they wanna a peace we gonna sit down and give 'em a peace. But if they wanna war – we gonna win.'

In nearby Peć the mood was angry, ugly even. The owner of the Prince café showed off where a hand-grenade had shattered the windows of the house next door. 'It's Serb terror,' he said. 'Someone chucked it from a car because he knew that we'd all been to the demonstration.' There was, however, another version of the tale of the hand-grenade. Just after the Drenica killings Rugova had ordered a day of mourning. But the owner of the Prince café had not closed his doors, leading to speculation that Albanian enforcers were at work. Whatever the truth, though, everyone remembered only too well that in both Croatia and Bosnia, the very first casualties of war ... were the cafés.

March snow swirled across the ancient city of Prizren. Churches and mosques blend here in perfect harmony against a backdrop of narrow hill-climbing alleys, tiny coffee shops, barbers, old-style draper's shops and jewellers specialising in the delicate filigree work that Albanians love so much. In his office a prosperous Albanian businessman said that if people would just get on with producing things and making money then 'we would not be in the situation we are now'. Then he asked for news of his son-in-law who, being a smart journalist, had incurred the wrath of the Serbs. Three weeks earlier he had applied for political asylum in Britain. Worried now, he said: 'Please, don't talk about him around town.' Asked if he thought that war was coming, he replied, a little stiffly: 'I hope it will not come to the worst.' But his eyes had filled with tears. 'It's the fear,' he said, 'the fear.'

Madeleine was keen to keep control

It was not only in Kosovo that paralysis had set in. While the diplomats criss-crossed Europe sending messages to Belgrade and Rugova, the Contact Group discussed limited sanctions, which were then imposed by the EU, the US and other countries, but opposed by Russia. However, a bitter stand-off now brought the State Department's effectiveness to a virtual standstill.[10] Many Kosovars believe that the US was hoping for or even encouraging Milošević to act quickly to crush the KLA, so that it could then move in afterwards to make some form of Dayton-style deal between the Yugoslav leader and Rugova. In fact, far from thinking so far forward, US diplomacy was snarled up in a banal power struggle involving strong personalities. Until now, the US special envoy to the region had been Robert Gelbard. Thanks to his February condemnation of the KLA as terrorists, he had already made himself enemies in Kosovo. Worried that the situation was slipping out of control, he now tried to play the hard man with Milošević, shouting at him and telling him what to do. Far from seeing in this behaviour a man with whom he could do business – à la Holbrooke – Milošević simply took against Gelbard and eventually refused to see him. As this end of the drama unfolded, another element was simultaneously being played out. Holbrooke was now working for the bank Credit Suisse First Boston. In mid-March he was in Berlin when he received a fax from Rugova asking him to become a mediator 'without preconditions'. Madeleine Albright, the US secretary of state, also received a fax from Rugova requesting Holbrooke's intervention. Mrs Albright was far from happy with this. According to one senior diplomatic source: 'Madeleine was keen to keep control and did not want Holbrooke back in the game. She wanted this as her Dayton.' And she wanted Gelbard as her man. Meanwhile, says the source, the US National Security Council (NSC), which advises the president on foreign affairs and security issues 'did not understand what was going on. So, in April, nothing happened.' It was only in May, then, that Holbrooke was taken on, after Albright had been persuaded by Strobe Talbott, her deputy secretary of state, and Sandy Berger, the president's national security adviser, that the US needed someone effective to lead its diplomatic thrust. This was becoming ever more urgent, because in March the European security organisation, the Organisation for Security and Cooperation in Europe (OSCE), and the EU had appointed Felipe González, the former Spanish premier, as their special envoy. The Contact Group had also asked him to see Milošević – but he refused to see him. 'So,' says the source,

> there was an eight-week period of no contacts and the situation was deteriorating. Madeleine was issuing statements with the 'Euros' saying something had to be done – and nothing was being done. Milošević would not see González for the OSCE, nor Gelbard and his forces were taking ugly actions. So, Madeleine reluctantly agreed that Holbrooke should take a trip.

The first meetings were to take place in early May. By then, compared to two months earlier, the situation on the ground had changed beyond recognition.

We are all KLA now

As young men slipped back across the mountains from Albania with guns and ammunition, or were organised into units with the weapons they already had, Serbian authority seemed to melt away before them. Apart from Drenica the KLA began taking over areas in central Kosovo and along the Albanian border. All these areas were connected by supply lines that led, over the mountains, into northern Albania. The idea was that this 'liberated territory' should expand and eventually surround the towns. However, it was essential that areas not yet connected to the supply lines should not begin anything premature, because then small rebel units might find themselves cut off, surrounded and hunted down. While the KLA at that time did not hold any towns but was spreading through the countryside, the Serbs still held all the main roads. In Priština, and amongst the Kosovars in general, a wave of euphoria accompanied this extraordinary and rapid expansion of Albanian power. It appeared that a rag-tag armed group had achieved more in a couple of months than Rugova and the LDK had in seven years. However, while it was true that the KLA was asserting its power over ever-larger areas, making them dangerous for the police to venture into, they were hardly fighting back, and the areas where the KLA was spreading had compact Albanian populations and very few Serbs. While there were was constant sniping and low-level skirmishing, this still remained, except along the Albanian border, very much a phoney war full of bizarre contradictions and oddities.

For example, while it was indeed the failure of Rugova's policy of passive resistance that made Kosovars ready and willing to contemplate an armed uprising, the vast majority of them still saw no contradiction between supporting both Rugova and the KLA. People said: 'We are all KLA now, the KLA is our army ... but Rugova is our president.' In the hamlet above Donji Prekaz where Tahir Mehaj's ruined house was, one man said, typically, 'Rugova is against the war, but if he says "Go to the KLA", we'll all go to war for him. Whatever he says, we'll do it.' Controversially Rugova now decided not to postpone planned elections for the parliament and presidency of the 'Republic of Kosovo', which he had already done several times, and the ballot took place on 22 March. It was a mark of the oddity of Kosovo at this point that, barring a few exceptions, the Serbian police did not intervene in the poll, in which Rugova also ran unopposed for president. While two weeks earlier they had shelled the compound of a man who wanted to secede from Serbia they left unmolested a general election they considered utterly illegal and presided over by a man who claimed that Kosovo had *already* seceded.

Kosovo's small opposition parties and the KLA were furious about the election because they said it should not be held while the nation was at war. It was 'treachery', they claimed, and called for a boycott. They were roundly ignored. The overwhelming majority of Kosovars, from peasants to middle-class sophisticates, crammed schools and other polling stations, voted overwhelmingly for Rugova and the LDK. And, not only that, the vast majority agreed that if Rugova chose to cut a deal with the Serbs, they would follow him. At the Xhevdet Doda School in Priština, for example, voters cast their ballots under the watchful eyes of the double-headed eagle of the Albanian flag which was nailed to the wall. Bekim Latifi, a rap musician of three albums' standing, said of Rugova: 'He knows what's best for us ... he is our light.'

One of those who did not share such an opinion was Veton Surroi, the editor of the influential daily paper *Koha Ditore*. Surroi was the man who, in 1991, had been involved in the secret negotiations with the Croats about securing safe passage for Kosovars deserting the Yugoslav army. Along with Blerim Shala, editor of *Zëri* magazine, he had founded the Parliamentary Party of Kosovo in 1990 but had found it impossible to break the virtual monopoly exercised over politics by the LDK. Still, along with Shkëlzen Maliqi, the philosopher, who had had a similarly dispiriting experience with his Social Democratic Party, they had become well known as part of that liberal intellectual circle called the 'Albanian Democratic Alternative'. Surroi, born in 1961, was the son of a former Yugoslav diplomat who had died in a mysterious car crash in Spain. He had been educated at American schools in La Paz in Bolivia and Mexico City and had studied literary criticism at university in Mexico. Scathingly, he remarked that 'anyone willing to show some kind of leadership, including military leadership, is welcome'. This was a clear vote for the KLA and he warned, prophetically as it turned out, that Serbian police action against what he called armed 'splinter groups' would transform them into a serious guerrilla movement.

And Surroi was right, too, to call the KLA 'splinter groups'. While there was a rudimentary *Shtabi i Përgjithshëm* or General Staff Headquarters, there was no one supreme commander giving orders. Of those that were issued, some were obeyed, some were ignored; and some groups, although calling themselves KLA – because that was what everyone else was doing – were really village groups knitted together by clan connections and fear. Everyone knew the local commander, few knew who commanded the next level up and were often unwilling to obey orders from unknown people who came from somewhere else. Still, it was also increasingly clear that the KLA was beginning to establish some sort of control. For every ten men under arms it appeared increasingly that nine were simple villagers while one, more often than not dressed in black fatigues, was a man they deferred to and who was giving the orders. Amongst them were men recruited by Thaçi and his group over the last few years and, increasingly, hard men returning from abroad who had been in contact with the LPK. That did not mean to say, however, that Drenica and other areas sealed off with KLA and Serbian checkpoints had yet begun to resemble the bloody and burned wastelands that they would soon become.

Forty minutes' drive from Priština lies the village of Obrinje, close to Glogovac. Just as Holbrooke shuttled between Priština and Belgrade trying to get talks started, two KLA commanders, who refused to give their names, arrived in a flashy red BMW, complete with a fluffy, cuddly toy dog in the back window. The older one wore camouflage uniform but the younger one, dressed in black fatigues with a Motorola two-way radio, did the talking. 'Weapons speak a different language,' he said dismissing Holbrooke's best efforts. Referring to Albanian politicians in Priština, he said baldly: '*This* is the army which is liberating people,' adding, 'our job is to free the whole of Kosovo, the Albanians of Macedonia and Montenegro too.'

His words were translated by a granite-faced 14-year-old girl dressed in uniform with flaking nail varnish, a Kalashnikov and pistol. Her blue polo-neck peeked out from under her fatigues. She had recently returned from Germany with her father who had come to fight. Her nickname was Shota – in honour, of course, of Shota Galica, the Amazon of Drenica.

At 11 a.m. precisely, Obrinje was rocked by the sound of a single artillery round. Whether it was incoming or outgoing was unclear and the two KLA men refused to say. Throughout the morning mourners came to pay their respects to the father of one of the commanders whose brother had been killed a few days earlier. Many of the mourners drove in from Serb-held territory and there were even regular buses which were crossing the line. This being a relaxed day in Obrinje, men at the KLA checkpoint, in fact local villagers, most of whom were not in uniform, were simply lounging in the sun, their anti-tank weapons ready by the side of the road.

Barely seven miles away, on the main east–west road between Peć and Priština, however, the atmosphere was very different. Here, angry Serb police were turning vehicles around, saying that the road was closed. A few miles further on, the KLA had succeeded in cutting off the road for the first time.

Back in Priština, Richard Holbrooke emerged after several hours of talks with Rugova. All he would say was: 'We're trying to get a process going ... without much progress.' Five minutes' drive away, on the other side of Priština, Isuf Hajdari, aged 60, shot dead in his vegetable patch early the day before (19 March), lay in his coffin while his family and friends sobbed quietly. A bullet hole was clearly visible under his ear. Exactly what had happened at 17 and 17A Kačanik Street was unclear. Kosovars who gathered outside the house said that the police had raided a student house at 17A and, after throwing a couple of grenades, had arrested them. They said that Mr Hajdari, who lived in number 17, had come out into his garden to see what was happening and then been shot or executed. Blood was congealing on his spring onions, a bullet casing still lay on a lettuce leaf. A police statement claimed that a group of 'terrorists' had attacked the police and had then fled back to their house. There they had seized large amounts of ammunition but the 'terrorists' had escaped. The statement added that one policeman had been wounded and that Mr Hajdari, who had been shot, 'had weapons and munitions'. His family said that he owned a legal pistol because he was a security guard.

Away from the areas where the KLA faced off with the police, in fact most of Kosovo, since at this stage KLA control covered at a maximum one-quarter of the province, peasants were working their fields. At night the cafés of Priština were full. No one knew what was happening, everyone asked what would become of them. Serbs knew that their army and police had the firepower to reduce the whole of KLA territory to rubble but as yet their police were barely reacting. Up the hill which led to Slatina airport and airforce base, police emerged silently from the bushes where they had been hiding. One said: 'You foreign journalists are all lying. Only the Chinese tell the truth!' Although not a single Chinese journalist had ever been seen in Kosovo, let alone ventured up the dirt tracks of Drenica, it was a mark of the effectiveness of Yugoslav propaganda that he believed this. In a closed information loop *Xinhua*, the Chinese news agency, repeated reports from *Tanjug*, the state-controlled Yugoslav news agency. Its Beijing correspondent then filed stories which were duly printed or broadcast back in Serbia saying that the Chinese press were reporting such and such from Kosovo, when in fact they were simply recycling *Tanjug* copy! Still, after a further harangue, the angry policeman came to the point: 'We could finish off those Albanian terrorists in 24 hours – but *you* won't let us!'

Clay pigeons

There was some measure of truth to what the policeman said, but in what measure the fear of triggering further sanctions – or worse – weighed up with Milošević we do not know. At this stage the army, plagued by low morale and desertions, was still playing a relatively minor role inside Kosovo, as opposed to the border regions. One reason for this was not only that General Momčilo Perišić, the chief of staff, was unwilling to be drawn in to what he considered essentially a police job but also that he believed that if soldiers were deployed in anything other than specialist roles in the fight with the KLA, then Serbia ran the risk of incurring NATO military action. And indeed, on 5 March Gelbard reiterated George Bush's 1992 'Christmas Warning' to Belgrade which had threatened US action in case Serbia used force to resolve the Kosovo question.

Several other factors may also explain the relative passivity of the Serbian security forces at this stage. Western leaders, keen to be seen to have 'learned the lessons of Bosnia', were rapidly escalating their rhetoric in a bid to be seen to be standing up to Milošević, before it was too late. Bearing this in mind, Milošević and his security chiefs may at this stage have decided that they should keep the level of violence down so as to keep Kosovo off the front pages of Western newspapers. By contrast, another theory current at the time was that the Serbian security forces were luring the KLA into a trap by inviting them to spread themselves thinly over a large area so that, when the counter-attack came, they would be unable to mount significant resistance. Certainly this theory was current in at least one stream of US thinking about the way the conflict was developing. Whatever the true reasons then for Serbian inaction, the merits of one theory over another were pretty academic for people on the ground. Radovan Urošević, now the director of the new Serbian media centre which had been established in Priština's Hotel Grand, literally shook with anger as he said: 'Our boys are being set up like clay pigeons ... and we cannot understand why.'

Milošević now settled on diversionary tactics while he shored up the SPS position at home. Although, as we have seen, an education agreement had been signed as far back as 1996, nothing had actually happened. On 23 March a follow-on agreement promised progress which did in fact come. It was of course too little and far too late to affect the relentless drift to disaster. Milošević also offered talks on the province's future, which appeared to respond to the increasingly strident demands for just such negotiations by the Contact Group. Rugova and the LDK rejected the offers, though, because it was their position that any talks needed a foreign mediator. They also objected to the fact that the delegation from Belgrade, led by Ratko Marković, a constitutional lawyer and the father of Yugoslavia's 1992 constitution, represented the government of Serbia and not the Yugoslav authorities. Unstated, of course, were two further reasons for spurning the offer. The first was that, just before elections to the Kosovar parliament, the LDK could hardly be seen to be talking to the Serbian authorities about autonomy when it had promised its supporters independence. The second was rather less prosaic – the fear of assassination at the hands of the KLA for treachery and talking to the enemy just as it had launched its liberation war.

Meanwhile, on 24 March, Milošević's SPS and the Yugoslav United Left, known by its initials, JUL, the party led by his wife, Mira Marković, entered into a coalition with the Serbian Radical Party, led by the extreme nationalist Vojislav Šešelj. There were two reasons for this. The SPS's position in the Serbian parliament was relatively weak, and in a conflict which could inflame nationalist passions it was better to have nationalist hardliners on the inside of government rather than taking advantage outside. However, more was at stake. Milošević had by now finally realised that, despite Dayton and his at first having being seen by many as a guarantor of the Bosnian peace deal, he would never be fully rehabilitated as a normal and respectable European statesman. So, by inviting Šešelj into government he was suggesting to Western governments that if they did not like him, they might like to consider the alternative. And he would not be a liberal, Western-friendly politician but a man who had formed a brutal paramilitary force to fight in Croatia and Bosnia. Bearing in mind what was to happen in Kosovo exactly one year later, it is worth recalling some of Šešelj's ideas, which were expressed in his party's programme. They included the expulsion 'without delay' of what it claimed were 360,000 post-war immigrants to

Kosovo from Albania 'and their descendants'. It also proposed the clearing of a belt '20 to 50 km wide as the crow flies along the Albanian border' of Kosovars, 'as it has transpired that Albania is a state lastingly hostile to Serbia'. The Radicals' programme also demanded that no parliamentary elections be held in Kosovo 'until the ethnic structure of the population is restored to the ratio which existed on 6 April 1941'. This point pandered to the Serbian myth, which is widely believed, that until the outbreak of the Second World War in Yugoslavia Serbs were the majority population in Kosovo.[11] If Milošević thought that by entering into a coalition with Šešelj he would persuade Western countries to decrease their pressure on him to cut a deal with the Kosovars, he was wrong. At no time, and despite his record in Croatia and Bosnia, did any of the diplomats he met ever understand that threats against hundreds of thousands of Kosovars, either implied or direct, were actually meant to be taken at face value. When he sometimes made these threats, in a seemingly half-joking fashion, they simply shrugged them off as incredible.

In another move aimed at deflecting Western pressure, the Serbian authorities now organised a referendum in which citizens were asked whether they wanted foreign mediation over the Kosovo issue. 'Once again,' declared Milošević:

> our country faces the threat of all possible forms of pressure. Those who want to dictate to the entire world how it should live and even think, have an extremely negative and aggressive stand towards our determined position to resolve our problems without foreign interference.
>
> Over the last few days, we have heard how they have nothing against our people, that they even love us and are sorry that the people will be subject to pressures because the leadership is taking such a stand. I believe that we cannot accept such cynicism which serves to justify pressure exerted in the name of democracy ... our refusal to allow foreign factors to participate in the resolution of the internal issue of the Republic of Serbia – Kosovo and Metohija ... represents a national policy, not a personal or party one. Whether this is true, can only be decided by the citizens.[12]

The poll was held on 23 April and, unsurprisingly following a media blitz persuading people which way to vote, the authorities announced that 94.73 per cent of those casting ballots had voted against foreign participation. As was now the established norm, ethnic Albanians boycotted the poll. The whole affair was somewhat mysterious as, instead of persuading foreign diplomats that the issue of Kosovo was nothing to do with them, it merely made Milošević look weak, as within days of the result he was talking about Kosovo with Holbrooke. In fact, in many ways this rejection of foreign mediation followed by its acceptance is symptomatic of Milošević's behaviour. However hard he protests about how he will never do this or that, he always ends by conceding far more than he was originally asked. In this case it is widely believed that Milošević vehemently rejected the Gonzalez mission because he feared that this diplomatic track would ultimately end with the specific demand for his removal, something he could be fairly sure that Holbrooke would not do. Milošević may, by this stage, have perceived that there were at least two streams in US diplomacy. One, represented by Madeleine Albright, was the hardline 'no-compromise' wing and the other, represented by Holbrooke, suggested that, bad as Milošević might be, it was in everyone's interest to do business with him.

As the Holbrooke mission got going, Milošević made sure that he kept Gelbard, Albright's man, out of the picture. This served Holbrooke's interests too, as he wanted to insert his own man into the diplomatic picture. This was Chris Hill, with whom Holbrooke had worked closely in Dayton, and who was now the US ambassador to Macedonia. Still, Holbrooke had to tread carefully. Albright told him, in no uncertain terms, that he had to take Gelbard with him, which he did, but he also took Hill. A period of intense telephone conversations then ensued between Milošević and Holbrooke who was then in Sweden. The Yugoslav leader insisted that he would not see Gelbard but Holbrooke told him that it was both of them or neither. According to one diplomatic source: 'Holbrooke had to do this to protect Gelbard but the real plan was to substitute him with Hill.' When they got to Belgrade Milošević demanded to know which of them was the leader of the delegation. Finally a fax arrived from Albright confirming that it was indeed Holbrooke.

Milošević declared that this was a top-level meeting and in this way Gelbard found himself shut out. Outside, and deeply depressed, Gelbard mused openly that his greatest success in life was his daughter. Milošević's sleight of hand meant that Holbrooke's internal office-politics coup had triumphed and shortly afterwards Hill formally became the US special envoy for Kosovo.

During the talks, Milošević stated that he was prepared to meet with Rugova, and Holbrooke began working on arranging the meeting. With the unfortunate Gelbard in tow, he now began shuttling back and forth between Priština and Belgrade. Rugova did not know what to do. He kept changing his mind. He caved in, however, when Holbrooke bought his assent with the offer of a meeting with President Clinton. Rugova also agreed that a team appointed by him would meet once a week with a team appointed by Milošević. To get round the problem of the Serbian rejection of foreign mediation, it was understood that Chris Hill, or his team, would be nearby while the talks were held – but not actually in the room. Satisfied that he had jump-started the talks, Holbrooke left the country. What was to follow did not augur well for the future. In Priština, Albanian politicians were wringing their hands, furious that Rugova appeared to have been forced into meeting Milošević and that he had dropped one of the LDK's hallowed tenets – that of no talks without foreign mediation. They were also angry that Rugova had agreed to the meeting without consulting the rest of the LDK's leadership.

Disregarding this, Rugova travelled to Belgrade on 15 May where, along with his closest adviser Fehmi Agani, Veton Surroi and two others, the Albanians met Milošević. At one point Milošević said something and Rugova doubled over with laughter. A camera crew from Serbian television caught the moment and the clip was repeated endlessly over the next few days. What Milošević said is inaudible. This did not go down well amongst Albanians. 'After all,' said one politician, 'while Rugova laughs, half of Kosovo is bleeding.' A source in Belgrade said: 'He was laughing, because he was nervous, all the Albanian delegation were. And there was Milošević like some great crocodile. They were frightened of him.' The repetition of the clip and the fact that the Serbian media made Rugova look like a provincial supplicant coming to beg favours from the big boss helped dispatch yet more angry volunteers to join the ranks of the KLA.

By now Rugova had named the so-called Group of Fifteen, who were a team chosen to advise him on the upcoming talks. Blerim Shala was a member and considering that he had also been chosen as its spokesman he had remarkably little to say. 'Confusion rules,' he said curtly. During these tense and crucial weeks politicians around Rugova became ever angrier with him for not telling them, or indeed anyone else, what was happening. Shala said: 'I could resign and then I would have a clear conscience, but of course I still would not be able to sleep at night. Resigning would be to play the Serbian game – divide and rule.'

On 22 May, in Priština, Ratko Marković and Fehmi Agani, as heads of their respective delegations, met and agreed on how talks should proceed. Surroi had been against this, because there had been an upsurge of fighting. He recalls that Holbrooke was flying to Detroit and that when they spoke, 'we were shouting for an hour'. Eventually he agreed to the meeting because he found himself alone in opposing it.

On 29 May Rugova travelled to Washington where, along with Agani, Surroi and Bukoshi, they met President Clinton in the Oval Office. Rugova was collecting his reward for meeting Milošević. That morning, in the hotel, Surroi received a call from Priština telling him that the Serbs had finally launched a counter-offensive against the KLA, around Dečani. They met Clinton, between his meetings in the National Security Council on the crisis which had just blown up between India and Pakistan. Despite this, says Surroi, Clinton was 'concentrated'. When they came out, Surroi called Holbrooke and, because of the Dečani offensive, said: 'We can't continue talks with Milošević doing this.' There had been only two meetings – the one with Milošević himself and the one between Agani and Marković – and the process was already dead.

The premature death of the peace process was hardly mourned by the KLA. One Sunday that May there was only one very old nun at home in the monastery of Dević. Driving there made the flesh crawl. There was this inexplicable feeling of being watched. You just had to hope that 'they' were watching you through their binoculars, not their gunsights. The nun said she was far too old to be frightened. Driving back down the hill, 'they' were waiting. Two large cars packed with uniformed KLA men. A thirty-something commander speaking impeccable English who said he had recently returned from Germany to fight checked documents. 'What were you doing at the monastery? What did the nun say?'

He was unimpressed by US attempts to get peace talks started. 'We're not interested in them,' he said dismissively. Surely, he was asked, he should be, since the Americans insisted that Kosovo could not be independent. 'And they said that none of the six republics of former Yugoslavia could be independent either,' he replied with impeccable logic. 'They'll come round.'

Whatever the men on the ground said, the senior ranks of the KLA were well satisfied with Holbrooke's work. In fact, this was nothing to do with his shuttle diplomacy but arose mainly from an inadvertent publicity coup they had managed to effect. On one of his recent trips to Kosovo Holbrooke had visited a local Albanian dignatory in the border village of Junik. While he was there a local KLA commander had barged in, sat down next to Holbrooke, cradling his Kalashnikov, and, before anyone knew what was happening a photo had been taken of the top US diplomat next to the armed man. When it was published both Albanians and Serbs interpreted this as a calculated signal of US support for the KLA – but it was not, and Holbrooke later found that when he told people the meeting was unplanned, nobody believed him.

Kosovo? Click!

For anyone who had witnessed the great sieges of the Croatian and Bosnian wars, the rocket duels fought by the Serbs and Croats over the old city of Dubrovnik in 1991 or the set-piece artillery barrages which had wrought such devastation from the Dalmatian coast to Vukovar, the fighting that spread through Kosovo that May and June was of a different order. It was guerrilla war of a type unseen so far in the wars of the former Yugoslavia and it resembled nothing so much as the ultimate Serbian nightmare: its very own Vietnam. This was, of course, ironic since Serbian leaders had long promised the West its own Balkan Vietnam should its forces intervene. The 'liberated' zones were expanding, Serbian civilians in small but significant numbers were being kidnapped and killed – to encourage stragglers to leave – and arms and ammunition were pouring across the border from Albania.

While policemen dug in, in bunkers surrounding the KLA-held zones, complaining that they were not being given the green light to 'finish them off', the military were keen to show that they were playing their role in defending the nation's borders. At Slatina airport, where airforce hangers could be seen dug in under the mountain which overlooked the runway, Yugoslav airforce fighters were scrambling but, certainly fearing the imposition of a NATO-enforced 'no fly zone', as had been the case in Bosnia, they had not resorted to air strikes or bombing.

At the base it was possible to hitch a ride on a Yugoslav airforce military transport helicopter. It flew dangerously low to avoid the risk of being shot down. The higher a helicopter flies, the longer an enemy can keep it in his sights and thus the greater his chance of bringing it down. As the helicopter jumped over gorges and skimmed wooded hilltops the gunner gripped his weapon as he leaned from the open door scanning the ground for targets. Within thirty minutes the helicopter touched down at the lonely Gorožup garrison, high in the mountains and on the slopes of Mount Paštrik, on the border with Albania. In April, things were so relaxed here that there was not even a sentry at the gate. A neat line of twenty pairs of socks and boots outside the barracks front door gave it the air of a scout hut. Now things were very different. Gunfire crackled in the distance while Serbian troops crouched in position. One mile away was an Albanian army barracks which had long since been abandoned. Gorožup's commander, Major Radomir Jović, proudly announced that since 26 April his men had thwarted eight attempts to smuggle arms across the border. In the early hours of the morning of 7 May his men had seized a haul which included 800 Chinese-made 'pineapple' hand-grenades and 5,000 rounds of ammunition. According to Major Jović the twenty KLA guerrillas who were carrying the arms fled back to Albania. The captured weapons, arranged in perfect order, were then shown off in the army headquarters building in Prizren while waiters in white gloves passed around coffees and canapés.

Despite Major Jović's boasts about how much weaponry his men were seizing it was quite clear that for every arms run intercepted several more were successful. A few days earlier, in a major escalation of the conflict, KLA fighters had surrounded the Serbian police in the village of Ponoševac, near Djakovica, close to another part of the frontier. The authorities subsequently reported that they had driven them off and that the fighting was over. It was not true. Artillery and mortar fire could still be heard nearby. The road to Ponoševac was strewn with dead cows and horses. A carrion crow, surprised by a car speeding to avoid snipers, was so bloated from its feasting that it had to struggle to get airborne. It was a terrible omen of the hellfire yet to come. At the edge of the combat zone was a friendly Serbian policeman from Belgrade. He spoke perfect English. He was asked how the police proposed to deal with the KLA. 'Ever seen *Lepa sela, lepo gore?*' ('Pretty villages, burn prettily' is a powerful film about the war in Bosnia in which life-long friends end up fighting on different sides and the Serb burns his Muslim friend's village.[13]) Reaching inside his flak jacket, he pulled out his lighter. Click!

At the same time, fighting was beginning to close in around the monastery at Dečani. Also close to the border, and in a valley, the KLA were crossing over from Albania, moving down the wooded valley and slipping across the road at the Serbian-held Dečani town into KLA-held territory on the other side of the road. Yugoslav soldiers, their faces done up in full camouflage paint, could be seen moving silently through the trees. Their job was to cut the weapons trail from Albania – but the KLA were slipping through their fingers.

On 7 May two elderly Albanians were found dead, 400 metres from the monastery. It was widely assumed that they had been executed by the KLA for 'collaboration'. On the evening of the next day four Serbian soldiers came to the cool monastery church to pray at the sarcophagus of King Stefan Dečanski. The monastery's Father Sava flew down the stairs, his black robes and blond beard flowing, to tell them that weapons were not allowed inside the monastery walls. While three of them went into the church, one then stood at the fortified gate guarding their weapons. In the refectory the monks said grace and prepared for dinner. On the terrace, overlooking the church, were a sobbing family. But, they had not just been chased away from their homes by the KLA, nor had anyone just died. 'Their son has come here to join the brotherhood,' explained Father Sava, with a big grin. 'It's always like this; because people were brought up in communism they think it is a terrible thing if their son wants to become a monk. My parents were just the same.'

Minutes later Dečani's calm was shattered by a short burst of loud gunfire. From beyond the gate came the shouts of '*Napad! Napad!*' – 'Attack! Attack!' The soldiers ran for their guns while Sava exclaimed in horror: 'It's never been this close before! I hope no one will attack us, we have done no evil to anyone!'

According to the survivors, masked men suddenly appeared on the road and ambushed a van driving a group of Serb and Albanian workers home from a nearby power plant. One died and four were injured. They survived because, despite the hail of bullets, the driver did not stop. With tyres and windows shot out he managed to get the van to the nearby police checkpoint. More than an hour later six truck-loads of soldiers, guns cocked and bristling, faces painted in camouflage green, were rushing into action. That night some of the remaining 300 Serbs who lived amongst some 55,000 hostile Albanians sought sanctuary in the monastery, too frightened to sleep at home. Sava fretted that seven elderly Serbs in the zone held by the KLA had disappeared and, rightly, he feared for their lives. The next day fighting cut the main road from nearby Peć to Priština. At the time, the attack looked like a brazen KLA show of force, right under the noses of the soldiers that surrounded the monastery in the woods. Months later Sava said that he had subsequently been told that the attack had been carried out by a unit of Serbian special police commanded by Frank 'Frenki' Simatović. Presumably they made a mistake, thinking that the men in the van were KLA soliders, rather than ordinary workers from the electricity company.

Three weeks later Serbian forces began the offensive around Dečani which was to scupper the talks process. Fighting swirled around the monastery, much of the town was looted and burned and large numbers of young Albanians who until then had equivocated about what they should do, flocked to join the guerrillas.

The day that the workers were attacked in their van was a

Thursday. Every Thursday the monks open the sarcophagus of Stefan Dečanski. They claim that when they do this they can smell a sweet smell of roses which emanates from the relics. From under his shroud King Stefan's little brown withered hand peeks out. As darkness fell that evening, the monks sang mass, and beeswax candles pricked the gloom before guttering and dying. Only wafts of pungent smoke lingered awhile before vanishing. The Serbs had not yet disappeared from Kosovo but the churchmen feared what was coming, they feared these could well prove to be the dying days of their ancient presence here. Some weeks earlier, in the aftermath of the Donji Prekaz massacre, Artemije, the Orthodox Bishop of Prizren and Raška, which covered Kosovo, made a statement which is all the more extraordinary now, because of its partly prophetic nature:

> After the massacre in Drenica, the chances of a dialogue as a way of resolving the problem have been missed. Now what remains is what the gentlemen in Belgrade have chosen – the loss of Kosovo, just like that of Krajina, in war. War in Kosovo would mean the definite loss of Kosovo. War would give the international community an excuse to get involved and in that case the Serbian army and police would be forced to withdraw as occupation forces. Even if Kosovo keeps some links with Serbia it would no longer be Serbian and isn't that the loss of Kosovo?
>
> If the destructive policies of the Belgrade regime continue, and everything points to that conclusion, Milošević won't sit down to sign Kosovo over to the Albanians but will prepare the situation for that, with him seemingly not being to blame.
>
> I think the sale of Kosovo has been signed somewhere already. We do not need mediators, people who impose solutions, but representatives who would listen to both sides in the Serbian-Albanian dialogue and inform the international community. They would not be an obstacle but are necessary. Serbia is not capable of offering a healthy dialogue without someone from outside. I don't understand why we are afraid of their presence when all the arguments are on our side: we have history on our side, we have the fact that Kosovo is part of Serbia.

Bishop Artemije had taken Father Sava as an adviser and spokesman, and the two of them travelled to Washington and Paris in a bid to persuade politicians that there was 'another Serbia' and to try and get their moderate, pro-talks views across. They also participated in several conferences abroad with Kosovar politicians where they made the acquaintance of people like Adem Demaçi and Veton Surroi, whom otherwise they would never have had the chance to meet. By now Sava was using this connection to have letters printed in Surroi's *Koha Ditore*, denying its accusations that the monastery was paying host to Serbian paramilitaries.

Artemije and Sava were also leading lights in the Serbian Resistance Movement (SRM), a group which had emerged in Kosovo over the previous two years. Its other main leader was Momčilo Trajković, a portly local businessman and former Priština SPS boss who had played an important role in the rise of Milošević and had even been a governor of Kosovo after 1989, until he had fallen out with the leadership in Belgrade. Although committed to retaining Kosovo for Serbia, the group did call for real dialogue with Albanians because they saw clearly that Milošević's policies were heading for disaster. The emergence of the SRM prompted the rebirth of an old pro-Milošević group called the Božur Association. However, as it too discovered, the authorities in Belgrade no longer had any interest in what Kosovo Serbs thought and so they remained irrelevant.

Just as Dayton and its failure to deal with Kosovo had traumatised Kosovo's Albanians, its Serbs had suffered a similar, shocking realisation. When the Croatian army stormed back into the Krajina region of Croatia and some 170,000 Serbs fled in three days, it finally dawned on many of the Kosovo Serbs that they, too, were doomed. Either because he could not or he would not, Milošević did not raise a finger to save Krajina, but it was he who had been responsible for arming the Serbs there and encouraging them and helping them rise in revolt against the Croats. Now, they had been driven from their ancestral homes. Kosovo's Serbs, amongst others, began to ask then why Milošević had encouraged their uprising if he was unable or unwilling to protect them. After all, unpalatable as it might have been for the Serbs of Croatia, and indeed difficult as it might have been, life in their homes in an independent Croatia would have been far preferable to a life in a damp, overcrowded collective centre in Serbia, without Yugoslav citizenship and with no prospects whatsoever. While, by the end of 1995, there were some 600,000 Serb refugees from Croatia and Bosnia in Yugoslavia, throughout most of Serbia they were invisible. That is to say, they were not immediately obvious as a large group, especially as they were, after all, Serbs living amongst Serbs.

By contrast, the 16,000 who were sent to live in Kosovo were a highly visible group. For example, at the school in the middle of Srbica or indeed in the Hotel Božur on Priština's main street, they were evident by their laundry perpetually flapping from balconies or outside. In the main they had come to Kosovo unwillingly, not wishing to be sent from one hostile environment to another and fearing that, sooner or later, they would again be on the run. Albanians despised them as 'colonists'. To some extent their presence did help radicalise the situation, because many Albanians believed that they were the advance guard of hundreds of thousands of others who would one day be sent to Kosovo to reverse the demographics in the province which were so unfavourable to the Serbs. By contrast, it was their visible presence which undermined Serbian morale in Kosovo. If Milošević had let the Krajina Serbs drop, then what guarantee was there that he would fight for Kosovo? The Kosovo Serbs were suffering from Krajina Syndrome.

As the spring of 1998 turned to summer, Serbs in Priština who were feeling far from confident and who lived in outlying areas were moving into the city centre to stay with friends and family. They felt safer clustered around the concrete symbols of Serbian power, especially the army and police headquarters. Although some Serbs, asked about Krajina, still said 'Kosovo is different', they did so without conviction. By the middle of May their fear and feeling of impending betrayal was beginning to boil over. As we have noted, the government had, on 23 March, agreed to abide by the education agreement, which had first been signed in 1996. It was now time to deliver. Tension began mounting then as Serbian students, many of whom were not Kosovo Serbs but from other parts of Serbia, began a sit-in at the building of the Technical Faculty, telling anyone who would listen that not only had they no intention of moving to make way for the hated 'Shiptars' (a derogatory term for Albanians), but that their fight was symbolic of the whole struggle for Kosovo. In the basement, they set up a 'Crisis Headquarters' where they made posters, some of which exhorted the police, who it was feared would soon move to turf them out, to 'Follow your hearts, not your orders!'

A rally inside the building gathered students and local Serbs. And despite the empty rhetoric of 'no surrender', one word recurred over and over again – 'Krajina'. Outside, crowds of Albanian students jeered at them. Stones were thrown and stone-throwing skirmishes fought with the police. Within 48 hours the Serbian students were gone, evicted by the police on the night of the 18 May, but not before they had rampaged through the building, destroying as much as they could. Even then it was not only some of the students who saw the symbolism of their very own battle of Kosovo as a portent of things to come.

The next day some returned to fight a rearguard action. Armed with rocks and clubs and under a skull-and-crossbones flag of the wartime royalist and nationalist Chetniks, they clashed with Albanian students. Shots rang out and then the police intervened. The Serbs then began to march through the city streets, screaming obscenities at the man they believed had betrayed them – Slobodan Milošević.

Back at the faculty building Albanian professors picked their way gingerly through the building that few of them had entered since the Albanian staff had been sacked almost a decade earlier. 'Oh, this was my office,' they were saying. Where the offices were locked they pulled up tables to peek through the fanlights. Just before the students left they had daubed the walls with graffiti denouncing Milošević and Albanians: 'Slobo – Shiptar! Death to Shiptars!' For good measure, one, making reference to the great Serbian Kosovo myth, added: 'Repent – The Empire of Heaven is Coming!'

Father Sava said that for years Milošević had simply been playing with the fears of the Kosovo Serbs:

> He doesn't care about the Serbian people. For him they are just animals. His wife too lives in the spheres of her own sick fantasy. Once she told Trajković that the Kosovo Serbs were 'primitives sitting around the fire talking about their myths'. She despises people here.

6 Quoth the Raven, 'Nevermore'

It was late July. Orahovac was shattered. Some Albanians remained there or had returned since the Serbs had retaken it. A man pointed out where he had buried his wife in a cornfield. Empty bullet casings littered the ground. 'This is where they were shot,' said someone, 'people were running away, just there ... *bah, bah, bah, bah.*' Her arms swung dramatically to show how the gun was fired. A young woman with sunken eyes held a baby that was as white as a sheet. Her husband was dead and she had been wandering the hills for days. Chris Hill was talking to the Serb mayor around the corner and said that things were 'looking up'. One his aides muttered that it was tough going trying to find the right KLA men to speak to. 'We still have to find their telephone number.'

In a tiny village in the hills children's shoes still lay on the road. Six people, including a pregnant woman, had died when a single Serb shell or rocket had hit the group. In the village of Klečka, the Serbs unearthed the remains of 22 civilians, including children, who they said had been murdered by the KLA who had then attempted to incinerate them in a lime kiln. As usual, civilians were paying the price of war.

To get back to Priština the road passed through the burned-out ghost town of Mališevo. Cows rooted for food in its smashed-up shops. Along the roads thousands of houses had been burned, put to the torch by the Serbs. In the fields cows were trampling the wheat and eating the corn. But in one field, a small group of Russians including Nikolai Afanasyevsky, the country's deputy foreign minister, were being shown a captured KLA trench by the Serbian police. Russia may be weak but it is still, after all, a nuclear power with pretensions to influence. 'Who are these KLA?' asked the Russian. 'I don't know. Do you know who they are? Anyway you can't negotiate with terrorists, even the Americans don't want to.' So, what, he was asked, would be a good solution to end Kosovo's agony? 'If you have an idea I'll give you a $1 million.' As the sun dipped behind the nearby hills, where tens of thousands were camping out under the trees, he jumped back in his car and was off.

Back in Priština, Radovan Urošević, the director of the Serbian media centre, was asked if he thought things were better than before. 'As you can see,' he replied briskly. And the future? His smile gone, he said simply, 'For that, we need a million Serbs.'

If you go on like this ...

The fighting around Dečani in late May and during the first two weeks of June was savage and thousands were sent fleeing for safety. The authorities had made safe the main road through Dečani but they had not broken the back of the KLA in the area. They had, by contrast, stiffened the resolve of the diplomats and Western leaders to be seen to being doing something. On the 11 and 12 June NATO defence ministers met in Brussels and ordered the organisation's military chiefs to prepare a range of options, should the use of force ever become necessary. Little did they realise then that not only did the fact of simply making plans, in the long run, fail to act as a deterrent to Milošević – which was the main aim – but that less than nine months later they would have to set them in motion. At the same time the EU and other Western countries banned all new foreign investment in Serbia and began proceedings to ban Yugoslav airlines from flying to their countries. On 12 June the Contact Group called for an immediate ceasefire and the 'withdrawal of security units used for civilian repression' from the province and demanded that the Kosovo Albanian leadership 'make clear its rejection of violence and acts of terrorism'. It added that their governments would 'ensure that all those seeking to escalate the crisis through violence are denied financial and material support'.[1] As they were to discover, however, stopping the flow of cash into the hands of the KLA was a far more difficult proposition than they could ever have imagined.

On 15 June NATO began a much-heralded aerial exercise called Determined Falcon which consisted of flying more than 80 planes – at a safe distance from the Yugoslav frontier – over Albania and Macedonia in a show of force. In fact, militarily speaking this was a limp gesture because it proved nothing more than the fact that NATO had planes in the region which could fly very fast. By contrast, it was important politically, because it was part of the ever-toughening Western stance. In effect, western leaders, convinced that sooner or later the Serbs and Albanians would be compelled to back down from all-out war and would be forced to compromise, were marching their troops to the top of the proverbial hill. When, by March 1999, and many more threats later, there was still no compromise, there was also no way back – and, short of a humiliating climbdown, force had to be used. In the meantime, more and more Kosovars were becoming ever more convinced that, like the Fifth Cavalry, NATO would soon be appearing on the horizon ready to rescue them. On 16 June Milošević went to Moscow to meet President Boris Yeltsin. The Russians were becoming increasingly alarmed by the hardening Western rhetoric and Milošević, keen to play up Russian fears, agreed with Yeltsin that he would refrain from repressive action and that he would restart talks with Rugova. This was, of course, rather like Determined Falcon, something of an empty gesture since he had not broken the talks off; the Albanians had done so in the wake of the Dečani offensive. However, as we shall see, the agreement with Yeltsin was to have important political consequences – but not yet.

As the fighting died down around Dečani, two things were clear. One was that the KLA were still in control of large areas, and the other was that the Serbian authorities now had to tread very carefully if they wished to keep Kosovo off the front pages of Western newspapers and so avoid further punishment. But what to do? For a brief period Kosovo was quiet again. Serbia's leadership looked to Milošević to tell them what to do. They were horrified. On 10 June the Main Board (formerly the Central Committee) of the SPS met in Belgrade. Those who attended wanted to know what Milošević was proposing while Kosovo was being lost and Western leaders were telling NATO to prepare for war. But, Milošević, according to one source, looked 'tired' and 'frightened'. He clearly did not know what to do.

Ostensibly the meeting had been called to deal with Kosovo but, in the event, the issue was barely discussed. Milošević, said the source, 'did not seem like the powerful man of a couple of months ago'. Instead of giving firm leadership he mumbled platitudes about 'the difficult situation'. The source added that: 'He seemed out of touch.' This performance led to speculation by those present that their leader was in the grip of depression. Over recent weeks he had been withdrawing for days on end and then reappearing, working frenetically, 'calling the police every hour' – and then disappearing again. Milošević was not so far out of touch, however, that he did not feel the need to tighten his grip on power. After failing to deal with Kosovo Milošević then moved that his party should formally hand all decision-making powers within the SPS to an inner circle of fifteen of his most trustworthy loyalists. This in turn fuelled rumours in Belgrade that he was nervous that his personal position might soon be threatened from within the party or state machinery.

The performance at the Main Board left army, police and security chiefs seething. This was hardly the time for the boss to lose his nerve and, as the source explained, 'Many people around Milošević are very frightened because they think that he and his government are the real target of the west – and not Kosovo.' This fear was real and it was to dog all Serbian calculations about how to respond to the crisis over the next year.

On the ground, in Drenica, a number of fortified police checkpoints suddenly disappeared. But on a road where there had been one Serbian checkpoint, there were now two manned by the KLA. Their command of the road gave them control of yet more territory in the province. The day after the SPS meeting two Serbian policemen were killed in an ambush near the settlement of Obilić, on the outskirts of Priština. A police commander said: 'It was an attack at close quarters. One of them had half his body blown off.' The next day the bullet-riddled police truck in which the men had been riding could be seen being brought back to Priština on the back of a lorry.

Policemen were angry. Just as in spring, they railed that they could destroy the KLA within ten days if the West had not tied their hands. However, the police were not trained as specialist anti-insurgency fighters and so they had no idea how to take on a vastly popular guerrilla movement without driving out the village populations who gave them shelter and burning their houses. This is what they done in Dečani and from the international perspective the operation had been entirely counter-productive. It resulted in television footage of the first groups of refugees to trek out to Albania, images of destruction horribly reminiscent of Bosnia – and instructions to NATO chiefs to look at the options for Kosovo.

From Priština, Western journalists fanned out every day, scouring the countryside for someone whom they could identify as the leader of the KLA. These trips were, for the most part, fruitless. Although there was a military headquarters and a 'political directorate', there was, as we have already noted, no overall commander, and outsiders found it hard to judge the seniority or importance of the KLA men they met. At this stage the KLA was still extremely difficult about news photographers doing their job, just as they were about cameramen filming. Preparing to make a documentary about Drenica, Dan Reed, a British director, was held up by a group led by a man whom he described as looking 'cold and ruthless'. Only later did he discover that he was Hashim Thaçi – a name which still meant absolutely nothing to outsiders and indeed, the vast majority of Kosovars. By contrast, the loosely organised KLA had, by now, produced a spokesman, Jakup Krasniqi, the former history teacher and LDK activist from Ćirez. Not only did his language leave an impression of an old-style petty Communist bureaucrat but his early pronouncements, on how the KLA was intent on forming a Greater Albania which would consist of Kosovo, Albania and Albanian-inhabited parts of Macedonia and Montenegro, did the organisation great harm. They helped convince Western chancelleries, at least at this stage, that while Milošević had to be stopped, the KLA should not be helped. For a while, then, rhetoric from Western politicians about air strikes quietened down. As a consequence, Krasniqi dropped this explanation of the KLA's objectives in favour of the more media-friendly aim of winning a pro-Western war of liberation against the 'savage' Serbs. This was, he explained:

> not a dream because dreams don't come true. Our dream is a reality based on the Albanian people, who have lived here for centuries. The ethnic make-up of Kosova is also a reality, within precise ethnic borders. The culture of independence and freedom are realities. Our aim is the

creation of a Kosovan state within its ethnic boundaries. We aim to create a free and democratic order, looking towards the West, just like the other nations of Europe.

With Serb forces now no longer on the offensive, Western leaders angry and KLA morale high, two individual commanders took the initiative. It was a turning-point in the war, and the decisions taken by these two were made without any apparent reference to KLA headquarters and without any thought of what the consequences might be. As we have noted, until now, the KLA had actually captured nothing of its own accord, but rather filled an ever-expanding vacuum in which Serbian authority was weak or even non-existent. On 23 June, however, one of the commanders seized the important coalmine at Belaćevac. The Serbs were driven out. Six days later, they retook the mine. Over the next few weeks, the situation took a dramatic turn for the worse. In a last-ditch effort to avert a Serbian rampage Britain dispatched its former ambassador to Belgrade, Ivor Roberts, to meet Milošević on 2 July. Roberts had struck up something of a rapport with Milošević during his tenure in Belgrade in the mid-1990s, but now he failed to persuade him to back down and look for a peaceful solution. If Milošević had, until now, been dithering, the KLA attack on Belaćevac and indeed the situation on the ground was now dictating the pace of events. On 15 July a KLA unit attacked the Trepča mine – in Serbian eyes an outrageously provocative thing to do. Within days, they had their revenge. At the border, close to the Albanian village of Padesh, the KLA suffered a catastrophic disaster when a group of up to 700 men was ambushed returning from Albania laden down with arms and ammunition. On the same day, 18 July, the second of the commanders acting without orders from above stormed the small central town of Orahovac. Within four days it was back in Serbian hands.

The initiative had passed from the KLA to the Serbs. The police, and now increasingly the army too, swept through Drenica and other KLA-held areas, sending tens of thousands fleeing before them. Houses were looted and burned and all of the KLA's strongholds, including the small town of Mališevo, next to Orahovac, tumbled like ninepins. As rapidly as they had surfaced, apparently from nowhere, the KLA seemed to disappear. Villages were burning, crops were burning, cattle were being machine-gunned and tens of thousands of people were now hiding in the hills and the woods. As the month drew to a close the political directors of the British, Austrian and German foreign ministries visited Kosovo and Belgrade. The authorities made no attempt to stop them seeing the devastation they had caused. In Belgrade the three men met Milošević where, in a meeting which had begun in a reasonably affable atmosphere, things soon turned sour. Milošević outraged the visitors by interrupting them and telling them that they were talking nonsense. When they told him what they had seen, recalls Emyr Jones Parry, the Briton in the party, 'he disputed it all'. According to Jones Parry, the three said: 'Mr President, it is either that your people are not telling you of the things we have seen or you are choosing to ignore them.' Milošević did not reply. As they left, Jones Parry said to Milošević: 'If you carry on like this the British government will take military action against you within six months.' Again Milošević said nothing.

If there had been qualms about direct contact with the KLA, the British and American governments now dropped them. The first formal contact between the US and the KLA took place on the 29 July in the Drenica village of Likovac. Chris Hill, travelling with Veton Surroi of *Koha Ditore* and Blerim Shala of *Zëri*, sought them out. Hill wanted not only to make contact but to urge them to look at his first draft proposals for a settlement of the crisis. He met Shaban Shala, the veteran militant and former human rights activist, who had now taken up arms.

The next day a British diplomat, travelling with Baton Haxhiu, the deputy editor of *Koha Ditore*, met KLA officials including Jakup Krasniqi in the village of Klečka to which the headquarters had been moved after the fall of nearby Mališevo. The diplomat was unimpressed and found Krasniqi 'incoherent, wooden, and not very creative'. He was just beginning to hear the name of a young man called Thaçi but he was not there because, as head of the KLA's Political Directorate, he had had to go over to Likovac to collect the draft peace agreement that Hill had left behind.

As the diplomats now began examining various possible solutions for Kosovo, they found dealing with the Kosovars extraordinarily difficult because, politically, they spent more time attacking one another than concentrating on uniting behind a common position and forming a common negotiating team. The Serbian authorities found it easy to tell the same diplomats that although *they* were happy to talk, they had no one to talk to.

By the 3 August the UN High Commissioner for Refugees (UNHCR) was estimating that 200,000 Kosovars had been displaced by the fighting. Very soon the pathetic pictures of these people eking out an existence in the woods and on hilltops began to head-line news programmes across the planet. While the Serbian authorities were trumpeting that they now had the whole of Kosovo back under their control, it was hard to know whether they really believed this – or just wanted to believe it. Despite having inflicted undoubted reverses on the KLA, they had in fact tumbled, like a lumbering giant, into a vast trap. As the Serbian security forces rampaged across the countryside the KLA simply pulled back, barely engaging them because, lightly armed, they would have stood little chance against the heavily armed Serbs. Indeed, there was relatively little fighting during this period in the interior of Kosovo, as opposed to along the border. However, by burning villages and sending tens of thousands fleeing and thus into the arms of television crews from across the world, the offensive turned out to be a complete disaster for the Serbs. There were few casualties on either side but the unfavourable publicity generated by the refugees was to have an extraordinary impact in galvanising Western opinion in favour of doing 'something'.

Let's finish it now

Over the border in Albania, from Padesh, you could see down the mountains into Kosovo. Plumes of smoke rose from not-so-distant blazing houses. Even without binoculars you could see the main road from Peć to Djakovica, a straight grey scar streaking across the hazy plain below. The August sun was baking and the thud of artillery reverberated in the distance. On a nearby plateau, wedged between high peaks, a lorry was disgorging munitions, flour and cigarettes, ready to be trekked across the border. In the shade of the bushes KLA soldiers were resting, waiting for dark, waiting for the moment when the order would finally come to cross the border to take the fight back home. As Serbian forces swept through the centre of Kosovo and the KLA melted away before them, conserving their energies for another day, the situation in northern Albania looked grim. Headquarters here were in a small building a good ten minutes' walk from the centre of Tropoja, a tiny village close to the border.

In the village school 160 men, exhausted and defeated, flopped down on the hard earth of the schoolyard. After four months of defending their village, Smolnica, which lies close to the border, they had been finally driven out by the Serbs. The men had walked all night before managing to slip across the frontier. There were old and young, some in uniform, some without. They had just arrived and sat in stunned silence. They were not much in the mood for talking. The next day two of the younger ones agreed to talk. They had just found their families who were filtering over in separate groups. 'None of us are going to go back and fight like that,' said one. 'If we have proper, heavy military equipment, then we'll go.' His friend said: 'It's useless to fight the Serbs with old guns and Kalashnikovs.'

They were not the only men to come in from Kosovo that week. Here was Jashar Salihu too. Gone were his suit and tie, briefcase and mobile phone, the uniform of the Swiss-based fund manager of the Homeland Calling fund. Now he was in fatigues, unshaven, and – despite the Serbian offensive – curiously elated. 'There's no point in being disappointed,' he said, 'It's normal that in a war the percentages go up and down.' Still he did not hide the fact that the Serbs had inflicted a heavy blow on the KLA. 'There was a kind of euphoria,' he said. 'Now we realise that the war is going to last for years.'

That summer, Tropoja was the nerve centre of the KLA's Albanian operations. There were training camps dotted about in the hills and it was from here that arms were collected and distributed. But there was no hiding the fact that this was far from a professional operation. The road from Tropoja to the plateau was a mud track, hard enough to drive up in summer. When the rains started to fall it was obvious it would be impassable. Still, for the moment, it was to here that, after the death of the Jasharis, young men hearing that the KLA had set up rear bases began to trek across the countryside and up over the mountains to get their guns. It was chaotic. Some had to buy their own weapons while others simply collected supplies for their villages. The new but feeble, Socialist-led Albanian government which had succeeded that of Sali Berisha in 1997 was horrified. Its sympathies lay with the Kosovars but its duty lay in preventing the war from spilling over into Albania. There was precious little it could do, however. Government writ simply no longer ran in northern Albania, much of it now being held in thrall by criminal gangs and bandits. The government was also frightened of another factor, from its point of view far more significant than Serbian retaliation over the border. They were afraid that Berisha, who unfortunately for them came from Tropoja, would use the KLA if they prevented them from getting arms. They were especially frightened that if the KLA was routed and thousands of armed men poured back into Albania – just like the men from Smolnica – then Berisha would use them for his own ends. They were frightened that he might tell them that they had been defeated because of Albania's policies and that he would mobilise them as a personal armed force, explaining that 'the road to Priština ran through Tirana'.

In fact, the situation in northern Albania was even more complex than this. Holed up in one of the camps near Tropoja were units of something called the Armed Forces of the Republic of Kosova, or FARK. These men owed their loyalty to Bujar Bukoshi and Ahmet Krasniqi, the man he had now appointed as his defence minister. Throughout the early summer there had been talk of a deal between Bukoshi and his government and the KLA. The nature of it was that, in a bid to unite, the KLA would become the army of the 'Republic of Kosovo'. Indeed, men like Xhafer Shatri in Geneva were desperate to take control of the KLA because, in view of its early phenomenal success, they were frightened that, if and when the Serbs were ejected from Kosovo, KLA people would take over – and they would be left on the scrapheap of history. Back in Switzerland men like Salihu and Mahmuti were telling Shatri and Bukoshi that the only thing they could do now was to hand over all the money they had collected since 1991, something they refused to do. This resulted in bitter polemics between the two, including unproven accusations that Bukoshi's people had stolen money from the funds and had also lost huge sums in Albania at the time of the collapse of the pyramid schemes. Bukoshi responded by dispatching former Yugoslav officers to Albania to set up FARK.

In the long run FARK was unable to influence the course of events. Many of its small number of men joined the KLA and were welcomed, since many of them, as former army officers, had specialist skills. As the war went on, units which had operated as FARK began calling themselves KLA too, which only added to the confusion, since it was not clear then to whom they owed their loyalty. At one point the KLA accused FARK of rank treachery in areas close to the border, but exactly what had happened there was murky in the extreme. In Tirana FARK maintained its own headquarters where Kosovars whom it deemed to be suspicious were held and interrogated after being kidnapped.

With one eye on FARK and one on the Serbs, the KLA in Tropoja carried on buying, collecting and distributing arms. Because of the nature of the business and the lawless environment, this was not an easy task. One KLA man was shot after it was discovered that he was buying arms and then selling them to the KLA at greatly inflated prices. This was hardly the patriotism that recruits who were now beginning to flow in from abroad were expecting. Like much of the weaponry they came north from Tirana, taking the ferry across the man-made fjord at Koman. Under the boiling sun it sailed slowly for two hours to Fierzë from where minibuses and taxis took them on to Bajram Curri and Tropoja. As the boat sailed down the fjord men on board would blast their guns at the towering mountains that tumble into the water and toss watermelon rind over the side.

All sorts of petty arms trading went on at the quayside and on the boat. A man could be seen with a rocket-propelled grenade working out a deal on his calculator here while another touted sniper sights amongst the young Kosovars going north to fight before opening the ferry's bar.

The Koman ferry became so infamous that, that summer, the UN and other international organisations in the area warned their people not to use it. They were frightened that, because of the arms and ammunition carried on board, either a Serbian commando squad would blow it up or it would explode anyway because much of the ammunition was old and unstable.

Recruits coming from amongst the *Gastarbeiter* communities abroad reported to Xhabir Zharku in Tropoja. He had returned to Albania from abroad to help set things up for the KLA in January, that is, just before the Donji Prekaz massacre which precipitated the war. Soft-spoken and bespectacled (hence his codename Blind), he had been born in Macedonia but later came to Kosovo. At the age of 17 he had been sent to prison for distributing leaflets. When he was released he wandered between Sweden, where he owned a pizzeria, the US, where he managed an insulation company, and Albania, where he unsuccessfully tried to import cars. Intense and intelligent, he seemed to have spent his whole adult life just waiting for this moment. He had a 9-year-old son. He said: 'If I don't do this job today I know my son will have to do it tomorrow. Let's finish it now.' In the courtyard of his headquarters building boxes of munitions were piled high while inside the satellite phone warbled softly, announcing calls from Switzerland or the frontline.

At the beginning of August he claimed that he had dispatched more than 4,000 men over the border. Asked about a number of ostentatiously Muslim recruits seen on the ferry whom UN sources said they too had seen but who then disappeared and were never seen again, Zharku said that the KLA wanted no help from Islamic fundamentalists. 'They came to offer their help but we declined. Once you accept you have to play their game and we're not interested in that. Some of us are Catholics and this is not a religious struggle.' In the event, and despite dire predictions, fundamentalists and indeed religion as a whole did not play a role in the war.

Salihu posed for pictures but then decided that they should not be used in a magazine article about the KLA. After all, there were 'security reasons', Western countries were threatening to block KLA funds and, as the head of the Homeland Calling fund, he had to travel on business. In July the Swiss and German authorities froze the fund's accounts, but as most of the money was in cash, this had a limited effect. With the KLA hard pressed in Drenica and now on the frontier, would it not now think of compromise, especially as the 'international community' insisted in every communiqué handed down from whatever international organisation, group or meeting that Kosovo had to remain part of Serbia or Yugoslavia? He smiled.

'You know what Edgar Allan Poe wrote? "Quoth the Raven, Nevermore."'

The threat

Back in Kosovo, in the hills, things were coming back to life, even though tens of thousands were still sleeping in the open air. Girls with flowing hair, neat black knapsacks and Kalashnikovs strolled to their positions along with the men. In areas where Serbian forces had moved on, traffic was flowing along a network of earth and back roads that the KLA had carved out so that people could travel about in cars without having to pass Serbian checkpoints. It was rapidly becoming clear that, despite their offensive, the Serbs simply did not have the manpower to leave men in every village. So, as they moved away, the KLA returned. They wandered around through charred villages and told anyone who cared to listen that they were happy about the offensive. 'Because,' said one soldier, 'it has shown anyone who ever doubted us, that we can never live with the Serbs again.'

That Serbs and Albanians could not or would not live together again was not what the diplomats wanted to hear. What they wanted was some form of credible pressure which would lead to talks and then to a solution, along the lines of the agreement over Bosnia. That is to say, either the so-called 'Three Republic' solution or some other sort of virtual independence for Kosovo, with safeguards for the Kosovo Serbs and Kosovo remaining, on paper, inside Yugoslavia or Serbia. Since both Serbs and Albanians rejected this option, the question was how to force them to accept it. While NATO readied its plans, it was, at the same time, far from clear whether they would ever be used. There was the fear that air strikes might provoke a full-scale KLA uprising, which was not the objective; there was the risk that Milošević might try and cleanse as much of Kosovo as he possibly could in as short a time as he could; and there was also the legal question. At what point could NATO use force, if ever, without a UN Security Council resolution, which would not be forthcoming because of Russian objections? While the fighting in the summer had been dramatic in terms of refugees, the number of casualties had been limited. The lawyers in the Foreign Office in London, and in foreign ministries across

Europe studied the facts and decided that there was no case for the use of air strikes without a Security Council mandate. Still, there were demands for action, but no one knew what it should be.

At the beginning of July Holbrooke had returned to Belgrade. He had studied the communiqué made by Milošević and Yeltsin in Moscow two weeks earlier and noted a line there about diplomats accredited in Belgrade being allowed full freedom of movement to monitor the situation in Kosovo. 'So,' he recalls, 'I invented the Kosovo Diplomatic Observer Mission – KDOM – on the spot.' Part of the strategy was, in effect, to humour the Russians and to make them feel as though they had an international role to play. Holbrooke went to the Russian embassy in Belgrade and told them of his idea. They were delighted, he says, because 'for them, it was all about respect', and he had pulled his idea out of the Yeltsin–Milošević communiqué. Within days, Russians, Americans, Britons and others were driving around Kosovo as official observers and reporting back home. With the exception of a tiny observer mission from the EU, a team from what was still called the European Community Monitoring Mission or ECMM, which had come from Bosnia, this was the beginning of the international presence in Kosovo which continues to this day.

The problem was that KDOM was toothless and could do nothing beyond observe. (Its members earned themselves the unenviable nickname of the Kondoms.) It was late summer now and fighting continued, albeit at a low level. Some 200,000 were displaced within Kosovo, 50,000 of whom remained out of doors and more than 98,000 had fled the province.[2] With winter coming, though, a catastrophe loomed. Somehow those still outside had to be brought under cover before the winter set in – or they would die. And, not only that, after so much huffing and puffing and threatening Milošević, Western governments would be humiliated by the spectacle of these poor people shivering every night on the television news. However, as Holbrooke puts it, 'Milošević kept doing his stuff, continued coming down on all Albanians, using his security forces to squash any sign of dissidence.'

Several things were happening simultaneously now – and all of them pointed to a need for action to prevent the situation spinning out of control. On 2 September Presidents Clinton and

Yeltsin agreed on a statement calling for an end to violence in Kosovo and for negotiations. One week later the Serbian police found a site at the village of Glodjane in which they claimed they had found 34 bodies, mostly Serbs but including eleven identified Albanians who they claimed had been executed by the KLA. On the same day the army began shelling villages in the Klina and Dečani areas. The next day Javier Solana, NATO's secretary-general, announced that the organisation had completed its plans for military intervention should it become necessary. On 12 September Azem Hajdari, a close aide to former Albanian president Sali Berisha, was assassinated. Over the next few days Tirana was in tumult with Berisha supporters storming parliament and the Albanian government subsequently announcing it had crushed a coup. As rumours circulated that Kosovars were involved in helping the Berisha supporters, alarm bells rang in the West, as pessimists warned that unless the situation in Kosovo was brought under control, the doomsday scenario of chaos engulfing Albania and Macedonia too might have already begun.

On the ground the Serbian police and military continued operations in Drenica. In New York the Security Council passed Resolution 1199 which demanded that Serbs and Albanians stop fighting and start talking. The next day, 24 September, the diplomatic spotlight shifted to a NATO defence ministers' meeting in Portugal. In the margins the ambassadors of the North Atlantic Council (NAC), that is, the ambassadors of NATO countries to the organisation, approved the issuing of a so-called Activation Warning (Actwarn). This, according to a NATO statement, took 'NATO to an increased level of military preparedness' in case it was subsequently authorised to begin a 'limited air option and a phased air campaign in Kosovo'. Referring to the UN Security Council Resolution, it demanded an end to Serbian 'repressive actions', a political solution and 'immediate steps to alleviate the humanitarian situation'.[3]

With the situation on the ground dictating events, the leaders of the Western alliance were facing an appalling and unenviable choice. The question was whether they could use force, in this case the instrument being NATO, against a sovereign country which had not attacked any of them without a Security Council mandate. On the face of it, Yugoslavia was putting down an armed uprising, which was an internal affair, and so the answer appeared to be no. The US, as we shall see, did not subscribe to this interpretation, however, and the British and French governments were increasingly leaning towards the view, which they eventually took, that they were faced with a humanitarian emergency, and in this case, according to the British government,

> in the exceptional circumstances of Kosovo ... a limited use of force was justifiable in support of purposes laid down by the Security Council but without the Council's express authorization when that was the only means to avert an immediate and overwhelming catastrophe.[4]

Because the Russians would not agree, there was no chance of getting a Security Council mandate to use force. The tricky question, then, if one accepted the legal argument that there might be exceptions to the rule, was: at what point did one judge that a country had gone beyond a certain undefined line – from which it could be as brutal as it wanted because it was crushing an illegal secessionist movement – to triggering foreign action because in putting down the rebellion it was creating a humanitarian catastrophe? No one knew the answer. The situation had no precedent and the question lies at the core of contemporary debate about the development of international law. With no final arbiter for such questions, each country has to make up its own mind, and final decisions are usually intertwined with issues of *realpolitik* and national interests. In other words, although you will not find an international lawyer or a foreign minister admitting this, the situation is a mess. To date, the answers to such questions are points of view, not points of law.

As the legal wrangling continued, two relatively limited but nasty enough atrocities were committed by Serbian forces. As September drew to a close, fierce bouts of fighting engulfed the area around Gornje Obrinje, close to where granite-faced Shota had translated for the two commanders in the red BMW. In the fighting at least fourteen Serbian policemen died. According to a detailed investigation by Human Rights Watch:

> Special police forces retaliated by killing twenty-one members of the Delijaj family, all of them civilians, on the

afternoon of Saturday, September 26. Fourteen people were killed in a nearby forest where they were hiding from government shelling, six of them women between the ages of twenty-five and sixty-two. Five of the victims were children between eighteen months and nine years of age. Of the three men killed in the forest, two were over sixty years old.[5]

On the same day, continues the report, the Serbian police rounded up 'a group of several thousand civilians who had fled the shelling in Golubovac, a village just kilometers away from Gornje Obrinje. Fourteen men were ultimately selected out, interrogated, physically abused for several hours and ultimately executed ... one of the fourteen men miraculously survived by feigning death.'[6] His name was Selman Morina. Interviewed on 1 October he described first the beatings they received and how the police kept saying that whoever said who amongst the group belonged to the KLA could go free. Morina said: 'There was no KLA among us, so we didn't know what to do.'

> I believe one policeman executed all of us. A policeman, a new one, came into the garden ... One man shot us, but the others were around in the garden. We were executed one by one. Each person was fired on twice with a burst from a machine gun. We had nowhere to escape. Some of us were begging to be released. No one tried to get up and escape ... Each person was shot twice. One person was shot a third time. I heard the police say 'One is still alive,' and they kicked him once and shot him again. They kicked me too, but I didn't move and then they didn't touch me again. I survived because I remained totally dead.[7]

These massacres and executions were revolting but, in terms of numbers, compared to say those killed in Bosnia at the beginning of the war in 1992 or the thousands killed in Srebrenica in 1995, they were negligible. Likewise, Serbs too were being kidnapped and murdered. However, their deaths did not have the same impact as the deaths of Albanians, because the backdrop to the killings of Albanians was the plight of the some 300,000 displaced, both inside and outside the province. Besides, in the wake of Vukovar and Srebrenica, the spectre of the past hung over Western policy makers, and their constant fear was that sooner or later a truly enormous massacre could take place, leaving them exposed to criticism for having failed to act. At the same time as these stories were hitting the headlines, Serbia's leadership was making a concerted effort to claim that the massacres were faked either by the Western media or the KLA, and that besides their operations had now come to a close. On 28 September, for example, Mirko Marjanović, the Serbian prime minister, announced the following:

> Today there is peace in Kosovo Metohija. Life in Kosovo Metohija has returned to normal. The Republic of Serbia has thwarted the secessionists' attempts to realize their intentions through terror. The terrorist gangs have been destroyed ... Serbia has once again shown that it is capable of resolving its problems alone, with full respect for the democratic countries' principles and standards regarding human, civil and minority rights. [8]

On the same day ambassadors from Contact Group countries visited Milošević who told them the same thing. They retorted that he had to abide by Security Council Resolution 1199. But what would they do if he did not? Robin Cook, the British foreign secretary, told his EU counterparts that Britain still wanted a Security Council resolution that would mandate the use of force if it came to that. But time was running out especially because pressure was now mounting from the US. Four days after the first massacres, news of a new one at Gornje Obrinje was splashed across the front pages. The impact was extraordinary. On 30 September the National Security Council began a series of meetings on Kosovo. Holbrooke recalls that on the front page of the *New York Times* that morning was a gruesome colour picture from the Gornje Obrinje massacre:

> Later [Joe] Lelyveld [the executive editor] told me there had been a big debate at the *Times* about whether to use it. People were horrified. It was at the top of the front page and it sat there like a mute witness at the NSC meeting in the Situation Room. There was an enormous debate, and it broke out with the picture stirring people. There was a decision then to press ahead for NATO action, to try and

sidestep the British, French, German and Russian view that you needed a Security Council mandate.

The US position was that NATO could do what it liked. The British and the other Europeans, however, had, as we have seen, been resisting this argument, although their opposition had been weakening. Still, the Americans were outraged because they said that if you always had to go to the Security Council, that gave the Russians a veto on US foreign policy. Holbrooke describes this as a 'theological debate' which in terms of international law, it was. However, in the real world, where policy decisions were needed *now*, what was important was how the allies lined up. Holbrooke says: 'On the one hand you have us and on the other you have the French. Then you have the Germans who usually go to us, reluctantly. Thus, Britain is often the key to NATO decision making.' Once the British made up their mind, the die would be cast, but, despite what Holbrooke says, the French position, at least on paper, was actually identical to the British. While, throughout the summer, the Foreign Office lawyers had argued that there was still no case in international law to use force, the atrocity stories, particularly the pictures of the tens of thousands of people in the hills, had been changing minds. Gerhard Schroeder, the new German chancellor, reluctant, as Holbrooke says, now told President Clinton that his country would support bombing. Clinton called French President Jacques Chirac and Tony Blair in London. Madeleine Albright went to Brussels to brief the NAC and then flew to London for the next Contact Group meeting. Both the British and the French were coming round. On 6 October President Chirac said that France considered that 'any military action must be requested and decided by the Security Council' but then went on to qualify this by adding that:

> the humanitarian situation constitutes a ground that can justify an exception to a rule, however strong and firm it is. And if it appeared that the situation required it, then France would not hesitate to join those who would like to intervene in order to assist those who are in danger.[9]

In general, foreign ministers and their aides are used to meeting in the plush surroundings of one another's ministries or at the very least, luxurious conference centres. By contrast, one of the most important meetings about Kosovo took place on 8 October in a crammed VIP lounge at London's Heathrow Airport. Robin Cook, Hubert Védrine, his French counterpart, Klaus Kinkel, the outgoing German foreign minister, Albright, Holbrooke, Igor Ivanov, the Russian foreign minister were all there, as were representatives of the OSCE, the Austrians in their capacity as current EU chairmen and several more ministers and aides. There were some 50 people crammed into the room. Ivanov had just flown in from Belgrade, as had Holbrooke. They could hear the planes roaring outside, and as Holbrooke says: 'There were also these British matrons serving tea and biscuits. It was mad.' A decision was made to go down to the level of foreign ministers plus a few other key players. 'So,' says Holbrooke, with about thirteen people in the room 'we got down to it.' They were arguing again about the question of force and the need – or not – for a Security Council mandate.

> Ivanov said: 'If you take it to the UN, we'll veto it. If you don't we'll just denounce you.' Kinkel says he wants to take it to the Security Council, as do the British and French. Madeleine and I say: 'That's insane!' So, Kinkel says: 'Let's have another stab at it.' But Ivanov says: 'Fine, we'll veto it.' And Kinkel asks again and Ivanov says: 'I just told you Klaus, we'll veto it …' He says: 'If you don't we'll just make a lot of noise …' It was all foreshadowed. The Russians can't do anything. NATO is the power …

NATO is the power, but enfeebled as it might be, Russia still has a formidable military arsenal and anti-aircraft systems which could wreak havoc on NATO planes. What had just taken place, then, was a watershed. The Russians had, in effect, told NATO that it would do nothing if it were to bomb. Even if they had been bluffing, the Russians could have upped the ante, kept NATO guessing and threatened to supply the Serbs with their anti-aircraft systems. But they did not. They simply shrugged and dumped them. What they were telling Milošević, though, remains open to question. Sources in Belgrade believe that one of the many reasons Milošević decided to defy NATO in March 1999 was because he believed the Russians would indeed supply him with these advanced weapons systems. But Western leaders already knew that the Russians were not even threatening to do any such thing.

Just before the Heathrow meeting began Madeleine Albright made a statement in which she forcefully expressed the US view that NATO had 'the legitimacy to stop a catastrophe'. It was time, she said, for NATO, 'to make the difficult but necessary decision to authorise military force' if Milošević failed to abide by the demands of Security Council Resolution 1199.

Over the last few days things had been relatively quiet on the ground, the KLA had declared a unilateral ceasefire and in a public show of compliance with the resolution, a number of police units were pulled back. Albright, however, was not impressed. In her statement she referred, indirectly, to the killings at Gornje Obrinje and Golubovac:

> We have to take into account not only this week's snapshot of events on the ground but Milošević's long-standing unwillingness to negotiate seriously, and the accumulated barbarity of the last three months. Time and again, Milošević has promised us to do things he had no intention of doing. Time and again, he has taken half measures to avoid the consequences of his actions. Yet, even in the last two weeks, even as he made cosmetic gestures in the direction of compliance, his forces committed some of the worst atrocities of the war. We must assume that Milošević will continue to do the minimum necessary to avoid NATO action. But he has to understand that the minimum is not good enough. The only thing that is good enough is full compliance. Milošević knows what he needs to do to avoid NATO action. He must immediately end all police and military actions in Kosovo; withdraw all units to their bases and cantonments in a way that can be verified; provide international organisations and diplomatic observers unfettered access to Kosovo; agree to a timetable for a political settlement based on the draft that the Contact Group has endorsed and cooperate with the War Crimes Tribunal .... We have made it very clear to Milošević and the Kosovars that we do not support independence of Kosovo – that we want Serbia out of Kosovo, not Kosovo out of Serbia. But one of the keys to good diplomacy is

knowing when diplomacy has reached its limits. And we are rapidly reaching that point now.[10]

The British and the French were persuaded. Holbrooke says: 'If you get caught up in the niceties of the lawyers of the Foreign Office you lose the game. Cook and Blair simply told the Foreign Office lawyers to "shove it". But it took all summer – which Milošević used to crush the KLA and fuel the resistance.' Unsurprisingly, if you ask officials at the Foreign Office about this interpretation of events, they take umbrage, denouncing Holbrooke's interpretation of events as 'a travesty'. They say that British attempts to secure a Security Council resolution were actually undermined by the US which, as we have noted, disagreed with the proposition that it should be consulted on this issue. Given, then, that Russian *and* US opposition blocked the use of the Security Council, they say that the reason for the British (and French) change of heart was nothing to do with pressure from the US, it was because the situation had changed. That is to say, that the magic line had been crossed between the lawyers' demand for a Security Council resolution to deter-mining that action could be taken without one because of an impending humanitarian catastrophe. On the same day, then, the NAC approved a plan for phased air operations. It was called OPLAN 10601 – Allied Force. Armed with this credible threat of bombing, Holbrooke returned to Belgrade to see Milošević. 'He and his military were sweating and they knew the bombing was ready to go.' He says: 'We had moved the B-52s forward from the United States to Great Britain. The planes were on the runways in Italy. The targets had been picked.'[11] With him was US general, Michael Short who would be commanding the air strikes. Nonchalantly Milošević said: 'So, you're the one who will bomb us.'[12] Holbrooke recalls that Short replied:

'I've B52s in one hand and U2 surveillance spy planes in the other. It's up to you which I'm going to use,' and Milošević knew he was telling the truth. Now that threat was completely real and it resulted in the ceasefire agreements which saved the lives of countless people who otherwise would have frozen to death out in the forests of Kosovo over that winter.[13]

Later, General Short gave a fascinating insight into the way the negotiations were held. Ten or twelve people would sit around the table, he said, and when the talks reached an impasse Milošević and Holbrooke would 'withdraw to a separate room'.

> The rest of us would hear raised voices, occasionally a hand slapping the table, and they'd come back out with some level of agreement and we'd press on. About the third day, I was invited back into that room – Mr Holbrooke, President Milošević and myself. We had reached the point in negotiations where we had agreed that we would fly airplanes in Kosovo to take pictures of his operations and he would have to move his [anti-aircraft missile] SA-6s and SA-3s out of Kosovo in order to allow my airplanes to fly without fear of being shot down. The three of us sat down around a small coffee table, and Mr Milošević – and you'll pardon my efforts at accent – he said, 'General, you cannot make me move my SA-6s. They have been in place for many years. A logistical nightmare. It would be very difficult for me. I cannot – do not ask me to do that. I will just turn them off and it will be all right.' At this point I'd been up for about 32 hours … I leaned forward and I said, 'Mr President, you're pounding sand up my ass.' And he leaned forward and he said, 'What means "pound sand up my ass"?' I explained to him I thought he was pulling my chain. I had been watching his SA-6s for the last six weeks; he was moving them every day; I knew very well he could move them, 'Now get them out of Kosovo!' And he said, 'You are right. I will move the missiles.'

Significantly, on the basis of these talks, General Short concluded that 'if you hit that man hard, slapped him up side the head, he'd pay attention.'[14] On 12 October Milošević and Holbrooke struck a deal. The Serbian military and police presence would be drawn down to its pre-war levels and serious negotiations with the Albanians would begin. Two thousand monitors, or verifiers as they were to be called, would come to Kosovo under the auspices of the OSCE and NATO would have the right to make aerial surveillance flights above the province to verify whether the authorities were living up to their promises. As the drama of the talks unfolded the NAC gave Holbrooke's threat backbone. They passed an Activation Order (Actord) which meant that, if there was no agreement, bombing, as envisaged by the Allied Force plan, would start in 96 hours. Holbrooke flew back to Brussels and Milošević issued a statement. 'Honorable citizens,' he began, 'the accords we have reached eliminate the danger of military intervention against our country.'[15]

The crisis was over, at least for the moment. Javier Solana and General Wesley Clark, the military head of NATO, whose formal title is Supreme Allied Commander Europe or SACEUR, went to Belgrade to meet Milošević. For Clark, it was the first of three meetings that would take place over the next few days. At one of these meetings Milošević told Clark about how the Partisans had finished off Shaban Polluzha and his men:

> He said, 'you know General Clark ... we know how to handle problems with these Albanian killers.' I said, 'Well, how do you do that?' He said, 'We have done this before.' I said, 'When?' He said, 'Drenica 1946.' I said, 'How did you handle it?' He said, 'We kill them, all of them.' He said it took several years but 'we kill them all'.[16]

Over the next few weeks meetings took place in Belgrade and indeed across Europe as plans for what was to be called the Kosovo Verification Mission (KVM) were laid. On 27 October, following the departure of 4,000 special police from Priština, the NATO ambassadors declared that Yugoslavia was complying with its commitments, but it also agreed to maintain the Actord in place. Simultaneously it began assembling what was to be a NATO 'Extraction Force' to be based in Macedonia. The idea was that these French-led troops could, if needed, storm in to Kosovo to rescue KVM members if they were ever held up or in trouble. Unstated, however, was the understanding that, in such an unpredictable situation, it was best to have troops beginning to be built up on the ground. Not only were they a covert threat to Milošević, but they might well come in handy for something else later on. This is not to say, however, that in the wake of the Holbrooke Agreement anyone was seriously thinking of a NATO-led ground force for Kosovo. Of course, in all of the plans that NATO had laid since the summer, there were contingency plans for either a NATO-led peacekeeping mission or even some form of invasion, but these were plans – for the sake of plans. The military had them because they had been ordered to prepare for every possible option. Indeed, the whole point of threatening air strikes at this stage was to try and avoid having to put NATO troops into Kosovo. This was one of the reasons why the US had pushed so hard to make the threat credible. In the run-up to the Holbrooke deal, Britain and one other minor NATO country had signalled their willingness to put troops on the ground as armed peacekeepers, but they had stood alone. In the end, given the lack of goodwill by the KLA and the Serbian authorities, an unarmed verification mission could not save the situation. However, the fact that the KVM was tried, and failed, was an important step in building consensus for the eventual use of force. As one senior Foreign Office official puts it: 'We were never that confident that it would work,' but there was the feeling in Whitehall, and elsewhere, that every possibility of resolving the conflict peacefully had to be exhausted.

In the short term the agreement was successful, because the displaced people began to come down off the hills and moved into shelter for the winter. However, the real problem was that the agreement had no enforcement mechanism. That is to say, if the parties did not comply, then what was supposed to happen next? Milošević had agreed to the plan because he wanted to avoid air strikes. The plan was acceptable to him in that it did not call for foreign troops in Kosovo, as the later proposed Rambouillet Accords did, and also possibly because he was given to understand that Western countries would now move to throttle the KLA's sources of arms and finance. However, whether history would have been different if Holbrooke had demanded armed verifiers – foreign troops – is a moot point. We do not know whether, at that point, Milošević would have accepted them, because he was not asked to. Firstly, as we have noted, there was no alliance push for troops; and the second reason Holbrooke did not ask him was that he had been specifically instructed not to. President Clinton, now facing impeachment because of sexual misdemeanours with Monica Lewinsky, the former White House intern, found it impossible to concentrate on his job and did not want to contemplate having to send US troops into any possible danger. Mid-term congressional elections were also forthcoming and talk of US troops going to Kosovo was simply a vote loser. William Cohen,

the US secretary of defence, would have opposed the proposition and Sandy Berger, the president's national security advisor
was ambivalent. In the event, however, the threat of bombing,
this time around, worked.

Apart from the fact that there was no enforcement
mechanism incorporated in the agreement, it rapidly became clear
that there was another serious flaw which, in their hurry to do a
deal with Milošević and avoid having to bomb, no one had dealt
with. The fact was that the Holbrooke Agreement was with
Milošević and the Serbs. The KLA were not party to it and, as far
as they were concerned, not bound by it either. As the Serbs
pulled back, the KLA followed in their wake, reoccupying the
positions they had withdrawn from during the summer. The
Serbs, understandably, were furious, but following their initial
redeployment they said they would abide by a ceasefire as, half-
heartedly, did the KLA. In fact the Holbrooke agreement had
come at just the right time for the guerrillas. They were hard
pressed and were holed up in the hills; now the agreement gave
them a reprieve, time to reorganise and rearm and, as they told
anyone who cared to listen, time to prepare for their spring offensive. The Serbs were listening. As soon as they had begun drawing
down their forces in accordance with the agreement, they began
putting them back in again. The omens were not good.

Spring comes early to Kosovo

The head of the KVM was William Walker, an American diplomat who had recently worked as head of the UN Transitional
Administration in eastern Slavonia, the formerly Serb-held
region of eastern Croatia. Ten years earlier, he had been the US
ambassador to El Salvador, at a time when the US was helping
the government there to suppress leftist rebels while simultaneously supporting the Contra guerrillas against the Sandinista
government in Nicaragua. Assuming, then, that his past must
presuppose a close relationship to the CIA, the Serbian authorities were deeply suspicious of Walker. However, this was to
some extent offset by the appointment of Gabriel Keller, a
former chargé d'affaires at the French embassy in Belgrade, a
position which Albanians suspected would mean he was partial
to the Serbs. The two diplomats loathed each other. Many if not

most of the men now arriving to take up positions in KVM were either serving or recently retired military officers. While their official loyalty lay with the OSCE, it is fair to assume that a good number of them also had strong ties with the intelligence services of the countries that sent them. While other nations 'folded' their KDOM observers into the KVM, the US did not. This led to suspicions that it wanted its men to have a certain independence, that is to say, to be able to continue working on the ground away from the prying eyes of friends and allies. Based in towns around Kosovo, men from the KVM in vehicles painted an unmistakable bright orange fanned out across the province every day – as did the American KDOM men. They made contact with the Serbian authorities and the KLA and filed detailed daily reports. During the period of the relatively slow build-up of KVM verifiers the situation on the ground was comparatively quiet, comparatively being the operative word. From 28 September to 19 October the Serbian authorities reported 117 attacks on the police and army resulting in the deaths of ten policemen and seven soldiers. Working on the basis of KVM, UN, KDOM and other reports, Kofi Annan, the UN secretary-general, reported on 12 November that:

> Recent attacks by Kosovo Albanian paramilitary units have indicated their readiness, capability and intention to actively pursue the advantage gained by the partial withdrawal of the police and military formations. Reports of new weapons, ammunition and equipment indicate that the capacity of those units to resupply themselves is still fairly good.[17]

His next report, on 4 December, noted that while the displaced and refugees were returning home, 'the return process is fragile, and those returning home often sleep with their belongings still packed beside them'.[18] On Christmas Eve another UN report noted that between 1,500 and 2,000 Albanians had been detained by the authorities since the Holbrooke Agreement and that an estimated 150 civilians had been kidnapped by the KLA.[19] Low-level conflict between the police and army and the KLA was not the only one being played out across the province. The KLA was also seeking to stamp its authority on areas that it controlled and to make sure that the LDK understood Mao's dictum that power grew from the barrel of a gun. LDK activists were arrested and according to one UN report the activity of KLA 'tribunals' suggested a 'pattern of arbitrary arrests and execution'. It cited a communiqué issued on 3 November which acknowledged that two individuals 'had been executed'. A few days later it abducted two Serbs in Srbica which resulted in Serbs in the overwhelmingly Serbian inhabited region of Leposavić abducting 25 Albanians from an intercity bus. Thanks to the intervention of KDOM, all of these civilians were released. [20]

The initial hopes that the Albanians and Serbs would use the breathing space afforded them by the Holbrooke Agreement to search for a peace deal were rapidly fading. The observers or verifiers were increasingly being sucked into negotiating hostage and prisoner releases and local ceasefires. Around the town of Podujevo, by the main road linking Kosovo with the rest of Serbia, the KLA began flagrantly constructing bunkers overlooking the town. In the centre of the province, anger boiled as the Serbian mayor of Orahovac led a demonstration of 700 Serbs into neighbouring KLA-controlled Dragobilje to demand the release of kidnapped Serbs. As their orange vehicles crisscrossed the province, the KVM men had the ever-stronger feeling that their mission was doomed. Referring to the conflict earlier in the summer Holbrooke said later:

> The KLA was arming, the KLA taking very provocative steps in an effort to draw the west into the crisis. That was ultimately successful, the Serbs were playing right into the KLA's hands by committing atrocity after atrocity, way overreacting, wiping out entire villages, outrageous actions which had to be responded to.[21]

The fear was that it would not be long before a new atrocity would, once again, play right into the KLA's hands. US intelligence, for one, was warning that the KLA 'intended to draw NATO into its fight for independence by provoking Serb forces into further atrocities'.[22]

The downward spiral was ugly. On 14 December the army killed some 36 KLA men, part of a group of 140 crossing back from Albania to Kosovo. That evening, masked men burst into the Panda café in Peć, gunning down six Serb teenagers who were playing pool. Adem Demaçi, who had by now been appointed as a spokesman for the KLA, denied that they were responsible. Whether they were, or whether the killings were committed by a rogue unit, as some of the diplomats believed, hardly mattered now. Five thousand angry, emotional and frightened Serbs turned up for the funerals. Several thousand also rallied in Priština to protest at the killings. On 18 December the police found the body of the Serbian mayor of Kosovo Polje who had been kidnapped from his home the night before. Foreign aid workers distributing aid to Albanians were held up by angry Serb civilians. The government said it would not let 'terrorists take over Kosovo' and that 'attempts by the armed groups to cross into Kosovo from Albania and killings of civilians would justify a renewal of operations against Kosovo Albanian paramilitary units.'[23]

In the first eleven days of January, 21 people died in what a UN report described as 'random violence in urban centres'. Three Serb youths died when a bomb exploded outside a Priština café 'triggering retaliatory attacks by Serbian civilians on Albanians'. On 8 January eight young soldiers were kidnapped by the KLA but their release was negotiated by the KVM. Although the Serbian authorities denied it, a straight swap had been arranged and, a short time later, nine KLA prisoners including one woman captured while infiltrating over the border were released.

In Washington and the other Western capitals it was clear that the Holbrooke Agreement was disintegrating. Braving an ice storm, President Clinton's foreign policy team met on the afternoon of the 15 January in the Situation Room in the basement of the White House. There, according to the *Washington Post*, 'they approved a 13-page classified "Kosovo Strategy" that policymakers referred to informally as "Status Quo Plus",' which outlined a vision of a highly autonomous Kosovo within Yugoslavia. On the ground Chris Hill and Wolfgang Petritsch, the Austrian ambassador to Belgrade who had been appointed the EU's special envoy, had been shuttling back and forth between Priština and Belgrade working on various draft plans for the future of Kosovo – but all to no avail. With the situation worsening by the day the *Washington Post* reported that an angry Madeleine Albright declared 'We're just gerbils running on a wheel.' Her conclusion was that 'muddling through was not working and that the time had come to tie the threat of force to a comprehensive settlement'. But her cabinet peers in the so-called Principals Committee, no less frustrated, were not yet ready to take that risk.[24] As they met, they had no idea that events on the ground had outstripped them.

On 8 January, in a well-planned ambush, the KLA killed three Serbian policemen at a village near the town of Štimlje. Two days later, in another nearby village, they killed another policeman. For the next four days the police and army began a build-up in the area. Early on 15 January fighting broke out around the village of Račak. A few hours later the KLA retreated and the police entered the village. Several people were shot over the next few hours. A group of 30 men and boys hid in the cellar of a house. Later, a 12-year-old boy who was in the group told Human Rights Watch that when they were found the men began screaming: 'Don't shoot! We are civilians!' Boys were taken out of the group, including a 15-year-old. According to Human Rights Watch: 'The conscious decision to return him, while later executing the others, suggests that the police had a clear order to kill the adult males of the village.' Twenty-three men were now taken away. Shooting was heard at 3.00 p.m.

A few hours later, a KVM team entered the village and took away five wounded. The villagers thought that the 23 had been taken to Štimlje police station, but during the night they scoured the area for more wounded. At 4.00 a.m., according to the testimonies given to Human Rights Watch, the villagers discovered the bodies. According to their report, it was 'clear that most of these men were fired upon from close range as they offered no resistance. Some of them were apparently shot while trying to run away.' The report continued that the men's

> clothes were bloody, with slashes and holes at the same spots as their bullet entry and exit wounds, which argues against government claims that the victims were KLA soldiers who were dressed in civilian clothes after they had been killed. All of them were wearing rubber boots typical of Kosovo farmers rather than military footwear.

The final death toll in Račak was 45, including a 12-year-old boy and two women. Nine KLA soldiers were also found dead. The next day, when William Walker arrived, he immediately accused the Yugoslav authorities of responsibility. Walker's chief of staff called the State Department from Račak and began dictating a report. But Madeleine Albright first heard the news on her clock radio at 4.30 a.m. Outraged by the massacre she called Sandy Berger and said: 'Spring has come early to Kosovo.'[25]

Over the next few days doubts began to be raised about Račak. Keller, angry perhaps that Walker (with whom relations had been deteriorating) had immediately condemned the Yugoslavs without waiting for concrete evidence, briefed French journalists indicating that he believed that there was something odd about Račak. Suspicions were raised that at least one group of dead men might not have been civilians or that they might have been killed in the fighting and that the KLA had moved their bodies to make it look as though they had been executed there. Some sources believe that Walker rushed to condemn the authorities because he wanted to provoke a showdown. There is, however, no hard evidence to support any of these theories. While it is true that the Serbian media centre in Priština told journalists that there had been a successful operation in Račak, and invited journalist to visit, this more than likely implies a lack of coordination between the media centre and the police rather than evidence that the Serbs were about to be 'set up'. One month later Dr Helena Ranta, in Kosovo as head of an EU forensic team, wrote in her report that: 'There were no indications of the people being other than unarmed civilians.'[26]

From the moment that agencies began to flash the news of Račak around the world, it was obvious to everyone concerned that nothing could ever be the same now. The authorities in Belgrade declared that the KLA had faked a massacre scene and ordered Walker out of the country. Under tremendous pressure they later 'suspended' this. Judge Louise Arbour, the head of the International Criminal Tribunal for the former Yugoslavia, tried to visit, and, having been refused a visa, she was turned back at the border. By doing this, the authorities immediately undermined their claim that they had nothing to hide. In Washington, Paris and London the diplomats and politicians began a frantic round of emergency consultations. Moving quickly, Albright began to build consensus for her idea that future diplomacy had to be backed by the threat of force. Across the Atlantic, British and French leaders agreed. Consulting with Russian foreign minister Ivanov, a new plan was hatched.

Serbs and Albanians were to be summoned to talk peace at a château 30 miles southeast of Paris in a town called Rambouillet. They were to negotiate on the basis of the draft proposals for Kosovo's future worked out by Chris Hill and Wolfgang Petritsch, who would be the negotiators along with a Russian called Boris Mayorski. Robin Cook and Hubert Védrine were to be the co-chairmen of the talks. While this was the diplomatic half of the strategy, the other half – the credible use of force – came in the form of threats delivered by NATO's North Atlantic Council on 30 January. It issued a statement thundering that the crisis was a 'threat to international peace and security' and continued:

> NATO's strategy is to halt the violence and support the completion of negotiations on an interim political settlement for Kosovo, thus averting a humanitarian catastrophe. Steps to this end must include acceptance by both parties of the summons to begin negotiations ... on an interim political settlement within the specified timeframe.

The Serbs were also told to reduce their army and police numbers to those agreed with Holbrooke in October and to end their 'excessive and disproportionate use of force in accordance with these commitments'.

> If these steps are not taken, NATO is ready to take whatever measures are necessary in the light of both parties' compliance with international commitments and requirements, including in particular assessment by the Contact Group of the response to its demands, to avert a humanitarian catastrophe, by compelling compliance with the demands of the international community and the achievement of a political settlement. The Council has therefore agreed today that the NATO Secretary General may authorise air strikes against targets on FRY territory. The NATO Secretary General will take full account of the positions and actions of the Kosovar leadership and all Kosovar armed elements in and around Kosovo in reaching his decision on military action. NATO will take all appropriate measures in case of a failure by the

Kosovar Albanian side to comply with the demands of the international community. NATO is also studying how to support measures to curb arms smuggling into Kosovo.[27]

Britain, France and Italy now began the job of assembling the peacekeeping force which they intended to deploy once the Serbs and Albanians had signed on the Rambouillet dotted line. Along with the US, which announced that it would join the peacekeeping force, Western leaders had simply decided that a peace deal without a NATO-led force would never be implemented. Russia made it clear that it had no opposition to a peacekeeping force, in which it was certain to participate, so long as it was invited in to Kosovo by the Yugoslav authorities. Although the troops now beginning to gather in Macedonia were from NATO countries, this was not officially a NATO force. The core was British and it was headed by the bluff, no-nonsense General Sir Mike Jackson. Britain pledged 8,000 troops to what was to be called the Kosovo Force or KFOR, the Germans 4,000 and the US 4,000.

7 Agreement for Peace?

At the time it seemed almost a foregone conclusion that Rambouillet would succeed. After all, the alternatives were so awful that it just seemed inconceivable that either side would scupper the talks. While the Serbs were being told that if they failed to sign up to the draft proposals they would be bombed, the Albanians were, in effect, being told that if failure was their fault, they would be left to the tender mercies of the Serbian security forces and paramilitaries. In other words, both were being told: 'Sign or die.' Given the starkness of this choice it is hardly surprising that most observers believed that, even while both sides would negotiate to the very last minute, they would close a deal. And, indeed, sources on both sides said, and believed, exactly that.

Still, while both sides were to turn up, it was not without much grumbling and complaint. Adem Demaçi counselled against going and was the most senior Kosovar not physically present in Rambouillet. As we shall see, however, he was very much able to inject himself into the working of the conference thanks to the delegates' mobile phones. On the Serbian side Živadin Jovanović, the Yugoslav foreign minister, wrote to the UN Security Council on 1 February saying that NATO's 30 January statement represented 'an open and clear threat of aggression'. He argued that because NATO's declaration did not have Security Council backing, it undercut 'the very foundations of the international legal order'.[1] His call for an emergency session of the council was turned down, because of US, British and French opposition, a move which according to Vladislav Jovanović, Yugoslavia's ambassador to the UN, represented a 'failure' of the council to 'perform its duties'.[2]

Four days later it was clear that, despite their reservations, both the Serbs and the Albanians would turn up. However, the first signs that the diplomats were beginning to get frightened that this modern version of gunboat diplomacy might actually fail came from one of the diplomatic crew. That evening, as gloom gathered over Whitehall, a British Foreign Office official who was putting the finishing touches to various documents to be presented to the parties confided that he was 'not particularly optimistic'. He had been at Dayton and in a chilling observation pointed out the crucial difference, in his view, between the Bosnian talks and these ones:

> In Bosnia everyone was ready – they were all exhausted. And, don't forget that three peace plans had already failed before we got to Dayton. The problem here is that we are trying to get them to agree to a deal before the war has really started. What we are concentrated on is a deal. It ought to satisfy both sides if they are rational about it … but both sides have not yet fought each other to a standstill …

Still, he noted that there was one ray of hope and that was that the Russians really seemed to be on board. 'It's been really striking. They've said, "We've had to be very brutal with Milošević and tell him that this is affecting our bilateral relations."' In the event, once the talks started, the Russians seemed to take a softer line on the Serbs, to the extent that many began to believe that they were acting as their attorneys rather than as a Great Power trying to solve a problem with other Great Powers.

The Bergerie Nationale

As far as the negotiators were concerned, most of the work on the future of Kosovo had already been done. Robin Cook, the British foreign secretary, said:

> Three quarters of the solution is already there … But we've done enough shuttling back and forth. In order to complete the work and fill in the remaining 25 per cent we have to have the parties together, which is the purpose of this meeting.

Bearing this in mind, and the fact that the major players believed they were holding guns to the heads of both the Serbs and the Albanians, there was a certain amount of theatre in what then followed. By chance, Rambouillet, an otherwise prosperous, suburban town, is home to the French *Bergerie Nationale*, which translates roughly as the National Sheep Pen or Sheep Farm. This venerable institution was founded by Louis XVI in 1786, just a few years before he lost his head. Its aim was, and remains, to train world-class shepherds and breed top-quality sheep. An explanatory leaflet shows a shepherd driving a flock through the farm's venerable portals with the practiced ease of a man well trained. The theatre lay in the fact that Robin Cook and Hubert Védrine hoped that by playing the role of stern euro-shepherds they could drive the respective delegations through the gates of the château where their sheep-dogs, in the shape of the negotiators, would corral them into doing what they wanted.

The first signs that things were not going to plan, though, was when the Albanian delegation did not turn up. An urbane British Foreign Office spokesman, trying to allay suspicions that panic was mounting behind the scenes, and unaware of the existence of the *Bergerie Nationale*, said: 'They are being gathered together and brought in.' In fact, an extraordinary problem was now developing. The Serbs declared that far from talking to delegates from the KLA, if they actually tried to come to the conference, they would arrest them. Ratko Marković, the constitutional lawyer who had been involved in the earlier abortive talks and who was the head of the Serbian delegation, declared that his team had no intention of talking to them and that the place for 'killers and kidnappers' was in court and not at the negotiating table. To this Wolfgang Petritsch remarked acidly: 'I really want to hear from him about how he envisages a real solution for Kosovo without the KLA.'

With a French military plane now on the tarmac waiting for the Kosovars at Priština airport, the KLA men, high in the hills, hesitated. Alerted by satellite phone as to the problem, their international diplomatic escorted convoy failed to move. Across Europe, mobiles were buzzing. Called from Rambouillet, one diplomat in Priština said: 'I don't know where they are. They haven't come down from the woods.' A rumour now spread across the continent. Because some of the KLA men, including Hashim Thaçi, had been indicted as criminals by the Serbian authorities, the French were said to have suggested that the KLA change their team. It hardly mattered whether the claim was true because tension was now turning into anger. From Geneva, Jashar Salihu barked that: 'If the KLA delegation is not allowed to leave, the talks are gone. We refused their proposal to form a new delegation and if the Contact Group can't get our delegation out and guarantee their lives then the talks are off.' Also in Switzerland, Bardhyl Mahmuti muttered darkly about a French 'conspiracy' to try and cut the guerrillas out of negotiations in a bid to secure a deal between the Serbs and Ibrahim Rugova.

Pulling out all the stops, the diplomats prevailed over the Serbs. The KLA men came down from the woods. The problem that some did not have passports was then overcome with the French issuing them with travel documents. Several hours late, the delegations marched up to the château. As if the trauma of the last few hours had not been enough, the Albanians were even more shocked at finding themselves all together, deadly enemies, some of whom had never met, some of whom had hated each other for years and some of whom had recently been making death threats against the others.

The sixteen-strong Albanian delegation was a veritable 'Who's Who' of the most important Kosovar politicians of the last decade. It included Rugova, Bukoshi and Agani for the LDK and the government-in-exile, Thaçi and Xhavit Haliti, two of the founders of the KLA, and Rexhep Qosja, the nationalist writer who commanded much respect and was now the leader of his own United Democratic Party, the LBD. The delegation also included Veton Surroi of *Koha Ditore* and Blerim Shala from *Zëri*. Because the LBD was close to the KLA, a vote on who should be the formal leader of the delegation selected Thaçi. However, it was also agreed that consensus would be needed for all decisions.

The contrast with the Serbian delegation was stark. It included no one of real stature, in the main because there is only one man who makes decisions in Serbia, and he was not there. The group was led by Ratko Marković and included Nikola Šainović, a Yugoslav deputy premier, Vladan Kutlešić, another constitutional lawyer and a Serbian deputy premier and Vladimir Štambuk, a lawyer who was also a senior member of JUL, Mira Marković's party.[3] Bishop Artemije also came to

Rambouillet saying that the delegation was unrepresentative, but he was not allowed in and had to brief journalists in the snow outside the château gates. The rest of Belgrade's team was made up of unknowns brought to Rambouillet to bolster Milošević's claim that his government was interested in a multinational Kosovo and that therefore representatives of *all* of its people, Gypsies (Roma), Turks and Slav Muslims had to be present. His delegation also included an Albanian called Faik Jashari, leader of an unheard-of pro-Serb party called the Albanian Democratic Initiative, otherwise reviled by the vast majority of Kosovars as a minuscule group of collaborationist traitors.

In principle, of course, Milošević had a point when he argued that representatives of all Kosovo's ethnic groups should have a say in the future of the province. The problem was that when he made such statements he was utterly insincere, just as when he insisted to the diplomats that his security forces were not doing what everyone had seen them doing. This is Chris Hill's assessment of such behaviour based on his months of negotiating with him:

> He tries to present himself as a model of ethnic tolerance. He points out that the test of democracy is not what it does for the majority but for the minority. There's a high bullshit quota there. There's a sense of being in another world. Either he is very poorly informed or he's a terrible liar or wishful thinking has encroached on his sense of reality. There is this concept of deluding yourself into believing you didn't do something you really did. Many criminals on death row think like this. It's a kind of self-hypnosis.

Not exactly the Congress of Vienna

For the people of Rambouillet, the war in Kosovo shattered their lives. On the morning of the day that it began, Saturday 6 February, a poster for the local paper screamed: 'Peace Conference: Market moved: Parking changed.' As grumbling market stallholders unfolded their trestle tables, evicted from their usual spot, the Quai d'Orsay, the French foreign ministry, was, like the Foreign Office in London, beginning to get that queasy feeling that maybe the threat of 'do or die' was not going to be enough to get the parties to sign up. And just in case it did not, the French were very gently beginning to downgrade Rambouillet even before it had started. 'Above all we do not want this to be seen as a test of Europe's common security and foreign policy,' said one official. It does not take much imagination to see how that would have changed if Rambouillet had succeeded. In a curious piece of symbolism, the French also insisted that what was about to happen was, contrary to false reports, not a *conférence* at all but simply a meeting. Presumably the arcane thinking behind this was that a conference could succeed or fail, while, people could just leave a simple *réunion*. Even more ominously, while saying little about the Serbs as potential deal-breakers, they began briefing senior French journalists about the threat from what they had taken to calling the 'Khmer Rouge' wing of the KLA.

As to the politicians who opened the talks, it is easy to be cynical about their lofty speeches, but in fact President Jacques Chirac made an undeniably noble and emotional appeal to the enemies. He compared their enmity with the Franco-German antagonism, which had led to three major wars between 1870 and 1945. It bears citing, especially in view of what would happen in the next few months:

> As you know, France has suffered the horrors of war. It has looked barbarity in the eye. But it has healed what were thought to be everlasting wounds. It has overcome supposedly ancestral hatreds. What France is saying today is that the will for peace can outweigh the temptation of war. This is particularly meaningful here where General de Gaulle and Chancellor Adenauer built a new future together. In building peace you must turn your gaze to a new horizon …. Let me say this to both parties, Serbs and Kosovo Albanians: peace is in your hands. I call upon your sense of duty. I call upon courage. Not the courage that leads to battle, to revenge and never-ending violence. But true courage, a greater and nobler form of courage. The courage to negotiate and make peace.

Robin Cook also noted that there was symbolism in the choice of location:

This château has not always been so peaceful. The castle which stood at this site has been attacked three times by the English. However, today Britain and France preside jointly over these talks – a symbol of the strong partnership which we have forged. Like all countries of the European Union we have learned that our peoples and their economies have gained far more from peace and stability than they ever gained from war or conflict.

As the delegates sat stiffly, in serried ranks, Serbs on one side of the room and Albanians on the other, he added:

A distinguished former resident of this château, President Clemenceau, once said: 'It is much easier to make war than make peace.' I understand the bitterness and distress created by the violence of the past year. But we do not honour those who have given their lives by prolonging the conflict in which more people will be killed.

In principle, the hosts had said the talks would last one week, after which there would be a review of progress and then, if necessary, the talks would be extended. The idea was that these should be proximity talks, that is to say that the negotiators would shuttle between the delegations. The Serbs, however, in a major U-turn, demanded face-to-face talks with the very same people who, only a few hours before, they had said should be in prison. The Albanians rejected this, arguing that they should start by drafting responses to the proposed Rambouillet text and should then (perhaps) meet only later. The negotiators were backed up by a formidable Contact Group legal team which was headed by the State Department's Jim O'Brien. He had played a key role in formulating the Dayton Accords and had garnered the nickname of Jim O'Brilliant.

The château was surprisingly small. One of the lawyers who was working inside commented that it 'was not exactly the Congress of Vienna' and that the Albanians found themselves lodged in small rooms, under the eaves, 'without en suite facilities'. Meanwhile everyone was furious when Italian diplomats, there as part of the Contact Group, the EU and the OSCE delegations locked up shower rooms and toilets for themselves and kept the keys. 'This was not five-star accommodation,' said the lawyer.

Both delegations were given formal conference rooms. The Albanians were given 'a fabulous marbled salon,' while the Serb room right above, 'was not so splendid'. Each room was equipped with a very obvious video camera and outside the château was a large lorry with blacked-out windows and cables trailing from it. Not unreasonably, the delegates assumed that nothing they said was private. Although they had sat next to each other during the opening speeches, neither would have to endure this painful ordeal again, apart from the odd ceremonial appearance. The large dining area was divided into two inter-connecting rooms with two buffets so the Serbs and Albanians neither had to eat nor queue together. Perhaps because he thought it beneath his dignity as 'president', Rugova did not serve himself from the buffet but had another member of the delegation do it for him.

As was to be expected, the meals were good and the average wine was a 1985 claret, good 'but not excessive,' according to the lawyer. At first, the delegates were given a choice of up to twelve different cheeses at every meal. However, in a previously unknown form of diplomatic pressure, this dropped to a single brie, at precisely the moment when the diplomats were at their most desperate to force the delegates to reach a deal. For future reference, an eminent international lawyer, who asks for anonymity, has dubbed this 'the cheese signal'. Simultaneously the French claimed there was no more cognac, but it is unknown whether this too will, in future, be cited as evidence of precedent, in the development of international law.

It is of course a cliché that the real work in international conferences is actually done in the corridors rather than around the negotiating table. Rambouillet proved the exception to the rule. Members of both delegations ignored each other when they passed in the corridors.

In general, the atmosphere inside the château was rather sober, except for quarrels within the Albanian camp, and increasing boredom amongst those members of the Yugoslav delegation who, as we have noted, were only there as token ethnic representatives. To the irritation of the Albanians and others, they tended to congregate in various public parts of the château and gossip, a fact which earned them the nickname of the 'tea club'. Even more irritating was the fact that they would

30. Rugova meets NATO during the bombing. On his left is Jamie Shea, NATO spokesman. 18 May 1999, Brussels.

31. *From left to right:* General Wesley Clark, SACEUR, US President Bill Clinton, NATO Secretary General Javier Solana. 5 May 1999.

32. United Front: Viktor Chernomyrdin (*left*) and Martti Ahtisaari (*right*) face Slobodan Milošević. On his right is Milan Milutinović, the president of Serbia.

33. Bernard Kouchner, Head of UNMIK.

34. Albanian refugees return home, KFOR deploys, June 1999.

35. KFOR troops in Priština, June 1999.

36. Revenge: Albanians looting the Serbian church in Vučitrn, June 1999.

37. Veton Surroi, (*left, in dark suit*) politician and publisher of *Koha Ditore* and Hashim Thaçi, KLA leader, (*right, in light suit*) Priština, June 1999.

38. British soldier, Albanian looter. Priština, June 1999.

39. Revenge: Three Serbs executed at Priština University. June 1999.

40. Slobodan Milošević and his wife Mira Marković go to the theatre.

41. Serbs flee Kosovo as NATO-led troops deploy and Albanian refugees return home.

KOSOVO POLJE

42. Kosovo Polje, 1389–1999. Serbs in flight.

keep much of the rest of the château awake by late-night carousing and the singing of Serbian songs, which induced the negotiators to complain. A piano was also brought in to the château but whether this was for the Serbs, or, as has also been suggested, for Boris Mayorski, remains a point of dispute.

While the Serbs had their Paris embassy as back-up, and teams of experts and ministries back home, the Kosovars, of course, did not. Likewise the only members of the Serbian delegation who counted were in fact the country's best constitutional lawyers. By contrast, the Albanian delegation was a collection of important personalities, politicians and fighters. They clearly lacked the skills necessary to examine complex legal documents and, without expert advice, would be vulnerable to, say, agreeing to one thing without understanding that it might be nullified by something else. To make up for this the Kosovars assembled a team of advisers, or rather Bujar Bukoshi thought it prudent to bring them. They included Morton Abramowitz, a former State Department official, the president of the International Crisis Group, and, not insignificantly, a close friend of Madeleine Albright. Also there were Paul Williams, a Washington-based international lawyer and Marc Weller, a German international lawyer who teaches at Cambridge University. The KLA men, who had, until Saturday, been fighting in the hills, were initially taken aback by this and were alarmed by the presence of advisers whom they regarded as having been recruited by the enemy, that is to say, the Bukoshi camp, and so they insisted on their own. Their principal external adviser was to be Shinasi Rama, a doctoral student at Columbia University in New York, who, although from Albania, had roots in Kosovo. He had also been acting as a KLA spokesman in New York.

At first the French had made no provision for the advisers and were keen to keep them out, but they were eventually forced to relent on this point, allowing each delegation five passes a day. Before this was sorted out, on Monday 8 February, Marc Weller had to spend five hours standing in the snow outside the château gates before being allowed in. The initial idea had been to segregate the delegates and indeed their passes were marked in such a way that the château guards would block their way if they tried to leave. In fact, such seclusion proved impossible, thanks to mobile phones. Lacking an embassy, important Kosovars milled around in the cafés of Rambouillet until their own press office was opened. Among the Kosovars briefing journalists, both on and off the record, were Visar Reka, Rexhep Qosja's son-in-law from Geneva, Pleurat Sejdiu from London, Ibrahim Kelmendi, the chairman of the Homeland Calling fund in Germany and important fund-raisers from the United States.

Que sera, sera

As the conference began, the delegations had two documents to consider. The first, which had actually been given to them a few days earlier, was a one-page list of 'non-negotiable principles' and 'basic elements' which had been endorsed by the Contact Group on 30 January. Besides making reference to the territorial integrity of Yugoslavia, human rights and the fact that what was to be discussed was an interim agreement for three years (not a final settlement of Kosovo's future), there were also some very vague points about implementation. For example: 'participation of OSCE and other international bodies as necessary'. In other words, there was no reference here either to NATO or to the necessity of any foreign troops to implement the agreement – but neither did these 'non-negotiable principles' rule them out.[4]

The second document given to the delegations was the Interim Agreement for Peace and Self-Government in Kosovo. While this talked about a ceasefire, an assembly and elections, certain key elements, including the provisions on implementation, were not included. So, on 8 February, Blerim Shala delivered an oral submission to the negotiators saying that as far as the Kosovars were concerned the document had to include, among other things, a clause on a referendum on independence and it had to define the future role of the KLA. The Albanians now set up a drafting committee nominally led by Fehmi Agani and including Jakup Krasniqi, the KLA spokesman, which with the help of its foreign advisers began working on written responses to the texts.

The Serbian delegation made opening comments and then to the surprise of everyone else fell more or less silent for the next ten days. Why they did this is anyone's guess. They tried to insist, for example, that both sides sign the 'non-negotiable principles', perhaps because of its insistence on Yugoslavia's territorial integrity and because it said nothing about implementation by foreign troops. Perhaps for the same reasons, the Albanians refused. The fact that the Serbs seemed to be doing nothing rapidly led to an increasing sense of frustration and eventually panic among the negotiators. The Serb move, or rather lack of one, appeared predicated on the assumption that the Albanians would ultimately reject the document and hence have to shoulder the blame for the conference's collapse. The reason for this was that they knew from the Russians that in Contact Group meetings before Rambouillet it had been agreed that the word 'referendum' could not appear in the final text, and this was because everyone understood that in the event of a referendum the Kosovo Albanians would always win thanks to their overwhelming numerical superiority in the province.

The tactic adopted by the Albanians was to say: 'Yes, but ...' That is to say that their comments on the text were generally prefixed by noting that they were 'acceptable' but that they should be supplemented by other points. The Albanians disliked provisions in the initial draft because they gave powers to the 'national communities' as well as an assembly and, above all the communes, i.e., local governments. In theory the powers given to the 'national communities' meant that no one group could dominate the other. The Albanians feared, however, that, in reality, this would give the Serbs a veto on anything and everything in Kosovo. By contrast, the Albanians liked the fact that there was virtually no reference to Serbia or Yugoslavia. They also believed that the reconstruction of the police on a local level meant that a good proportion of KLA members could simply change uniforms and so take over the police force in most regions. They submitted their points ... but got no reply. In fact, the legal adviser Marc Weller now concludes that simply by being so cooperative to begin with, the Albanians were sending out the wrong signals. He has written:

> Unfortunately, Kosovo's reasonable written comments may have deceived the negotiators into thinking that the Kosovo delegation was fully united behind the Rambouillet project and willing to sign up to any political settlement provided it brought NATO enforcement with it.[5]

This attitude of taking the Albanian delegation for granted meant that the negotiators were simply putting off dealing with very fundamental problems. In the short term, though, they were worried by the lack of any Serbian reaction to the initial draft. This prompted Hill to fly to Belgrade on 16 February where he met Milošević who had already been phoned by Madeleine Albright earlier in the day. Immediately afterwards the Serbs produced a major document responding to the draft. This enraged the Albanians because they felt they had been made fools of. Not only was it obvious that the Serb delegates in Rambouillet had no power but it now looked as though the real work on the papers was being done back in Belgrade and not in the château. In the meantime the Contact Group extended the conference until 20 February. The negotiators now formulated a new text, which they produced 48 hours before the scheduled end of the meeting, which left the Albanians in state of shock. Not only did it incorporate certain key Serb demands but it ignored most of the Kosovar comments which they had been formulating over the last ten days. An important consideration was, as Weller points out, that 'the new draft reintroduced the issue of the legal status of Kosovo ... and sought to resolve it firmly in favour of Belgrade'.[6] Looking back, Weller says now: 'It was such a foolish thing to put in. It was this moment where 100 years of foreigners imposing their will on Albanians appeared to come true again.' The document also reintroduced a more formal veto mechanism for the 'national communities'. Faced with this the Kosovars came to close to walking out – but did not because this was exactly what the Serbs had been hoping they would do all along. They were, however, beginning to ask themselves why they were there.

Until this point all the work on the Albanian side had been done by the small drafting committee. In meetings of the whole team Rugova said virtually nothing and thus contributed nothing either. Bukoshi was very quiet until just before the end. Thaçi took little interest in what the committee was doing and there were embarrassing scenes with the negotiators when, at certain key points, it became evident that he did not know what was happening. Much of his time was spent wandering about the château talking on his mobile phone to people outside while failing to give leadership inside. Chris Hill says he thinks that

Thaçi never read the documents. By contrast, Jakup Krasniqi, who until now had gained the reputation of being a Stalinist schoolmaster from Drenica, not only read the documents but contributed to the debate. He had been surprised by Thaçi's emergence into the public eye over the last few weeks, especially as he had wanted to be the first premier of the new Kosovo himself. Managing these disparate elements fell to Veton Surroi who, according to one observer present, was not just 'the voice of reason' but, towards the end, 'the only one who could get anything moving'.

That the proceedings were going seriously wrong now began to be reflected in the contradictory and even erratic statements that the negotiators were making in public. For example, on 18 February, Chris Hill, asked at a press conference about the military implementation part of the proposed deal, said that there had been a 'very full discussion of the military aspects … and I think, speaking from the point of view of the United States, we consider these military aspects essential to the completion of this settlement.' Boris Mayorski immediately chimed in, saying: 'I can add to this that there was no official presentation of any military annexes to the delegations up to now.' He then continued:

> 'Que sera, sera.' I hope you know this song, and you know the name of the film from which it was taken. I think it was called 'The Man who Knew too Much'. Doris Day and … And the second thing is that, if there were discussions on military – active discussions on military aspects of the – Now, speaking as a Russian representative, I can assure you that we were not taking part in those discussions.[7]

In fact, it seems that the military annexe had been presented or certainly would be presented on the same day, but, with the countdown to the end of the talks now having begun, it was clear that the central problems had neither been resolved nor even properly tackled. The KLA also now went into shock because, for the first time, they were having to face the reality, as it was explained to them by a senior US military man, that they 'would disappear'. This prompted statements from KLA spokesmen abroad and officers on the ground that neither would they disappear nor had they any intention of disarming. Upping the ante, Pleurat Sejdiu said: 'The armed struggle will not stop until the independence of Kosovo,' and added that he did not consider that the arrival of NATO troops in Kosovo would mean its liberation. 'Our forces will be those who liberate Kosovo,' he said.

The problem, when it came to the Serbs, was different. First of all, Appendix B, as it was called, (it has also been referred to as Annex B) gave NATO troops:

> together with their vehicles, vessels, aircraft, free and unrestricted passage throughout the FRY including associated airspace and territorial waters. This shall include, but not be limited to, the right of bivouac, maneuver, billet, and utilization of any areas or facilities as required for support, training and operations.[8]

Later the Serbs would claim that this was tantamount to an attempt to occupy the whole of Serbia and hence one of the major reasons why they rejected the whole package. In fact, what is far more likely is that the 'cock-up' theory of history should apply. That is to say that the annexe had been drawn up by NATO officers who, having been told that that implementation was non-negotiable, proceeded to draft a sort of military wish-list. Although it was based on standard UN peacekeeping drafts, it was indeed somewhat more expansive than the norm. However, since the Serbs now, as earlier, refused to discuss the principle of a NATO-led implementation force, these points were not raised at Rambouillet. If they had been, and the Serbs had accepted the principle of some form of foreign military deployment, then, in exchange, such rights could certainly have been whittled down significantly. As it was, Serb officials just kept repeating that there could be no deployment of foreign troops, a message which was reinforced in the wake of Hill's visit to Belgrade. A statement released following his meeting with the Yugoslav president reported that:

> Milošević said that the negative attitude to the presence of foreign troops is not that of the government alone, but is shared by the people as well. It is also … the unanimous position of the popular representatives in the national parliament, regardless of party affiliation.[9]

Other major problems with the draft were that no one knew what the mechanism would be for determining Kosovo's fate after three years, and the Kosovars were still insisting that there *had* to be a referendum on independence. So, while there were indeed significant sections of the various drafts that both sides could agree to, neither side was any the closer to accepting the very essence of the deal. That is to say, Serb acceptance of NATO deployment in exchange for the Albanians giving up their demand for a referendum. In this way, the diplomats counted on freezing the conflict, perhaps for far longer than the three-year interim period now under discussion, and anyway they hoped that by that time Milošević would be gone, so making it easier to strike a final status deal with a more flexible government in Belgrade.

Diplomats will never admit to panic. They prefer to concede weasel words like 'extremely concerned' and then smile knowingly. If ever there was a textbook case of 'extreme concern', then this was it. The talks were due to finish at midday on 20 February – and, as we have noted, there was still no agreement on fundamentals. With both sides rejecting key parts of the proposed text that they had seen, and the Serbs still refusing to agree to any military implementation force, the negotiators resorted to a desperate manoeuvre. With no final document to sign, and just a few hours before the deadline, they simply asked both sides to sign a letter which, in effect, said that they both accepted the agreement apart from a few technical details. Unsurprisingly, neither side even contemplated signing what amounted to a blank cheque. On 19 February Hill went to Belgrade again, where Milošević refused to meet him. He did, however, find time to meet a delegation from the Cypriot parliament whom he informed that his government 'would not give Kosovo–Metohjia away even at the cost of bombardment'.[10]

Staring failure in the face, the Contact Group decided to extend the talks for another three days. By now, the British and French foreign ministers appeared to have faded from the scene and Madeleine Albright herself had been deployed in a bid to apply extreme pressure. The key meetings took place with Milan Milutinović, the Serbian president, now working out of the Yugoslav embassy in Paris, and Hashim Thaçi. After meeting Milutinović, Albright said that although he had told her that he could accept the political deal, 'the Serb refusal to even consider the presence of a NATO-led military implementation force … is largely responsible for the failure to reach full agreement.' Urging Milošević to 'wake up and smell the coffee' she said that the Serb refusal to 'engage at all on the security part … is a complete non-starter, because a political agreement without the military annexes is just a piece of paper. The security annexes are needed in order to implement the political agreement.'[11] One source recalls how Madeleine Albright then came to appeal to the whole Albanian delegation:

> She said: 'We are not asking you to abandon your dreams but to show a sense of realism.' They were utterly unmoved. They didn't care. Personally they admired her and they didn't want to offend her, but the delegation had not discussed what it was supposed to sign. She said, 'look at the text' – but there wasn't one. The understanding was that there would be bombing [if they signed and the Serbs did not] but they didn't take it seriously. They were not persuaded of it.

Pleurat Sejdiu says that it is an 'open secret' that while sequestered with Hashim Thaçi, Albright was telling him that his delegation had to sign because otherwise NATO could not carry out its threat. If that was not enough, though, Jamie Rubin, the State Department spokesman, who had struck up a relationship with Thaçi and was walking with him in the gardens of the château, now made it as clear as he possibly could, without actually being crude, what the Albanians were being told. On 21 February he briefed the press, saying:

> We believe it is extremely important to put pressure on the Serbs. We cannot put the full amount of pressure if we don't get an agreement from the Kosovar Albanians. Contrary to what many of you seem to believe, it has never been the view of NATO or the United States that a Serb refusal along with a Kosovar Albanian refusal would necessarily lead to NATO military action. All of the officials who have worked on this have made very clear that in order to move towards military action, it has to be clear that the Serbs were responsible.[12]

The problem was that the Kosovars would not budge. Not knowing, of course, that at the very last minute the Serbs might not suddenly agree to the deal, they were frightened that they might sign and without an explicit commitment to a referendum, find themselves trapped inside Yugoslavia forever. It is important to remember that even the best-informed Serbs still believed that at the very last minute Milošević would indeed strike a deal. So, to reassure the Kosovars, the source who had been at the meetings with Albright and others recalls that they were being told that, in the event of a deal, 'You'll get NATO to protect your people. Don't mind the small print because you will be running the show and many of the problems in the text will be irrelevant.' But when the delegates pointed out that they would have difficulty selling an agreement which did not include their central demand of a referendum, they were told that although they could not have independence (at least for now), they could still go back to their constituents 'and say that nothing had been abandoned'. Meanwhile the negotiators had by now come up with a formulation of words which they hoped might entice the Kosovars. They are enshrined in the document that they did sign two weeks later. Instead of a referendum, it stated that:

> three years after the entry into force of the agreement an international meeting shall be convened to determine a mechanism for a final settlement for Kosovo, on the basis of the will of the people, opinions of relevant authorities, each Party's efforts regarding the implementation of this Agreement, and the Helsinki Final Act ...[13]

The Kosovars were faced with a terrible dilemma. If they refused the deal then the war would go on, they would lose international sympathy and indeed they might lose an historic chance to begin a process which might (or might not) end in independence. Whether or not it could have been done, they were also being told that western countries would take vigorous action to choke off diaspora funding for the KLA, and that troops from NATO countries might be deployed on the Albanian border with Kosovo to cut arms supplies; and the threat that the US and other Western countries might yet declare the KLA a terrorist group hung in the air. On the other hand, as the lawyers pointed

out, the wording of the new key paragraph was cleverly constructed so that it gave something to the Serbs as well. The
Helsinki Final Act guarantees the territorial integrity of states
and so, even if the 'will of the people' did mean a referendum on
independence, it did not mean that any 'international meeting'
was bound to respect that over respect for international borders.

For Albright, a huge amount of prestige was now riding on
Rambouillet, or at least getting the Albanians to sign. But she
simply could not understand why Thaçi was holding out,
especially as it was clear that, unless the Serbs changed their
mind, an Albanian signature could trigger the bombing. According to one senior US diplomat, Albright was now living through
'the most difficult moments of her secretaryship'. Originally, he
said, she had thought Thaçi 'wonderful', now he was 'odious'
but later he would be restored to favour again. Still, as the
diplomat points out, 'when she realised that those little assholes
were going to stick it to the Secretary of State she had some
rough moments'.

For Thaçi, far more than prestige was at stake. His life was on
the line. On the phone he was being hectored by Demaçi who
was screaming at him that the commanders in the field would
never accept the deal without a cast-iron guarantee of an
independence referendum after three years. So, if he signed a
document which did not contain the magic word, he risked
being condemned as a traitor. Since he had been one of the men
in charge, he well knew that the price of treachery was death.
Meanwhile, the Serbian authorities, in a bid to try and prompt an
Albanian walk-out from Rambouillet, not only stepped up
military activity on the ground but asked Interpol to issue an
international arrest warrant for Thaçi.[14] He was also receiving
death threats. By now, he was so paranoid that when one of
the diplomats offered him a glass of wine he refused saying
that people were out to poison him. He drank half a bottle of his
own whisky instead. The diplomat recalls that, uncertain what
to do, 'Thaçi was almost in tears.' But he decided to stand his
ground.

A full meeting of the Albanian delegation now voted on
whether or not to sign up to the deal, even though they still did
not have the full text in front of them. It was nine to seven
against. Thaçi, the four other KLA men and Qosja and his

people voted against. Rugova, Bukoshi, the three other LDK delegates plus Veton Surroi and Blerim Shala voted in favour.

During the night of 21–2 February the American lawyers in the château spent more time working on the Albanians. At 5.25 on the morning of the 22 February they delivered a draft letter which was supposed to be signed by Madeleine Albright, if things had gone to plan. The disputed words 'will of the people' were substituted by 'expressed will of the people'. A covering letter was appended to the sheet with the suggested new wording, which read as follows:

> Rambouillet, 22 February 1999
> This letter concerns the formulation (attached) proposed for Chapter 8, Article 1 (3) of the interim Framework Agreement. We will regard this proposal, or any other formulation, of that Article that may be agreed at Rambouillet, as confirming a right for the people of Kosovo to hold a referendum on the final status of Kosovo after three years.
> Sincerely,
> Madeleine Albright, Secretary of State

According to Marc Weller, 'The US took the position that it [this proposal] would only be available should Kosovo sign the agreement by the deadline.'[15] The Kosovars did not sign there and then and, as the morning wore on, Russia and the other Contact Group countries discovered what had happened and began to protest. One source says: 'The Russians said: "Are you mad? 'Expressed' means a referendum!"' So, the Contact Group refused to endorse the proposal and the KLA refused to sign. 'Everyone ambled about,' says the source, 'Agani was pacing up and down the room in silence. He thought it was good deal.' By the morning of 23 February a final text was ready. Shinasi Rama, the adviser from New York, who had been against acceptance, found himself barred when he tried to enter the château. Back in Brooklyn Florin Krasniqi, the KLA's chief fund-raiser in the US, had been receiving menacing telephone calls from people who did not identify themselves but warned him that unless he did something to encourage acceptance his operation would be closed down. Although his instincts were against signing, he says, 'they were tapping my phones' so he called

KLA commanders on the ground on the satellite phones he had bought them and told them they should back the deal. 'I agreed because of the pressure. There was no way out.'

Back in Rambouillet the Albanians found their emotions now under pressure – not just their sense of *realpolitik*. Ismail Kadare, the most famous living Albanian author, a man considered a veritable icon by Kosovars and who now lived in Paris, wrote to them appealing for their signature. His letter was read out by his friend Qosja, 'with great pathos,' says the source. Later Kadare recalled that, that night, he could not sleep for worry. 'So, between three and four in the morning I wrote the letter and then I calmed down. At nine o'clock my wife typed it.' The Albanian embassy then delivered the missive. 'It was necessary. I understood that they were hesitating, they were tired, they could not judge things and so I took the responsibility upon myself.'

Kadare's letter was followed by an appeal by Paskal Milo, the Albanian foreign minister who had been flown in specially. He told them that unless they signed, Kosovo would be isolated and indeed virtually 'cease to exist'. It was enough. Almost everyone was ready to sign. Except Thaçi. As he stood alone now, he said that he had resigned as leader of the delegation. Still, he was summoned anew for a session with Madeleine Albright but he only succeeded in infuriating her with his stubbornness. Back in the delegation conference room Jakup Krasniqi pounded the table, informing everyone that he intended to be prime minister. After his session with Albright, Thaçi returned and assumed the chairmanship of the meeting. 'No one dared remind him that he had resigned,' says the source. Thaçi thundered that if the others went ahead and signed he would say that the KLA disowned the agreement. Krasniqi remained silent but the other KLA men made clear they would side with Thaçi. At this point Surroi began working on a solution, because he understood the disastrous implications for the Albanians if the Serbs could pin a failure on them. From Kosovo, though, came alarming news. To their horror, the delegates heard that Adem Demaçi appeared to have orchestrated some form of *coup d'état*, saying that the KLA men in Rambouillet did not represent the organisation and naming Sylejman Selimi, the Drenica commander, as its new head.

An hour past the deadline, Hill entered the room and asked the delegates if anyone was ready to sign the document. This led to an awkward silence. One of the problems was that according to the rules of the delegation, any decisions required a consensus. According to Surroi, 'Thaçi mumbled something,' and then Rugova piped up, suggesting that he sign in his capacity as 'President of the Republic'. Thaçi responded that if he did this, he would oppose the agreement. Everyone else shuffled uneasily, not knowing what to do. A new silence was broken by Surroi, who announced that they had, indeed, reached a consensus. It was untrue but, bearing in mind the gravity of the situation, Surroi was thinking fast, trying to salvage the situation. He said that the Kosovars would accept the agreement in principle but needed time to consult with people back home. Meanwhile, as the Serbs were now talking seriously about the political side of the agreement, Surroi's move sought to freeze the document, to ensure that it could no longer be changed in favour of the Serbs. As these discussions carried on, one of the Russians delegates kept coming in and out of the room to find out what was happening and to report back to the Serbs.

Surroi moved over to the computer along with Jim O'Brien, the State Department lawyer, and Dukagjin Gorani, one of the delegation translators, who was also one of his *Koha Ditore* journalists. The lean, goatee-bearded Gorani sat down to type. Hill and Thaçi milled around while the rest of the delegation waited. In his hand Surroi had three scribbled versions of his consensus idea. While charges of treason came from Demaçi back home, Surroi says that the problem was not about 'signing a postponement but whether to sign at all. However instead of saying that we were asking for a delay we said we were ready to sign but needed to consult about the document in its entirety.' So, the letter they typed to the negotiators began: 'This declaration is given with full consensus. The Delegation of Kosova with consensus understands that it will sign the agreement in two weeks after consultations with the people of Kosova, political and military institutions.' It went to on to state that NATO deployment was an 'essential part of the agreement' and that it was understood that 'at the end of the interim period of three years, Kosova will hold a referendum to ascertain the will of the people ...' Finished, the letter was handed over to the negotiators at 4.00 p.m. At this point Edita Tahiri, Rugova's foreign affairs adviser, and the other Kosovar women in the room including translators, began crying, believing that everything was over. Everyone, including the negotiators, was thoroughly confused, no one really understanding what had or had not been agreed to. Still, one senior US diplomat goes as far as to say that 'Surroi saved the US government by keeping the talks in suspension.' Hill, borrowing an American football term, called the manoeuvre the 'Hail Mary pass'.

There was no less tension in the Serbian camp. Milošević's strategy appeared to be based on two factors. The first was his gamble that the Albanians would refuse to sign and the second was scepticism that NATO countries really intended to carry out their threat to bomb. As the conference drew to a close, it was becoming clearer that he might well have miscalculated.

A few days earlier the Yugoslav press reported with glee that on 18 February Russian President Boris Yeltsin had said that he had 'conveyed to Clinton my view, both by phone and by letter, that this [threatened military strikes against Yugoslavia] will not work ... We will not let you touch Kosovo.' Apart from the fact that the White House denied it had ever got such a message, it was also clear by now that the US and the other leading NATO countries, while politely acknowledging Russian objections, were not going to listen to them either. 'The United States and Russia would both prefer a political settlement, but NATO has made it clear it is prepared to take action,' said a White House spokesman.[16]

If this strategy looked as if it was failing, then Milošević would have to hope that the Albanians refused to sign. The problem was that, just like everyone else, he did not know what they would do. This is reflected in the series of three letters sent by Ratko Marković to the negotiators as the conference drew to a close. The first contained a list of elements that the Serbs agreed upon and also enumerated points on which 'we did not reach agreement'. A few hours later a second letter arrived asking for a date on which to resume talks, and adding that the Yugoslav government had agreed to discuss 'the scope and character' of an 'international presence' in Kosovo to 'implement the agreement to be accepted in Rambouillet'. This was not exactly an endorsement of a NATO-led force – but it did not rule out discussion of it either. At 4.00 p.m. another letter arrived. This came at a point where Hill had thought that the Albanians had agreed to sign, and where, in fact, they began the discussion about acceptance in principle. Keen not to be caught out, and also keen, like the Albanians, to 'freeze' the document where it stood, Marković in this letter dropped any reference to points of disagreement, simply reiterating lines of fulsome praise from the earlier letters about the 'major progress' that had been achieved and noting that the delegation looked forward to 'continue the work, in line with the positive spirit of this meeting'.[17]

Bearing in mind this series of messages coming from both the Albanians and the Serbs, it is hardly surprising that the negotiators and their political masters emerged somewhat dazed and confused from the conference. In a concluding statement the co-chairmen, Cook and Védrine, said that 'a political framework is now in place' and that 'the groundwork has thereby been laid for finalising the implementation Chapters of the Agreement, including the modalities of the invited international civilian and military presence in Kosovo'. The first part, about an agreement being in place, was simply not true, because although the Serbs had talked of major progress, even their letter had not suggested that they agreed with everything. However, confusion arose because, in a final meeting, Milošević had given the foreign ministers the impression that he had agreed to the political part of the agreement. It was not enough, though, so, by inviting the delegates back to Paris on 15 March, the diplomats were throwing the Serbs a lifeline. Although, in theory, implementation was 'non-negotiable', they were in effect giving Milošević time to prepare for a climbdown and even time for some form of compromise to be worked out on this question. For example, although the US and Britain had made it very clear that the implementation force had to be NATO-led, with NATO 'command and control' structures, if Milošević had asked for a face-saving deal whereby these troops would wear UN blue berets but still be NATO commanded, then it is more than likely that such a deal could have been struck.

Three months later, during the bombing of Yugoslavia, Chris Hill sat in the garden of the US embassy in Skopje. Asked whether he and his fellow negotiators would indeed have agreed to such a face-saver for Milošević, he said that there is no doubt they would have done. The problem was, he recalls, that the Serbs simply 'would not engage' on the question at all. He added: 'If the Serbs had said "Yes" to the force but "No" to the independent judiciary – and insisted on all sanctions relief – do you think we could have bombed?' Hill believes that Milošević was open to a political deal but wanted to avoid the military lement that came with it because 'he felt that the true intention of the force was to eliminate him – and/or detach Kosovo from Serbia. In fact, there was nothing in the political agreement which was unsellable to Serbs … the agreement reiterates the sovereignty of Yugoslavia.'

Before they left Rambouillet the Albanians did one more thing which was to have long-term consequences. The KLA men, Rugova and Qosja signed an agreement on the formation of a 'provisional government'.

Of course, in the first couple of days after Rambouillet, it was still not clear that a deal would not be struck in Paris. In the meantime the Kosovars returned home and Thaçi travelled through KLA-held areas where he discovered that not only did the vast majority of Kosovars want the deal but also that there was less to Demaçi's 'coup' than he had been led to believe. Only a few commanders were really dead set against the deal. Abandoning his previous stance he began to convince the doubters that the Kosovars had to sign. Pleurat Sejdiu recalls: 'He wanted people's approval, especially in places like Drenica, but he didn't care about those who weren't fighting, like in Priština.' To encourage the Albanians, Madeleine Albright also despatched Bob Dole, the former Senate majority leader who had first visited Kosovo in 1990 and had since been a strong supporter of their cause ever since. According to one diplomatic source, 'It was an inspired idea. Dole had a lot of leverage over the Albanians and Albanian-Americans and he told the Kosovars, "We'll abandon you if you don't sign".' Refused a visa by the Yugoslav authorities, who did not want the Kosovars to be talked into signing, he met them in Skopje.

If both sides had agreed to Rambouillet, both Serbs and Albanians would have lost something but both would have gained something too and thousands who were die in the next few weeks would still be alive. NATO would have deployed a force of some 30,000 men. Over the next six months Serb and

Yugoslav forces would have been withdrawn. However, 1,500 lightly armed border troops would have remained, plus 1,000 support personnel. The police would have been cut down to 2,500 but that force would have been replaced after a year by a local police force in which it was intended that local Serbs would have participated. The KLA would have been 'demilitarised' but exactly how, or to what extent, was not clear. Although Kosovo would have been a highly autonomous part of Serbia, it would still have sent deputies to the Serbian and Yugoslav parliaments. The problem that Milošević had pinpointed in the late 1980s, i.e., that while Kosovo had a say in the running of Serbia, Serbia had no say in Kosovo and in particular could not safeguard the Serbs there, would have been circumvented by the establishment of institutions for he 'national communities' which were supposed to operate alongside the national and locally elected bodies. The Kosovars believed that the interim deal would have led to independence, but this was not a foregone conclusion. The institutions of the 'national communities' could have protected the interests of the Serbs, who although life might have been difficult, would not have had to face the incandescent anger of vengeful Albanians returning home after what was to become a 78-day orgy of violence and ethnic cleansing. Some Serbs passionately believe that Rambouillet was a disaster and was but an interim measure to ease Kosovo on the way to independence. By contrast, others believe it was a unique opportunity and the last chance to strike an historic compromise. By definition, nobody knows. Rambouillet is now the great 'what if...?' of modern Balkan history.

In the days running up to the reconvening of the talks, all the signs were that an Albanian signature would be forthcoming while hopes of a last-minute change of heart from Milošević began to recede. Rumours swirled round Belgrade that Milutinović wanted a deal, but that hardliners, such as General Dragoljub Ojdanić, chief of the Yugoslav army general staff, Serbian interior minister Vlajko Stojiljković, and foreign minister Živadin Jovanović were dead set against. Perhaps they believed that the NATO threat was a bluff, or they could not believe that the Albanians really would outmanoeuvre them by signing. After a few days, shrill commentaries in the press made it clear which way Milošević was going to jump. Besides, as we shall see, military and other preparations were being set in train. Until the archives are opened (or one of Milošević's tiny group of confidantes tells us), this could either mean that he was keeping his options open to the very last minute or that he had already decided to gamble on a rejection.

Now an enthusiastic convert to Rambouillet, Thaçi shocked his own delegation on the return to Paris on 15 March. Having realised that, in the age of the mobile phone, it was impossible to isolate conference delegates, the French did not bother to try this time. The new round of talks was held in the International Conference Centre on the avenue Kléber. When the negotiators opened the first session with the Albanians, Thaçi embarrassed his colleagues by announcing that they would be 'honoured to sign the Agreement in your presence at a time and place of your choosing'. The other delegates had not been informed of what was coming. Because the negotiators were still trying to engage the Serbs, they asked Thaçi to wait before signing. Over the next few days the Albanians were treated to lectures on implementation by NATO officers and, in the words of one source, the KLA and LBD members, 'sat around plotting to remove Rugova'. They did not appear to take much notice of the increasing fighting on the ground nor to be thinking much about the inferno that was to come.

The reception received by the negotiators when they met the Serbs was different to say the least. Far from wanting to discuss implementation, the delegates handed the negotiators a new version of the Rambouillet agreement. About half of the original text had simply been struck out and a Serbian wish list had been written in. The word 'peace' had been crossed out and every mention of the word 'Kosovo' had also been crossed out and replaced with the Serbian 'Kosmet'. That meant that the title now looked like this:

~~Interim~~ Agreement for ~~Peace and~~ Self-Government in ~~Kosovo~~ Kosmet

Even Boris Mayorski, the Russian negotiator, was shocked. Paragraphs and even whole chapters that had taken months of work were simply crossed out and replaced with other clearly unacceptable paragraphs or nothing at all. The whole chapter on humanitarian assistance and reconstruction had simply gone and

the final key lines about the 'will of the people' and a substitute
Serbian paragraph looked like this:

> ~~Three years after the entry into force of this Agreement, an~~
> ~~international meeting shall be convened to determine a~~
> ~~mechanism for a final settlement for Kosovo, on the basis~~
> ~~of the will of the people, opinions of relevant authorities,~~
> ~~each Party's efforts regarding the implementation of this~~
> ~~Agreement, and the Helsinki Final Act, and to undertake a~~
> ~~comprehensive assessment of the implementation of this~~
> ~~Agreement and to consider proposals by any Party for~~
> ~~additional measures.~~
>
> After three years, the signatories shall comprehensively
> review this Agreement with a view to improving its
> implementation and shall consider the proposals of any
> signatory for additional measures, whose adoption shall
> require the consent of all signatories.[18]

Wolfgang Petritsch recalls that Ratko Marković was silent and
apparently embarrassed by what had happened. Some of the
other delegates were not. One source recalls how the negotiators
fled the Serbian room looking shaken and either pale or red-
faced, as they were greeted with a hail of invective such as 'Have
you come to fuck us again?' Another diplomat believes that the
Serbian fury was in part provoked because they had been caught
off guard:

> At Rambouillet I think that Serbian Intelligence had
> picked up that they were not going to sign but it let them
> down over Paris. I was in the coffee bar in the Kléber
> Centre and the Yugoslav delegation were all there
> laughing. Then, a junior foreign ministry official, whom
> I recognised, came running in and said: 'They are going to
> sign!' Their faces dropped and they all charged out.

In this situation there was little to be done. On 18 March the
Kosovars signed the Agreement. While Hill and Petritsch
witnessed the signatures, Mayorski refused to. Since he had
never indicated there was a problem with the text before, this
was somewhat surprising, but clearly, in view of what was
happening and about to happen Russia had decided to
distance itself from the process. After all, Russia was about to

be humiliated by its failure to stop NATO taking action, but perhaps even more humiliating was Russia's failure to influence the leadership of a small Slav state with a population little bigger than Moscow's. For all their sympathies with the Serbs and their identification of Kosovo with Chechnya and other troublesome (and Muslim) republics, Russian leaders and diplomats made little secret of the fact that they loathed Slobodan Milošević.

After one more fruitless attempt to engage the Serbs, the British and French co-chairmen 'adjourned' the talks. They said they would not begin again unless the Serbs 'expressed their acceptance of the Accords'.[19] They did not.

Živadin Jovanović, the Yugoslav foreign minister, says that 'there were never any negotiations at Rambouillet,' because 'except for a photo opportunity with Her Majesty Mrs Albright' the two delegations never met. 'They were never started, they were never held.' His view is that Rambouillet was:

> all about geopolitics not about human or minority rights ... it was a pretext to expand NATO and the US presence to south-eastern Europe, as they could not enjoy hospitality any more in Germany. It was a cover-up for shifting NATO from north to south and south-east so that Europe could get closer to important international highways, roads, railways, waterways and sea. It was to do with a military, strategic and economic presence, a rich world presence in the Caspian Sea and the Persian Gulf and for this Yugoslavia has always been perceived as an obstacle.

These ideas may seem eccentric to western readers but it is important to understand that, especially as politicians like Živadin Jovanović repeat such things every day, a large number of Yugoslavs believe them. Both Serbs and Albanians also have a propensity to believe that Serbia and Kosovo are fantastically important, rich and strategic corners of Europe. While it is true, for example, that a major European motorway and rail link does connect Croatia, Hungary, Greece and Bulgaria through Serbia, the fact that this link was more or less closed to large-scale international commercial traffic for much of the 1990s did not impoverish most of the rest of Europe or North America, especially since there are other routes. Still, Jovanović contends: 'I understood the geostrategic objectives from the very beginning.' In September 1999 he was staying in a suite at the Plaza Hotel in New York where he was attending the UN General Assembly meeting. Outside, as if nothing had happened, a vast Yugoslav flag flew next to the UN flag and the Stars and Stripes. 'Rambouillet was a theatre designed to provoke us,' he said.

> As the strategic interests of NATO were involved they had made their plans before Rambouillet to attack Yugoslavia because Yugoslavia would not submit voluntarily to occupation. It was clear they would attack us ... their strategy was conquering a nice piece of European territory.

Jovanović contends that his country's delegation went to Rambouillet in good faith but that: 'we were tricked by sneaky methods. They tricked us and the Russians ... They were cheating. It was not goodwill and they were not treating the Yugoslav delegation in an honest way but favouring a separatist, terrorist group.' Asked why Ratko Marković had written such a positive final letter before leaving, he claims that this was because the Yugoslav delegation was 'never informed' about the key implementation parts of the deal and only found out about them later. 'This was not honest behaviour on the part of the negotiators. They were holding those voluminous 80 pages of text behind their backs like a sword.' Warming to his theme, he said:

> It was clear they would attack because Yugoslavia would not submit to capitulation. Yugoslavia has never capitulated in all her history. Some think that history is a burden but we think it is a teacher. Everything else is hypothesis, maybe yes, maybe no. The Serbs have never accepted capitulation or occupation. In the fourteenth century the Serbs resisted and won. We resisted Austro-Hungary in 1914 and we know how it turned out, Serbia won. Again in 1941–45 Serbia defeated Hitler, and that was not because we were helped by the US or the Russians but simply because we don't know how to do anything else but resist. In 1948 Yugoslavia was surrounded by a steel wall of tanks, but Yugoslavia did not submit. In 1968 Yugoslavia rose up against Brezhnev's theory of limited sovereignty. We

condemned the occupation of Czechoslovakia. So, today, we don't buy that limited sovereignty idea and we're damn strong in our convictions!

Back in Belgrade, Milošević was making some final arrangements for the future. In fact, these had begun as early as November 1998, when he had fired the army chief of staff, Momcilo Perišić. He had been replaced by a hardliner cum yes-man General Dragoljub Ojdanić. Perišić's sacking had come a few weeks after the dismissal of another former loyalist and longtime confidant, Jovica Sanišić, his intelligence chief. Milošević no longer had anyone in the inner circle who was prepared to give him bad news. The sacking of the two men who might also have played a major role if ever there was to have been a coup or some form of 'change from the inside' was a key moment. From then on in, the tone had hardened. Milošević was surrounded by men who were not counselling caution and compromise. On 25 December the reshuffles at the top continued. General Nebojša Pavković, who headed the Priština Corps, was made commander of the Third Army, which included Kosovo. Now, on 22 March, two days before the bombing started, Milošević completed his purges. Holbrooke visited Milošević and told him that unless he backed down, air strikes would begin. Aleksandar Dimitrijević, the head of military intelligence, was dismissed. He had advised Milošević not to call NATO's bluff. 'When I heard Dimitrijević was sacked,' says Braca Grubačić, the editor of Belgrade's English-language *VIP* newsletter and one of Serbia's sharpest analysts, 'I knew we were going for war.'

Some 2,000 people were believed to have died in the conflict in Kosovo so far.

8   You will bomb us

No one could quite believe it. Milošević had decided to gamble
on fate. He had made up his mind. He was going to risk the
bombs and go for broke. There is no doubt that he knew what
was coming because Holbrooke had told him – and he was
hearing from other sources too. This is Holbrooke's account of
their last meeting, on 22 March:

> I said to him, 'You understand what will happen when I
> leave here today if you don't change your position, if you
> don't agree to negotiate and accept Rambouillet as the basis
> of the negotiation?' And he said: 'Yes, you will bomb us.'
> And there was a dead silence in the room er … uncharac-
> teristic and I said: 'I want to be clear with you, it will be,'
> and I used three words I had worked out very carefully
> with the US military, 'it will be swift, it will be severe, it
> will be sustained.' And he said, in a very matter-of-fact
> way, very flat: 'No more engagement, no more negotia-
> tions, I understand that, you will bomb us. You are a great
> and powerful country, there is nothing we can do about it.'
> And I said, 'It will start very soon after I leave,' and there
> was, again, dead silence and I looked at my watch and I saw
> it was noon and I said, 'You know it's 6.00 a.m. now in
> Washington, people are getting up. I have to report to
> Washington and to our allies in London and Paris and
> Bonn and Brussels, where we stand.' And I waited, last
> chance. And he said: 'There is nothing more I can say,'
> and so I got up and we left and exactly 34 hours later the
> bombing began, and it was swift, severe and sustained.[1]

But there was one more thing Milošević wanted to say. Just
as Holbrooke left, he asked him, 'Will I ever see you again?'
Holbrooke replied, 'That's up to you, Mr President.'

The KVM had already left Kosovo on 20 March. Over
the next few days aid workers, employees of most other

international organisations and many diplomats left Kosovo, Serbia and Belgrade. After the Americans cleared their desks at their Belgrade embassy they smashed their computer hard drives with sledgehammers. But many of those who left did not think they would be gone that long. A good number of the KVM verifiers, now in Macedonia, thought they would be back within days. Maki Shinohara, a UNHCR official, at that point in Geneva but in touch with the organisation's staff in Kosovo and Serbia, recalls: 'We never thought it was going to get as serious as it did. We thought we would be able to go back in a day or so and resume our assistance ... our staff on the ground simply didn't think the air strikes would happen.' There had, after all, over the last few years been a lot of threats – and far less action.

There is no mystery about why NATO bombed Yugoslavia for 78 days beginning on 24 March. Quite simply, the leaders of NATO countries thought it would only last a few days and so did Milošević. Jamie Shea, NATO's spokesman who was soon to become a familiar figure around the world – a hated man amongst Serbs and a hero to Albanians – sums up what was about to happen in typically pithy fashion: 'In football the winner is not the team that plays the best but the one that makes the least mistakes.'

Ideological *jihad*

Madeleine Albright and the other Western leaders had put their faith in diplomacy backed by a credible threat of force. The problem was that Slobodan Milošević did not think it was credible. In October, when he had backed down in the face of earlier threats, he had. Now he had changed his mind. While Holbrooke notes that in October, 'we were asking for less, we were not asking for ground troops', he also believes that there was another factor involved. In December 1998, in Operation Desert Fox, Britain and the US had bombed Iraq, accusing its leader, Saddam Hussein, of obstructing UN arms-inspection monitors. The monitors were withdrawn and the bombing lasted 70 hours. After that the monitors never went back. For Saddam Hussein that was a victory of sorts. Of course, relatively small-scale bombing of Iraq has continued ever since, but

Milošević certainly calculated that such a casual and on-going bombing campaign in the middle of Europe would not be acceptable to public opinion in the countries doing the bombing. Holbrooke says: 'My instinct tells me that he got information via intelligence, from one of the NATO countries or the Russians, that it would be light.' But it was not just Milošević who was expecting what was jokingly called 'bombing-lite'. Jamie Shea says: 'Don't forget, many were predicting that he would buckle after 24–48 hours.'

In fact, in the weeks and months running up to the bombing almost everyone predicted that any campaign would be short. A fashionable theory at the time was also that Milošević 'needed a little light bombing' in order to justify his backing down and accepting a peace deal enforced by foreign troops. In other words, that bombing would provide him with the alibi he needed. The problem was, as Holbrooke has indicated, that Milošević and Western leaders became trapped by a sort of information short-circuit. That is to say, because he knew that they believed the bombing would be short, he believed it too and, encouraged by hardliners in his entourage, he believed he could weather a short campaign and extract some sort of benefit. Indeed, in the days running up to the campaign, the fact that NATO leaders believed that the air strikes would be of short duration was explicit. Lamberto Dini, for example, the Italian foreign minister, said that he expected that after the initial attack there would be a pause and peace talks could begin.

There was also another vague hope on the part of the Western leaders. Somewhere along the line the intelligence services had suggested that in the course of bombing there was a possibility that Milošević might be overthrown. Perhaps this arose from out-of-date information based on guesswork concerning the motivations of the now sacked Perišić and Stanišić and the powers and possibilities of the Montenegrin leaders. Weeks earlier, at a crucial point in the talks in Rambouillet, one diplomat took one journalist aside for a briefing in a local café. As the journalist's 10-year-old son was there, the diplomat slipped him 10 francs and he retired happily to the pinball machine. Madeleine Albright was due to arrive the next day. Warming to his theme the diplomat reached a fever pitch of excitement as he said: 'If it comes to bombing, it's going to be heavy, not pinprick stuff, and I seriously doubt whether Milošević is still going to be there at the end of it!'

In Belgrade Braca Grubačić, the editor of *VIP*, who realised that war was coming when Dimitrijević, the head of military intelligence, had been sacked, recalls that when his contacts close to Milošević's inner circle said, 'He's going for war,' at first, he simply couldn't believe it. 'They were talking about creating a Vietnam, saying we'll win this or that ...' In other words, just as Western leaders slid unwittingly into war, so did the Serbs. While the inner circle believed it would be short-lived, they made rough plans for a one-month conflict. Grubačić traces the roots of Milošević's decision to challenge the West to the October agreements with Holbrooke. He says that in the wake of the deal that set up the KVM regime Milošević was angry and believed that his old negotiating partner had betrayed him:

> He thought the US would close the border with Albania to prevent arms smuggling, that the US would freeze the KLA's assets and make arrangements to terminate the KLA's influence ... When Milošević understood that Holbrooke would not fulfil such a 'promise' he went for war. He thought the only goal was NATO in Kosovo, and after Rambouillet, when he saw that the West wanted to allow NATO to pass through Yugoslavia he was afraid that someone like Walker would turn up and say: 'You are no longer president.'

Indeed, when Milošević had met Walker he had taken against him. 'Walker made Milošević suspicious and furious,' recalls Grubačić. After the meeting, the president had concluded: 'They want to get rid of me.' He refused to go to Rambouillet because he could not stand the idea of being put on a par with a man like Thaçi whom he considered a terrorist and a pipsqueak to boot. He did not want to risk arrest by the Hague Tribunal under one of the 'sealed' or secret indictments, and thought that Rambouillet would mean the loss of Kosovo for the Serbs. Grubačić says Milošević thought, 'If I sign we will lose it, but, if I don't there's a possibility that our grandchildren will get it back.'

Grubačić's suspicions about how Milošević was thinking on

the eve of war are borne out by Milisav Pajić, a senior foreign ministry official, who had worked in Yugoslavia's London embassy until the bombing began and relations were broken off. Although he had officially been number two in the embassy, he was widely believed to be the *de facto* ambassador and a relatively powerful voice in his own right. As workmen with cranes struggled to rebuild those parts of the foreign ministry struck by cruise missiles weeks before, Pajić articulated the official Yugoslav view of why NATO had gone to war:

> I don't think Kosovo and Metohija was the real goal. It was to oppose the leadership of this country and introduce NATO here. It was a sort of ideological *jihad*. We did not want to accept the military occupation of this country and the legal basis for the separation of Kosovo and Metohija. As far as Rambouillet was concerned, the document was imposed on us. There was not the slightest chance that we would accept it. The Americans prevented an agreement. They were looking for excuses because their intention was to bomb Yugoslavia. Their plans were ready but an excuse was needed.

When trying to comprehend Milošević it is vital to understand that the man has no long-term vision. His main interest is power and keeping it, and what he is best at is manoeuvring from day to day. On occasions, such as the spring of 1998, he lies low, dithers, is uncertain how to react, but finally he decides to pursue a particular course of action – but again is uncertain how it will end. On the eve of war Milošević contemplated a number of possibilities but, like a gambler, had no idea how things would end up. He did not know if he would win, lose or come out quits.

Since he had sacked people like Stanišić, Perišić and now Dimitrijević, those in charge of the security services were relatively new and eager to please. They were confronted by an anti-war wing of ministers such as Bogoljub Karić, a Kosovo Serb and big businessman, who understood that war would devastate the country's industrial and business interests. The hardliners in the military and police and their allies, like foreign minister Živadin Jovanović, were ultimately able to prevail. Poor Western intelligence failed to predict the correct balance of power in the inner circle, as did, to be fair, most well-informed Serbs.

According to Serbian sources the army chiefs were 'very tough'. For them, this was not just a matter of a David and Goliath military struggle, but one which would restore their pride after their humiliations in Slovenia, Croatia and Bosnia. This time, there was no doubt: this was to be a Serbian army defending Serbian land – and in Kosovo, sacred land at that.

The military chiefs told Milošević that they calculated that, with their existing air-defence systems, they could, in a relatively short time, shoot down ten to twenty NATO planes. However, if, as they hoped, the Russians would give them their more sophisticated missile systems, they could 'massacre' NATO jets. They also had several other important cards up their sleeves. Freed from the constraints of the KVM they thought they could destroy the KLA within a week. They told Milošević that they would rapidly spread the war into Bosnia and Macedonia and have the West looking for a quick exit. They would do this in several ways. The first was to order the Bosnian Serb army to begin a guerrilla war against NATO in Bosnia and the second was to foment unrest in Macedonia. In the event of a ground war – an invasion – they did not believe that they could 'win', but they did tell Milošević that they could extract heavy casualties from NATO. This would give Milošević time for some form of talks which might, in turn, allow them to pull back half-way across Kosovo (a line from Podujevo to Peć was mentioned) which might then freeze into a partition, rather like in Bosnia. In the event, their plans came to nothing, indeed, they backfired horribly for them by helping to cement a shaky Western alliance. But none of these half-baked plans was to backfire quite as spec-tacularly – and disastrously – as the idea of either physically deporting hundreds of thousands of Kosovars or terrifying them into flight.

On the broader political front Milošević's calculations were equally catastrophic. He believed that Russia had to support him with more than rhetoric or the consequences for President Boris Yeltsin would be disastrous. Milošević had a very personal connection to Moscow in that he had made his brother Borislav ambassador there. When it came to the West, the calculation was that if the war did not end in days, then discord between alliance members would either cripple NATO, or, in the run-up to its 50th-anniversary Washington summit on 23 and 24 April, force a climbdown to cover the embarrassment of its having failed to impose its will on a small Balkan country.

Facing the black hole

In the weeks before the bombing began, the fighting between the Serbian security forces and the KLA had worsened. On 19 March, the day after Thaçi had signed the Rambouillet Accords in Paris, the UNHCR reported that there were 250,000 people displaced within Kosovo. At the same time Western governments were receiving reports that 40,000 police and soldiers plus 300 tanks were either poised to enter Kosovo or already there. The next day, as the KVM verifiers pulled out, there were reports that a major Serbian military campaign was under way. Three days' fighting in Drenica was reported to have resulted in a fresh wave of 25,000 people in flight. There was no telling how it would end.

On the eve of war, Western leaders declared that their aim was to prevent a worse humanitarian catastrophe than the one which was already unfolding. There is no reason to disbelieve that this was one of their main motives – but it was also the legal cover needed to go to war. This was, of course, disputed, but as we saw earlier, the British and French foreign ministry lawyers clearly believed that the use of force was legal if a Security Council mandate could not be obtained and a humanitarian catastrophe was looming. But their motives were mixed. The humanitarian catastrophe *was* a part of the reason but the other part was a modern-day version of gunboat diplomacy. When Holbrooke returned for his last meeting with Milošević he asked him to stop his offensive in Kosovo. However, that was not the point he chose to highlight when he described the meeting in the account at the beginning of this chapter. Instead of mentioning that tens of thousands were again in flight, he says he told Milošević that Serbia would be bombed, 'if you don't change your position, if you don't agree to negotiate and accept Rambouillet as the basis of the negotiation'.

There were strategic objectives too, if only in the negative, preventative sense. For years it had been feared that a war in Kosovo would spill over into Macedonia. That would pit the country's ethnic Albanian minority, perhaps one-quarter of the population, against its Orthodox Slav majority. There was no love lost between the two and it was feared, rightly, that a war could drag in Albania on the side of its kin and the Serbs on the side of the Macedonian Slavs, and thus provoke a wider south-east European war. What would the Bulgarians with historic claims to Macedonia do, and if Albania at war chose to invoke its defence agreement with Turkey, how would Greece react? What would happen if, in these circumstances, either of these two NATO members decided to make a pre-emptive move in Cyprus? All of these were legitimate concerns, and speaking to the nation as the air strikes began, President Clinton addressed them: 'Let a fire burn here in this area and the flames will spread. Eventually, key US allies could be drawn into a wider conflict, a war we would be forced to confront later – only at far greater risk and greater cost.'[2] By contrast, Javier Solana, NATO's secretary-general, chose to emphasize the moral imperative:

> We have no quarrel with the people of Yugoslavia who for too long have been isolated in Europe because of the policies of their government. Our actions are directed against the repressive policy of the Yugoslav leadership. We must stop violence and bring an end to the humanitarian catastrophe now taking place in Kosovo. We have a moral duty to do so.[3]

It was possible that Western leaders felt obligated by a moral duty but, in the days running up to the beginning of the campaign, some people at the very hearts of Western establishments were suddenly contemplating the appalling situation which NATO might now be facing. In Germany, for example, senior British and German officials, soldiers and politicians, including Britain's Sir Charles Guthrie, the chief of the defence staff, met on the occasion of an annual Anglo-German Königswinter Conference. One of the subjects they were supposed to examine was the 'New NATO' – the organisation had just admitted former Warsaw Pact members Hungary, Poland and the Czech Republic. Inevitably, the discussion was sidetracked by the situation in Kosovo. While most expected the impending conflict to be short, private fears were also being expressed that the conflict could last much longer than had been anticipated. Over coffee a senior British military figure was even heard to say that, if it did, he was worried that Britain's expensive and hard-fought-for cruise missile stocks might soon run out.

As the conference came to a close on 20 March, a report on the 'New NATO' session was written in the style of a memo to Tony Blair and the new German Chancellor Gerhard Schroeder. It reflected the fears and doubts that that were being expressed.

> There are never military solutions to difficult political problems. Political will to see through NATO's threat of military action is not guaranteed if it does not achieve results in 4 to 6 days ... <u>At this very moment in Kosovo, the alliance is now damned if it does, and damned if it doesn't</u> ... NATO's credibility will be destroyed if it dithers indefinitely and fails to deliver on its threats (however justified the military fears). Conversely, the military black hole into which it is heading can just as well devastate that credibility ... Listening to those from the military and political, the options now for the New NATO of nineteen are deeply – deeply – uncomfortable .... Everyone hopes by some miracle for a climbdown from Belgrade, which means NATO's response need be much less. But the reality now is ominous. NATO – an alliance for mutual defence – is sliding inexorably into possible war fighting.

The report then went on to ask whether the British and German establishments and indeed those of all the nineteen NATO countries had made any serious preparation of public opinion. Roger Liddle, Blair's special adviser on European policy, who was there and was particularly concerned about the effect on public opinion, took one of the 'memos', saying: 'I think Tony had better see this.'

> Politicians should plan for the worst, not hope for something much better. But they have not yet signalled that they have embraced this nasty reality and considered the impact on public opinion – especially if – as expected –
>
> ● the military options become ever messier after a few days of air strikes;

- when the chances of NATO declaring victory (or some other such phrase) become slimmer and slimmer;
- and when the first images of humanitarian suffering and probably Serb revenge slaughter of Albanians start hitting the TV news bulletins.

Before that, the military want to be sure that the political process and dialogue with Belgrade has to be seen to go the last kilometre AND BEYOND. The public have to be convinced before NATO bears such high risk.[4]

But the military were not to get their reassurances. Milošević had, as we have seen, already decided to gamble. The problem was, as the report indicated, that NATO could not afford to lose. If it did, its credibility would be devastated.

When the war was over many of NATO's senior military officials claimed that they had known all along that Milošević would not buckle after only a few days. In some cases, this might be an example of being wise after the event, but in others it means that either they did not make strenuous enough efforts to warn their political masters that they were wrong – or their masters were not listening. Air force General Joseph Ralston, vice-chairman of the joint chiefs of staff and successor to General Wesley Clark as SACEUR, said at a lecture in London after the bombing:

> I do not believe it was a surprise to anyone in uniform that the operations in Kosovo lasted as long as they did. Indeed, I counselled at the very beginning that we needed to be prepared to go for many months, if not years. So, don't start an operation unless you are prepared to do that.[5]

Gerhard, Bill, Tony ...

For NATO the technical basis on which it was to go to war was derived from the Actord it had passed in October. Following the Holbrooke deal it had not been rescinded but as Jamie Shea describes it, 'We changed the traffic lights from green to red.' The reason for this was was two-fold. Firstly NATO wanted to keep up a form of pressure but secondly it had to be done this way otherwise the planes, the other hardware and the troops assembled would have had to be stood down. Five days before the air strikes began, the NATO ambassadors met to set the wheels in motion. Shea recalls that in the run-up to the bombing of the Bosnian Serbs in August 1995 there had been 'a great deal of discussion and long meetings'. This time things were different. 'It was remarkably fast. Everyone was very grim faced but composed.' The ambassadors gave Solana the authority to begin the strikes but told him that he had to consult with all 19 capitals first. 'He spent four days calling them. Shea says, "it was Gerhard, Bill, Tony, you know we are ready. I am going to instruct SACEUR to begin. Are you okay with that?" They were.'

As Solana made his phone calls, Holbrooke made his last, futile visit to Belgrade. After the mission failed he flew to Brussels where he gave Solana a report in a sealed envelope. From then on, he said, everything was in the hands of NATO. On 23 March the Yugoslav government declared a state of emergency. During the day Serbs began stocking up with essentials, including bottled water and candles. That night *TV Pink*, a television station run by a leading member of JUL, Mira Marković's party, dropped their scheduled American film, *Twins*, and replaced it with the Serbian film *Battle of Kosovo*. A few hours later police burst into the premises of the independent, or perhaps more correctly described anti-Milošević, radio station B-92 and closed it down. General Nebojša Pavković, the commander of the Yugoslav Third Army which covered Kosovo, told the Kosovo Serb newspaper, *Jedinstvo:* 'The defence of Kosovo is a strategic task and our major national interest. If we lose Kosovo, we will lose Serbia, the FRY and our freedom which is sacred to all citizens.'[6] Everyone was bracing themselves.

The attacks began on 24 March at 8.00 p.m. local time. Amongst the first targets, in the suburbs of Belgrade, were the Military–Technical Institute, a military academy, the air base of Batajnica and the major communications mast on Mount Avala. Some 40 military targets, from a list of 51 selected for this first phase of the war, were also hit. Because the Serbs knew full well what was on the target list – either through guesswork or good intelligence or, as has consistently been rumoured but never proven, thanks to leaks coming from one NATO member – all the military facilities were empty. Also amongst the targets were Yugoslavia's air-defence systems. According to the newsletter *VIP*, as the bombs and missiles began to hit, Serbian state television played patriotic songs ('We love you, our fatherland …') and showed the feature film *Kozara*, evoking the Second World War battle between Yugoslav Partisans and the Germans. News broadcasts ended with the message: 'At this hour, the most important thing is to stay calm. The NATO criminals and their evil masters can inflict casualties on us, but they cannot vanquish us.' Milošević appeared on television to address the nation: 'At stake is not only Kosovo, although it is of great importance to us, but also the freedom of our whole country.'[7] In view of what was happening, the speech was curiously low key.

The next day, life in Belgrade continued more or less as usual. But this was an illusion. A profound psychological homogenisation was beginning to take place. Over the next few days all the bitter divisions in Serbian society simply vanished. The rule of Milošević, an issue which had caused such dissension in recent years, and particularly in middle-class society, became irrelevant. There was only one issue now, which was that the country was being attacked. With a State of War now declared, those few that did not feel swept away by Serbia's 'Blitz spirit' deemed it prudent to keep quiet. Opposition journalists were hauled in for prolonged sessions of questioning by the secret police and some Serbs who had worked for foreign embassies were picked up and also subjected to gruelling interrogations. The security services appeared convinced that Western agents had been distributing types of electronic beacons at strategic points which could guide in NATO missiles and warplanes. On the 11 April, Slavko Ćuruvija, the editor of the daily *Dnevni Telegraf* and the magazine *Evropljanin*, was murdered in a professional assassination as he entered his home in the centre of Belgrade. Ćuruvija had once been a political insider and friend of Mira Marković. However he had fallen out with the Miloševićs and had begun to denounce the regime in no uncertain terms. If NATO bombs were not enough to silence Milošević's foes the murder of Ćuruvija was. It terrorised journalists, academics and other anti-Milošević activists. Many were now convinced that a bloody purge was about to begin or would do so as soon as the bombs stopped falling. Some left for Montenegro, some found refuge abroad, while the rest, feeling angry and betrayed by the West, kept silent, wondering if they might be killed by a NATO bomb – or an assassin's bullet. Censorship meant that the media now toed a single 'party line' and indeed one of the slogans broadcast on television was, 'All of us are one party now – its name is freedom.'

What the (still unresolved) murder of Ćuruvija meant, however, along with the assuming of full control of the media plus the wartime curtailing of civil liberties, was that, as the analyst Denisa Kostovičová has noted, 'the homogenisation of the Serbs...did not come about bottom-up, but it was imposed top-down'. She adds that the choice of targets, 'including bridges and power plants...played directly into Milošević's hands and, appeared to contradict the claim that the enemy was Milošević and not the Serbian people.'[8]

Back in NATO headquarters, bureaucrats and soldiers bustled through the corridors going about their work. Still, as Shea recalls, 'The first few days were difficult. It was rather like the phoney war of 1939–40. The weather was incredibly bad and an enormous number of missions had to be canceled.' However, there was, above all, 'a feeling of everyone being in the same boat, all the politicians and parties too, so it was not just make or break for NATO'. One of the ambassadors says:

> You would not convey the right impression if you did not convey the fog, the fog of war. We were working 20 hours a day, there was fatigue, there was an overwhelming amount of information and intelligence ... but half of it was wrong.

Shea's phoney war did not last long. Within days of the bombing beginning, tens of thousands of Kosovars were flooding across the borders of Albania and Macedonia. At first NATO officials and Western leaders were stunned and horrified. Milošević thought he had played his trump card. In fact, he had lost the game.

We lived off revenge

Two days after the bombing began, the UNHCR representative in Tirana briefed diplomats, including the American and British ambassadors, the staff of UN agencies in Albania and the director of the Albanian government's Office for Refugees. The representative told them about the few recent arrivals (there had been none that day) and the state of the organisation's preparedness.[9] During the meeting no one mentioned that anything untoward was about to happen. One week later 300,000 people had crossed the border of Kosovo into Albania and Macedonia.

A few days later Joschka Fischer, the German foreign minister, told the *Berliner Zeitung* that on 26 February Serbian forces had set in motion a plan called Operation Horseshoe which aimed at expelling Kosovo's ethnic Albanian population. He added that he deeply regretted 'that he did not take Milošević seriously when the Yugoslav leader told him in early March that Serbian forces could empty Kosova "within a week"'.[10] After that, without any firm evidence, it appeared to become established as fact in the Western media that the German intelligence services had indeed discovered this alleged plan, and various organisations such as the UNHCR were accused of not having prepared accordingly. In fact, if this was the case, it soon became clear that either no one knew much about it or were not told about it at all. A bitter post-war report by UNHCR notes that in the weeks leading up to the crisis Western governments, far from urging the organisation to prepare for a massive influx of people, were in fact trying to persuade it to 'get prepared for the early implementation of the Rambouillet Accords'. The report continued:

> It seems unlikely that these same governments would have responded to a request from UNHCR for massive contingency preparations predicated on the failure of their own peace efforts ... UNHCR received no advance warning from any government or other source.[11]

Asked whether the intelligence services in Britain had warned senior officials of what was about to happen, one said:

> No, not in anything like those explicit terms. The first I heard of Operation Horseshoe was after the bombing started. But, no we didn't get a warning in advance that bombing would lead to a pre-triggered plan to drive people out. When it happens people say 'We knew, but ...' We

were very conscious that people would be driven from their homes but it was the scale that was unexpected.

A senior US state department source says that 'Bulgaria and some other states in the region' had passed some information to the US about Operation Horseshoe or 'Operation Winter' before the bombing but implied that it was extremely vague and certainly not taken too seriously. 'We knew it was there, in the abstract,' he says. So, asked if the US was surprised by the scale of the exodus, he says, 'Quite a bit!'

While there was without doubt a major plan to crush the KLA which would have resulted in large numbers of refugees, until the archives are opened in Belgrade, the real picture will remain unclear. In fact, all that can be deduced from refugees' accounts is that the situation inside Kosovo during those crucial weeks was very confused. On the night of 14 March – 1 April tens of thousands were rounded up at gunpoint from two areas of Priština, pushed on to trains and deported. In the end almost 850,000 were either deported or fled Kosovo and hundreds of thousands more were displaced inside. No one has yet managed to piece together a comprehensive picture of exactly what happened, or rather why, because confusion reigned. A large proportion left out of fear, wanting to go before they were pushed. Another large proportion were simply marched around the province, told to go in one direction, then sent home, then sent elsewhere and then finally expelled. What the logic behind all of this was is unclear. Within days of the bombing beginning, virtually every single Albanian was expelled from Peć, but after the clearing of two districts of Priština, there were no more large-scale clearances of the capital. Braca Grubačić is probably right then in his analysis of what was really going on:

> There were differences between the police and the army. The police were in favour of expulsions because they could steal money from people. The intelligence guys were against it though because they said it was bad for us. There were vague ideas about expulsions, but I doubt that there was a real Horseshoe plan. I think that when the bombing started they just did it. The worst were paramilitaries and locals. Before the bombing it was common knowledge that

they would expel Albanians but it was more of a case of 'we'll fuck 'em if they start!'

That is not to say that Milošević did not have vague ideas about expulsions – and no one can accuse Grubačić of being wise after the event. On 27 March he wrote in his *VIP* bulletin:

> Milošević will try to destabilize the entire southern Balkans and expand the conflict to Macedonia, Bosnia and Albania in order to scare his adversaries in NATO. He intends to expel a large number of Albanians from Kosovo in order to provoke a reaction from Western Europe, which already does not know what to do with the masses of Albanian refugees and fake asylum-seekers.[12]

Some of the most fascinating eyewitness testimony about what was happening in Kosovo after 24 March comes from Nataša Kandić, the head of the Belgrade-based human rights group, the Humanitarian Law Center. After the bombing started she went to Kosovo to look for her staff. Although she had problems she was able to drive around relatively freely, the police she met not being particularly suspicious because she was a Serb and a woman. On 30 March she says the streets of downtown Priština were 'almost deserted'. She went to a part of town where every-one was Albanian. There she 'encountered groups of people discussing what to do: should they make their way to the border or stay until the police ordered them out of their homes?' She then joined a column of hundreds of cars heading for the border, apparently without having been coerced. There:

> rumours flew around that the border was closed, that police were taking cars, that they were separating out the men ... The sight of police with masked faces in the column frightened us and we decided to return to Priština. No one prevented us. As we drove back, we saw that there were more than 2,000 cars in the column. We also saw groups making their way on foot, all gripped by a terrible fear.[13]

On 23 April Kandić met a large group of people 'who were walking towards Vučitrn. These people were returning to their homes having spent two weeks in the woods hiding, and were anxious whether the police would allow them to go back and whether their houses were still standing.' Later, she says, they were expelled and as she passed the town on 5 May she saw that it was empty 'and many houses were on fire'.

> The same day, I passed through Mitrovica. There were neither police nor military in the town center. There wasn't a soul to be seen. Large sections of the town had been destroyed. One could see that houses had been plundered first, and then set on fire. There were some people in the suburbs. Serb parts of town were intact. Afterwards, when I talked to Albanians from Mitrovica who had come to Montenegro, I found out that approximately 30,000 Albanians were expelled from Mitrovica on 15 April, and that they had been ordered to leave for Montenegro. They traveled on foot, it took them three days to reach Dubovo, a village 80 kilometers away from Mitrovica where the Yugoslav army stopped them. The army kept them there for three days, when three officers announced there had been an 'order for refugees to return home'. They were put on buses and shipped back to burnt down Mitrovica. Hunger and fear made many of them leave Mitrovica again and go to Montenegro.[14]

Father Sava, the monk from Dečani, was horrified when, with Bishop Artemije, he witnessed the cleansing of Peć at the end of March. They were passing through the town on their way to Montenegro:

> I saw a lot of paramilitaries in different uniforms, with baseball hats and Nike caps, camouflaged faces and masks. I saw Albanian civilians with children and plastic bags. Near the centre of town there were trucks full of women and children. We drove quickly, it was obvious what was happening. The road up to Rožaje was blocked. There were hundreds, thousands of people, with cars and on foot. They told us they had been given 10 minutes to go. I was crying, it was the road of sorrow. I was so shocked. There was mist at the top of the pass. I saw a woman in slippers. The bishop was shocked and petrified. I said, 'I can see the Serbs leaving Kosovo very soon.'

Thousands of refugees, especially from western Kosovo, crossed the border at a place called Morina, near Prizren. From there, they came down the steep road to the tiny town of Kukës, where those who stayed were put up in vast tent cities erected for them. Hava, a six-months pregnant 32-year-old woman, tearful and in shock, spent her first night in Albania in late April on the floor of the municipal library. Her story was typical. She came from the village of Dulje. At the beginning of the bombing 'the police came and everyone ran away'. They went to the hills but were shelled so they moved to another village called Dragačin, 'because we thought it would be safer'. Because there were KLA nearby, there was fighting around the village. The police were in Dragačin 'where they held us in houses for three days. They took girls away. Then they took us back to Dulje and held us in a school, where we were robbed. They said, "Get your money out or we'll cut your throats."' Women were molested and Hava had a gun put to her head. The police were asking the women where their men were – some were abroad, some were undoubtedly in the KLA and some were hiding. After some soldiers had been killed in what she said was a 'bombing', soldiers came to the school and demanded money, saying: 'Serbs have been killed and we need money to send their bodies home.' Then the women were robbed again. Finally they were told to bake bread and told, 'You'll be safer in Albania.' At this point a bus was brought to drive them to Žur, close to the Morina frontier where they were told to walk across 'but to follow the white line in the middle of the road'. Presumably this was to avoid mines planted along the side.

From town to town and village to village, experiences were different. Peć was almost completely cleansed, and much of the old centre was torched. Priština was partly cleansed but much of the population fled. Prizren was partly cleansed but doctors there were a particular target, arrested in their white coats and dumped at the border. In Djakovica the experience was different again. Here, parts of the old town were torched and people were expelled, but Albanian doctors and their families, who still worked in the Serbian hospital system, were saved and sheltered by Savo Stanojević, the Serbian director of the hospital. According to Dr Agron Binxhiu, Stanojević got special passes from his brother (a top Djakovica official), so that using ambulances the doctors were able to collect their families who then lived in the hospital for the whole period of the bombing. There they were safe, because the hospital was guarded; but elsewhere para-militaries were roaming the streets, periodic expulsions were organised and in some parts police and army had moved into people's houses, as they did all over Kosovo because they could not live in barracks any more for fear of being hit by NATO bombs and missiles. Stanojević and Binxhiu were both natives of Djakovica and had shared digs as medical students in Skopje. Binxhiu said of Stanojević, who fled after the war: 'He was a doctor, a big nationalist but not a criminal. He was a good man.'

Because of Stanojević's actions some 100 Albanians were able to live out the war in relative safety. But, there was a sting in the tail here. This was not simply a 'Schindler's List' story translated to Kosovo. As Binxhiu says: 'The police and the army needed us because we worked for them. If it had not been for Savo the hospital would have closed.' Although most seriously injured police and soldiers were looked after by military doctors elsewhere and then, if need be, evacuated to the military hospital on the outskirts of Belgrade, there were still not enough Serbian doctors to look after the troops that came through the ordinary hospital. Stanojević told his friend that if he wanted to leave he would escort him to the border with Albania but Binxhiu refused. He told his friend he would only leave 'when the last Albanian' had left Djakovica. This action was regarded as far from heroic by the KLA men who, after the Serbian collapse, came into the town. One said: 'Those Albanian doctors were bastards. We had people dying of minor injuries because we had no doctors. We sent them messages asking them to come over to us, but they would not. Even those that left went to Tirana and did not come and help us.'

Although the picture across Kosovo was confused, some-times a pattern can be identified. In certain operations the army would secure the perimeter of an area while paramilitaries went in, often killed a few people – not very many probably, because you only needed to kill a few to prompt everyone else to flee – and then proceeded to loot. Some paramilitaries were groups of local Serbs, some were recruited in Serbia proper and, in the days before the bombing began, an unknown number were recruited from Serbian jails where they were given amnesties in exchange for fighting. All of them, however, operated under the umbrella of the authorities and alongside various units of the police and military structures. Some paramilitary members were later tracked down in Montenegro by two intrepid American reporters. The testimonies they managed to collect give an extraordinary, chilling and unique insight into the minds of killers. Milan (a pseudonym), a Bosnian Serb, told them that he was recruited by members of the Serbian Radical Party, whose hardline nationalist leader, Vojislav Šešelj, was Serbian deputy premier. The man who recruited them:

> provided us with weapons, ammunition, satellite phones and walkie talkies. That was the middle of March 1999, ten days before NATO began bombing. We trained for three days at a camp in Leskovac (Serbia). There were 20 in my unit, and most of the guys came with war experience from Bosnia and other places. Three of them were former members of the Yugoslav state security service in Croatia. Many of them were criminals. The goal was to fight against the KLA and to cleanse away their support. I am a Serbian patriot. I fought for the Serbian cause. And also for the sake of money. Money was the main thing. We heard that members of the Serbian secret police were transporting Albanian civilians in the trunk of their cars for $2,700. There were some members of my unit who would take the money and just kill the guy. I didn't do such things. I took them to the border. When the NATO bombing intensified, I started doing the same thing – taking the money and killing them ... A Yugoslav army officer – Major Radičevíc – was supplying us with food and ammunition. Every three days, the truck would come with ammunition and food. And other things from the army – like travel documents, to allow you to pass checkpoints. We also had travel documents from the police inspector at the training camp in Leskovac, Stojković.

In one operation Milan's unit entered a village where they suspected there had been KLA men:

> There was this village elder, some old Albanian guy, who refused to leave. I mean the guy was just pathetic. We

ordered him to go to the border to Albania, but he just
refused. So we put a bullet in his forehead. The others were
taken to the border while we burned everything in that
village. The whole village. We'd hear about what was
happening to Serbs every day on the news. When you see
that NATO is bombing the center of a town or the television station in Belgrade, and every day friends, comrades
died, you don't care about the Albanians. Why would you?
We lived off revenge. Sweet revenge. During the history of
the Serbian nation, everybody has hated us. We suffered
many casualties during the First World War and the
Second. Our nation was always threatened ... you have to
strike back, pay back that evil. Back then, revenge felt very
good. Especially when we killed the KLA. That was back
then. Now I can't sleep, I can't eat. It hasn't lasted.

Marko, a criminal, was in prison before he was recruited by an
agent of Željko Ražnatović, the warlord known as Arkan who
had fought in Croatia and Bosnia and then been elected in 1992
to parliament as a deputy from Kosovo. He said that 50 men had
joined up at the same time, just before the bombing started, and
added, 'Let me tell you, that for freedom we would do just about
anything.' He was sent to Kosovo on 1 April and his unit was
charged with arresting people. 'We would receive a list of names.
Bring this person in alive or dead. I was assigned to arrest people,
and had permission to kill them if necessary.'

We didn't arrest just anyone ... we arrested important
people, political types, functionaries. We didn't arrest
people we weren't supposed to, but you know you have
crazy people everywhere. People who would rape everyone from Serbia to Albania ... The lists came from all over,
police, city authority, because they had been collecting this
kind of information for years. Who were the rich ones,
where they lived, who were the important ones, where
they lived. And we had local spies to help us on operations.
We would use locals from a particular village to guide us,
tell us where so-and-so lived, and they might get some
money, if they were Serbs. We also had Albanian spies and
Gypsies, too.

Many of those Albanian and Gypsy 'spies', of whom there were probably more than one might expect, were targets of instant revenge as soon as the Serbs pulled out of Kosovo. In the first few days after NATO entered the province on 10 June, scattered bodies, or small groups of bodies, were often described to journalists as Albanians killed by the retreating Serbs. Four of them, for example, lay in hedges and ditches near the village of Bela Crkva where a massacre of Albanians had taken place during the bombing. But a week after the Serbs had left, the bodies of these men, all bound, and one stripped and badly bruised, looked suspiciously fresh. Of course the story told to journalists by the locals could have been true but equally these four could have been Serbs or perhaps, even more likely, local Albanians marked down for execution by the now-victorious KLA as 'collaborators'.

Some of the paramilitaries were more brutal than others. Marko described a group called *Munja* or Lightning, which operated around Peć.

> *Munja* was given names of people, on lists, to liquidate, or arrest, and usually the others were moved out. But *Munja*'s main interest was in robbing people and in raping women. They were a dirty group of men who had no qualms about killing women and children, whether or not they were ordered to do it. They weren't disciplined like us. We carried out orders, and we were not ordered to kill women and children. We killed men, we killed those we were ordered to kill. That's the difference. We were professionals. We were organized, had our tasks and carried them out. We did what we were ordered to. Now, if I had been ordered to kill women and children, I would have. But I wasn't. Men, yes. These guys from *Munja*, I mean they would just go in and kill. It didn't matter, women, children … It's not really war. It's total destruction. That was the way cleansing happened. I mean, you used the guys who were really hungry, full of lust, to go into some of these places. And in return, like us, they got a chance to make money. We were all, in a way, working for the same boss – Milošević – it's just that some people went about their jobs differently … I don't have any regrets. It was either us or

them. I mean, look at what is happening now. But I'm not for killing women and children. I'm a professional.[15]

Most Yugoslav officials are not keen to talk about this period and what happened in Kosovo. The official line is that people left because they were frightened of NATO bombs, but even to raise the issue with Živadin Jovanović, the Yugoslav foreign minister, is to provoke his rage. He says that NATO countries were responsible for 'genocide against the Serbian and Montenegrin people' and therefore even to ask about the exodus of the Kosovo Albanians is to attempt 'to accuse the victims [i.e., the Serbs] for their [i.e. NATO's] crimes.' It is an attempt to 'divert attention from the problems they provoked from killing thousands at random'. By contrast, Vladislav Jovanović, the Yugoslav ambassador to the UN in New York, has a much more considered response. Although he agrees that 'the bombing and aggression' were 'the main cause', he says, 'our army were expecting a ground operation much earlier.' They deployed along the frontiers, but when the bombing began Thaçi and the leadership of the KLA, 'called for a general uprising and for an attack on our army from behind. No army could accept that ...'

> so, there was a very serious danger for the security of our army and its communications, especially in Drenica and it was essential to do away with that. There was a need for quick action and it was not particularly gentle. There were a lot of fights. Our army wanted to do away with those strongholds and so, in densely populated parts of Kosovo, people had to leave in order to preserve their lives. Some remained inside while some went to Macedonia and Albania. I have no evidence that our security forces were encouraging the departure of these people, but it is possible that some private paramilitaries were taking advantage to achieve some goals, robbing and killing to settle some scores or to get property. It was a messy situation and it was impossible to keep law and order and some dishonest Serbs wanted to take revenge and kill ... and some private paramilitaries exploited the vacuum to impose their own law.

According to Jovanović, this period of lawlessness lasted some weeks but after that the army and police managed to reimpose law and order 'as much as they could in such circumstances'. He says that President Milošević 'stated that 350 individuals were caught and sentenced' for crimes. 'When the Serbian government invited people to come back, nearly 100,000 did. Although rather unclear, it may be that here he is talking, at least in part, about columns of refugees blocked at the frontier who suddenly 'disappeared' rather than cross, presumably having been ordered back home. Still, Jovanović contends that refugees:

> were told by KLA propagandists not go home. They tried to keep them in the camps to show them to the world's TV. They told them. 'Don't go' but some went back, they trusted, somehow, in the Serbian government. But, on the way back their columns were targeted and some were killed. Most were from Priština and then Priština was heavily bombed so they were forced to flee again. Some NATO personalities said, 'Don't go back before the end of the war.' It was in someone's interests to keep them out of Kosovo temporarily for their extraordinary usefulness for propaganda.

From the Serbian point of view, this explanation appears utterly logical. However, it is perhaps more likely that it attempts to turn on its head what might otherwise be interpreted as the greatest single mistake made by Milošević during the war. As we have seen earlier, there may have been some haphazard expulsion plans. These, coupled with what Grubačić describes as the 'we'll fuck them' attitude, plus fighting, terror, a lack of food and all the other circumstances of the war led to the exodus. By the end of the bombing, according to UNHCR 848,100 Kosovo Albanians had left the province. Of these 444,600 went to Albania, 244,500 to Macedonia, 69,900 to Montenegro and 91,057 were airlifted from Macedonia to other countries.[16] A large, unknown number were also hiding in the hills of the interior. To the extent that Milošević makes long-term plans he certainly considered the fact that, in the wars of the former Yugoslavia, the vast majority of refugees have not returned home if their home remains controlled by the enemy ethnic group. So it seems logical that he concluded that the bombing gave him a window of opportunity to deport, or terrify into fleeing, a large number of people who would never return. As they left, the police stripped most refugees of their documents, and in this way Milošević may have hoped to make it impossible for them to come home later as they would have no way of proving that they were Yugoslav, as opposed to Albanian or Macedonian citizens. Perhaps he also calculated (this seems logical but there is no evidence for it) that he could later repopulate Kosovo with some of the 600,000 Serb refugees in Yugoslavia from Croatia and Bosnia. In this way he would solve their housing problems and completely alter the ethnic structure of Kosovo to the advantage of the Serbs in one fell swoop. His problem was that the expulsions backfired immediately.

For the first few days of the NATO bombing operation, Western television viewers saw nothing but the results of bombs and missiles falling on Serbia – which was explained to them by the fact that there was a humanitarian catastrophe to address but, as we saw from Holbrooke's explanation, was as much to do with gunboat diplomacy as anything else. If this situation had continued for much longer there is little doubt that uproar would have ensued. The question would have been asked, 'How can we bomb a small country – whatever we think of its government – because it refuses to sign an agreement about the future of part of its own territory?' However, within days of the start of the bombing the refugees began flooding out and Milošević lost his advantage. Television news in the West was now dominated by the apocalyptic scenes of hundreds of thousands of refugees. Since Western journalists were no longer free to travel wherever and whenever they wanted inside Serbia and Kosovo, Milošević had scored a disastrous own goal and the main focus of the war now became the return of the refugees. Critics sometimes charge Western leaders with having changed the objectives of the war as it progressed. This is true, but then, having blundered into the conflict thinking it would be short-lived, they genuinely found that the nature of the conflict changed. There should be nothing surprising about this. Wars are by definition dynamic and so circumstances change. Britain and France went to war in 1939 ostensibly to defend Poland. They did not end the war fighting for Poland.

On 2 April, 45,000 Albanians flooded in to Macedonia in one day. Apart from the fact that Milošević was happy to get rid of these Albanians for good, he also hoped, as we have mentioned, to export the war. Just as deporting people turned out to be a policy which backfired, this too turned out to be a miserable failure. The Macedonian authorities, alarmed and frightened by this human tidal wave into a country of barely 2 million, tried various schemes to block the refugees, including refusing on 3 April to let them in at all. This led to 65,000 being trapped at the Blace border point. The authorities feared – as Milošević hoped – that the influx of these Albanians who they too thought would never go home would upset Macedonia's fragile ethnic balance and thus tip the country into war between its Slav majority and Albanian minority. The Macedonians also feared that amongst the young men coming across there might be considerable numbers of KLA fighters who if NATO did not win the war would start it again from Macedonia.

Although, as we have seen, the UNHCR and Western countries in general were by no means prepared to deal with the influx, Milošević had miscalculated their ability to react extremely quickly. Early on the morning of 4 April, Easter Sunday, Robin Cook called his staff and said: 'How can we cope with all these people? I want an answer by 11 o'clock. Come up with a policy.' The answer was blindingly simple. Although Milošević had rejected the Rambouillet package, there were by now 8,000 NATO troops in Macedonia under General Jackson who were being assembled for the post-peace deal peacekeeping force. They were ordered to build refugee camps.

In this way the 'refugee bomb', as it was sometime described, was defused. Refugees were marshalled into the giant Stenkovec camps built just over the border, the main one based at an old airfield and a number of smaller ones. Troops from NATO were also rapidly deployed to help contain the problem in Albania with camps being built in Kukës and refugees being distributed across the country.

Although there was much criticism of the UNHCR at the time, in fact, working with NATO, governments of NATO and other countries, plus dozens of non-governmental organisations, it responded rapidly and well to the crisis. The camps were hardly comfortable, but under the circumstances they were well run, there was food and water, medical supplies, doctors and even satellite phones for those prepared to queue. Compared to refugee camps in Africa or other parts of the Third World, these were certainly at the luxury end of the market. In Macedonia, the authorities, recovering their balance after the initial shock, enforced a ban on people leaving the camps. This was because they did not want refugees to move out to friends or family in Skopje or in ethnic Albanian-inhabited western Macedonia. What this resulted in was a curious class division by which middle-class and professional Kosovars and those with contacts mostly never even went into the camps but rather went straight to Tetovo in western Macedonia or elsewhere, while most ordinary people ended up in tents. One of the more bizarre elements of the crisis was the way in which the whole of Priština's café society appeared to have been transported, *en bloc*, to the cafés of Tetovo.

When the refugees began to come out, NATO officials were at first horrified. Jamie Shea says: 'We were faced by accusations of turning a disaster into a catastrophe.' A senior State Department source says he 'would never admit, ever, to panic,' but says that in the US administration there was 'a feeling of being "real concerned"'. Shea goes on to say that if it had not been for the fact that NATO already had troops on the ground, the situation would have been very different. He also relishes the fact that the expulsion proved to be a disaster for Milošević. During the early days of the conflict, NATO's media operation was overwhelmed by the sheer number of journalists descending on Brussels and the demands of the world media. Tensions also grew with the military side of NATO which was either reluctant to give enough information or extremely slow. However, Alastair Campbell, Tony Blair's press secretary, plus an experienced media team were sent to Brussels to help direct the news management of NATO's operation. Some journalists did not appreciate this, believing that they were being fed stories which were not true. Still, Campbell's catch-phrase was 'no picture, no story' and the fact was that until the exodus began Milošević had the upper hand in the all-important battle of the media, because as Shea says 'until then, he could say NATO was killing people'. After that he no longer had the upper hand in the media war. The images of the refugees and their stories now solidified NATO unity. Legitimate questions abut the legality of the campaign were undermined by the expulsions and, given the accusations that were coming from those who opposed the bombing that NATO had actually *caused* the exodus, there was now no way back. The credibility of NATO meant that the exodus had to be reversed. Everyone understood this, including the leaders of Greece, whose pro-Serb population was massively against the bombing. The Greek government, which like every other member of NATO could have stopped the bombing whenever it liked, simply decided to ride out the storm because, considering its security in general, it made the crude calculation that it feared the Turks more than it liked the Serbs. As one NATO source says:

> The Greeks were wonderful. We understood their situation. Their leaders made fiery speeches in Greece which we didn't mind and in exchange they never broke the consensus. They worked very hard with their bilateral contacts with the Serbs and with Milošević but in the end, they realised there was no alternative strategy.

Few Serbs understand that just one vote from one country of NATO's nineteen members could have prevented or stopped the bombing but, presumably with an eye to rich post-Milošević business opportunities, Greek leaders are keen to cultivate the impression that they were helpless to stop the bombing. They were not.

The wars that never happened

The exodus was certainly Milošević's biggest mistake, but it was not his only one. Since the collapse of the old Yugoslavia in 1991, the Serbian intelligence and security services had maintained cordial relations with their counterparts in Skopje. Through them, according to sources in Belgrade, they helped organise demonstrations of ethnic Serbs in Macedonia (a very small minority) and Macedonians who, fearing the territorial and secessionist ambitions of their own Albanian minority, identi-fied with the Serbs. At times these demonstrations turned violent but, as the campaign continued they fizzled out, largely because the refugee problem had been contained by NATO and the authorities in the camps.

The second biggest miscalculation made by Milošević was in believing he could export the war to Bosnia, where there are some 30,000 troops in the NATO-led Stabilization Force, SFOR, keeping the peace. On 1 March SFOR announced that it had taken the radical action of disbanding the Bosnian Serb army's 311th infantry brigade because its members had been caught smuggling weapons. Troops from SFOR had seized two civilian trucks in which they discovered anti-tank weapons, multiple rocket-launchers and eighteen SA-7 air defence systems. Another haul of weapons was also discovered elsewhere.[17] The arms were destroyed. When, a few weeks later, NATO began bombing Serbia, the Yugoslav army which had previously either controlled or exerted enormous influence over the Bosnian Serb military including paying officers' salaries, ordered it to begin a guerrilla war against NATO troops in Bosnia. According to a senior SFOR source, 'They wanted to engage NATO in Bosnia because they were convinced that there would be a ground attack from there.' Bosnian Serb chief of staff General Momir Talić was 'shattered' by what had happened to the 311th infantry brigade and so when the orders came to start a guerrilla campaign he was disinclined to obey. Troops from SFOR were immediately sent to blockade weapons depots and Talić was told by General Mike Willcocks, the deputy commander of SFOR, that if his men tried anything, all of his weapons would be destroyed – just as some of them had been a few weeks earlier. Talić told him about his orders and that he had refused. The Bosnian Serb military had no appetite for another war and, now under such strict control, there was little it could do anyway. On 25 August Talić, attending a conference in Vienna about post-war Bosnia, was arrested and sent to the International War Crimes Tribunal in The Hague on the basis of a 'sealed' or secret indictment relating to his activities during the Bosnian war.

Milošević's other strategy for spreading the war to Bosnia also ended in failure. Probing NATO at the beginning of the bombing, two Yugoslav Mig-29 jets flew into the east of the country and were immediately shot down.

Throughout the 78-day bombing campaign the government of Montenegro, led by President Milo Djukanović, constantly raised the alarm, saying that Milošević was attempting to mount a 'creeping coup' in the republic by using the army. Although there is little doubt that, if he had thought it possible and could have toppled the government in Montenegro without opening a debilitating 'second front', Milošević would have proceeded with his plans here, like those for Macedonia and Bosnia, they came to nothing. So, with this string of failures behind him, Milošević's options were narrowing. But now that the campaign was in full swing, it was hard, short of a humiliating surrender, to back down. Politically speaking, he battened down the hatches, sent out the odd feeler about wanting to make a deal and waited to see what would happen next.

The grey zone

According to Živadin Jovanović, NATO had 'announced a victory before they started'.

> They said they would make Milošević and the Yugoslav government bow down in three days. Then they post-poned that to one week and then it was months. So, we saw the targeting of civilians and our civilian infrastructure. They were targeting refugees, our electricity system, hospitals, schools, refineries, heating systems and they were always expanding the list of civilian targets. Because they realised that they could not win. They were attacking the morale of people to provoke the suffering of civilians so the government would be obliged to stop its defence. They were killing three to four times as many civilians as soldiers.

While NATO officials would hotly deny that they were targeting civilians and refugees and indeed insist they took extreme care to avoid the risk of civilian casualties, there is of course some truth in what Jovanović says. When Milošević's expected early collapse did not come, NATO's original 51-item target list was expanded on 28 March. That NATO increasingly aimed at demoralising Serbia's population is, of course, correct.
    When the bombings were over NATO commanders criticised their political masters, saying that they had told them that the strategy of 'bombing-lite' was wrong and that they

should have prepared for a massive blow at the very beginning rather than a slow build-up. General Michael Short, for example, told the Senate Armed Services Committee:

> I'd have gone for the head of snake on the first night. I'd have turned the lights out the first night. I'd have dropped the bridges across the Danube. I'd have hit five or six political–military headquarters in downtown Belgrade. Milošević and his cronies would have waked [sic] up the first morning asking what the hell was going on.[18]

Short was a Vietnam veteran who had flown 276 combat missions there and his own son was flying missions over Yugoslavia. With no sign of buckling General Wesley Clark rapidly stepped up the campaign, moving from the use of some 400 planes to more than 1,000. It was only in early May, however, that NATO planes began attacking the Serbian electrical system. At first they used new graphite bombs which cause short-circuits, but on 24 May 'heavier munitions took the grid out completely'. In a highly revealing article for the *New Yorker*, the writer and broadcaster Michael Ignatieff examined the way Clark ran the war and wrote that until that point, 'as Clark puts it, "this was the only air campaign in history in which lovers strolled down riverbanks and ate at outdoor cafés and watched the fireworks"'.[19] This was, of course, hardly the way that most Serbs saw the campaign. Apart from the fear the problem was that some 60 per cent of eventual targets were what is called dual use, that is to say they had both military and civilian uses. They included factories, oil refineries and depots, roads, bridges, railways and communications facilities. According to one study, 25 per cent of targets was purely military and 15 per cent was air defence.[20] So, with this massive overlap, came a legal grey zone. All targets were referred to a military lawyer who, wrote Ignatieff,

> sitting at his computer screen, would assess the target in terms of the Geneva conventions governing the laws of war. He would rule whether its value outweighed the potential costs in collateral damage. A military lawyer also applied 'the reasonable-person standard' to the fine line separating military and civilian targets.[21]

The Geneva Conventions prohibit attacks on dual-use sites if the 'incidental loss of civilian life ... would be excessive in relation to the concrete and direct military advantage' of the attack.[22] So, when it came to electricity it would, at first glance, seem a fair enough target in that the military used it too, the risk of civilian casualties would be low and the population would be demoralised by power cuts. However, as Ignatieff has pointed out:

> The irony here was obvious. The most effective strike of the war was also the most morally problematic. Hitting the grid meant taking out power for hospitals, babies' incubators, water-pumping stations. The military lawyers made this clear to Clark. One of them recalls, 'We'd have preferred not to have to take on these targets. But this was the commander's call.'[23]

In fact, the military lawyers are only reported to have rejected a target once – an electricity plant in Niš.[24] After the bombing Human Rights Watch took NATO to task for attacking such controversial tagets and the War Crimes Tribunal in The Hague also conducted a review of NATO's actions albeit without releasing any public information on its report.

While it is clear why telecommunications systems, electricity plants and bridges are dual use and hence are both military targets and civilian infrastructure, it is less clear why factories were so often targets. There are several reasons. Some worked for the military as well as having civilian uses. Some were linked to big businessmen close to the regime or even ministers in the government; a clear decision was made to hit their assets to make their continued support of Milošević increasingly expensive. A third reason was the redeployment of military hardware into industrial zones. NATO planes and missiles repeatedly came back to hit barracks and other such military targets. But before the strikes began, they were evacuated and the soldiers billeted elsewhere; in Kosovo, of course, Albanians were expelled from their flats to make room for them and factories were also taken over. Until a final reckoning is made, we will not know how much of the industrial infrastructure was now being used by the military. However, it is more than likely that the experience of the industrial zone in the provincial town of Čačak was relatively common. According to Velimir Ilić, the mayor, local people began protesting when the military hid a tank repair facility inside the building of the Sloboda plant which made vacuum cleaners and other electrical appliances. He says that NATO detected that something was going on in the plant and spy planes and satellites had also detected soldiers crossing the industrial zone where fruit-drying machines were made along with textiles and construction materials. As they did not know exactly what was happening or where, says Ilić, 'they destroyed the whole industrial zone'. Similarly, perhaps, the major Zastava plants in Kragujevac were hit: Zastava made cars and Kalashnikovs.

During the bombing the Yugoslav authorities compiled details of the NATO strikes with forensic detail which they subsequently published in a two-volume 'White Book' called *NATO Crimes in Yugoslavia*. The volumes are crammed with detail and appalling unflinching pictures of burned and contorted bodies. But in terms of the historical record the book is of limited value because of its selective use of facts. These, for example, are entries about the attacks on the Sloboda plant, which of course makes no reference to there having been military facilities hidden there.

> On 4 April 1999, at 3.20 a.m., 'Sloboda' household appliances factory Čačak was hit again by eight missiles; plant for quartz stoves production and enamel processing was struck. Three workers – Tomislav Dobrosavljević (1959), Miroslav Randjić (1969) and Predrag Djukić (1950) sustained minor injuries.
>
> On 6 April 1999, at 11.00 p.m., facilities of 'Sloboda' household appliances factory ... Čačak were hit by four missiles.[25]

The US Department of Defence claimed that up to 2 June, in other words virtually up to the end of the campaign, 99.6 per cent of some 20,000 NATO missiles and bombs hit their targets.[26] This appears absurdly optimistic, but even if it is true, 80 bombs or missiles, that is, the 0.4 per cent that did not hit their targets, can still kill a lot of people. When asked about this, NATO officials shrug and say that 'in war, accidents happen', and that in fact fewer accidents happened in this war than in almost any other one in history. This is probably true, but since modern communications make it possible for us to view the results of such accidents almost immediately, whereas old-fashioned censorship could keep a lot of news off world television screens, NATO found itself embarrassed by the results of the accidents that did take place. Indeed, its credibility was seriously damaged by them. The 'White Book' chronicles the minutiae of such accidents. These are extracts from one autopsy report from the section devoted to the blowing-up of a passenger train which began crossing a bridge near Leskovac the split second after a NATO pilot had fired his missile.

> IDENTIFICATION: No relatives inquired about this victim. No clothes, footwear, or personal documents were found on the victim.
>
> A male corpse. The remaining part of the body is 145 cm long. When shrinking as a result of carbonization is taken into account, and when the length of the amputated shins is added, the victim was about 180 cm tall. The appearance of the thigh and shoulder muscles indicates that the victim was about 50 years old.
>
> The vertex and the superior cerebrum regions are completely carbonized. The entire skin on the body and the underlying muscles are also completely carbonized.
>
> The carbonization of the head and neck transformed these parts of the body into a brittle black, and amorphous mass. Identification of certain parts of the head and neck parts is impossible.[27]

Amongst the worst NATO accidents were strikes on an Albanian refugee convoy near Djakovica and another on refugees that resulted in perhaps some 50 dead in the village of Koriša. What is uncertain in both these cases is whether the military was in the area at the time. Jamie Shea says that at the time NATO suspected that the Serbs were using refugees as a cover to help them move about, by mixing military vehicles in with refugee tractors. In the case of the Djakovica convoy, another NATO source says:

> Some pilots had gone over and said it was too risky ... another squadron came over. One will err on the side of caution and the other will be more gung-ho. There are the

airborne forward air controllers too. One more gung-ho than the other.

For Shea, the Djakovica convey disaster was the worst moment of the war. It was the first major accident, it took five days for the military at NATO to give him proper information and 'many believed we'd lost our moral rectitude'. He adds, though:

> The cause is not any the less worthwhile even if the price goes up. Conflict does not immediately bring order where there is disorder. If you have an ulcer, the doctor says he can take it out – but he'll have to open you up and it will be bloody.

Similar questions about whether the Serbian military were in the area linger over an attack on the Dragiša Mišović hospital in Belgrade which resulted in several dead. Sources in Belgrade and journalists who visited the site said that they believed that either soldiers were billeted in one part of the hospital or that the actual target was a military facility next door. The most spectacular mistake was an attack on the Chinese embassy on 7 May. Afterwards questions were raised as to whether the building was actually being used by the Yugoslavs to transmit military signals. If it had been, though, it would seem puzzling that President Clinton deemed it necessary to apologise so abjectly to the Chinese, and that US and NATO officials kept repeating that the embassy had been hit because the CIA had selected a target on the basis of an old map.[28] On 23 April the main building of Serbian television was hit. Western journalists received warnings, via a contact at CNN, not to go to the building. At least fourteen died in the attack. Afterwards the families of those who died began legal proceedings against the management because they said that they knew the attack was coming but had told the employees to stay. The attack aroused much anger both in Serbia and the West but, if the families of the dead are right, their loved ones were sacrificed by the authorities precisely because they wanted to arouse Western anger, cause dissension in NATO ranks and rally support at home for the continued defence of the nation.

Whatever or not there were 'good' reasons why mistakes were made and innocent civilians died, NATO's explanations could hardly be expected to win the hearts and minds of ordinary Serbs, many of whom, at least to start with, spent their nights in uncomfortable, damp basements and shelters. After the bombing, Jasmina Tešanović, a Serbian writer and film-maker, published extracts from her diary that she kept during this period.

18 April. It is Sunday, but who cares? We've been living the same day ever since the war started. In Belgrade there are efforts at normality – the traditional marathon was held in heavy rain; there was a big wedding on TV – but personally I'm done with anything that resembles human life. I'd rather be a cockroach, at this point, much safer.

Last night three factories in Pančevo were hit again, including the chemical factory, where there was an acid leak. Some people are being evacuated. We in Belgrade had a good wind, we were lucky once more. In Batajnica, near the airport, a three-year-old girl was killed by falling glass after an explosion. Her father said she'd been difficult in the night. First she wanted to go to the bathroom, then she didn't, then she did. And then he let her go in and she never came out.

26 April. The shops are still full but people are talking about radioactive vegetables. They are also predicting a future without bread, water or electricity. No visible signs of that yet, only fear. The shortages are still cigarettes and petrol – and of course peace.

Today the famous NATO star Jamie Shea announced that Serbian citizens feel safe with the NATO bombs: we don't stop working when we hear the sirens. Well, maybe not, but that's because the work has to be done, not because we feel safe. I don't feel safe with NATO or any other bombs. I don't feel safe without bridges, I don't feel safe in a boat, on a horse, on a bicycle, against a NATO bomber; I don't feel safe without schools, universities, libraries, against highly technological NATO countries. I am not afraid, not any more, but my legs still tremble when I hear bombers above my head.[29]

Although the now-censored Yugoslav press was full of triumphant reports about the dozens of NATO planes that the military were shooting down – in fact it only shot down two, but that included an advanced Stealth fighter – there was little doubt that morale was far lower than the authorities pretended. One of the more interesting attempts at morale boosting was the attempt to show Serbs that there were massive demonstrations of support for them around the world. In fact, though it was true that there was anger in Greece and Italy and discomfort in many other parts of the world, many of the demonstrations shown on television in Serbia were in good part small demonstrations of diaspora Serbs who had shown up because they had been told the time and dates of the protests by Serbian television's satellite broadcasts. Clever camera work then made these demonstrations look bigger than they were and the fact that the protestors were either Serbs or organised by far-left political groups was minimised. To what extent this and the constant showing of Second World War films actually managed to bolster spirits is questionable. In a similar vein the authorities at one point began attempting to give the serious impression – or began deluding themselves – that Yugoslavia was about to join the union of Belarus and Russia, which is in any case more of a notional construct than a reality. While such fantasies may have temporarily raised spirits by giving the impression that the great Slav brothers were about to come to Serbia's aid, the Serbs were soon to be made well aware that the Russians had no intention of giving them any serious help.

While some proclaimed that if NATO launched a ground war they would volunteer to fight, a far less vocal number of young men fled to Montenegro or abroad or began hiding because they feared a general mobilisation and had no intention of dying for Kosovo, even if it was 'holy land'. In May came stories of desertions from Serbian ranks in Kosovo and of units which refused to go back to the front from provincial towns like Kruševac. Although these may have been less significant in terms of numbers than NATO officials thought, they certainly caused alarm in the Yugoslav military. The high command remembered that Milošević had been forced to call a halt to the war in Croatia in 1991 when units from provincial towns in Serbia also began deserting, refusing especially to fight and die in the mud and gore of the eastern Croatian town of Vukovar. Unlike the murderous paramilitaries, most conscripts or reservists were in Kosovo because they had to be. Many of them spent much of the war hiding in empty houses and villages. Food was poor and otherwise minor problems like the army's inability to provide new underwear helped erode morale.

In Čačak a small, unofficial 'citizens' parliament' made a highly unusual call on the Serbian authorities to 'protect Albanian families and their civil rights, and to enable them to return' to Kosovo. It was unusual because most Serbs either did not believe that Albanians were being expelled by their forces or thought that they deserved it for having been responsible for the air strikes. On this point Denisa Kostovičová has noted that the NATO bombing campaign directly fed the Serbian 'proverbial sense of martyrdom', leading the Serbs to believe that the bombing was:

> concrete proof that they were the victims of the US-led New World Order. The fact that they were being bombed by the world's mightiest military alliance ... nourished their sense of martyrdom. In this context the plight of the Albanians was completely irrelevant from the vantage point of bombed Serbia.

The widespread Serbian contempt of the Kosovars and approval of their fate was, of course, to be repaid in kind. When the refugees returned from the camps, most of them tacitly approved of the expulsion of the Kosovo Serbs.

A key moment for Serbs and for their understanding of the situation they were in came on 26 April when Vuk Drašković, by now a deputy prime minister, made a blistering attack on Milošević and his entourage. Speaking on Studio B television, which he controlled, Drašković said: 'The people should be told the truth: we are on our own.' The national interest, he explained, lay in 'understanding and realising reality' and that involved putting aside visions of union with Russia and Belarus. 'I do not believe there is any sense in the heads of those who are invoking World War Three and lying to the people that Russia would be involved in World War Three.' From that point, believes Braca Grubačić, editor of *VIP*, 'although the propaganda stayed, no one thought we could win any more and that there had to be a deal'.[30]

There are no precise figures as to how many civilians died as a result of NATO's bombing campaign. The numbers range from 500 to 2,000. The number of wounded, however, appears constant and is always given as 6,000.

9 We will win. Period. Full stop.

Anti-aircraft units were deployed on the hills around Belgrade. They would keep some of their guns in people's garages. Most of their anti-aircraft fire, both around the capital and across the rest of the country, was futile in that the gunners were unable to shoot down planes. But they were not wasting their time. Anti-aircraft fire meant that NATO's planes had to stay high, mostly, but not always, at 15,000 ft. This was to have a major impact on the war. While it did not affect striking fixed targets like buildings, it made it very difficult to hunt down small groups of men and equipment who, in Kosovo, were hiding in houses, often with tanks parked under trees in people's gardens. The Yugoslav military also played cat-and-mouse with NATO with its radars. Either they were not turned on, or they were switched on briefly – which meant that attacking planes could detect them and fire special anti-radar missiles at them. At this point the radars were turned off, so the missiles, which home in on their beams, no longer knew where they were going and droned on until they ran out of fuel. In this way at least seven missiles ended up in Bulgaria, one of them exploding in a bathroom in Sofia. No Bulgarians were killed by any of these strays.

The jewel in the crown

The fact that NATO found it difficult to go after men on the ground and that Milošević showed no sign of giving in after a few days meant that the daily running of the campaign was going to get a lot harder. General Clark, a graduate from West Point who had also been a Rhodes Scholar at Oxford, was an army general in charge of an air campaign. The fact that it was difficult to hunt down men on the ground soon led to tensions with General Short, his senior air force commander. Short, a Vietnam veteran, objected to Clark's demands that his men risk their lives on what he derisively called 'tank plinking' exercises and, as we noted earlier, had argued that air power should have been used harder at the beginning and against major strategic targets. Just before one such target was due to be hit, the police headquarters in Belgrade, he said: 'This is the jewel in the crown.' Clark hit back saying: 'To me, the jewel in the crown is when those B-52s rumble across Kosovo.' Short said: 'You and I have known for weeks that we have different jewelers.' Clark said: 'My jeweler outranks yours.'[1]

Later, Short told *Air Force* magazine: 'I never felt that the 3rd Army was a center of gravity ... Body bags coming home from Kosovo didn't bother [Milošević], and it didn't bother the [Yugoslav] leadership elite.' A report in the *Washington Post* citing that interview says that:

> Short said that Clark urged him even before the conflict started to 'get down amongst' Yugoslav armored vehicles and troops in the field. Eventually, he said, 'we the airmen of the alliance were able to convince General Clark' of a need to conduct sustained operations against 'more lucrative and compelling targets ... in Serbia proper'.[2]

But hitting major strategic targets entailed its own problems, not least that of infrastructure which had civilian uses as well. With nineteen countries in NATO, it was clearly impossible to run the war by committee, but that did not mean that the generals could do what they wanted. When it came to the selection of sensitive targets, General Clark still needed to seek permission, at least from the big three countries, the US, Britain and France. After the war was over, US generals complained that the French kept placing restrictions on targets and that a lot of time was wasted by General Clark having to persuade them to relent. In return, the French complained that the US often bypassed the NATO command structure by using only American planes and missiles. Both complaints were true. There were tensions between NATO commanders and between NATO members in general; however, there was far less dissension between the states than was thought at the time.

Because he had no men on the ground to act as forward air-controllers – i.e. as men who would guide in the bombs, Clark had to devise a new system for finding targets. Although there was some liaison with the KLA over this, NATO commanders were often wary of using their information. For one thing they were frightened that somehow Serbian intelligence would manage to pass on disinformation this way, thus resulting in accidents or, of course, the bombing of the KLA by NATO. In one infamous incident, a small KLA barracks at Košare, just inside Kosovo, was indeed bombed, but how this happened was a mystery, since it had been featured on television news programmes the world over for the last couple of weeks. Michael Ignatieff writes that Clark

> was forced to rely on *airborne* forward controllers, aloft in thirty-year-old Lockheed EC130Es. Clark went to his Air Force commanders – including General Short ... but at first they didn't understand what he wanted. They told him, Give us the targets and we'll take them out. He recalls replying, 'You don't get it. You *develop* the targets.' 'But we don't do that,' his commanders replied. 'So we had to fix that,' Clark says tersely. He realized that they had to reduce the reaction times of the airborne controllers so that they could exploit targets of opportunity as soon as they appeared on their radar screens.[3]

Every morning Clark held two video teleconference meetings. The first was with top NATO officers and the second was with the commanders of US forces in Europe, EUCOM. For very important targets Clark had to talk to the politicians to get the go-ahead. In April, for example, the French balked at the targeting of the headquarters of Milošević's SPS which also housed the offices of his daughter Marija's Košava radio and television station and had a television mast on top of the 23-storey building. It was hardly surprising that they objected because the document circulated to Clinton, Blair and Chirac noted: 'Collateral damage: Tier 3 – High. Casualty estimate: 50–100 Government/Party employees. Unintended civ casualty est: 250–Apts in expected blast radius.'[4] In fact the building stands alone so these were extremely pessimistic calculations. Still, they were warning that up to 350 people could die in a target whose military connection was tenuous to say the least. The US argued that that the SPS building, 'was really an alternative headquarters for the Milošević regime' and worked hard at persuading the French of this. According to General Henry Shelton, the chairman of the US joint chiefs of staff: 'It was tough ... We kept at it. Persistence wore them down, and I think they eventually saw exactly what we were talking about.'[5] When the building was finally hit no one was killed but there is evidence to suggest that the Yugoslavs knew, or perhaps had even been warned, that the attack was coming. Jean-Claude Galli was staying in the Hyatt Hotel opposite the bombed-out building and working for TF1, the French television station. He says:

> The morning after the attack I was interviewing Goran Matić, the government's minister of information, at the foot of the building. He said: 'I called a friend who was still in the building at 10.00 p.m. and told him to get out immediately.' From then on I understood that the Serbs knew what was going on. In fact American and French journalists had, anyway, received several calls from their governments to warn them not to hang around the Serbian TV building five days before it was attacked. So, you can imagine that the authorities knew what was going on, since all our phones, and especially those in the Hyatt, were bugged.

Whatever the Yugoslavs did or did not know, and whatever NATO generals said about the military value of this building, everyone understood that its real importance was symbolic. NATO was striking the SPS and heart of the regime.

In particular the French did not want the Belgrade bridges targeted and they also wanted to protect Montenegro as much as was possible. This was perfectly logical since President Milo Djukanović could easily have been overthrown if it was seen that his anti-Milošević stance was, in the end, worth nothing. However, taking advantage of this, the Yugoslav army, according to one report:

> began hiding helicopters and fighter jets in bunkers at an airbase near Podgorica ... For the first time, radar there and on Yugoslav ships at the Montenegrin port of Bar also began tracking NATO warplanes.

Arguing that Milošević was trying to use Montenegro's neutrality as a shield, NATO commanders wanted to destroy the Podgorica air base. But first, they had to get past France's opposition to bombing Montenegro.

At a morning intelligence briefing, Clark was informed that Yugoslav artillery in Montenegro was shelling northern Albania.

'Forget the French!' Clark thundered, according to the participants. 'No, no, no, wait! Hold off on that,' he said. 'I'll get French permission. I'll get it.'

Within hours, Clark and three of the Clinton administration's top players – Albright, national security adviser Samuel R. 'Sandy' Berger and defense secretary William S. Cohen – dialed their counterparts in Paris. By the next morning, Clark had political approval for the strike.[6]

On the diplomatic front, the top five NATO countries liaised daily in the 'quints' group. This brought together either the foreign ministers of Britain, France, the US, Germany and Italy or their political directors. Sometimes they talked by phone several times a day, either as a group or individually.

As the air campaign ground on, there was the increasing realisation that NATO would have to prepare for a ground war to drive the Serbs out of Kosovo, unless Milošević accepted a peace deal involving NATO troops. At the beginning of the war, still banking on a rapid climbdown from Milošević, President Clinton made one of the cardinal errors of the campaign. On the day it started, he told the American people: 'I do not intend to put our troops in Kosovo to fight a war.' The problem was that he could not tell the Americans alone. He was, of course, telling Milošević and his generals as well. Despite Clinton's statement, NATO officers had, in fact, drawn up various plans, including invasion plans, as early as the spring of 1998. By October, the time of the Holbrooke deal, they were very advanced. This did not mean that they had any intention of invading Kosovo but simply that it was deemed prudent to be prepared for every possibility and to have contingency plans.

As an organisation, NATO itself never ruled out the ground option. There were several versions. One came to be called Operation B-Minus, which foresaw 50–60,000 men entering Kosovo as 'heavy peacekeepers', rather than having to fight their way in. A full-scale invasion would have entailed between

175,000 and 200,000 men. Britain was the first major power to press for the allies to start making decisions about whether there was a going to be a ground war, while the US, in view of what Clinton had said, and also fearing casualties, was reluctant. The Americans began calling the British prime minister 'Winston' Blair, and when he went to Washington for NATO's 50th anniversary summit, on 23–4 April, he tried to persuade Clinton not to shy away from thinking the impossible. Blair had an ally here. General Clark agreed that decisions would soon have to be made, because time was running out to prepare for a ground war. At one point the British thought NATO would need four months from the time a decision was made until it could start. A huge arsenal would have to be assembled, roads and infrastructure repaired or built in Albania and extreme political pressure applied to the Macedonians whose parliament had passed a resolution prohibiting the use of its territory for a ground war. Of course, even if a decision was made, it was still hoped that the ground war would not happen, rather that the preparations would be enough to force a capitulation from Milošević. Still, the Americans were embarrassed by Blair's calls and, just before the Washington summit, Clinton called him and asked him to tone down the rhetoric on the subject. In exchange, Clinton agreed that the existing plans be looked at again and refined.

Clark produced new plans in mid-May but the US joint chiefs of staff were not keen on the idea. They believed that the air campaign was working and that it needed more time. Significantly though, Clinton publicly backtracked from his earlier ruling on US troops. On 18 May he said: 'All options are on the table.' At same time preparations were agreed for some 45,000 troops to be stationed in Macedonia, including 7,500 Americans, who 'would serve as part of a NATO occupation force if Belgrade capitulated, but as the core of a potential invasion force if not.'[7] On 27 May the defence ministers of France, German, Italy, Britain and the US met in Bonn to decide how to proceed. Cohen was against beginning ground war preparations. 'I argued for intensifying the air war,' he said later. George Robertson, his British opposite number, argued in favour, saying that Britain would commit 50,000 soldiers, half the regular army. The French thought there was already no longer time to get an invasion force ready before winter and the Germans and the

Italians were nervous but did not reject the idea. No decision was taken beyond agreeing that a decision had to be taken within a week and that all nineteen NATO defence ministers needed to be consulted too.[8]

In Britain Tony Blair ordered preparations for a call-up of the Territorial Army, the country's reserve force. Thirty thousand letters were typed up and addressed.[9] In Washington, on 2 June Sandy Berger consulted a group of experts including former diplomats and military figures about the option of a ground war. He told them the US objective was: 'Serbs out, NATO in and the Albanians back.' He went to say that there were 'four irreducible facts':

> One, we will win. Period. Full stop. There is no alternative. Second, winning means what we said it means. Third, the air campaign is having a serious impact. Four, the president has said he has not ruled out any option. So go back to one. We will win.[10]

The next day, Milošević capitulated.

Jamie Shea says that, for an invasion to have begun in the first week of September, the orders to begin preparing would have had to have been given that week, the first week in June.

> It was very unpalatable, yes, it would have been difficult, but even in the US they were coming around to the view 'whatever it takes'. War had a solidifying effect. No decision had been made, but there was a political usefulness in talking about it. The mistake was ruling it out at the beginning, that's a lesson – that nothing should ever be ruled out. Milošević would have had to concentrate his forces but without the threat he could disperse them. They would have been easier to strike on the border of FYROM[11] but instead he could break them up into packets making them harder for NATO to hit. In the end the unthinkable was being talked about. It was no longer totally excluded, but, before the discussion was heavily engaged, he threw in the towel.

Asked whether, if Milošević had not given in when he did, there would have been a ground war, Strobe Talbott, the US deputy secretary of State, says: 'We would have done what it took to get it. Yes. In my view a ground war was risky, dangerous, undesirable and perhaps even inevitable.'

Hammer and anvil

One of Milošević's cardinal errors was to hope the Russians were going to help him. On the one hand, it was true that, because of their own problem in Chechnya, the Russians had to support Serbia's claim that whatever happened in Kosovo was its own internal affair. Serbia, as a fellow Slav and Orthodox country, also aroused considerable sympathy in Russia. On the other hand, Russia is poverty-stricken, needs Western help to survive and, whatever the legal merits of Serbia's case, Russia's reputation in the West could hardly be enhanced by consistently defending Milošević. On top of this, Russian officials detested Milošević because he humiliated them, just as he did Western officials, by making promises to them and signing agreements which he had no intention of keeping. And, finally, the Russian establishment had never forgiven Milošević for his support of the coup plotters who sided against Boris Yeltsin when they tried to overthrow President Mikhail Gorbachev in 1991.

Milošević hoped, as noted earlier, that the Russians would send him advanced anti-aircraft systems, which would have posed a major threat to NATO planes. The Russians did not have to consider this for very long. According to Strobe Talbott, the US told Russia 'repeatedly and explicitly' not to provide the Serbs with 'any military assistance – material, know-how, personnel ... We didn't mince words.' The Russians were told that any help they might give to Milošević would have a 'devastating' effect on US–Russian relations, and of course, the money that came with them.[12] Still, for a former superpower, this was a humiliating position to be in, especially as it underscored the fact that while Russian concerns might be listened to politely, NATO countries did not feel that they needed to worry unduly about brushing them aside. As the air strikes began, Sergei Lavrov, the Russian ambassador to the UN, vented his country's fury. 'Russia,' he said, was 'profoundly outraged by NATO's military action against sovereign Yugoslavia, which is nothing less than an act of open aggression.' He warned of the spread of the 'virus of illegal unilateral approaches' and said:

> A dangerous precedent has been created regarding the policy of diktat and force, and the whole of the international rule of law has been threatened. We are basically taking about an attempt by NATO to enter the twenty-first century in the uniform of the world's policeman. Russia will never agree to that.[13]

Kofi Annan, the UN secretary-general, took a curiously ambivalent approach which, if one was to be uncharitable, one might think looked rather like an attempt to sit on the political fence. He said that it was 'tragic' that diplomacy had failed, but noted that 'there are times when the use of force may be legitimate in the pursuit of peace'. He then qualified this by saying that the Security Council 'should be involved in any decision to use force'.[14] Two days later the Russians circulated a draft resolution in the Security Council demanding an immediate end to the air strikes. This was rejected by twelve votes to three. What this meant for the legality of the action was unclear, since it was now arguable that the Security Council, which obviously had not mandated NATO's action, had now had the opportunity to stop it but had not done so. In a similar vein, a Yugoslav attempt to get the International Court of Justice in The Hague to order an immediate end to the bombing was blocked on procedural grounds. However, the Yugoslav charge of unlawful use of force and genocide against ten NATO members remains to be adjudicated.[15]

On 30 March, Russian prime minister Yevgeny Primakov flew to Bonn from Belgrade. Milošević had offered to reduce his troop numbers in Kosovo if the air strikes stopped. This was rejected. However, in his meetings with the Germans Primakov took a hard line condemning NATO. 'He spoke in this turgid bureaucratic language of the old communist past,' recalls Michael Steiner, Gerhard Schroeder's chief diplomatic adviser and an old Balkan hand. 'What he had to say was essentially that Russia defended Milošević's position.' The Germans were disappointed but the Americans were unsurprised. They had distrusted Primakov 'ever since his attempt to interject himself as a mediator on behalf of Saddam Hussein during the gulf war in 1991'.[16]

It was simply too early for the diplomacy to start. While NATO countries were still waiting for Milošević to give in, Milošević was still counting on NATO becoming crippled by its own divisions and for the Russians to give him more than verbal support. On 9 April the Yugoslavs were encouraged by Yeltsin saying on television that Russia would respond to any NATO ground operation and he even raised the spectre of a new world war. He then proceeded to dash Serbian hopes by saying that he opposed supplying Yugoslavia with arms.

For the first few weeks of the campaign, then, Western diplomacy was aimed not at finding a settlement *per se* but rather at shoring up the alliance and encouraging and cajoling Serbia's neighbours into giving their full support to the operation.

On 14 April, Yeltsin appointed Viktor Chernomyrdin as his special envoy. A former premier, he had good relations with the US, especially Al Gore, the vice-president. He also did not like Milošević. Ten days later, during NATO's Washington summit, Yeltsin called Clinton and started exploring diplomatic options with him. At this point, one month into the air campaign, Clinton was facing the unwelcome British pressure to begin preparing for a ground war. Yeltsin too was desperate to get the bombing over with. As Talbott recalls:

> It was hell for the Russians. Not only was NATO still in business, it was expanding, there was talk of bringing in the Balts and now NATO was at war against Orthodox Slavs. It was harming relations with the west and Yeltsin was being denounced. He wanted the thing over.

Like Milošević, Yeltsin had believed that the bombing would cause NATO to split and in this he was counting on the French. However, Chirac went to Moscow where, according to Talbott, 'He took a tougher position than everyone else.' Yeltsin was getting calls from other Western leaders too and, says Talbott, 'was getting sick and tired'. So, he surmises, he appointed Chernomyrdin, telling him; 'I don't care what you have to do, just end it, it's ruining everything.' That is not to say that the Russians were about to become NATO's 'postmen', but rather that the time was now ripe to reopen the diplomatic channels.

Diplomacy is often viewed as a rather impersonal affair, in which men and women represent their countries and, in that sense, are all simply interchangeable. In fact, diplomacy is like anything else and personalities, contacts and friendships all count for something. What was happening now was that the US and Russia (the EU countries rather seem to have faded from the scene here), having decided that it was now in their common interest to end the war, began serious discussions on the ways and means to do so. On 3 May, after a 90-minute meeting with Clinton, Chernomyrdin went to his friend Al Gore's house where he told an American team, which included Strobe Talbott, of his 'hammer and anvil' plan. He said: 'I represent Russia and will go and pound away but, I want someone else to pound against.' What he told the Americans was that he needed a partner, because it would not be politically acceptable for Russia to be seen to be accepting Serbia's surrender.

At the time of the Washington summit, Kofi Annan, trying to resurrect the fortunes of the UN, which had been completely sidelined by now, raised the idea of a UN envoy. He gave the Americans a list of candidates, one of whom was President Martti Ahtisaari of Finland. The Americans were not keen to let the UN play a role because they felt that Milošević had, during the wars in Croatia and Bosnia, treated UN envoys with contempt. They did, however, like Ahtisaari. The next morning, talks continued over breakfast with Madeleine Albright. As Chernomyrdin outlined his 'hammer and anvil' plan again, she suggested that maybe Ahtisaari was the man they were looking for. Chernomyrdin shouted '*Voht!*' – 'That's It!'[17]

Everything was coming together now. Ahtisaari was the ideal candidate for several reasons. He had had a distinguished diplomatic career and had headed the UN's operation to bring Namibia to independence in 1978. Finland was a Western country and an EU member but, by virtue of its relationship with Russia, it was also a neutral country. So Ahtisaari was acceptable to the Russians and to the Americans, who trusted him, and would have to be to Milošević, too, since Finland was not a member of NATO. Ahtisaari also had some considerable experience of peacemaking in the Balkans, having played a key role in Lord Owen's team until he left to become President of Finland in 1994. In 1992, he had begun work on asking the three parties in Bosnia what they would and would not find acceptable in a post-war Bosnian constitution. He sent them all questionnaires, which they ticked off and faxed back to him in Geneva. This was the first of a thousand drafts which would eventually culminate in the document accepted by all parties in Dayton in 1995.

Chernomyrdin and Ahtisaari would now be working with Talbott. By a quirk of fate, Talbott had actually been born in Dayton in 1946. He had, however, other more significant qualifications for the job. He had known Clinton since they were both Rhodes Scholars and room-mates at Oxford. After university Talbott went to work for *Time* magazine which, in 1971, made him Eastern Europe correspondent based in Belgrade. Apart from knowing Serbia well, Talbott had also been fascinated by Russia since the Soviet Union launched the Sputnik satellite when he was 11 years old. He was a fluent Russian speaker and he had translated and edited two volumes of Krushchev's memoirs. When he met with Chernomyrdin, they talked Russian together. Everything was beginning to fall into place and the three-way diplomatic marathon now got under way. As Talbott describes it:

> The objective was to get Russia to come as close as possible to the NATO position. Milošević was trying to use perceived differences between alliance members and between the alliance and the Russians ... We were determined to head him off, so that wherever he turned he was told the same thing, 'here's what you have to do.'

Within days came the first diplomatic breakthrough. Meeting in Germany, the foreign ministers of the Group of Seven leading industrial democracies plus Russia – the G-8 – agreed on a broad group of 'general principles' for a settlement. They included all the key points that would later be enshrined in the UN resolution that ended the conflict. For example, they called for the 'withdrawal from Kosovo of military, police and paramilitary forces' and the deployment there of 'effective international civil and security presences'.[18] Over the next month, Ahtisaari, Talbott and Chernomyrdin would have more than 50 hours of talks in four major sessions in Helsinki, Bonn and twice in Moscow, as they tried to give flesh to these G-8 bones. The Serbs indicated to Chernomyrdin, who visited Belgrade alone, that they would accept these principles but they wanted to keep some troops in Kosovo and keep NATO out.

The two Moscow sessions were held in a guest house in the grounds of Stalin's dacha in a birch forest outside the city. It was a bizarre experience for Talbott who knew about this place from his translations of Krushchev. 'Stalin brought his politburo out here to watch American films,' he recalls 'and decided who to kill the next day.' Sometimes, as they were talking, Madeleine Albright would call on his mobile phone. 'I would ask her if she wanted to speak to Chernomyrdin. Her Russian is good. He'd light up. He'd call her "mother boss".' The talks were held around a triangular table. To 'represent' Milošević, Talbott invented a device called 'the empty chair'. He says:

> At first, it was rhetorical, but then we got an empty chair and put it at the corner of the table. So I, or Ahtisaari or Chernomyrdin, would point at it and say, 'But, what about the guy in the empty chair?' We were trying to generate the impression, and the reality, that here were three serious guys and three serious countries working on a serious problem – and a guy in an empty chair.

Throughout the sessions, the Russians held out in defending the Serbian position that some of their troops had to stay in Kosovo. They also could not agree on how Russian troops would fit in with any peacekeeping force, let alone whether it would be a NATO one. As the talks continued, the Americans became increasingly alarmed by the resistance to any concessions that came from within Chernomyrdin's delegation, especially from the military representatives. The final talks took place in Germany, in the Petersberg castle overlooking the Rhine, at the beginning of June. At 4.00 a.m. on 3 June, after thirteen hours of discussion, the positions of the negotiators had not moved. Then, suddenly, the Russians made a major concession. The diplomats believe that Yeltsin called Chernomyrdin and just told him to come to an agreement as soon as possible. So Chernomyrdin simply agreed that 'all' Serbian forces should leave Kosovo. By way of a compromise, it was also agreed that an unspecified number of them would later be allowed to return to perform four specific tasks. There was still no agreement on how the post-war peacekeeping force would work or about the Russian place in it, but all three sides believed that they still had time to deal with this. For the purpose of getting Milošević to accept the deal, they also worked out a formula of words which both the US and the Chernomyrdin found acceptable. The document specified that the 'effective international civil and security presences' called for by the G-8 document should come under UN, not NATO, auspices but then added that this should have 'substantial' NATO 'participation' and had to be deployed under a 'unified command and control'.[19] The military in the Russian delegation were outraged. They declared that they did not approve of the two-page document that was now being drawn up to present to Milošević. Chernomyrdin hit back, saying, according to one diplomat who was there: 'The only thing that matters is that I have the approval of the president of the Russian Federation.'

Chernomyrdin and Ahtisaari left for Cologne military airport and flew to Belgrade. Just before they left, Chernomyrdin said to the Americans: 'I want your word that if we can get Milošević to accept this you'll stop bombing.' When they got to Belgrade, Chernomyrdin and Ahtisaari sat, side by side, peering at Milošević over an extravagant ornamental flower display. Ahtisaari read the document and also warned Milošević that, unless he accepted, the bombers would step up their destruction of Serbia's infrastructure, including the telephone system. Milošević asked if the terms were negotiable and Ahtisaari said they were not. He then warned him that, if he turned them down, any future terms would be even stiffer. Serbian President Milutinović tried to argue, but Milošević said that he would send the document to parliament and asked Ahtisaari to address the deputies. He refused – and he then turned down an invitation to dinner, as did Chernomyrdin. According to Braca Grubačić, Milošević was furious. 'It showed him that the time for jokes over dinner was over.'

Milošević now called Drašković and Šešelj and told them that parliament would meet the next morning and it would accept the deal. Drašković agreed but Šešelj refused. In the chamber his people began arguing but they were outnumbered and the parliament voted to accept. Milošević met Chernomyrdin and Ahtisaari again. At that moment a NATO jet streaked across the city, causing a loud sonic boom. Milošević was the only one in the room not to flinch. 'We accept your terms,' he said. The Yugoslavs were now given General Clark's telephone number, plus several others at NATO, and then Chernomyrdin and Ahtisaari left. They flew to Cologne to brief Talbott who then went to Brussels to brief the NATO ambassadors. According to one report: 'The meeting started at 8.30 p.m., and General Clark was late. When the general walked into the room about 30 minutes later, he announced he had just received a call from the Yugoslav military.'[20]

On 5 June talks began in an Albanian-owned café, just over the Kosovo border at Blace in Macedonia. It was just a few hundred yards from where tens of thousands of refugees had, in April, been briefly prevented from entering the country. General Sir Mike Jackson was charged with negotiating a Military–Technical Agreement on the mechanics of the Yugoslav pull-out. Once a 'verifiable withdrawal' had begun, the air strikes would be called off. After one major hitch, when the Yugoslavs tried to negotiate but soon realised that they were in no position to do so, the agreement was signed on 9 June. The talks had by now been moved to a large tent at Kumanovo, Macedonia's northernmost city, close to the border with Serbia. General Jackson says the atmosphere was 'Perfectly workmanlike. There was no overt hostility. They wanted to get it done. They were more resigned than bitter. There was no animosity.' But, as the Serbs signed what amounted to their capitulation, they must have felt the presence of the ghosts of their grandfathers – who had 'avenged Kosovo' and redeemed it for Serbia in 1912 at the Battle of Kumanovo.

Paying for the hill

Several factors induced Milošević to back down. All of his calculations had failed. NATO had not split, he was unable to spark new wars in Macedonia and Bosnia and, in the end, the Russians had proved unwilling or unable to help him. If he thought that discontent in Russia over its treatment of Serbia would lead to political changes there, he was also wrong.

Milošević enjoys being the centre of diplomatic attention. He enjoys the prestige of the visits of envoys from world powers.

Now he understood, though, that all of this was over. Unlike Bosnia, there would be no Dayton and no glittering signing ceremony in Paris either. All that was impossible now. On 27 May he was indicted for war crimes in Kosovo by the International Criminal Tribunal for the former Yugoslavia in The Hague. He, and four others, stood accused of 'Crimes against Humanity' and 'Violations of the Laws and Customs of War'. The massacre at Račak was cited as a specific case along with the later massacre at Bela Crkva and 'the unlawful deportation and forcible transfer of thousands of Kosovo Albanians from their homes'. Until now, the Yugoslav leadership had not taken the Hague Tribunal seriously, and had anyway always regarded it as an anti-Serb kangaroo court. After the indictments were read out, Milutinović called an aide who had been watching the proceedings on satellite television and said: 'So, what did they bullshit about Slobo, then?' He was shocked when his embarrassed aide told him that he, too, was on the list. The indictment said:

> The planning, preparation and execution of the campaign undertaken by forces of the FRY and Serbia in Kosovo was planned, instigated, ordered, committed or otherwise aided and abetted by **Slobodan MILOSEVIC,** the President of the FRY; **Milan MILUTINOVIC,** the President of Serbia; **Nikola SAINOVIC,** the Deputy Prime Minster of the FRY; Colonel General **Dragoljub OJDANIC,** the Chief of the General Staff of the VJ [Yugoslav Army]; and **Vlajko STO-JILJKOVIC,** the Minister of Internal Affairs of Serbia.[21]

The Serbian leadership, and indeed the Serbs in general, thought that the indictment, especially coming when it did, was proof, if any more were needed, that the court was simply a political instrument of the US and her allies to be used against the Serbs. The court, of course, denies this saying that the indictment was published when sufficient evidence had been collected. However, court sources do not deny that Lousie Arbour, the outgoing Canadian prosecutor, had speeded up proceedings, because, knowing that the Chernomyrdin–Talbott–Ahtisaari talks were at a sensitive stage, she wanted to close off any possibility that either Milošević might secretly be guaranteed some form of *de facto* immunity from prosecution or that he might be offered the possibility of exile. At the time, South

Africa, Belarus and China were all rumoured to be possible destinations for the Milošević family. Indeed, in an interview broadcast on 26 April, Arbour had actually said that she wanted to make sure that the Tribunal 'moved sufficiently rapidly' with its work so that, 'if and when the time comes for some kind of political settlement, that amnesty doesn't become a currency in the talks'. When she was asked if it might be a problem if Milošević had been indicted but would also have to be involved in the peace process, she said that that was 'frankly, not much of a concern to this office'.[22]

As far as Milošević was concerned, the indictment not only condemned him to personal isolation as president, but it also confirmed to him what was in general true, that he and Serbia's élite were increasingly in NATO's sight. One of the recent NATO targets had been his house. So, Milošević was encircled diplomatically and militarily, and was promised worse to come by NATO. Ordinary people were suffering more and more, the Russians undoubtedly told him they could not head off a ground war and Mira, his wife, always prone to depression, was now breaking into floods of tears, even crying in front of students during a class she taught at university. Milošević calculated it was time to cut his losses.

Živadin Jovanović says the failure of the Russians to back the Serbs to the end was, 'I must admit, very relevant'. But he says that the main reason that Yugoslavia accepted the deal was that:

> Hospitals were left without electricity ... you can't even store vaccines and heal wounded people. Civilian struc-tures were being targeted. It was a most inhumane war. They tried everything but nuclear weapons ... I think they were getting out of their minds. NATO commanders were seeking excuses to burn the country and commit further massive killings. So the government, considering that the document guaranteed the territorial integrity and sovereignty of Yugoslavia, the equality of all in Kosovo–Metohija and the turning over of competencies from NATO to the UN, decided not to risk massive genocide by NATO against the whole population. It was also fair to conclude that we would preserve our defensive capacity and so the government and leadership opted to accept the

deal based on sovereignty and territorial integrity, the guarantee of a political solution based on autonomy and the resolving of problems by the rules of the UN rather than NATO force.

There are, however, two other factors we need to consider here. On the ground in Kosovo, the first few days and weeks of the campaign had seen the KLA not routed but certainly on the run. The security forces pushed the guerrillas into the hills and chopped up the zones where they operated into small enclaves. In the middle of March, however, Agim Çeku, who as a captain in the Croatian army had made those approaches with General Tom Berisha to Bukoshi in 1991, slipped back into Kosovo to assume control of the KLA. Since 1991, Çeku had risen through the ranks until in August 1995 he was one of the five commanders of Operation Storm which, in three days, swept away the Serbian enclave of Krajina and cleansed, or sent into flight, almost its entire population of some 170,000 people. After that, he worked with a group of retired US officers, who maintained close contacts with the US defence establishment, and who came from a company called Military Professional Resources Inc., or MPRI. They worked together on the transformation of the Croatian army into a Western-style fighting force. After Operation Storm, MPRI were credited with, or accused of, having helped prepare the Croatian army for the assault. How useful Çeku's contacts via MPRI were when he became KLA chief of staff remains to be seen.

Çeku says that when he returned to Kosovo he was sure 'war was coming'. First, he says, 'I needed time to see all my commanders and to organise and lead them and to involve the remaining FARK elements.' Once the air campaign started and the KLA was driven into enclaves, its operations were hampered by the fact that it had to help care for the thousands of refugees who had also fled into the hills. In some cases, where food was running low, it encouraged people to leave for the camps outside.

Çeku is adamant that the KLA received no physical help from NATO countries. He says that during the bombardments he had 12,000 men under arms inside Kosovo with 8,000 outside being trained in Albania. According to NATO estimates, he had fewer men. The real problem for the KLA, in the enclaves inside Kosovo, was that they were cut off. While small groups could trek out to Albania and Macedonia and back, it was impossible to infiltrate large numbers of men, with arms, ammunitions and supplies. The Serbs largely succeeded in driving the KLA off the main roads, but they were unable to crush them and increasingly the KLA operated in small guerrilla units, picking off soldiers here and there.

The situation in the interior was very different compared to that on the border with Albania. Here at Košare, behind Junik, the KLA managed to carve out a small enclave into which it brought volunteers coming home to fight from abroad. The strategy was to punch through two corridors from the border to the interior. Arms came from Albania and from abroad. Planes organised by Albanian–Americans brought boots, uniforms, satellite phones and some arms too. According to one source, high-power sniper rifles were sent to Albania via a loophole in US law. It was discovered that it was legal to export rifles to registered hunting clubs, so, says the source, 'we set one up in Albania!'

The number of Kosovars who poured into Albania in 1998 and 1999 was impressive. Thousands came from Germany, Switzerland and the other countries of the diaspora. They undertook short training courses in Kukës or other camps, such as Helshan. A group of 217 came from the US and fought under the title of the Atlantic Brigade. Although the KLA in Albania gave an impression of poor organisation, the fact that Serbs were not pouring home from abroad said much about the long-term determination of both peoples and the future of Kosovo. In the end, the simple fact was that most Albanian Kosovars lived in Kosovo but only 2 per cent of 10 million Serbs did.

On 26 May the KLA began a major offensive to try and break out of the Kosare enclave. From across the border, they had the support of Albanian army artillery. The fighting on Mount Paštrik was extremely tough and, as we have seen, time was now running out to make a decision on a ground war. General Clark gave the order to intervene directly. 'That mountain is not going to get lost. I'm not going to have Serbs on that mountain ... We'll pay for that hill with American blood if we don't help [the KLA] hold it.'[23] On 7 June Yugoslav forces were bombed by US B-52s. Two days later the Military–Technical Agreement was signed and sealed. Çeku says:

> One of the reasons Milošević had to end the war was because we were attacking from the border and he was obliged to bring in many units who made good targets. Before, they had been dug in, but our attack made them come out. NATO enjoyed *that* bombing! The Serbs were faced with low morale and no one wanted to go to Paštrik or Košare. Milošević was in danger of losing his army. One B-52 killed 224 soldiers.

It is quite possible that the fear of a KLA breakthrough on the border which could have led to thousands of men pouring down the mountain was one more reason why Milošević decided to back down when he did. However, after the war, when NATO military investigators went to Mount Paštrik and looked over their bomb craters, they found no evidence whatsoever that large numbers of men had died there. One report also notes that 'NATO commanders were surprised to see the robust columns that eventually withdrew from Kosovo and they concluded that the Yugoslav 3rd Army could have held out for weeks or even months.'[24]

There is another mystery that remains to be solved. Some believe that Milošević was given a secret promise, that, if he agreed to the Chernomyrdin–Ahtisaari deal, Russian troops would be flown into Kosovo. They would then peel off and establish a sector in the north, around Mitrovica and the Trepča mines which, at some later stage, Milošević might be able to hive off in any partition of Kosovo. On 11 June some 200 Russian troops from SFOR left Bosnia and drove to Kosovo where, after a triumphal entry into Priština, where they were greeted by ecstatic Serbs, they moved to secure the nearby Slatina airport. According to senior official sources, the Russians then filed flight plans with the Bulgarians and Romanians who stunned them by refusing them permission to fly over their countries. One source says: 'We had reports that the planes were already in the air. In fact this was not true, but it was what we were hearing.' General Clark now ordered General Jackson to move his troops, who had not yet entered Kosovo, to seize the airport. Jackson responded, famously, that he would not start World War

Three for him. It is of course an intriguing theory but there is no hard evidence that the Russians were either capable of or willing to mount such an operation. Within days, the Russian troops at the airport had to ask the British for bread.

Dear Citizens

On 10 June NATO suspended its bombing and the UN Security Council passed Resolution 1244 which sanctioned the entry of NATO troops into Kosovo and guaranteed Yugoslav sovereignty. Milošević appeared on television. 'Dear Citizens,' he said. 'The aggression is over. Peace has overcome violence ... I wish us happy peace.'

> At this moment, our first thoughts should go to the heroes who gave their lives in the defense of the fatherland, in the struggle for the freedom and dignity of their people ... All their names will be made known, but now I want to inform you that 462 members of the Yugoslav Army and 114 members of the police force of the Republic of Serbia were killed in the war ... Our entire nation has taken part in this war – from babies in maternity wards to patients in intensive care to soldiers in air-defense trenches and patrolmen on the borders. No one can forget the heroism of the defenders of the bridges, of the citizens who defended factories, squares, their cities, their jobs, their country, their people. Our nation is a hero. That may be the shortest conclusion about this war. Our nation is a hero and that is why it must feel heroic, and that is why it must act heroically, which means with dignity, generously and responsibly. Early this year there were numerous rallies throughout our country. One slogan could have been heard there: we won't give up Kosovo. We haven't given up Kosovo ...[25]

10 Tomorrow's Masters of Kosova

Early on the morning of the 10 June, British troops began moving into Kosovo. One of the first people they met on the road from Macedonia was Xhabir Zharku or Blind, the KLA man who had owned a pizzeria in Sweden and managed an insulation company in the US before he had left for Tropoja to help organise the struggle. He was now the KLA commander in Kačanik, and, as the Serbian police left, he moved into the local police chief's office.

The British, and the troops that followed them, thought they were coming to protect Kosovo's Albanians. But, from the very first day, as they watched the Serbian police and army pull out, on schedule and according to the Military–Technical Agreement, they began to realise that Kosovo had changed. Just as everyone had been vaguely aware, to borrow Braca Grubačić's phrase again, that, in the event of bombing a 'let's fuck them' attitude would mean Serbs taking revenge on Albanians, but with no one knowing how bad it would be, the same was true again. Just as the policy makers underestimated the Serb will to expel or encourage the flight of as much of the Kosovar population as possible, they now underestimated the unrelenting thirst for revenge amongst the Albanians returning home.

Within days, the borders from Macedonia and Albania were jammed solid as hundreds of thousands of Kosovars streamed back home. Within three weeks, half a million out of those who had left the province during the bombing were back. By late November, the figure stood at 808,913 out of a total of 848,100.[1] It was the quickest and biggest refugee return in modern history, and also the quickest role reversal. As they came home, tens of thousands of Serbs did not wait to find out what would happen next. They knew. So, as the police and army pulled out, they packed their cars and tractors and left. There would be no bombing to secure their homecoming.

After her tour of northern Albania and Kosovo in 1908,

Edith Durham wrote that it was 'the fashion among journalists and others to talk of the "lawless Albanians"; but there is perhaps no other people in Europe so much under the tyranny of laws'. The problem was the nature of that law: 'The unwritten law of blood is to the Albanian as is the Fury of Greek tragedy. It drives him inexorably to his doom. The curse of blood is upon him when he is born, and it sends him to an early grave.' She went on to add: 'And lest you that read this book should cry out at the "customs of savages", I would remind you that we play the game on a much larger scale and call it war.'[2] But this was war, or rather the next chapter of the war, and not necessarily the last.

By November, the Yugoslav Red Cross had registered some 247,391 people, mostly but not only Serbs and Gypsies, who had been driven out or had fled.[3] Since an autumn KFOR survey indicated that there might be 100,000 Serbs left in Kosovo, this appeared to suggest that either this figure was wrong, or there were fewer refugees, or that there had been more than 200,000 Serbs in the province before the war. It was also unclear whether the some 16,000 Krajina refugees in Kosovo had now been registered again – as Kosovo refugees. Another theory was that Serbian emigration from Kosovo over the last 25 years had, in the last ten years, been offset by the immigration of bureaucrats, policemen and their families plus Serbian students who had been sent to Priština University.

He took my tractor!

Outside Dečani, Father Sava's monastery, was an imposing tank. Italian soldiers in sunglasses and designer stubble lounged on top. Every few hours a couple of monks would advance out of the monastery gate carrying a tray of small Turkish coffees for them. The monks were delighted that the Italians had secured Dečani. After all, it was not the first time. In 1941, when the area had been incorporated into Mussolini's Greater Albania, Albanian nationalists and Fascist Blackshirts had come to burn down the monastery and drive out the monks. But the monks had called for help from the regular Italian army, which had duly come to save them. When this new generation of Italians was deployed here, the Italian KFOR commander had come to visit the monks. They got down the visitors book from 1941 and looked up what his predecessor had said …. He had written that he liked the monastery's mineral water.

Twenty minutes away, in Peć, frightened Serbs were taking refuge in the Patriarchate Church. During the bombing, the monks at Dečani had taken in and looked after Albanians from town. Now they had gone home and local Gypsies or Roma had taken their place. Along with the Serbs, the Gypsies would also become an Albanian target for vengeance since they were widely believed to have collaborated with the Serbs and to have looted Albanian homes. Father Sava was matter-of-fact about the future: 'Kosovo has the same destiny as Asia Minor, once full of wonderful Christian sites and now all ruins and ash, or Constantinople now a Muslim city, or Palestine which once had flourishing Christian communities.'

Durham wrote that, amongst the 'Dukaghini tribes' of northern Albania and parts of Kosovo, the council of the elders 'has the power not merely to burn [someone's] house' when it came to a question of revenge, but also 'to destroy his crops, fell his trees,' and 'slaughter his beasts'.[4] During the past year the Serbian police and the paramilitaries had done this to Albanians and now the Kosovo Serbs would pay the price. In the village of Drsnik, near Klina, armed men roamed through houses which after looting they put to the torch. One man explained that the best way to set a house on fire was to begin with a pile of paper and cover that with branches. Perhaps embarrassed in front of a foreigner, he then said: 'They burned my house so I'll burn their houses.' Asked why, if his house had been destroyed, he did not move into the Serb house since the owners had fled, he looked incredulous. 'Because, one day, they might come back, and then I would have to move out.'

KFOR's soldiers had no idea how to deal with all of this. The experience of the British, the French, the Americans and the Russians in Bosnia had no relevance whatsoever here. There, armies had had to be placed under control and ethnic cleansing having been more or less completed, Serbs, Muslims and Croats had already been winnowed out into separate regions. The British adopted a superior attitude towards their KFOR colleagues. 'This is Northern Ireland,' said one officer. 'We know what to do. We have the experience. The others don't.' It was not much consolation for the Serbs of Priština, which fell in the British sector. The Serbian population fell from some 20,000 to less than 1,000. Ordinary Serbs were murdered, and when armed men showed up telling them to 'go back to Serbia' because their flats were now required for Albanians, there was not much they could do. To give them their due, the British began to guard Serbs when they found out where they were and they began helping the elderly to survive, but the pressures were too great for most Serbs in Priština and other towns to withstand.

In Vučitrn, within days of the French deployment there, one soldier struggled to protect an old woman from a mob of recently returned Albanians. She called the French, who had a checkpoint at the top of the lane where she lived, when neighbours had broken into her house. The French were already involved in a quarrel with Albanians who had reported an old Serb man, claiming that he was 'a sniper'. The French soldier said: 'He doesn't look like a sniper … they just want to get him out.' Now, the old woman and her neighbours were screaming at each other. She was shouting: 'They are stealing my stuff!' Opposite her house was the burnt shell of her neighbour's house. An Albanian was screaming: 'It cost me 200,000 marks to build it … her son did it … she stole my stuff.' She shouted: 'You're KLA! You're terrorists!' The Albanians shouted: 'You're a Chetnik! Go back to Serbia!' The soldier said: 'You must leave her alone in her house!' The Albanian neighbour said: 'There are 35 people in my family – where am I going to put them? She is alone in that big house!' The woman disappeared. The soldier said: 'You will not take her house!' The Albanian shouted: 'Her son is a paramilitary member. He fought in Drenica. He took my tractor! He killed one hundred people and he's got a big beard!' The soldier said: 'I don't care about her son!' The old woman returned with a crowbar. A few hundred metres away plumes of smoke rose from Gypsy houses which were being set on fire while people staggered out from inside laden down with furniture and clothes. The Frenchman said that if there was more trouble she should call him. 'But aren't you going to stay by my house?' she said. 'They'll come in the night and slit my throat.' The Frenchman said: 'The minute we go from here they'll kill each other.' He meant, when KFOR left Kosovo, but the reality was that the killings had already begun.

Several hundred Serbs died in the months after KFOR deployed. Albanians were killed too, either because they had been collaborators with the Serbs or thanks to crime which flourished in this lawless environment.

For years Human Rights Watch from New York had been chronicling the abuses committed by the Serbian authorities in Kosovo. Seven weeks after their departure they issued a damning report about the new reality:

> Ethnic Albanian civilians have taken part in much of the burning and looting of Serb and Roma property, and in a few instances, in violent attacks on their neighbors. Returning refugees, many of whom lost their own property through theft and arson prior to June, have been particularly implicated in the expulsion of Serbs and Roma from their homes. The most serious incidents of violence, however, have been carried out by members of the KLA. Although the KLA leadership issued a statement on July 20 condemning attacks on Serbs and Roma, and KLA political leader Hashim Thaçi publicly denounced the July 23 massacre of fourteen Serb farmers, it remains unclear whether these beatings and killings were committed by local KLA units acting without official sanction, or whether they represent a coordinated KLA policy. What is indisputable, however, is that the frequency and severity of such abuses make it incumbent upon the KLA leadership to take swift and decisive action to prevent them.[5]

This never happened. Indeed, even after the demilitarisation of the KLA, killings continued, sometimes committed by the 'secret police' which was connected to Thaçi's ministry of the interior. In a café, one of its members boasted that he had taken a wrong turn in a Serbian area in the north while driving with his girlfriend. An old man waved his fist at him. He stopped, reversed, pulled down the window and told his girlfriend to give him his pistol, which was in the glove compartment. 'Boom,' he said to his friends in the café. The girlfriend was impressed.

In Prizren, Human Rights Watch talked to Maria Filipović and Trifun Stamenković, who on the morning of 21 June had gone shopping. During the few days before they, and their spouses, had been harassed and beaten by 'men in KLA uniforms'. As the report points out: 'While KFOR has found that some persons arrested in KLA uniform have proven to be criminals unaffiliated with the KLA, nothing indicates that these persons were not KLA members.' Trifun Stamenković, aged 85, told Human Rights Watch:

> I left at about 10.00 a.m. and when I returned at 11.00 a.m. I couldn't find my wife. When I came inside, I saw the broken windows and everything broken. I was in the door-way and I went back outside and I saw a German patrol, two jeeps. I told them my wife was missing, that she wasn't in the house. When I entered the house with them I saw only my wife's knees. Her knees were bloody. I didn't see the rest of her body; the Germans took me outside. They saw her dead; they didn't let me inside to see her.

When they were interviewed, both Filipović and Stamenković were, with other Serbs, taking refuge in the Serbian Orthodox seminary where Edith Durham had lunched with the director and his frightened wife in 1908 (see p.13). She had written then: 'I could not but admire the imaginative nature of the Serb, who will lead a forlorn hope and face death for an idea.'[6] But years later, these were not Serbs who wanted to die for an idea. They were just innocent old people.

> When Maria Filipović returned from her shopping, German KFOR troops had already discovered that her husband had been attacked as well, and was dying from his stab wounds. As Maria stood in front of her home crying, her Albanian Catholic neighbors told her that KLA members had committed the killings. Both victims had their throats cut. German soldiers told Human Rights Watch that Marica Stamenković had been nearly decapitated.[7]

General Klaus Reinhardt, who took over from General Mike Jackson as head of KFOR in October 1999, said that with such levels of hatred his troops faced 'a very difficult job':

> The desire for revenge is very deep and, by being here, we can preclude there being constant clashes and outbreaks of

violence, but to keep that stable we have to win hearts and minds and there is no tolerance now.

In November 1999, the UNHCR, together with the OSCE, published a damning report on the situation. It said that non-Albanians, including Slav Muslims, faced:

> a climate of violence and impunity, as well as widespread discrimination, harassment and intimidation directed at non-Albanians. The combination of security concerns, restricted movement, lack of access to public services (especially education, medical/health care and pensions) are the determining factors in the departure of Serbs, primarily, and other non-Albanian groups from Kosovo to date ... This widespread disrespect for human rights has increasingly also affected moderate Albanians and those who are openly critical of the current violent environment.[8]

The last remark was a reference to Veton Surroi. After the collapse of the last talks in Paris he had, contrary to advice, returned to Priština. When the bombing started he had not fled, like many of the other Albanian leaders, but shaved off his beard and gone into hiding. 'I was in a kind of depressive mood,' he says. Later, he found that, even if he had wanted to leave, it had become too dangerous to do so. At the beginning of the bombing Bajram Kelmendi, a prominent human rights lawyer, had been murdered by men in uniform. Rugova was under effective house arrest, but after having been forced to appear on television with Milošević, was released and went to Italy. Fehmi Agani was killed, by the KLA according to the Serbian police but by the police according to an account given by his son. Surroi said that his family knew he was all right because, once a week, someone would telephone the outside with the message that his aunt Mahida 'and everyone' – i.e. he – 'was okay'. Staying with different families, Surroi was in despair:

> I thought I would try and be here and help people and suddenly I'm in a situation where I can't even help myself and am even endangering the people I'm staying with. I thought, 'What would happen if the Serbs get here, get me,

and as a reprisal hunt all the families I have been with, burn all their homes and shoot and kill them?'

Now the situation had reversed itself. Surroi was reopening the Priština office of *Koha Ditore*, which, during the bombing and thanks to British money, had been published in Tetovo in Macedonia. He decided to use its pages to speak out.

> In the past month an old woman has been beaten to death in her bath; a two-year-old boy has been wounded and his mother shot dead; two youths have been killed with a grenade launcher; and a woman dares not speak her name in public for fear that those who attempted to rape her will return.

The article went on to point out that these were 'not isolated incidents' and that frightened Serbs had locked themselves in their homes 'terrified by an atmosphere in which every sound seems threatening and every vehicle that stops might take you away to your death'. Albanians had been warned not to 'feed Serbs', he said.

> I know how Kosovo's remaining Serbs, and indeed Roma, feel, because I, along with nearly 2 million Albanians, was in exactly the same situation only two and a half months ago. I recognise their fear ... This is why I cannot hide my shame to discover that, for the first time in history, we Kosovo Albanians are also capable of such monstrous acts. I have to speak out to make it clear that our moral code, by which women, children and elderly should be left unharmed, has been and is being violated.
>
> I know the obvious excuse, namely that we have been through a barbaric war in which Serbs were responsible for the most heinous crimes and in which the intensity of the violence has generated a desire for vengeance among many Albanians. This however is no justification.

What was happening, thundered Surroi, was 'the organised and systematic intimidation of all Serbs simply because they are Serbs and therefore are being held collectively responsible for what happened in Kosovo'. Everyone understood this to mean the KLA.

Such attitudes are fascist. Moreover it was against these very same attitudes that the people of Kosovo stood up and fought, at first peacefully, and then with arms, during the past 10 years. The treatment of Kosovo's Serbs brings shame on all Kosovo Albanians ... from having been victims of Europe's worst end-of-century persecution, we are ourselves becoming persecutors and have allowed the spectre of fascism to reappear.

Anybody who thinks that the violence will end once the last Serb has been driven out is living an illusion. The violence will simply be directed against other Albanians. Is this really what we fought for?[9]

Surroi was widely praised abroad for his courageous stance. But not at home. On 2 October *Kosovapress*, which had been the mouthpiece of the KLA and was now linked to Thaçi and his provisional government, attacked Surroi and Baton Haxhiu who was now editing *Koha Ditore* (Surroi is the proprietor). It warned that they risked 'eventual and very understandable revenge,' said that 'such criminals and enslaved minds should not have a place in the free Kosovo' and accused them of having a 'Slav stink' about them. If Surroi had expected that by putting his head above the parapet he could now expect that others would follow, he was to be disappointed. In fact, many of Priština's other intellectuals thought that he was 'panic mongering', that talk of 'fascism' was over the top and that there was no proof that Serbs were being persecuted by the KLA or organised elements. The situation was, they thought, simply that people wanted revenge or, having had their houses destroyed by the Serbs, wanted to take theirs. In fact, just as most Serbs had so recently been either indifferent to the fate of the Albanians, or thought they deserved to be expelled for 'asking for NATO air strikes', now most Kosovars were indifferent to the fate of the Serbs. Indeed, many thought that they deserved to be expelled, for having tried to expel them. Likewise, if anyone in authority had the power to stop this persecution and decided not to do so, it was well understood why. It was because, with every Serb that left, Serbia's claim to the province for any but legal and historical reasons became that much weaker.

But Surroi was not wrong. During the autumn of 1999, as

Rugova's war-shattered LDK began reorganising, party officials were threatened, harassed and at least one was killed. Their offices were also bombed. At the same time, firm foreign friends of Kosovo and the Albanians were disgusted and embarrassed. What had happened gave ammunition to those who, as we saw with Durham in 1908, argued that all Balkan people were savages and 'as bad as each other', and so, if they wanted to fight and kill one another, it was nobody else's business and we should let them get on with it.

After the initial wave of Serb flight and cleansing, the situation stabilised. Few Serbs remained in the big towns like Priština, Prizren and Peć; however, in some towns like Gnjilane and Orahovac small ghettos formed where Serbs were relatively free to walk about inside but risked being lynched if they ventured out. In mixed towns where there had been a large proportion of Serbs, like Kosovo Polje and Obilić, Serbs were threatened or felt they had no future and so they began to sell their houses and leave. In more solidly Serbian areas like Gračanica, KFOR-guarded enclaves formed. But as Serbs from the enclaves moved out, other Serbs from more exposed areas moved in. However, in such a situation it was obvious that, unless things changed, which did not seem very likely, the enclaves had no long-term future. Priština, for example, is a ten-minute drive away from Gračanica, but since it was too dangerous for Serbs to go there, it might as well have been on the moon. Unless they were escorted out by KFOR, it was too dangerous to leave the enclave. One woman said;

A village can't survive without a town, so, if nothing changes we'll have to leave. When KFOR first arrived we had some hope but now we're all pessimists. In the whole of Kosovo there'll only be old people waiting to die, the poor and a thousand people who believe that things will get better. We have no hospital or university faculty for my sons to go to. There are hardly any doctors. My husband has had five double bypass operations, so what happens if there is a problem? Since the Albanians took over the telephone exchange in Priština we've only been able to call inside the village, apart from that we're completely cut off.

There was one area where the situation for Serbs was different. This was in Leposavić and the northernmost part of the province where there were compact areas of Serbs in areas adjoining Serbia. Connected to this region was the town of Mitrovica. As it had had a relatively large pre-war Serbian population, tensions were extremely high as Albanians began returning and French KFOR troops began deploying. Through June and July, a sort of violent but spontaneous division took place, with Serbs gravitating to that part of town north of the River Ibar, and Albanians to the south. With French troops clashing frequently with rioters on the bridge that divided the two halves of town, it came to resemble a sort of Kosovo Mostar, the Hercegovinian town divided between Croats and Muslims. Just as west Mostar and western Hercegovina had become an adjunct of Croatia, so northern Mitrovica and adjoining areas were starting to become, or rather remain, unlike the rest of Kosovo, adjuncts of Serbia proper. With the Trepča mines nearby, there was increasing speculation that, in an attempt to salvage something from the war, Milošević might now be setting the stage for the eventual partitioning of the province. Indeed, Kosovo Serbs who had left, fled or been driven out from other parts were beginning to settle here, and other Serbs from Kosovo who had already gone to Serbia proper were being encouraged to come and live in northern Mitrovica.

The past is a foreign country

In the first few days and weeks after KFOR moved into Kosovo, places like Priština did not look and feel radically different from before – except that Albanian flags had replaced Serbian ones. A few months later, the transformation was striking. Shops had changed, signs had changed – all the ones in cyrillic and the old bilingual ones had gone – and the sound of Serbian 'turbofolk' music had been replaced by Albanian 'turbofolk'. Kiosks which once sold pictures of Arkan now sold pictures of Adem Jashari, KLA trinkets and small statues of Skanderbeg, the Albanian medieval hero. The surly Serbs who worked in the Hotel Grand had been replaced by surly Albanians, many of whom had been sacked almost a decade ago and had now reclaimed their jobs. Apart from 42,000 KFOR troops (another 10,000 were also stationed in Albania and Macedonia), thousands of foreigners criss-crossed Kosovo, working for the UN, the OSCE, the EU and scores of non-governmental organisations. To anyone who had known the province before, it was evident that 'Kosovo' was the past. It was, in fact, a foreign country. This was now Kosova. While Serbs, and probably the other small minorities, had no future here, the vast majority of Albanian Kosovars regretted nothing. Independence seemed inevitable and, anyway, they were happy that Serb rule was gone.

Driving through the city, one began to see foreign police and the first graduates of the UN's Kosovo Police Service. At a British army roadblock a Jordanian policeman asked the writer Migjen Kelmendi for his papers. He, his wife and friend had already been searched for weapons by the British soldiers. Kelmendi did not have any papers and so the polite Jordanian asked him to 'please, carry them in future'. Kelmendi's car had an Italian number plate. Most cars in Kosovo no longer had number plates or they had foreign ones. This was because, as Kosovars left during the bombing, the Serbs took the number plates, along with most people's identification papers, because they hoped that if they were still in control, which they assumed they would be, they would then be in a position to prevent a good number of people from returning later. Another reason why cars had no plates, or foreign plates, was because many of the cars were stolen or bought abroad and not registered because there was no authority to register them. The UN announced it would start registration within weeks and the British soldier growled aggressively that Kelmendi had better get the car registered or 'shit happens – understand?' Driving away, the happy Kelmendi said: 'If it had been before and he had been a Serb I would have been frightened. That's the difference.'

But would it stay like this? The UN Security Council resolution 1244 of 10 June, which had ended the bombing and ushered in NATO's presence, had also set up the UN Interim Administration Mission in Kosovo (UNMIK). Its role was:

> to establish an international civil presence in Kosovo in order to provide an interim administration for Kosovo under which the people of Kosovo can enjoy substantial

autonomy within the Federal Republic of Yugoslavia, and which will provide transitional administration while establishing and overseeing the development of provisional democratic self-governing institutions to ensure conditions for a peaceful and normal life for all inhabitants of Kosovo.[10]

One of UNMIK's tasks was to organise, before 'a final settlement', elections to 'provisional institutions for democratic and autonomous self-government pending a political settlement'. What this amounted to was a seemingly impossible and contradictory task which was to be overseen by Bernard Kouchner, the head of UNMIK and flamboyant French politician, activist and founder of *Médecins sans frontières*. It was contradictory because the Resolution stated clearly that Kosovo was part of Yugoslavia but it also told UNMIK to prepare the province for something the vast majority of its people did not want, i.e., autonomy within Yugoslavia. What would happen if, after having vigorously promoted democracy, the assembly that the Kosovars elected was told by the international community that it could not do the only thing it wanted to do, which was to declare independence? Would KFOR and the UN become seen as the occupying enemy, rather like the Serbs before them?

While not really wanting to discuss this problem, officials of UNMIK were, for practical reasons, already giving the province all the attributes of statehood. With all Yugoslav authority gone, the UN had established customs on the borders of Macedonia and Albania and was using the revenue to fund its administration of Kosovo. There were no Serbian banks left and so, for all practical purposes, the Yugoslav dinar was abolished in favour of the mark. The UN was planning to start issuing identity cards and travel documents along with number plates.

Despite Kosovo's small size, UNMIK was also discovering that it was impossible to govern the province alone. In part, this was thanks to the fact that in the chaotic days following the ending of the bombing, the KLA had seized effective power in much of the province and its people were either governing or appointing people to do so. The 'provisional government', which had been set up at Rambouillet and which, at that point, had no real function, also moved into a building in the centre of

Priština and, as much as it was able, tried to govern. With two sources of power, then, UNMIK and the 'provisional government', the UN decided it had to try to co-opt local politicians including Rugova, who appeared politically paralysed in the new situation, and even Bujar Bukoshi, who had returned still claiming to be prime minister. The first move towards this was the Kosovo Transitional Council, which was supposed to advise Kouchner. The Serbs, represented by Momčilo Trajković and Bishop Artemije, were also members, but they left, on 22 September, saying that their voice counted for nothing and they did not want to play the role of court or token Serbs.

Specifically the Serbs objected to the way in which the KLA was demilitarised as Resolution 1244 required it to be. After long negotiations, the KLA leadership agreed that the organisation should be dissolved. However, a new formation was created called the Trupat Mbrojtëse të Kosovës or Kosovo Protection Corps (KPC). It was to consist of 3,000 men with 2,000 reservists and, according to the agreement, it was to be a 'civilian emergency service agency' whose tasks were:

> to provide disaster response services; perform search and rescue; provide a capacity for humanitarian assistance in isolated areas; assist in demining and contribute to rebuilding infrastructure and communities.[11]

In fact, the agreement was a compromise between the KLA and KFOR. The KLA handed in more than 10,000 weapons, 5.5 million rounds of ammunition and 27,000 grenades and agreed to stop wearing uniforms. Recruitment then started amongst former KLA members, inviting them to apply to join the KPC, which would only be allowed to keep 200 weapons. As it was dissolved, KLA leaders said they wanted the KPC to be seen as the nucleus of the future army of Kosovo, and they made little secret of the fact that a good proportion of their arms had not been handed in. A large part of their former weaponry was also believed to be hidden in Albania, where it remained when the war ended. General Çeku and the rest of the former KLA leadership then transferred to the leadership of the KPC. At a distance, the symbol of the KPC looks identical to that of the old KLA. But instead of the Albanian double-headed black eagle on a red background, the KPC symbol is black map of Kosovo on a red background. To all intents and purposes, the KPC is the KLA in mothballs. An alternative translation of its name from Albanian into English is the rather more martial-sounding Kosovo Defensive Troops. Asked about its future, Pleurat Sejdiu referred to its Albanian initials TMK and said: 'You know what the students say? Tomorrow's Masters of Kosova.'

A year earlier, Sejdiu had still been driving a minicab in London and operating out of an office in an Albanian car-wash off the city's Finchley Road. Now he was deputy foreign minister in the provisional government in Priština. The foreign minister was Bardhyl Mahmuti who had come home from Vevey. Their friend Jashar Salihu, the head of the Homeland Calling fund, had come home but gone abroad again for medical treatment as he was found to be seriously ill. Hashim Thaçi the prime minister, worked in the office next door to Sejdiu. Together, they had all formed a political party which had grown out of the old LPK and KLA. But its future was not guaranteed. With little law and order, people blamed the KLA for having brought crime in its wake and were frightened of former KLA men, or people who claimed to be KLA men, appropriating flats and shops and businesses at gunpoint. Many of these criminals were believed to be mafiosi from Albania. The effect of this was to restore Rugova's popularity, even though following his return he was virtually invisible, making very few public appearances. The Albanians could now, more than ever, have done with Fehmi Agani with his discreet, behind-the-scenes fixing and deal-making and his calming influence. His murder had caused irreparable damage to the Kosovar body politic.

At the turn of the millennium, Kosovo seemed set fair for independence, but there was no telling how long this process would take or how it would come about. Sejdiu said: 'Now we are living in a new reality. Serbia, Yugoslavia cannot decide.' Diplomats and UN officials in Priština said they hoped the problem would go away because they expected the entire region to change. Striking a compromise between Yugoslav sovereignty and the Kosovar Albanian desire for independence, a revived Rambouillet Accord, perhaps, might be possible once Milošević had gone. Apart from the fact that Albanian politicians rejected this possibility, there was no reason to assume that any post-Milošević government would be any more pliable on this question, especially as it could not afford to lay itself open to charges of betraying the nation. Besides, things could also change for the worse. If Montenegro declared independence, then there might be a new war to worry about.

While on the one hand there was no appetite in Western capitals to support the secession of Kosovo, on the other there was no desire to support the claims to territorial integrity of a country led by an indicted war criminal. But some diplomats in Priština said they thought that sticking their 'heads firmly in the sand' was not much of a policy. 'Either we accept independence as inevitable,' said one, 'and deal with the remnant Serb populations or we try and somehow convince Albanians that they'll never be independent and try to restore their contacts with Yugoslavia immediately.' Neither of these things looked likely to happen. So, in the long run, Kosovo might remain a unique and expensive protectorate in which its guarantors, NATO and the UN, just hope they do not become the eventual targets of Albanian rage. Still, optimistic UNMIK officials say that the future of Kosovo is 'a process' which has only just begun. Citing the examples of Northern Ireland, South Africa and Israel and the Palestinians, one said that, before any talks began, it would be 'difficult and unnecessary to focus on the endgame'.

For some Kosovars, of course, independence was not the endgame. It is the eventual unification of all the lands inhabited by Albanians into a Greater Albania. Of course, in the short term, this is a remote possibility. Albania is an economic basket-case and the government in Tirana is so weak it can barely govern all of Albania let alone consider absorbing Kosovo. However, the long-term aim of many Kosovar politicians, such as Rexhep Qosja, is the union of Kosovo and Albania. In the past this question was somewhat academic since Kosovo was part of Yugoslavia and only a tiny handful of Kosovars had ever been to Albania. The war changed all that. Five hundred thousand Albanian Kosovars were sheltered there during the period of the NATO bombing, an enormous proportion of the population, and while they appreciated the welcome, the experience also shattered any enduring myths about 'Mother Albania'. Kosovars were shocked by the poverty and the corruption of the country they had grown up idealising and there was bitterness too when many of the refugees were robbed. Having been expelled from your house in the morning by Serbs, only then, in the afternoon, to be robbed by fellow Albanians of your tractor on which you were hauling your family to safety, was a salutary experience for a good number of Kosovars. So, for many, independence is increasingly seen as an end in itself rather than an interim stop on the way to uniting all Albanians in one state.

Six months after the end of the war the whole question of a possible future union remained something for the distant future. However, there were already hints that fierce clashes could lie ahead. Migjen Kelmendi decided he would now write his weekly column for *Koha Ditore* in the Gheg dialect spoken in northern Albania and Kosovo. He said: 'This is the last taboo.' In 1972, academics from Kosovo, including Qosja, had signed an agreement on the adoption of a common standard literary Albanian language. One of the signatories from Albania was the writer Ismail Kadare, who had made that appeal to the Kosovars in Rambouillet. In fact, most of the standard literary language was based on the Tosk dialect spoken in the south of the country where Enver Hoxha (and Kadare) came from. Hoxha was deeply suspicious of anything northern because his Communists came mainly from the south while Albania's wartime anti-Communists came mainly from the north. However, the adoption of this standard Albanian suited Kosovar academics because it made an ideological point, which was that all Albanians were one and that by implication Kosovars were not Yugoslavs. So, from then on, Kosovars were taught in school to write in a way they did not speak.

As Kelmendi raised the issue, many were discomfited because the language question raised the broader political question. That was, that if there could be two different but legitimate forms of Albanian, then, of course, there could be two different Albanian states. Indeed, some said, why should there not be two? Germany, Austria and German-speaking Switzerland all co-existed happily without having to be combined into one state. The irony of the war was that while Serbia's actions made more likely the long-term formal secession of Kosovo, it diminished the chances of a future Greater Albania which the Serbs had always, and not incorrectly, accused Albanians of wanting.

Waiting for Adenauer

In Belgrade the post-war period was marked with bitterness. At the end of the bombing Milošević celebrated a victory. But no one really believed him. Despite official talk of Resolution 1244 guaranteeing Yugoslav sovereignty, officials began to rail at Kouchner, and KFOR, accusing them of working towards secession and of playing with fire. Živadin Jovanović, the foreign minister, went further, saying that the West had:

> exchanged a friendly ally for the devil's pumpkins! They will backfire on their heads! They are drugs traffickers and terrorists! It will backfire! Kosovo will never be lost. It is Serbian and will remain Serbian forever despite the temporary ambitions of Mr Kouchner as a *gauleiter* in his image as a small Napoleon. He will never have approval for what he is doing.

After the bombing stopped, Serbia's opposition thought that the time was right to organise rallies and to topple Milošević or to call for early elections. But its leadership was as divided as before and they failed to raise enough support. Some people began to talk of the 'Ceauşescu scenario', believing that Milošević would only leave power like the Romanian dictator Nicolae Ceauşescu who was executed at Christmas 1989, once enough people inside the system had decided it was in their interests for him to go. As summer turned to winter, fewer and fewer people were interested in politics. Vuk Drasković survived an apparent assassination attempt, but, on 15 January 2000, Arkan did not. Following the damage caused to Serbia's power and heating systems by NATO, heating became the national obsession. There were also worries about the long-term environmental impact of the bombing, quite apart from the destruction of factories and the consequent loss of jobs.

A UN Balkans Task Force (BTF) was established. Its job was to investigate the environmental impact of the war, both the NATO bombings and the consequences of the fighting in Kosovo. Its conclusion was that 'the Kosovo conflict has not caused an environmental catastrophe affecting the Balkans as a whole'. However, while it noted that at four main sites, Pančevo, Kragujevac, Novi Sad and Bor, 'environmental contamination

due to the consequences of the Kosovo conflict was identified',
it was hard to ascertain what had been caused by the bombing
and what pre-dated the conflict.[12] Addressing the question of
depleted uranium (DU), a substance used in some cruise missiles
and airborne-launched shells, the task force tested for contamination around sites attacked in Priština and took measurements
from damaged military vehicles but found 'no indications of
contamination'. However, as there was 'a lack of information
from NATO confirming that DU was or was not used' and, if it
was, where and how much, it was impossible to come to any
conclusions.[13]

The fact that the Balkans Task Force report was rather
inconclusive was unfortunate because it meant that all sorts of
conspiracy theories could continue to grow and to be believed
by an ever-wider range of people. We must remember that
people in Serbia had, by now, lived with war, sanctions and
isolation for almost a decade, even though war in the physical
sense of death and destruction only came to Serbia proper with
the beginning of the NATO bombing. However, in the months
after the bombing it was ever clearer that the isolation of almost
a decade had taken a terrible toll in people's perception of Serbia
and its place in the world. Intelligent and educated people were
increasingly prey to bizarre, crackpot theories. For example, it
came to be widely believed that Milošević was 'America's man'
and always did what the US wanted, including, for example,
having his country bombed for some unclear purpose. A
common view from one highly educated person was this:

> The US wants the biological extinction of the Serbs.
> Educated people like me will all leave and so our children
> will assimilate in other countries and no longer be Serbs. In
> this way Serbia will be left with uneducated riff-raff,
> peasants and refugees. The reason for this is that the
> Americans are low-grade biological material, being the
> descendants of slaves, criminals and people who left
> Europe because they came from bad families. Milošević is
> Clinton's man and, naturally, he does whatever Clinton
> orders him to.

Of course, not everyone believed this sort of thing. However, and
equally seriously, the bombing had left many of those who

wanted a genuine Western-style democracy disillusioned and angry because democracy had now become associated with what most Serbs considered the unjust rule of force. Also, whereas some Serbs might have been willing to express regret for some of the terrible things done in their name in Kosovo during the conflict, the fact that almost a quarter of a million Serbs and others had now fled or been ethnically cleansed, under the noses of the UN and KFOR, meant that this seemed confirmation, if any was necessary for them, that Milošević had been right about Kosovo all along. That is to say, the only way to keep the province in check was to rule it with an iron hand and, in the event of war, it was 'us or them'. In fact, in this way, the Serbs of Kosovo who had featured so prominently in the rise of Milošević, could now be used again as their plight played into his hands.

Serbia began the new millennium isolated and poverty-stricken. It was a pariah throughout Europe and the West in general, although, as Milisav Pajić of the foreign ministry noted, in Serbia's view his country was 'not isolated'. On his visit to the UN General Assembly in New York in September 1999, Živadin Jovanović had met with his counterparts from many countries who had told him that they supported Yugoslavia. Unfortunately for Serbia, most of those countries were neither potential trading partners nor investors. Yugoslavia also retained the support of Russia and China, but, as was evident from their failure to prevent the bombing of Yugoslavia, their global power and influence was limited.

The anger and bitterness of ordinary Serbs was also aroused by the fact that they believed that they had been victimised and picked on because it was politically *possible* to bomb *them*. They drew attention to Turkey's war with the Kurds which they said was ignored because Turkey was a valuable Western ally, or Russia's brutal wars in Chechnya which the West was unwilling or unable to do anything about because Russia was a nuclear power. The same applied to Tibet and China.

Although Serbia remained in a parlous state after the bombing, some infrastructure, such as bridges, were rebuilt quickly. Western countries, however, ruled out the lifting of economic sanctions and the reintegration of Serbia into the European mainstream while Milošević remained in power. Nevertheless, some questioned whether this was a sensible policy. They pointed out that the only time that Milošević's power had been seriously threatened was during the demonstrations of 1996 and 1997 when, following the end of the Bosnian war, life for ordinary Serbs had begun to improve again. Their expectations had been dashed again, and all people could worry about was heating and keeping their families. Also, as we have seen, the enforced isolation and poverty of Serbia had a dangerous side-effect, in that since most Serbs could not travel for lack of money and visas, and because ever wilder conspiracy theories were gaining credence, the country became ever more unstable in the same way that Weimar Germany had been unstable. People were looking for enemies, hunting for scapegoats and prone to manipulation. While Serbia's main opposition leaders travelled the world looking for support, Western policy-makers tended to overlook the fact that Serbs had another alternative to Milošević and the bickering opposition leaders favoured by the West. That was Vojislav Šešelj and his extreme nationalists.

In the meantime, the Yugoslav army growled that under the terms of Resolution 1244, a small number ('hundreds not thousands') of Yugoslav troops were due to be allowed back into Kosovo – and they wanted to go.[14] In fact, this was, as they knew, hardly realistic as their presence would undoubtedly provoke a bloodbath, but still, although some said that they believed that most Serbs understood that Kosovo was lost forever, this was not to be taken for granted. The army, as General Radovan Lazarević, commander of the Priština Corps, explained, considered that it had acquitted itself with honour in the conflict, was undefeated and wanted to go back:

> The Priština corps had three tasks prior to and during the war: protect itself, the Serb people and the borders of Yugoslavia towards Albania. We achieved all those tasks more than successfully while we were in Kosovo. While we defended Kosovo, the enemy did not expel the Serbs from that territory. And, what is also important, until we withdrew he did not capture a single foot of our country. Wars, as we know, are waged because of just that.
>
> The fact that we are not in Kosovo now, where our main zone is, cannot be seen as a military defeat. As an officer

and as a man, I would like more than anything in the world to have remained in Kosovo after completing our three tasks. The unfavourable developments on the international scene, to our misfortune, caused us to leave Kosovo. That is our great misfortune. It was imposed by those who started the war. I personally hope that this will end also.

Our return is our obsession. We are constantly turned towards Kosovo. We are on our territory now and with our people, but our people are also on the other side of the rim in Kosovo. We are still the Priština Corps and we will always be that. Under the constitution, our place is in Kosovo ... We are prepared to take back Kosovo by force. The refusal of the international community to implement the agreement means that we would have to take back our territory by force which they turned into an occupation zone. If the UN do not respect their agreements and decisions, then this state has the right to protect its territory and people and that has to be clear to everyone. If we are forced to do this, we are prepared. The return to Kosovo is the obligation of this unit, this command and my own. We will return to our zone and the Serbs and Montenegrins to their homes.[15]

After the bombing, Duška Anastasijević, a journalist from the Belgrade magazine *Vreme*, made the astute comment that things might look better if 'Serbia found its Adenauer and Kosovo its Mandela'. Konrad Adenauer was West Germany's first post-war chancellor who not only rehabilitated the country and reconciled it with its former enemies but presided over its rapid economic reconstruction. Nelson Mandela oversaw the peaceful transition of South Africa from apartheid while preaching a message of reconciliation. Serbia and Kosovo are still waiting.

1389, 1999, 2609

In the wake of the bombing, eminent foreign-policy journals were filled with ponderous essays on the 'Lessons of Kosovo'. Written in the main by people in faraway think-tanks, paid to write about the 'lessons' of things, these articles left one wondering whether the real truth was that there were no particular lessons. Of course, if one was paid by a think-tank to draw conclusions and one wrote that, actually, there weren't very many, one might risk the sack. Leaving aside certain tangential conclusions, for example that the European NATO countries were shocked by their military technological backwardness and reliance on US hardware, then many of the other questions raised by Kosovo have not been answered, as many partisan writers would have us believe.

Let us take the question of the legality of military intervention in the event of a humanitarian catastrophe. Some argue that a case has now been established, but others that it has not. In fact, no one knows; and whether countries do, or do not, have the right to intervene remains a matter of opinion and of a branch of international law that is still in a state of evolution. Catherine Guicherd, deputy for policy coordination at the NATO Parliamentary Assembly, has argued that 'international law has serious gaps in matters of humanitarian intervention' and that:

> instead of looking for convoluted and unconvincing justi-
> fications on the one hand, or issuing blatant condemnation
> on the other, advocates and adversaries of the NATO
> operations should focus on consolidating embryonic
> practices into a clear and strong body of law to allow
> intervention on humanitarian grounds.[16]

The OSCE has begun to try and do this but the fact remains that, whether there is a justification or not, countries can only inter-vene when it is politically possible and when there is a will to do so. Just as Russia was powerless to stop NATO's bombing of Yugoslavia, Western countries were powerless to stop poor but nuclear-armed Russia bombing Chechnya. Likewise, Western countries may well sympathise with the plight of the Kurds or the Tibetans, but *realpolitik* means that there is little they are willing, or able, to do to help them. The same goes for the Sahrawis of Western Sahara, whose country was conquered by Western-friendly and anti-fundamentalist Morocco in 1975 and who are still waiting for the UN-sponsored referendum that they have been promised.

Western countries intervened in Yugoslavia for a number of reasons, only one of which was a humanitarian consideration. Another was frustration with a leader who provoked the destruction of the old Yugoslavia and who had effectively held much of south-eastern Europe captive to his policies, and their consequences, for almost a decade. Western leaders also feared condemnation if they did nothing while his forces, pursuing the quite legal task of fighting secessionists, did so by burning villages and sweeping hundreds of thousands of people out of their homes. If this was not checked, they believed that it could eventually lead to war in Macedonia and then the rest of south-eastern Europe.

As Serbs like to point out, Kosovo is hardly a unique problem. In other parts of Europe, too, governments have had to deal with separatist guerrillas or terrorists. However, for all their faults and mistakes, the British, Spanish and French governments, for example, have not tried to crush the IRA, ETA or Corsican bombers by village burning and ethnic cleansing. If they had, then there is little doubt that these relatively tiny groups would have grown too, just as Milošević's policies turned the KLA from a couple of dozen men, a few groups of armed farmers and ideologues, into a serious guerrilla force. As we have seen, almost everything Milošević tried to do was a failure. If one could conclude from this that Milošević should have pursued a political strategy of dialogue, but against secession, which would have had the support of the West, then this would hardly be much of a lesson.

In the months after the war, those who supported the bombing, and those who did not, engaged in what could only be described as ideological warfare. However, their selective use of facts, or ignorance, often made many of their arguments tenuous in the extreme. During the bombing, NATO gave the impression that it was hitting thousands of different targets, including a large amount of tanks and artillery. A lot of this turned out to be false. Thanks to the Serbs' deft use of decoys and deception, much NATO weaponry was hitting things like tanks made out of plastic sheeting with telegraph poles for gun barrels. After a reassessment, NATO officials came back and said they believed that 93 tanks had been hit. This was not true, claimed others, who believed that as few as 13 had been destroyed. In fact, the argument was somewhat academic, since the most potent weapon in ethnic cleansing is the cigarette-lighter needed to set houses on fire. Of course, tanks would have been relevant if there had been a ground invasion, but there was not. Likewise, it also became clear that NATO bombed many of the same sites, to the mystification of local people, over and over again. One had to wonder whether, given the fact that Milošević was not backing down, that this was being done simply to create a favourable impression back home.

Another debate concerned the alleged 'lack of bodies'. During the bombing, Western leaders sometimes used exaggerated numbers of missing, and possibly dead, to justify the campaign. In fact, there was no reliable information on what was going on inside Kosovo during the bombing, and so, given that Serbian forces had just expelled or forced out 850,000 people (not counting those camping on the hills inside Kosovo), some of these claims *might* have been true. No one knows how many died but the International Criminal Tribunal in the Hague says that, as of the winter of 1999, it had excavated 195 grave sites out of 529, found 2,108 bodies but had reports of 11,334 dead from eyewitnesses.[17] This concurred with a post-war British estimate of 10,000 dead, although we do not know whether that figure, or that of the Tribunal's missing, included combatants. Still, the number of those exhumed was latched on to by people who argued that Western leaders had 'lied' because 'only' 2,108 had been killed.

In the Preface of this book there is an account of the people who had just been forcibly expelled from the village of Meja where their menfolk had died in a massacre some hours before. In June, the evidence of a massacre was clear. In the field where the men had last been seen alive, the ground was still covered in a black crust of dried blood. Scattered about were documents, pens, penknives, cigarette tins, pills, false teeth and an umbrella stuck in the ground. A couple of putrid corpses lay in a hedge. Villagers who had remained behind confirmed that the killings had taken place on 27 April but that on 28 April at 10.15 p.m a bulldozer came and removed the bodies. To this day, nobody knows where or how they were disposed of. The Tribunal says it also has plenty of evidence that mass grave sites have been tampered with and bodies removed.

That an unknown number of men have disappeared without trace has been ignored by those who say that Western leaders 'lied' to justify the bombing. In fact, as we have seen, Western

leaders blundered consistently from one mistake to another –
and this appears to have been another one. They were, after all,
haunted by the spectre of Srebrenica and their failure to act and
to comprehend that thousands *could* be slaughtered in a couple
of days. As we have argued, Western leaders believed that, by
using the threat of force, they could make Milošević come to a
compromise deal over Kosovo. Then they believed that the
bombing would last three days. As one senior diplomat said:
'American and British intelligence throughout the war was
dreadful.' Getting things wrong is different from lying, but it
does not fit any particular argument. Just as we have seen how
Milošević gambled on the bombing, and its results, Western
leaders gambled too. They found themselves trapped in an
unenviable situation in March 1999 where the strategy of
threatening force no longer worked, and so either they had to
use force or be humiliated by their failure to do so and risk a
genuine humanitarian crisis becoming a catastrophe. They opted
for the first, because they believed the campaign would be short.
They even thought that Milošević might welcome a little 'light
bombing' so that he could then make a face-saving compromise
deal and thus tell his people that he had at least tried to stand up
to the world's most powerful military alliance. The fact that by
then he had other plans, which turned out to be a disaster, and
that NATO hopes also turned out to be wrong, simply do not
lend themselves to any very profound conclusions. *They all just
got it wrong.* There were no diabolical Western conspiracies.
If Milošević had backed down after three days, Western leaders
would have congratulated themselves on a fantastically successful policy. Milošević thought, 'We'll fuck them.' It did not work
out that way.

Now Kosovo is in limbo, Serbia a broken pariah and the West
engaged in the region for probably generations to come. British,
French and American troops spent half a century in Germany
after the war and, in view of the Soviet threat, had a job to do.
Now they have nothing to do in Germany and a job to keep the
peace in the Balkans. It is quite possible that this job will last for
half a century too. The US military for one appears to have
understood this. Close to Uroševac it is constructing Camp
Bondsteel, the largest US base built since the Vietnam War. Apart
from solid housing for 5,000 soldiers it is also a helicopter base.

Paraphrasing the nineteenth-century French writer Stendhal, Aleksa Djilas, the Serbian historian and commentator, says: 'The possibility of revenge increases the desire.' This has certainly been borne out by the treatment meted out to the Serbs by Kosovo's Albanians in the wake of the bombing. But Djilas is looking ahead. While Albanians take their revenge today, the time may yet come when Serbs can take theirs. The way the Serbs have lost Kosovo means that, for the foreseeable future, they will have no chance to get it back. How could they while it is occupied by NATO troops? But what will happen in ten or twenty years? A decade ago, no one could have predicted the shape of the world today. What if, in twenty or thirty years, America is locked in isolationism, Russia rearmed and strong and Europe weak and divided? Djilas says that the spirit of revanchism may grow. 'Of course,' he adds, 'I would not support such a thing, but the Serbs are not exactly a "forgive and forget" nation. If they have remembered the 1389 defeat for 610 years, why not this one?'

Appendix One: Population of Kosovo

Census Data: 1948, 1953, 1961, 1971, 1981, 1991

	1948 Population	%	1953 Population	%	1961 Population	%	1971 Population	%	1981 Population	%	1991 Population	%
Albanians	498,242	68.5	524,559	64.9	646,805	67.2	916,168	73.7	1,226,736	77.4	1,607,690*	82.2
Serbs	171,911	23.6	189,869	23.5	227,016	23.6	228,264	18.4	209,498	13.2	195,301	9.9
Montenegrins	28,050	3.9	31,343	3.9	37,588	3.9	31,555	2.5	27,028	1.7	20,045	1.0
Muslims	9,679	1.3	6,241	0.8	8,026	0.8	26,357	2.1	58,562	3.7	57,408	2.9
Gypsies	11,230	1.5	11,904	1.5	3,202	0.3	14,593	1.2	34,126	2.2	42,806	2.2
Turks	1,315	0.2	34,583	4.3	25,784	2.7	12,224	1.0	12,513	0.8	10,838	0.5
Croats	5,290	0.7	6,201	0.8	7,251	0.8	8,264	0.7	8,717	0.6	8,161	0.4
Others	2,103	0.3	3,541	0.3	8,316	0.7	6,248	0.4	7,260	0.4	12,498	0.7
Total	727,820	100.0	808,141	100.0	963,988	100.0	1,243,693	100.0	1,584,441	100.0	1,974,747	100.0

*Estimate of the Federal Institute for Statistics, based on the data on the natural augmenation and migrations during the previous period (1981–1990).

Sources: Julie Mertus, *Kosovo: How Myths and Truths Started a War* (Berkeley and Los Angeles, 1999), from 'Jugoslavija 1918–1988, statistički godišnjak' (1989), pp.42–3; 'Statistički godišnjak Jugoslavije za 1992, godinu' (1992), pp.62–3, as cited in Milan Vučković and Goran Nikolić, Stanovništvo Kosova u razdoblju od 1918. do 1991. godine (Munich, 1996), pp.108–9

Appendix Two: United Nations Security Council Resolution 1244

RESOLUTION 1244 (1999)

Adopted by the Security Council at its 4011th meeting, on 10 June 1999

The Security Council,

Bearing in mind the purposes and principles of the Charter of the United Nations, and the primary responsibility of the Security Council for the maintenance of international peace and security,

Recalling its resolutions 1160 (1998) of 31 March 1998, 1199 (1998) of 23 September 1998, 1203 (1998) of 24 October 1998 and 1239 (1999) of 14 May 1999,

Regretting that there has not been full compliance with the requirements of these resolutions,

Determined to resolve the grave humanitarian situation in Kosovo, Federal Republic of Yugoslavia, and to provide for the safe and free return of all refugees and displaced persons to their homes,

Condemning all acts of violence against the Kosovo population as well as all terrorist acts by any party,

Recalling the statement made by the Secretary-General on 9 April 1999, expressing concern at the humanitarian tragedy taking place in Kosovo,

Reaffirming the right of all refugees and displaced persons to return to their homes in safety,

Recalling the jurisdiction and the mandate of the International Tribunal for the Former Yugoslavia,

Welcoming the general principles on a political solution to the Kosovo crisis adopted on 6 May 1999 (S/1999/516, annex 1 to this resolution) and welcoming also the acceptance by the Federal Republic of Yugoslavia of the principles set forth in points 1 to 9 of the paper presented in Belgrade on 2 June 1999 (S/1999/649, annex 2 to this resolution), and the Federal Republic of Yugoslavia's agreement to that paper,

<u>Reaffirming</u> the commitment of all Member States to the sovereignty and territorial integrity of the Federal Republic of Yugoslavia and the other States of the region, as set out in the Helsinki Final Act and annex 2,

<u>Reaffirming</u> the call in previous resolutions for substantial autonomy and meaningful self-administration for Kosovo,

<u>Determining</u> that the situation in the region continues to constitute a threat to international peace and security,

<u>Determined</u> to ensure the safety and security of international personnel and the implementation by all concerned of their responsibilities under the present resolution, and <u>acting</u> for these purposes under Chapter VII of the Charter of the United Nations,

1. <u>Decides</u> that a political solution to the Kosovo crisis shall be based on the general principles in annex 1 and as further elaborated in the principles and other required elements in annex 2;

2. <u>Welcomes</u> the acceptance by the Federal Republic of Yugoslavia of the principles and other required elements referred to in paragraph 1 above, and <u>demands</u> the full co-operation of the Federal Republic of Yugoslavia in their rapid implementation;

3. <u>Demands</u> in particular that the Federal Republic of Yugoslavia put an immediate and verifiable end to violence and repression in Kosovo, and begin and complete verifiable phased withdrawal from Kosovo of all military, police and paramilitary forces according to a rapid timetable, with which the deployment of the international security presence in Kosovo will be synchronized;

4. <u>Confirms</u> that after the withdrawal an agreed number of Yugoslav and Serb military and police personnel will be permitted to return to Kosovo to perform the functions in accordance with annex 2;

5. <u>Decides</u> on the deployment in Kosovo, under United Nations auspices, of international civil and security presences, with appropriate equipment and personnel as required, and welcomes the agreement of the Federal Republic of Yugoslavia to such presences;

6. <u>Requests</u> the Secretary-General to appoint, in consultation with the Security Council, a Special Representative to control

the implementation of the international civil presence, and further requests the Secretary-General to instruct his Special Representative to coordinate closely with the international security presence to ensure that both presences operate towards the same goals and in a mutually supportive manner;

7. Authorizes Member States and relevant international organizations to establish the international security presence in Kosovo as set out in point 4 of annex 2 with all necessary means to fulfil its responsibilities under paragraph 9 below;

8. Affirms the need for the rapid early deployment of effective international civil and security presences to Kosovo, and demands that the parties cooperate fully in their deployment;

9. Decides that the responsibilities of the international security presence to be deployed and acting in Kosovo will include:

(a) Deterring renewed hostilities, maintaining and where necessary enforcing a ceasefire, and ensuring the withdrawal and preventing the return into Kosovo of Federal and Republic military, police and paramilitary forces, except as provided in point 6 of annex 2;

(b) Demilitarizing the Kosovo Liberation Army (KLA) and other armed Kosovo Albanian groups as required in paragraph 15 below;

(c) Establishing a secure environment in which refugees and displaced persons can return home in safety, the international civil presence can operate, a transitional administration can be established, and humanitarian aid can be delivered;

(d) Ensuring public safety and order until the international civil presence can take responsibility for this task;

(e) Supervising demining until the international civil presence can, as appropriate, take over responsibility for this task;

(f) Supporting, as appropriate, and coordinating closely with the work of the international civil presence;

(g) Conducting border monitoring duties as required;

(h) Ensuring the protection and freedom of movement of itself, the international civil presence, and other international organizations;

10. Authorizes the Secretary-General, with the assistance of relevant international organizations, to establish an international civil presence in Kosovo in order to provide an interim administration for Kosovo under which the people of Kosovo

can enjoy substantial autonomy within the Federal Republic of Yugoslavia, and which will provide transitional administration while establishing and overseeing the development of provisional democratic self-governing institutions to ensure conditions for a peaceful and normal life for all inhabitants of Kosovo;

11. Decides that the main responsibilities of the international civil presence will include:

(a) Promoting the establishment, pending a final settlement, of substantial autonomy and self-government in Kosovo, taking full account of annex 2 and of the Rambouillet accords (S/1999/648);

(b) Performing basic civilian administrative functions where and as long as required;

(c) Organizing and overseeing the development of provisional institutions for democratic and autonomous self-government pending a political settlement, including the holding of elections;

(d) Transferring, as these institutions are established, its administrative responsibilities while overseeing and supporting the consolidation of Kosovo's local provisional institutions and other peace-building activities;

(e) Facilitating a political process designed to determine Kosovo's future status, taking into account the Rambouillet accords (S/1999/648);

(f) In a final stage, overseeing the transfer of authority from Kosovo's provisional institutions to institutions established under a political settlement;

(g) Supporting the reconstruction of key infrastructure and other economic reconstruction;

(h) Supporting, in coordination with international humanitarian organizations, humanitarian and disaster relief aid;

(i) Maintaining civil law and order, including establishing local police forces and meanwhile through the deployment of international police personnel to serve in Kosovo;

(j) Protecting and promoting human rights;

(k) Assuring the safe and unimpeded return of all refugees and displaced persons to their homes in Kosovo;

12. Emphasizes the need for coordinated humanitarian relief operations, and for the Federal Republic of Yugoslavia to allow

unimpeded access to Kosovo by humanitarian aid organizations and to cooperate with such organizations so as to ensure the fast and effective delivery of international aid;

13. Encourages all Member States and international organizations to contribute to economic and social reconstruction as well as to the safe return of refugees and displaced persons, and emphasizes in this context the importance of convening an international donors' conference, particularly for the purposes set out in paragraph 11 (g) above, at the earliest possible date;

14. Demands full cooperation by all concerned, including the international security presence, with the International Tribunal for the Former Yugoslavia;

15. Demands that the KLA and other armed Kosovo Albanian groups end immediately all offensive actions and comply with the requirements for demilitarization as laid down by the head of the international security presence in consultation with the Special Representative of the Secretary-General;

16. Decides that the prohibitions imposed by paragraph 8 of resolution 1160 (1998) shall not apply to arms and related matériel for the use of the international civil and security presences;

17. Welcomes the work in hand in the European Union and other international organizations to develop a comprehensive approach to the economic development and stabilization of the region affected by the Kosovo crisis, including the implementation of a Stability Pact for South Eastern Europe with broad international participation in order to further the promotion of democracy, economic prosperity, stability and regional cooperation;

18. Demands that all States in the region cooperate fully in the implementation of all aspects of this resolution;

19. Decides that the international civil and security presences are established for an initial period of 12 months, to continue thereafter unless the Security Council decides otherwise;

20. Requests the Secretary-General to report to the Council at regular intervals on the implementation of this resolution, including reports from the leaderships of the international civil and security presences, the first reports to be submitted within 30 days of the adoption of this resolution;

21. Decides to remain actively seized of the matter.

Annex 1
Statement by the Chairman on the conclusion of the meeting
of the G-8 Foreign Ministers held at the Petersberg Centre
on 6 May 1999
The G-8 Foreign Ministers adopted the following general
principles on the political solution to the Kosovo crisis:
- Immediate and verifiable end of violence and repression
  in Kosovo;
- Withdrawal from Kosovo of military, police and
  paramilitary forces;
- Deployment in Kosovo of effective international civil
  and security presences, endorsed and adopted by the
  United Nations, capable of guaranteeing the achievement of the common objectives;
- Establishment of an interim administration for Kosovo
  to be decided by the Security Council of the United
  Nations to ensure conditions for a peaceful and normal
  life for all inhabitants in Kosovo;
- The safe and free return of all refugees and displaced persons and unimpeded access to Kosovo by humanitarian
  aid organizations;
- A political process towards the establishment of an
  interim political framework agreement providing for a
  substantial self-government for Kosovo, taking full
  account of the Rambouillet accords and the principles of
  sovereignty and territorial integrity of the Federal
  Republic of Yugoslavia and the other countries of the
  region, and the demilitarization of the KLA;
- Comprehensive approach to the economic development
  and stabilization of the crisis region.

Annex 2
Agreement should be reached on the following principles to
move towards a resolution of the Kosovo crisis:
1. An immediate and verifiable end of violence and repression
in Kosovo.
2. Verifiable withdrawal from Kosovo of all military, police and
paramilitary forces according to a rapid timetable.
3. Deployment in Kosovo under United Nations auspices of
effective international civil and security presences, acting as may

be decided under Chapter VII of the Charter, capable of guaranteeing the achievement of common objectives.

4. The international security presence with substantial North Atlantic Treaty Organization participation must be deployed under unified command and control and authorized to establish a safe environment for all people in Kosovo and to facilitate the safe return to their homes of all displaced persons and refugees.

5. Establishment of an interim administration for Kosovo as a part of the international civil presence under which the people of Kosovo can enjoy substantial autonomy within the Federal Republic of Yugoslavia, to be decided by the Security Council of the United Nations. The interim administration to provide transitional administration while establishing and overseeing the development of provisional democratic self-governing institutions to ensure conditions for a peaceful and normal life for all inhabitants in Kosovo.

6. After withdrawal, an agreed number of Yugoslav and Serbian personnel will be permitted to return to perform the following functions:

- Liaison with the international civil mission and the international security presence;
- Marking/clearing minefields;
- Maintaining a presence at Serb patrimonial sites;
- Maintaining a presence at key border crossings.

7. Safe and free return of all refugees and displaced persons under the supervision of the Office of the United Nations High Commissioner for Refugees and unimpeded access to Kosovo by humanitarian aid organizations.

8. A political process towards the establishment of an interim political framework agreement providing for substantial self-government for Kosovo, taking full account of the Rambouillet accords and the principles of sovereignty and territorial integrity of the Federal Republic of Yugoslavia and the other countries of the region, and the demilitarization of UCK. Negotiations between the parties for a settlement should not delay or disrupt the establishment of democratic self-governing institutions.

9. A comprehensive approach to the economic development and stabilization of the crisis region. This will include the implementation of a stability pact for South-Eastern Europe

with broad international participation in order to further promotion of democracy, economic prosperity, stability and regional cooperation.

10. Suspension of military activity will require acceptance of the principles set forth above in addition to agreement to other, previously identified, required elements, which are specified in the footnote below.[1] A military–technical agreement will then be rapidly concluded that would, among other things, specify additional modalities, including the roles and functions of Yugoslav/Serb personnel in Kosovo:

Withdrawal
- Procedures for withdrawals, including the phased, detailed schedule and delineation of a buffer area in Serbia beyond which forces will be withdrawn;

Returning personnel
- Equipment associated with returning personnel;
- Terms of reference for their functional responsibilities;
- Timetable for their return;
- Delineation of their geographical areas of operation;
- Rules governing their relationship to the international security presence and the international civil mission.

Notes
[1] Other required elements:
- A rapid and precise timetable for withdrawals, meaning, e.g., seven days to complete withdrawal and air defence weapons withdrawn outside a 25-kilometre mutual safety zone within 48 hours;
- Return of personnel for the four functions specified above will be under the supervision of the international security presence and will be limited to a small agreed number (hundreds, not thousands);
- Suspension of military activity will occur after the beginning of verifiable withdrawals;
- The discussion and achievement of a military-technical agreement shall not extend the previously determined time for completion of withdrawals.

Notes

Author's note

1 Metohija, derived from a word meaning monastic lands, is the western part of Kosovo which Albanians call Dukagjin.

Introduction

1 The Kossovo Day Committee, *Kossovo Day (1389–1916)* (London, 1916), p.26. All the details of the events or 'celebrations' as they were called, come from this pamphlet. As to posters, another one, featuring a cartoon of 'Heroic Serbia', was also distributed and, as the pamphlet notes, 'For weeks these posters were much in evidence all over London and the provinces.' (pp.12–13).

2 *Ibid.*, p.26.
3 *Ibid.*, p.14.
4 *Ibid.*, p.28.
5 Edward Crankshaw, *The Fall of the House of Habsburg* (London, 1963), p.377.
6 Edith Durham, *High Albania* (London, 1985), p.32.
7 *Ibid.*, p.31.
8 *Ibid.*, p.263. 'Servia' and 'Servians' were the names in common use during this period.
9 *Ibid.*, p.294.

1 History: War by Other Means

1 Anne Kindersley, *The Mountains of Serbia: Travels through Inland Yugoslavia* (Newton Abbot, 1977), p.90.

2 The Serbian authorities have since made a rather feeble effort to ascribe the destruction of the building to NATO. In *NATO Crimes in Yugoslavia: Documentary Evidence 24 March – 24 April* (Belgrade, 1999), a book which chronicles destruction and deaths caused by NATO's bombings, pictures of the still-smouldering buildings are shown on pp.227–8. Although most other entries record the time and circumstances of the NATO attack, this entry only notes that the building was 'demolished' on 28 March 1999.

3 Noel Malcolm, *Kosovo: A Short History* (London, 1998), p.57.

4 Mark Krasniqi, 'The Role of the Serbian Orthodox Church in Anti-Albanian Policies in Kosova', in Jusuf Bajraktari *et al.* (eds), *The Kosova Issue – A Historic and Current Problem* (Tirana, 1996), p.75.

5 Anne Pennington and Peter Levi, *Marko the Prince: Serbo-Croat Heroic Songs* (London, 1984), p.13.

6 Kindersley, *The Mountains*, p.121.

7 Pennington and Levi, *Marko the Prince*, pp.17–18.

8 Thomas Emmert, 'The Battle of Kosovo: Early Reports Victory and Defeat', in Wayne S. Vucinich and Thomas A. Emmert (eds), *Kosovo: The Legacy of a Medieval Battle* (Minneapolis, 1991), p.24.

9 Paul Rycaut, *The History of the Turks Beginning with the Year*

1679 (London, 1700), p.351.
10 *Ibid.*
11 *Ibid.*, pp.367–8.
12 H.N. Brailsford, *Macedonia: Its Races and Their Future* (London, 1906) p. 265.
13 *Ibid.*, p.277.
14 Milan St Protić, Migrations Resulting from Peasant Upheavals in Serbia during the 19th Century', in Dimitrije Djordjević and Radovan Samardžić (eds), *Migrations in Balkan History* (Belgrade, 1989), p.94.
15 Macolm, *Kosovo*, p.226.
16 James Pettifer and Miranda Vickers, *Albania: From Anarchy to a Balkan Identity*, (London, 1997), p.96.
17 Brailsford, *Macedonia*, p.263.
18 Edith Durham, *High Albania* (London, 1985), p.275.
19 Brailsford, *Macedonia*, p.276.
20 Dimitrije Djordjević, 'The Tradition of Kosovo in the Formation of Modern Serbian Statehood in the Nineteenth Century', in Vucinich and Emmert, *Kosovo: The Legacy*, p.317.
21 Thomas Emmert, *Serbian Golgotha: Kosovo 1389* (New York, 1990), p.129.
22 Ivo Banac, *The National Question in Yugoslavia: Origins, History, Politics* (Ithaca and London, 1992), p.293.
23 *Ibid.*
24 Leon Trotsky, *The War Correspondence of Leon Trotsky: The Balkan Wars, 1912–13* (New York, 1995), p.62.
25 Emmert, *Serbian Golgotha*, p.133.
26 Malcolm, *Kosovo*, p.254.
27 Carnegie Endowment for International Peace, *Report of the International Commission to Inquire into the Causes and Conduct of the Balkan Wars* (Washington DC, 1914), pp.151. (Republished in 1993 under the title *The Other Balkan Wars*.)
28 *Ibid.*, p.151.
29 Trotsky, *War Correspondence*, p.120.
30 *Ibid.*, p.290.
31 Rebecca West, *Black Lamb and Grey Falcon: A Record of a Journey through Yugoslavia in 1937*, 2 vols (London, 1943), vol.1, p.604.
32 Nicolas-Jiv Petrovitch, *Agonie et résurrection: Récits de la prise de Belgrade de la retraite en Albanie et d'un séjour au lazaret de Corfou* (Courbevoie, 1920). In the text I have transliterated his name back to Petrović.
33 The Kossovo Day Committee, *Kossovo Day (1389–1916)* (London, 1916), cover page.
34 Banac, *National Question*, p.298.
35 West, *Black Lamb*, vol.2, p.326.
36 Banac, *National Question*, p.299.
37 *Ibid.*
38 Malcolm, *Kosovo*, p.272.
39 *Ibid.*, p.282.
40 Banac, *National Question*, p.301.
41 Malcolm, *Kosovo*, p.286. Figures given by Albanian historians are much higher. See, for example, Enver Maloku, *Expulsions of Albanians and Colonization of Kosova* (Priština, 1997), pp.50–1.
42 Ibrahim Berisha *et al.* (eds), *Serbian Colonization and Ethnic Cleansing of Kosova: Documents & Evidence* (Priština, 1993). The convention is reproduced on pp.43–55.
43 *Ibid.*, p.15.
44 *Ibid.*, p.21.
45 *Ibid.*, p.23.
46 *Ibid.*, pp.24–5
47 Banac, *National Question*, pp.302–3.
48 Malcolm, *Kosovo*, p.274.
49 Banac, *National Question*, p.305; see also Malcolm, *Kosovo*, pp.276–8.
50 West, *Black Lamb*, vol.2, p.390.
51 Emmert, *Serbian Golgotha*, p.140.

52 Winston S. Churchill, *The Second World War*, vol.3: *The Grand Alliance* (London, 195), p.148.
53 Smijla Avramov, *Genocide in Yugoslavia* (Belgrade, 1995), p.186.
54 See Malcolm, *Kosovo*, pp.312–13 for a detailed discussion of numbers killed.
55 Vladimir Velebit, *Yugoslavia in the Second World War* (Belgrade, 1987), p.42.
56 *Ibid.*, p.52.
57 Bernd J. Fischer, *Albania at War: 1939–1945* (West Lafayette, 1999), p.184.
58 *Ibid.*, pp.185–6.
59 *Ibid.*, p.186.
60 *Ibid.*, p.187.
61 General Fabijan Trgo, *The National Liberation War and Revolution in Yugoslavia (1941–1945): Selected Documents* (Belgrade, 1982), p.363.
62 Malcolm, *Kosovo*, p.308.
63 Miranda Vickers, *Between Serb and Albanian: A History of Kosovo* (London, 1998), p.142.
64 Trgo, *National Liberation War*, p.585.
65 Miranda Vickers, *The Albanians: A Modern History* (London and New York, 1995), p.165, citing *Zëri i Popullit*, 17 May 1981.
66 Malcolm, *Kosovo*, p.319.
67 Berisha, *Serbian Colonization*, pp.85–6.
68 *Ibid.*, p.94.

2   Slobodan.Milosevic@gov.yu

1   http://www.gov.yu/ institutions/president/ presidentspeech.html
2   Sabrina P. Ramet, *Nationalism and Federalism in Yugoslavia 1962–1991*, 2nd edn (Bloomington and Indianapolis, 1992), p.229.
3   Anton Logoreci, 'A Clash of Two Nationalisms in Kosova', in Arshi Pipa and Sami Repishti (eds), *Studies on Kosova* (Boulder, 1984), p.190.
4   Shkëlzen Maliqi, *Kosova: Separate Worlds, Reflections and Analyses 1989–1998* (Priština, 1998), p.20.
5   Julie A. Mertus, *Kosovo: How Myths and Truths Started a War* (Berkeley and Los Angeles, 1999), p.76. In her book, Hyseni is not identified but given the pseudonym of Afrim. Because she had done her interviews during the period of Serbian rule and because her book was published during NATO's bombing of Yugoslavia, Mertus concealed his identity. With any risk now gone, I have quoted Hyseni by name, with her kind permission to do so.
6   Alex Dragnich and Slavko Todorovich, *The Saga of Kosovo: Focus on Serbian–Albanian Relations* (Boulder and New York, 1984), p.165.
7   *Ibid.*
8   *Ibid.* See also Miranda Vickers, *Between Serb and Albanian: A History of Kosovo* (London, 1998), p.198 and Noel Malcolm, *Kosovo: A Short History* (London, 1998), p.355.
9   Malcolm, *Kosovo*, p.335.
10 Maliqi, *Kosova*, p.21.
11 *Ibid.*
12 Mark Thompson, *A Paper House: The Ending of Yugoslavia* (London, 1992), p.128.
13 Maliqi, *Kosova*, p.225.
14 *Ibid.*, p.226.
15 Dragnich and Todorovich, *The Saga*, pp.166–7.
16 *Ibid.*, p.167.
17 See Appendix One for population statistics.
18 See Malcolm, *Kosovo*, pp.317–18.
19 Information supplied by the Turkish Embassy, Belgrade.

20 Vickers, *Between Serb*, p.187
21 Smilja Avramov, *Genocide in Yugoslavia* (Belgrade, 1995), p.198.
22 Denisa Kostovičová, *Parallel Worlds: Response of Kosovo Albanians to Loss of Autonomy in Serbia, 1989–1996* (Keele, 1997), p.17, citing 'A Report of the Independent Commission on Kosovo', *Vreme* (Belgrade), 12 November 1990.
23 Kosta Mihailović and Vasilije Krestić, *Memorandum of the Serbian Academy of Sciences and Arts: Answers to Criticisms* (Belgrade, 1995), p.129. See Mertus, *Kosovo* for a detailed discussion of the Martinović case and, as the title of her book suggests, 'myths and truths' that started a war.
24 Laura Silber and Allan Little, *The Death of Yugoslavia* (London, 1995), p.35.
25 Robert Thomas, *Serbia under Milošević Politics in the 1990s* (London, 1999), p.37.
26 In the headquarters of Human Rights Watch in the Empire State Building in New York there is a wall of pictures celebrating the champions of human rights and free speech from Eastern Europe and the Soviet Union from the 1970s onwards. There is one gap, where Ćosić's picture used to be, although his name is still there. According to one source: 'People began to scratch him off until there was nothing left.'
27 Thomas, *Serbia*, p.41; see also Branka Magaš, *The Destruction of Yugoslavia: Tracking the Break-up 1980–92* (London and New York, 1993), p.49.
28 Mihailović and Krestić, *Memorandum*, p.133.
29 *Ibid.*, p.125.
30 *Ibid.*, p.119.
31 *Ibid.*, p.127.
32 *Ibid.*, p.128.
33 *Ibid.*, pp.129–30.
34 *Ibid.*, p.140.
35 *Vreme, Dossier: From the Memorandum to War* (Belgrade, n.d.). The *Dossier* cites the internal bulletin of the Communist League of the Federal Secretariat of Interior Affairs, *Naše aktuelnosti*, of June 1987, as its source.
36 Slavoljub Djukić, *Izmedju slave i anateme: Politička biografija Slobodana Milosevića* (Belgrade, 1994), p.14.
37 *Ibid.*
38 Aleksa Djilas, 'A Profile of Slobodan Milošević', *Foreign Affairs*, vol. 72, no.3, p.86.
39 Silber and Little, *Death*, p.36.
40 *Ibid.*, p.37.
41 Djukić, *Izmedju slave*, p.49.
42 All the various branches of the Communist party in Yugoslavia were called the 'League of Communists' rather than Communist Party.
43 Djilas, 'Profile', p.90.
44 Kostovičová, *Parallel Worlds*, p.20.
45 Thomas, *Serbia*, p.45.
46 Kostovičová, *Parallel Worlds*, p.20.
47 Silber and Little, *Death*, p.66.
48 Maliqi, *Kosova*, p.82; for details of the strike as well, see pp.82–4.
49 Kostovičová, *Parallel Worlds*, p.23.
50 Silber and Little, *Death*, p.77.
51 See Maliqi, *Kosova*, p.85.
52 Warren Zimmermann, *Origins of a Catastrophe: Yugoslavia and its Destroyers* (New York, 1996), p.17.
53 Milorad Vučelić, *Conversations with the Epoch* (Belgrade, 1991), p.109.
54 *Ibid.*, pp.47–8.

3 Phantom state

1 Every republic and both provinces had reserve Territorial Defence forces. In Slovenia and

Croatia the organisations were important as first steps to creating armies for them.

2   Miranda Vickers, *Between Serb and Albanian: A History of Kosovo* (London, 1998), p.264, quoting Rugova from *Impact International*, 10 April – 7 May 1992, p.10.

3   Denisa Kostovičová, *Parallel Worlds: Response of Kosovo Albanians to Loss of Autonomy in Serbia, 1989–1996* (Keele, 1997), p.32.

4   *Ibid.*, pp.33–4.

5   *Ibid.*, p.35. See also Kostovičová's essay 'Albanian Schooling in Kosovo: 1992–1998: "Liberty Imprisoned"', in Kyril Drezov, Bulent Gokay and Denisa Kostovičová, (eds), *Kosovo: Myths, Conflict and War* (Keele, 1999) and the International Crisis Group (ICG), *Kosovo Spring* (Priština and Sarajevo, 1998), pp.20–5.

6   ICG, *Kosovo Spring*, p.21.

7   UN Commission for Human Rights Special Rapporteur for the Former Yugoslavia, 'Report on the Situation of Human Rights in the Former Yugoslavia', 1 November 1993. See Marc Weller, *The Crisis in Kosovo 1989–1999: From the Dissolution of Yugoslavia to Rambouillet and the Outbreak of Hostilities* (Cambridge, 1999), vol.1 p.161.

8   Shkëlzen Maliqi, *Kosova: Separate Worlds, Reflections and Analyses 1989–1998* (Priština, 1998), p.100.

9   *Ibid.*, p.101.

10 Kostovičová, *Parallel Worlds*, p.32.

11 Sources are a combination of author's interview with Bujar Bukoshi, July 1997, and ICG, *Kosovo Spring*, pp.5–6.

12 ICG, *Kosovo Spring*, p.21 and Kostovičová, 'Liberty Imprisoned', p.15.

13 *Ibid.*, p.19.

14 Noel Malcolm, in his *Kosovo: A Short History* (London, 1998), cites 'Kosova Communication' of 5 December 1995 and says on p.345, 'A UN expert on toxicology did later conclude ... from analyses of blood and urine samples, that the substances Sarin or Tabun (used in chemical weapons) were present, and in 1995 evidence emerged that the Yugoslav army had manufactured Sarin.'

15 ICG, *Kosovo Spring*, p.26.

16 Barton Gellman, 'How the US and Allies Went to War', *Washington Post*, 18 April 1999.

17 Maliqi, *Kosovo*, pp.40–1.

18 Laura Silber and Allan Little, *The Death of Yugoslavia* (London, 1995), p.213.

19 At an annualised rate this is 851, 000, 000, 000, 000, 000, 000, 000, 000, 000, 000, 000, 000, 000, 000, 000, 000, 000, 000, 000, 000, 000, 000, 000, 000, 000, 000, 000, 000 per cent.

20 In December 1994, at its Budapest summit, the CSCE became the Organisation for Security and Cooperation in Europe, the OSCE.

21 Human Rights Watch/Helsinki, *Open Wounds: Human Rights Abuses in Kosovo* (New York, 1993), p.xiii.

22 *Ibid.*, pp.7–8.

23 UN Commission, in Weller, *The Crisis*, p.160.

24 ICG, *Kosovo Spring*, p.7.

25 Fabian Schmidt, 'Show Trials in Kosovo', *Transition*, vol.1, no.20, 3 November 1995, p.37.

26 *Ibid.*, p.36.

27 Human Rights Watch/Helsinki, *Open Wounds*, p.67.

28 *Ibid.*, pp.25–6.

29 UN Commission, in Weller, *The Crisis*, p.160.

30 Human Rights Watch/Helsinki, *Open Wounds*, p.2.

31 UN Commission, in Weller, *The Crisis*, p.160

32 Human Rights Watch/Helsinki, *Open Wounds*, p.2.

33   Letter from Lord Carrington, Chairman, Conference on Yugoslavia, to Dr I. Rugova, 17 August 1992, in Weller, *The Crisis*, p.86.
34   Weller, *The Crisis*, pp.76–7.
35   Maliqi, *Kosova*, p.24. In fact, Maliqi wrote this in 1993 but I have cited it as it still accurately summarises the Kosovar situation before the Dayton Accords of November 1995 which ended the Bosnian war.

4   Homeland Calling

1   Rebecca West, *Black Lamb and Grey Falcon: A Record of a journey through Yugoslavia in 1937*, 2 vols (London, 1943), vol.2, pp.341–2.
2   The quote about the war-cries on the hills and the songs were given to me by Dan Reed, a British documentary maker. His extraordinary and award-winning film, *The Valley*, about the war in Drenica, was first shown on Channel 4 on 18 February 1999.
3   In Britain a minicab is a taxi which has to be called by phone and does not have the right to ply the streets for business.
4   Before the Second World War Bajram Curri was called Kolgecai. The Communists renamed in honour of the pre-war Kosovar *kaçak* leader.
5   Julie A. Mertus, *Kosovo: How Myths and Truths Started a War* (Berkeley and Los Angeles, 1999), p.77. See note 5 in Chapter 2.
6   Milan Mijalkovski, 'Profile of an Average Albanian Terrorist', in *Serbia: News, Comments, Documents, Facts, Analysis*, no.34, October 1994, p.3.
7   *Ibid.*, p.5.
8   See Maliqi quote, Chapter 3, p.98.
9   Roger Cohen, *Hearts Grown Brutal* (New York, 1998), p.449.
10   Richard Holbrooke, *To End a War* (New York, 1999), p.370.
11   *Ibid.*, p.372.
12   *Ibid.*, p.234.
13   Gafurr Elshani, *Ushtria Çlirimtare e Kosovës: dokumente dhe artikuj* (Aarau, 1998), pp.23–4.
14   *Ibid.*, pp.24–5.
15   *Ibid.*, p.32.

5   Friends from the woods

1   International Crisis Group, *Kosovo Spring* (Priština and Sarajevo, 1998), p.23.
2   *Ibid.*, p.29. See also Miranda Vickers, *Between Serb and Albanian: A History of Kosovo* (London, 1998), p.313.
3   Human Rights Watch, *Humanitarian Law Violations in Kosovo* (New York, 1998), p.27.
4   ICG, *Kosovo Spring*, p.30.
5   *Ibid.*, p.29.
6   *Ibid.*, p.31.
7   *Agence France Presse*, 23 February 1998.
8   For accounts of what happened on 28 February see Human Rights Watch, *Humanitarian Law*, pp.19–26. Also Anthony Loyd, 'The Dogs of War', *Esquire*, September 1999.
9   Human Rights Watch, *Humanitarian Law*, p.28. For details of the whole operation see pp.28–32.
10   The Contact Group brought together Russia, the US, France, Germany, Italy and Britain when they needed to discuss events in the former Yugoslavia.
11   Sonja Biserko and Seška Stanojlović, Helsinki Committee for Human Rights in Serbia, *Radicalisation of the Serbian Society: Collection of Documents* (Belgrade, 1997), pp.162–3.

12 FRY: Yugoslav President Milošević calls for Referendum, 2 April 1998. See Marc Weller, *The Crisis in Kosovo 1989–1999: From the Dissolution of Yugoslavia to Rambouillet and the Outbreak of Hostilities* vol.1, (Cambridge, 1999), p.351.

13 When the film was released in the English-speaking world, its name was changed to *Pretty Village, Pretty Flame.*

6 Quoth the Raven, 'Nevermore'

1 Contact Group and the foreign ministers of Canada and Japan, Statement, London, 12 June 1998, in Marc Weller, *The Crisis in Kosovo 1989–1999: From the Dissolution of Yugoslavia to Rambouillet and the Outbreak of Hostilities* vol.1, (Cambridge, 1999), p.236.

2 The UN High Commissioner for Refugees' estimate of Kosovo displaced and refugees at 13 October 1998 stood at:
Kosovo 200,000
Montenegro 42,000
Other parts of Serbia 20,000
Bosnia–Hercegovina 8,600
Albania 20,500
Turkey 2,000
Slovenia 2,000
Former Yugoslav Republic of Macedonia 3,000
TOTAL 298,100
The figures do not include those who sought refuge in other countries.
Source: UNHCR figures cited in 'UN Inter-Agency Update on Kosovo Situation', 21 October 1998, in Weller, *The Crisis,* p.300.

3 Statement by NATO secretary-general following Actwarn decision, Vilamoura, 24 September 1998, in Weller, *The Crisis,* p.277.

4 United Kingdom Parliamentary Testimony on the Threat or Use of Force, November 1998 and January 1999, in Weller, *The Crisis,* p.285. See also the British Foreign Office note circulated to NATO countries concerning legal justifications. Adam Roberts, 'NATO's "Humanitarian War" over Kosovo', *Survival,* Autumn 1999, vol.41, no.3.

5 Human Rights Watch, *A Week of Terror in Drenica: Humanitarian Law Violations in Kosovo* (New York, 1999), pp.1–2.

6 *Ibid.,* p.3.

7 *Ibid.,* pp.52–3.

8 *Ibid,* p.63.

9 President Chirac, press conference in Florence cited in Catherine Guicherd, 'International Law and the War in Kosovo', *Survival,* Summer 1999, p.29.

10 Statement by Secretary of State Madeleine K. Albright, 'Situation in Kosovo', 8 October 1998, in Weller, *The Crisis,* p.278. The War Crimes Tribunal she refers to is the UN's International Criminal Tribunal for the Former Yugoslavia based in The Hague.

11 BBC 2, *Newsnight,* 20 August 1999.

12 Barton Gellman, 'How the US and Allies Went to War', *Washington Post,* 18 April 1999.

13 *Newsnight,* 20 August 1999.

14 Hearing of the Senate Armed Services Committee, 'Lessons Learned from Military Operations and Relief Efforts in Kosovo', *Federal News Service,* 21 October 1999.

15 'President Milošević Announces Accord on Peaceful Solution', Belgrade, 13 October 1998, in Weller, *The Crisis,* p.279.

16 *Newsnight,* 20 August 1999. Milošević's mention of 'Drenica 1946' is a reference to the crushing of Shaban Polluzha's rebellion of 1944–5.

17 Report of the Secretary-General, 12 November 1998, in Weller, *The Crisis*, p.302.
18 Report of the Secretary-General, 4 December 1998, in Weller, *The Crisis*, p.310.
19 UN Inter-Agency, Update on Kosovo Humanitarian Situation, 24 December 1998, in Weller, *The Crisis*, p.314.
20 Report of the Secretary-General, 4 December 1998, in Weller, *The Crisis*, p.310.
21 *Newsnight*, 20 August 1999.
22 Gellman, 'How the US and Allies Went to War'.
23 Report of the Secretary-General, 24 December 1998, in Weller, *The Crisis*, p.315.
24 Gellman, 'How the US and Allies Went to War'.
25 *Ibid.*
26 Report of the EU Forensic Team on the Račak Incident, 17 March 1999, in Weller, *The Crisis*, p.334.
27 Statement by the North Atlantic Council on Kosovo, 30 January 1999, in Weller, *The Crisis*, p.416.

7 Agreement for Peace?

1 Letter from Yugoslavia to the President of the Security Council, 1 February 1999, in Marc Weller, *The Crisis in Kosovo 1989–1999: From the Dissolution of Yugoslavia to Rambouillet and the Outbreak of Hostilities* (Cambridge, 1999), vol.1, p.418.
2 Yugoslavia has an anomalous relationship to the UN. In principle, it is a member but rights of participation and voting have been suspended, even though it still has to pay its dues. Yugoslavia maintains a diplomatic mission to the UN but when its ambassador, in this period Vladislav Jovanović, is called to speak, he does so under a formula derived from the period of the Bosnian war. That is to say he can address the Security Council in his capacity as simple 'Mr' as opposed to 'Ambassador' Jovanović. For a Yugoslav view of the matter see Vladislav Jovanović, 'The Status of the Federal Republic of Yugoslavia in the United Nations', *Fordham International Law Journal*, vol.21, no.5, June 1998.
3 The Yugoslav and Serbian governments had five deputy premiers each.
4 The Contact Group, Non-Negotiable Principles / Basic Elements, issued on 30 January 1999, in Weller, *The Crisis*, p.417. See also Marc Weller, 'The Rambouillet Conference on Kosovo', *International Affairs*, vol.75, no.2, April 1999, pp.225–6:
General Elements
• Necessity of immediate end of violence and respect of cease-fire;
• Peaceful solution through dialogue;
• Interim agreement: a mechanism for a final settlement after an interim period of three years;
• No unilateral change of interim status;
• Territorial integrity of the Federal Republic of Yugoslavia and neighbouring countries;
• Protection of rights of the members of all national communities (preservation of identity, language and education; special protection for their religious institutions);
• Free and fair elections in Kosovo (municipal and Kosovo wide) under supervision of the OSCE;
• Neither party shall prosecute anyone for crimes related to

the Kosovo conflict
exceptions: crimes against
humanity, war crimes, and
other serious violations of
international law);
• Amnesty and release of
political prisoners;
• International involvement
and full cooperation by the
parties on implementation;
Governance in Kosovo
• People of Kosovo to be self-
governed by democratically
accountable Kosovo
institutions;
• High degree of self-
governance realised through
own legislative, executive and
judiciary bodies (with
authority over *inter alia*,
taxes, financing, police,
economic development,
judicial system, health care,
education and culture (subject
to the rights of the members
of national communities),
communications, roads and
transports, protection of the
environment);
• Legislative: Assembly;
executive: President of
Kosovo, government,
administrative bodies;
judiciary: Kosovo court
system;
• Clear definition of
competencies at communal
level;
• Members of all national
communities to be fairly
represented at all levels of
administration and elected
government;
• Local police representative
of ethnic make-up with
coordination on Kosovo
level;
• Harmonisation of Serbian and
Federal legal frameworks with
Kosovo interim agreement;
• Kosovo consent required
inter alia for changes to
borders and declaration of
martial law;

Human Rights
• Judicial protection if human
rights enshrined in
international conventions and
rights of members of national
communities;
• Role of OSCE and other
relevant international
organisations;
Implementation
• Dispute resolution
mechanism;
• Establishment of a joint
commission to supervise
implementation;
• Participation of OSCE and
other international bodies as
necessary.

5 *Ibid.*, pp. 229–30.
6 *Ibid.*, p.230.
7 Press briefing by the Contact
Group negotiators, 18 February
1999, in Weller, *The Crisis*, p.442.
8 Interim Agreement for Peace
and Self-Government in
Kosovo, 23 February 1999.
Appendix B: Status of
Multi-National Military
Implementation Force, in
Weller, The Crisis, p.469.
9 *VIP Daily News Report*
(Belgrade), 18 February 1999.
10 *VIP Daily News Report*
(Belgrade), 22 February 1999.
11 Secretary of State Albright,
press conference on Kosovo,
France, 20 February 1999, in
Weller, *The Crisis*, pp.449–50.
12 James Rubin, press briefing on
the Kosovo peace talks,
Rambouillet, France, 21
February 1999, in Weller, *The
Crisis*, p.451.
13 Interim Agreement, in Weller,
The Crisis, p.469.
14 Weller, *The Crisis*, p.404.
15 Draft for Chapter 8, Article 1
(3), 22 February 1999, 05.25 hrs,
and proposed draft side letter, in
Weller, *The Crisis*, p.452.
16 *VIP Daily News Report*
(Belgrade), 19 February 1999.
17 All three letters are reproduced
in Weller, *The Crisis*, p.470.

18   Federal Republic of Yugoslavia
     Revised Draft Agreement, 15
     March 1999, in Weller, *The
     Crisis*: title, p.480, final
     paragraph, pp.489–90.
19   Statement by the Co-Chairs of
     the Contact Group, France, 19
     March 1999, in Weller, *The
     Crisis*, p.493.

8   You Will Bomb Us

1   BBC 2, *Newsnight*, 20 August
    1999.
2   President Clinton, Address to
    the nation, Washington DC, 24
    March 1999, in Marc Weller,
    *The Crisis in Kosovo 1989–1999:
    From the Dissolution of
    Yugoslavia to Rambouillet and
    the Outbreak of Hostilities* vol.1
    (Cambridge, 1999), p.499.
3   Press Statement by the NATO
    secretary-general following the
    commencement of air
    operations, 24 March 1999, in
    Weller, *The Crisis*, p.497.
4   Proceedings of the 49th
    Anglo–German Königswinter
    Conference, 'Europe on the
    Move', Königswinter, Germany,
    18–20 March 1999; from the
    report on Study Group 3, Nik
    Gowing, 'A New NATO'.
5   Royal United Services Institute,
    12 November 1999.
6   For the Pavković quote and
    other details in this paragraph,
    see *VIP Daily News Report*
    (Belgrade), 24 March 1999.
7   *VIP Daily News Report*
    (Belgrade), 25 March 1999.
8   Denisa Kostovičová, 'NATO
    Intervention in Yugoslavia: The
    Serbian Response', lecture
    delivered at the NATO and
    Central and Eastern European
    Security Conference, Paris,
    15–16 October 1999.
9   House of Commons,
    International Development
    Committee. *Fourth Special
    Report: Government Response*

      *to the Third Report from the
      Committee, Session 1998–99:
      'Kosovo: The Humanitarian
      Crisis'* (London, 1999),
      Appendix Two: 'Response to
      the Committee's Third Report
      from the United Nations' High
      Commissioner for Refugees',
      p.xii, n.3.
10   Radio Free Europe/Radio
     Liberty, *Newsline*, vol.3, no.67,
     7 April 1999.
11   House of Commons,
     International Development
     Committee Report, p.xi.
12   *VIP Daily News Report*
     (Belgrade), 27 March 1999.
13   Nataša Kandić, Humanitarian
     Law Center, Belgrade, Report
     YHRF no.8, 29–30 March
     1999.
14   Nataša Kandić, Humanitarian
     Law Center, Belgrade, Report,
     YHRF no.11, 12 May 1999.
15   The journalists were Michael
     Montgomery and Stephen
     Smith. Their story was
     broadcast on National Public
     Radio's *All Things Considered*
     on 25 October 1999. The
     interviews quoted here were
     taken from transcripts posted at:
     www.americanradioworks.org/
     features/kosovo/More1.htm.
16   UNHCR, *Refugees*, vol.3,
     no.116, 1999, p.11. Most of the
     issue is taken up with detailed
     articles about Kosovo, the
     Albanian refugees and then the
     Serb ones. For more analysis see
     Forced Migration Review, no.5,
     August 1999.
17   Radio Free Europe/Radio
     Liberty, *Newsline*, vol.3, no.42,
     2 March 1999.
18   'Lessons Learned from Military
     Operations and Relief Efforts in
     Kosovo', Hearing of the Senate
     Armed Services Committee, 21
     October 1999.
19   Michael Ignatieff, 'The Virtual
     Commander', *The New Yorker*,
     2 August 1999.
20   Anthony H.Cordesman, *The*

Lessons and Non-Lessons of the
Air and Missile War in Kosovo:
Report to the USAF XP Strategy
Forum (Washington, 1999),
p.60. See: www.csis.org

21   Ignatieff, 'Virtual Commander'.
22   Dana Priest, 'France Balked at
     NATO Targets', Washington
     Post, 20 September 1999.
23   Ignatieff, 'Virtual Commander'.
24   Priest, 'France Balked'.
25   Federal Ministry of Foreign
     Affairs, NATO Crimes in
     Yugoslavia: Documentary
     Evidence, 24 March – 24 April
     1999 (Belgrade, 1999), p.353.
26   Cordesman, The Lessons,
     p.46.
27   NATO Crimes, p.295.
28   See, for example, 'Truth behind
     America's Raid on Belgrade',
     Observer, 28 November 1999.
29   Jasmina Tesanovic, 'The Diary
     of a Political Idiot, Belgrade,
     March 1998 – June 1999',
     Granta, no.67, Autumn
     1999.
30   VIP Daily News Report
     (Belgrade), 26 April 1999.

9   We Will Win. Period. Full Stop.

1   Dana Priest, 'Tension Grew
    with Divide Over Strategy',
    Washington Post, 21 September
    1999. This article is one of a
    highly detailed and valuable
    trilogy.
2   Ibid.
3   Michael Ignatieff, 'The Virtual
    Commander', New Yorker, 2
    August 1999.
4   Dana Priest, 'France Balked at
    NATO Targets', Washington
    Post, 20 September 1999.
5   Ibid.
6   Ibid.
7   Steven Erlanger, 'With Milošević
    Unyielding on Kosovo, NATO
    Moved toward Invasion', New
    York Times, 7 November 1999.
    For some of the details in this
    section I am indebted to this
    article and Dana Priest's 'A
    Decisive Battle that Never Was',
    Washington Post, 19 September
    1999.
8   Priest, 'Decisive Battle'.
9   Erlanger, 'Milošević
    Unyielding'.
10 Ibid.
11 The Former Yugoslav Republic
    of Macedonia. Due to Greek
    insistence, Macedonia must be
    called FYROM by all
    international organisations and
    officials. The Greeks believe
    that the name Macedonia, used
    by the former Yugoslav
    republic, implies a territorial
    claim on the whole area of
    geographic Macedonia which
    includes its northern province
    and a part of eastern Bulgaria.
12 Ignatieff, 'Virtual Commander'.
13 Security Council Provisional
    Record, 3988th Meeting, 24
    March 1999, 5.35 p.m. (NY
    time), extract in Marc Weller,
    The Crisis in Kosovo 1989–1999:
    From the Dissolution of
    Yugoslavia to Rambouillet and
    the Outbreak of Hostilities
    (Cambridge, 1999), vol.1,
    p.500.
14 Radio Free Europe/Radio
    Liberty, Newsline, vol.3, no.59,
    25 March 1999.
15 The International Court of
    Justice is not to be confused
    with the International Criminal
    Tribunal for the former
    Yugoslavia, also based in The
    Hague.
16 Blaine Harden, 'A Long
    Struggle that Led Serb Leader to
    Back Down', New York Times,
    6 June 1999.
17 Ibid.
18 The G-8 principles of 6 May
    were later incorporated in UN
    Security Council Resolution
    1244, which is given in full in
    Appendix Two.
19 This document became Annex 2
    of UN Security Council

Resolution 1244; see Appendix Two.

20 Harden, 'A Long Struggle'. I am indebted to this article for various quotes and details used in this section and also to William Drozdiak's 'The Kosovo Peace Deal: How It Happened', *Washington Post*, 6 June 1999.

21 The International Criminal Tribunal for the Former Yugoslavia. *The Prosecutor of the Tribunal against Slobodan Milošević ...*, 27 May 1999.

22 BBC 1, *Panorama*, 26 April 1999.

23 Priest, 'Decisive Battle'.

24 *Ibid.*

25 *VIP Daily News Report* (Belgrade), 11 June 1999.

10 Tomorrow's Masters of Kosova

1 Source: United Nations High Commissioner for Refugees (UNHCR).

2 Edith Durham, *High Albania* (London, 1985), pp.40–1.

3 Source: UNHCR. See also UNHCR/OSCE 'Overview of the Situation of Ethnic Minorities in Kosovo' 3 November 1999.

4 Durham, *High Albania*, p.33.

5 Human Rights Watch, *Abuses against Serbs and Roma in the New Kosovo*, vol.11, no.10 (D), August 1999, p.2.

6 Durham, *High Albania*, p.275.

7 Human Rights Watch, *Abuses*, p.8.

8 UNHCR/OSCE, 'Overview'.

9 The original article appeared in *Koha Ditore* but these English-language extracts were taken from a version published in the Institute for War & Peace Reporting IWPR's *Balkan Crisis Report*, no.69, 25 August 1999. See: www.iwpr.net

10 UN Security Council Resolution 1244; see Appendix Two.

11 UN Interim Administration Mission in Kosovo (UNMIK), press release, 21 September 1999.

12 United Nations Environment Programme (UNEP)/United Nations Centre for Human Settlements (UNCHS/Habitat) Balkans Task Force: *The Kosovo Conflict: Consequences for the Environment and Human Settlements* (Geneva, 1999), p.10.

13 *Ibid.*, p.62.

14 UN Security Council Resolution 1244; see Appendix Two.

15 Interview with General Radovan Lazarević in *Nedeljni Telegraf* republished in *VIP Daily News Report* (Belgrade), 8 September 1999.

16 Catherine Guicherd, 'International Law and the War in Kosovo', *Survival*, vol.41, no.2, Summer 1999, p.20.

17 IWPR, *Balkan Crisis Report*, no.92, 12 November 1999.

Select Bibliography

Anzulovic, Branimir. *Heavenly Serbia: From Myth to Genocide* (New York, 1999)

Avramov, Smilja. *Genocide in Yugoslavia* (Belgrade, 1995)

Bajraktari, Jusuf, *et al.* (eds). *The Kosova Issue – A Historic and Current Problem* (Tirana, 1993)

Banac, Ivo. *The National Question in Yugoslavia: Origins, History, Politics* (Ithaca, 1992)

Berisha, Ibrahim, *et al.* (eds). *Serbian Colonization and Ethnic Cleansing of Kosova: Documents and Evidence* (Priština, 1993)

Biserko, Sonja and Stanojlović, Seška, Helsinki Committee for Human Rights in Serbia. *Radicalisation of the Serbian Society: Collection of Documents* (Belgrade, 1997)

Brailsford, H.N. *Macedonia: Its Races and Their Future* (London, 1906)

Carnegie Endowment for International Peace. *Report of the International Commission to Inquire into the Causes and Conduct of the Balkan Wars* (Washington, DC, 1914) (Republished in 1993 under the title *The Other Balkan Wars.*)

Cordesman, Anthony H. *The Lessons and Non-Lessons of the Air and Missile War in Kosovo: Report to the USAF XP Strategy Forum, Center for Strategic and International Studies* (Washington, 1999) See: www.csis.org

Djilas, Aleksa. *The Contested Country: Yugoslav Unity and Communist Revolution 1919–1953* (Cambridge, 1991)

Djordjević, Dimitrije and Samardžić, Radovan (eds). *Migrations in Balkan History* (Belgrade, 1989)

Djukic, Slavoljub. *Izmedju slave i anateme: Politička biografija Slobodana Miloševića* (Belgrade, 1994)

Dragnich, Alex and Todorovich, Slavko. *The Saga of Kosovo: Focus on Serbian–Albanian Relations* (Boulder and New York, 1984)

Drezov, Kyril, Gokay, Bulent, and Kostovičová, Denisa. *Kosovo: Myths, Conflict and War* (Keele, 1999)

Doder, Dusko and Branson, Louise. *Milosevic: Portrait of a Tyrant* (New York, 1999)

Durham, Edith. *High Albania* (London, 1985)

Elshani, Gafurr. *Ushtria Çlirimtare e Kosovës: dokumente dhe artikuj* (Aarau, 1998)

Emmert, Thomas. *Serbian Golgotha: Kosovo 1389* (New York, 1990)

Federal Ministry of Foreign Affairs. *NATO Crimes in Yugoslavia: Documentary Evidence, 24 March – 24 April 1999* (Belgrade, 1999)
——. *Nato Crimes in Yugoslavia: Documentary Evidence, 25 April – 10 June 1999*, vol.2, (Belgrade, 1999)
Fischer, Bernd J. *Albania at War, 1939–1945* (West Lafayette, 1999)
Glenny, Misha. *The Balkans 1804–1999: Nationalism, War and the Great Powers* (London, 1999)
Hodgkinson, Harry. *Scanderbeg* (London, 1999)
Holbrooke, Richard. *To End a War* (New York, 1999), revised edn
Human Rights Watch. *Open Wounds: Human Rights Abuses in Kosovo* (New York, 1993)
——. *Humanitarian Law Violations in Kosovo* (New York, 1998)
——. *A Week of Terror in Drenica: Humanitarian Law Violations in Kosovo* (New York, 1999)
——. *Abuses against Serbs and Roma in the New Kosovo*. vol.11, no.10 (D), August 1999
Jakupi, Ali. *Two Albanian States and National Unification* (Priština, 1997)
Jelavich, Barbara. *History of the Balkans*, 2 vols (Cambridge, 1989–93)
Judah, Tim. *The Serbs: History, Myth and the Destruction of Yugoslavia* (New Haven and London, 1997)
Kindersley, Anne. *The Mountains of Serbia: Travels through Inland Yugoslavia* (Newton Abbot, 1977)
The Kossovo Day Committee. *Kossovo Day (1389–1916)* (London, 1916)
Kostovičová, Denisa. *Parallel Worlds: Response of Kosovo Albanians to the Loss of Autonomy in Serbia 1989–1996* (Keele, 1997)
Mackenzie, Georgina and Adelina Irby, *Travels in the Slavonic Provinces of Turkey-in-Europe* (London, 1877)
Magaš, Branka. *The Destruction of Yugoslavia: Tracking the Break-up 1980–92* (London and New York, 1993)
Malcolm, Noel. *Kosovo: A Short History* (London, 1998)
Maliqi, Shkëlzen. *Kosova: Separate Worlds, Reflections and Analyses 1989–1998* (Priština, 1998)
Maloku, Enver. *Expulsion of Albanians and Colonisation of Kosova* (Priština, 1997)
Mertus, Julie. *Kosovo: How Myths and Truths Started a War* (Berkeley and Los Angeles, 1999)
Mihailović, Kosta and Krestić, Vasilije. *Memorandum of the Serbian Academy of Sciences and Arts: Answers to Criticisms* (Belgrade, 1995)
Mihaljčić, Rade. *The Batttle of Kosovo in History and in Popular Tradition* (Belgrade, 1989)
Motes, Mary. *Kosova, Kosovo: Prelude to War 1966–1999* (Homestead, Florida, 1999)
Owen, David. *Balkan Odyssey* (San Diego, 1995), updated edn
Pavlowitch, Stevan K. *A History of the Balkans 1804–1945* (London, 1999)

Pennington, Anne and Levi, Peter. *Marko the Prince: Serbo-Croat Heroic Songs*, with introductory notes by Svetozar Koljevic (London, 1984)

Pettifer, James and Vickers, Miranda. *Albania: From Anarchy to a Balkan Identity* (London, 1997)

Pipa, Arshi and Repishti, Sami (eds). *Studies on Kosova* (Boulder, 1984)

Pulaha, Selama. *L'Autochtonéité des Albanais en Kosove et le prétendu exode des Serbes à la fin du XVIIIᵉ siècle* (Tirana, 1985)

Ramet, Sabrina P. *Nationalism and Federalism in Yugoslavia 1962– 1991*, (Bloomington and Indianapolis, 1992), 2nd edn

Rycaut (also sometimes, Ricaut), Paul. *The History of the Turks Beginning with the Year 1679* (London, 1700)

Samardžić, Radovan and Duškov, Milan. *Serbs in European Civilization* (Belgrade, 1993)

Silber, Laura and Little, Allan. *The Death of Yugoslavia* (London, 1995)

Thaçi, Miftar Spahia. *About Kosova* (Tirana, 1998)

Thomas, Robert. *Serbia under Milošević: Politics in the 1990s* (London, 1999)

Thompson, Mark. *A Paper House: The Ending of Yugoslavia* (London, 1992)

Trotsky, Leon. *The War Correspondence of Leon Trotsky: The Balkan Wars, 1912–13* (New York, 1991)

UNEP/UNCHS Balkans Task Force: *The Kosovo Conflict: Consequences for the Environment and Human Settlements* (Geneva, 1999)

Veremis, Thanos and Kofos, Evangelos (eds). *Kosovo: Avoiding Another Balkan War* (Athens, 1998)

Vickers, Miranda. *Between Serb and Albanian: A History of Kosovo* (London, 1998)

——. *The Albanians: A Modern History* (London and New York, 1995)

Vučelić, Milorad. *Conversations with the Epoch* (Belgrade, 1991)

Vucinich, Wayne S. and Emmert, Thomas A. (eds). *Kosovo: The Legacy of a Medieval Battle* (Minneapolis, 1991)

Weller, Marc. *The Crisis in Kosovo 1989–1999: From the Dissolution of Yugoslavia to Rambouillet and the Outbreak of Hostilities* vol.1 (Cambridge, 1999)

West, Rebecca. *Black Lamb and Grey Falcon: The Record of a Journey through Yugoslavia in 1937*, 2 vols (London, 1943)

Zimmermann, Warren. *Origins of a Catastrophe: Yugoslavia and its Destroyers* (New York, 1996)

Index